MW00831703

Rock Creek Canyon
Bear Creek Spire
13,720ft
ROCK CREEK
(8,600 ft)
Mount Morrison
12,268ft
Laurel Mountain
11,812ft
Mammoth Mountain
11,053ft
Lakes Basin
Devils Postpile National Monument
Tom's Place
SWALL MEADOWS
PARADISE
Sherwin Grade
CROWLEY LAKE
Convict Lake
SUNNY SLOPES
DREAMERS
Owens River Gorge
River Gorge
Whitmore Hot Springs
MAMMOTH LAKES
7,800ft
Crowley Lake
× POCKETOPIA CATACOMBS
(7,100 ft)
Browns
The Owens River
Sherwin Plateau
Long Valley Caldera
Caso Diablo Mountain
Volcanic Tableland
Mono County
Benton Range
CHALFANT
CALIFORNIA
White Mountain Peak
14,246ft
Bristlecone Pine Forest
4,000 year old trees
10,000ft
Sierra View Outlook

© Mick Ryan 2007

Bishop
Bouldering

Expanded 2nd edition

THIS BOOK BELONGS TO: ____________________

____

BISHOP BOULDERING SECOND EDITION

Words: Wills Young.
Fieldwork and research: Wills Young, Mick Ryan.
Maps and topos: Mick Ryan, Wills Young.
Photographs: Wills Young, Mick Ryan, unless otherwise credited.
Published and distributed by Wolverine Publishing, LLC.

Cover photo:
Kevin Jorgeson swings around on the pinch of *Saigon Direct* (v9) at the Buttermilk Boulders. Photo: Jim Thornburg.

Opening page photo:
Jeremy Smith says "Bishop Bouldering needs YOU!" Thanks Jeremy. Photo: Wills Young.

International Standard Book Number:
ISBN: 978-0-9826154-1-6

Library of Congress Catalog in Publication Data:
Library of Congress Control Number: 9780982615416

Wolverine Publishing is continually expanding its range of guidebooks. If you have a manuscript or idea for a book, or would like to find out more about our company and publications, contact:

Dave Pegg
Wolverine Publishing
1491 County Road 237
Silt
CO 81652
970-876-0268
dave@wolverinepublishing.com
www.wolverinepublishing.com

Printed in China.

WARNING

DO NOT USE THIS GUIDEBOOK UNLESS YOU READ AND AGREE TO THE FOLLOWING:

Bouldering is a dangerous sport that can result in death, paralysis or serious injury.

This book is intended as a reference tool for advanced/expert boulderers. The activity and the terrain it describes can be or is extremely dangerous and requires a high degree of ability and experience to negotiate. This book is not intended for inexperienced or novice boulderers, nor is it intended as an instructional manual. If you are unsure of your ability to handle any circumstances that may arise, employ the services of a professional instructor or guide.

This book relies upon information and opinions provided by others that may not be accurate. Opinions concerning the technical difficulties, ratings, and dangers of a boulder problem or lack thereof are subjective and may differ from yours and others opinions. Ratings may differ from area to area, holds may break, fixed protection may fail, fall out or be missing, and weather may deteriorate. These and other factors, such as rock fall, inadequate or faulty equipment, etc., may all increase the danger of climbing a boulder problem and may contribute to the climb being other than as described in the book. Furthermore, errors may be made during the editing, designing, proofing, and printing of this book. Thus, the information in this book is unverified, and the authors and publisher cannot guarantee its accuracy. Numerous hazards exist that are not described in this book. Climbing or bouldering on any terrain described in this book, regardless of its description or rating, may result in your death, paralysis or injury.

Do not use this book unless you are a skilled and experienced boulderer who understands and accepts the risks of bouldering. If you choose to use any information in this book to plan, attempt, or climb a particular boulder problem, you do so at your own risk. Please take all precautions and use your own ability, evaluation, and judgment to assess the risks of your chosen climb, rather than relying on the information in this book.

THE AUTHORS AND PUBLISHER MAKE NO REPRESENTATIONS OR WARRANTIES, EXPRESSED OR IMPLIED, OF ANY KIND REGARDING THE CONTENTS OF THIS BOOK, AND EXPRESSLY DISCLAIM ANY AND ALL REPRESENTATIONS OR WARRANTIES REGARDING THE CONTENTS OF THIS BOOK, INCLUDING, WITHOUT LIMITATION, THE ACCURACY OR RELIABILITY OF INFORMATION CONTAINED HEREIN. WARRANTIES OF FITNESS FOR A PARTICULAR PURPOSE AND/OR MERCHANTABILITY ARE EXPRESSLY DISCLAIMED.

THE USER ASSUMES ALL RISKS ASSOCIATED WITH THE USE OF THIS BOOK INCLUDING, WITHOUT LIMITATION, ALL RISKS ASSOCIATED WITH ROCK CLIMBING AND BOULDERING.

Table of Contents

MAMMOTH MOUNTAINEERING
GEAR EXCHANGE
Used Gear & Consignment For All Sports
298 N. Main St, Bishop
760-873-4300
MAMMOTH MOUNTAINEERING
3189 Main Street, Mammoth Lakes
760-934-4191 888-395-3951
Mammoth
Mountaineering
Supply
Both Stores Entire Selection Available At
www.mammothmountaineering.com
photo Justin Lawrence, climber Lisa Bedient

ADVERTISER INDEX

INTRODUCTION

Bishop is a boulderer's paradise, one of the few places in the world where a high concentration of world class bouldering combines with magnificent scenery, convenient amenities, and near-perfect weather. More than 2000 problems on two principal rock types provide a range of options from the pocketed Bishop tuff of the Volcanic Tableland and Sherwin Plateau, to the generally crimpier though occasionally frictiony quartz monzonite in the Buttermilk Country.

Climbers are simply spoiled for choice not just by the quantity and variety of climbing, but by the radically different environments. The shallow canyons of the Happy and Sad Boulders—with their fascinating jumbles of blocks and their long, winding walls and alcoves—have a completely different feel to the higher altitude, more exposed, and sometimes intimidating giant eggs of the spectacular Buttermilks.

The freedom to hike and explore this expansive wonderland in search of new or unrecorded lines, either on the Tableland, the Sherwin Plateau, or in the Buttermilk Country, is another great plus. With so much rock still to be climbed, Bishop will be a boulderer's paradise for many years to come.

GETTING TO BISHOP

Bishop is at 37.2 degrees north latitude, on the east side of the Sierra Nevada Mountains in California, west of the White Mountains, and not far from the Nevada border. Bishop is 230 miles north of Los Angeles and 170 miles south of Reno. London is 5265 miles away, Tokyo 5340 miles, Rio de Janeiro 6400 miles, Sydney 7585 miles, and Johannesburg 10320 miles.

Unquestionably, the best way to get to and around Bishop is to fly into one of the closer and cheaper airports, such as Reno (Nevada), or Los Angeles (California), and rent a car. A car is nearly essential for getting to and from the climbing areas in Bishop. For those who are not planning to arrive by car—perhaps meeting others, or hoping to "wing it" when they get here—see "Flights & Busses/Coaches" (opposite).

The times listed below are for good driving conditions and no speeding. Visitors from out of state or other countries are warned that Hwy395 is extraordinarily well-patrolled by the California Highway Patrol.

Highway information is available by calling 1-800-427-7623 which is a free call from within California, or dial 1-916-445-7623 from outside California. This is especially useful for mountain travel. You will be asked to state the number of the highway you are interested in (you can also input the numbers directly). Unless you are told a road is closed or has intermittent traffic due to work, you can assume it is open and flowing freely. You can find the same information online at www.dot.ca.gov/hq/roadinfo/hi.htm.

San Diego, California

356 miles, 6 hours.

No matter where you are in San Diego aim for Escondido. From the airport take the 163 freeway north (other options are available). Join the 15 freeway through Escondido. Pick up the 215 freeway north of Temecula and head north through San Bernardino and eventually rejoin the 15 northward. Go uphill about 15 miles to the high desert, where you exit onto Hwy395 for Bishop.

Los Angeles, California

273 miles, 5 hours.

From the International Airport aim for the 405 freeway north. Take the 405 north toward Sacramento for about 25 miles and then take the 5 freeway north for just a couple of miles to get onto the 14 freeway north toward Palmdale and Lancaster. Follow the 14 to Mojave (where it becomes Hwy14), and on, eventually joining Hwy395 north to Bishop.

San Francisco, California

a. 300 miles 5 1/2 hours, via Tuolumne Meadows in summer.

b. 430 miles 7 hours, via Reno in mid winter.

c. 514 miles 8 1/2 hours, via Bakersfield as a last resort.

Driving directions from San Francisco—and for all points on the west side of the Sierra, including Yosemite Valley—are complicated by the Sierra Nevada Mountains. The passes through these mountains are closed for most of winter and spring due to snowfall, and the options are too complicated for complete information to be provided here. Get a map, check out the various routes, and confirm information regarding closure (or not) of the various highways. It is worth noting here that the Sherman Pass Road/Kennedy Meadows Road, the first pass through the Sierras south of Sequoia National Park is not a good option under any circumstances.

a. When it is open, during summer and fall, Hwy120 via Tuolumne Meadows and over Tioga Pass is the best option. This 9,943ft (3030m) pass is the highest drivable in California and is open (like all the passes) on an entirely weather-determined schedule, but usually from around the end of May through early November and occasionally into mid December.

b. When all the smaller high passes are closed, there are two options: Interstate 80 between Sacramento and Reno is usually the quickest. It is kept open in all but the most horrendous conditions and even then will shut only briefly.

c. If you've heard there's a rare and horrible storm, and you don't want to risk crawling at 10 mph through snowfall for hours at a time, the last resort is to go south around the southern end of the Sierras via Bakersfield and Tehachapi. This is a really long, monotonous, yet uneventful and "easy" drive.

Reno

200 miles, 3 1/2 hours.

From the Reno/Tahoe International Airport take Hwy395 (initially freeway) south. After 7 miles exit the freeway rightward in order to STAY on Hwy395, which leads all the way to Bishop.

Salt Lake City

520 miles, 8 1/2 hours.

From the Salt Lake City International Airport, or, indeed from anywhere near Salt Lake City, take Interstate 80 (freeway) west toward Wendover and Reno. Take exit 410 at Wendover and head toward Ely by Alt Hwy93 south. From Ely take Hwy6 to Tonopah. It seems there are more cop cars here than any other form of transport. Go north toward Reno on Hwy6/Hwy95 turning left toward Bishop after 40 miles. Stay on Hwy6 to Bishop. Don't run out of gas on these vast stretches of empty road.

Las Vegas

275 miles, 5 hours

From McCarron International Airport, or anywhere in Vegas, get on the 95 freeway north (you will need the 15 freeway north through Vegas to get started). The 95 leads through the desert for 160 miles or so to a left onto Hwy266, which meets California Hwy168. Follow the 168 over Westguard Pass, descend to Hwy395 and follow this north to Bishop.

Driving Times From Other Climbing Areas:

Yosemite, California: 3 hours via Tuolumne when the pass is open.

Joshua Tree, California: 5 hours.

Red Rocks, Nevada: 5 hours

Smith Rock, Oregon: 10 hours.

City of Rocks, Idaho: 12 hours.

Boulder, Colorado: 15 hours.

Hueco Tanks, Texas: 15 1/2 hours.

Red River Gorge, Kentucky: 33 hours.

The Gunks, New York: 40 hours.

Flights & Busses/Coaches

Seasonal flights intended for skiers visiting the Mammoth Mountain ski area will run during peak ski season, such as mid-Dec to mid-April. Check www.alaskaair.com or www.visitmammoth.com for information about air service, which may be extended or canceled according to demand. Alaska Airlines/Horizon Air operates flights to and from Mammoth Lakes (city code MMH) and Los Angeles, San Jose (near San Francisco), Portland (Oregon), and Seattle.

There is another simple way to get to Bishop, which is to fly into the Reno/Tahoe International Airport. Buses of the Carson Ridgecrest Eastern Sierra Transit (CREST) at time of press leave this airport for Bishop on Monday, Tuesday, Thursday, and Friday, at 1:50pm. Please call 800-922-1930 for confirmation or look up details online at http://easternsierratransit.com.

Coming from Los Angeles, you can also make your way to Bishop and back on public transport. Check at the website listed above for the northern part of this journey. On Mondays, Wednesdays, and Fridays, busses run to and from Lancaster Metrolink station, which in turn has trains (and some busses) running to Los Angeles and other cities (see www.metrolink.com). Sadly, you need three or four different services to make it from the LAX Airport to Bishop. The trip will not be expensive, but it could take a long time. Buses for one stretch may not run on exactly the same days as for other stretches of the route. In short, this journey is possible, but may not be a great option.

From Las Vegas, aim for Mojave and connect north from there. From San Francisco, aim for Reno and connect south.

WEATHER: A CLIMATE OF EXTREMES

Sunset at the Happy Boulders. Photo Wills Young.

In general, the best weather conditions for climbing are between fall and spring—that is between mid-October and mid-May. September and late May can have some very hot spells, they can be okay but aren't the best choices. The rest of the summer is usually scorching, though even then, you could still seek climbing at higher elevations at dawn or dusk if you're utterly incorrigible or immune to heat and pain. During the winter, despite the cold it is typically very sunny here, and there is rarely a three day stretch during which you cannot reasonably get outside and climb.

Bishop sits in a rain shadow cast by the 400-mile-long chain of the Sierra Nevada Mountains. This creates a climate ideally suited to rock climbing. While the Sierra's western slopes receive an average of 40 to 80 inches (100-200cm) of precipitation from the prevailing west winds, Bishop's rain gauges collect barely 6 (15cm). For 200-plus days of the year there is not a cloud in the sky. Ninety more days are just partly cloudy.

With the clear sky, the daily fluctuation in temperature is vast. Swings of 30F or even 40F (17C to 22C) between the mid-afternoon high and the overnight low are not unusual for Bishop. In winter, after enjoying a warm 65F (17C) sunny afternoon, you might shiver through a 20F (-7C) night. Up in the mountains, or at higher elevation campgrounds, expect some severe cold.

Extreme low and high temperatures can also arrive dramatically with storms or huge weather systems spinning in from the ocean, from Canada, or from the Gulf of Mexico, to create a degree of unpredictability that keeps even longtime locals on their toes. In 2006 a couple of 90F (32C) late May days were suddenly followed by a night that was barely above freezing. Winter storms can also be dramatic, but even the worst of those usually blow through in a matter of days.

On bright days, the difference between sun and shade is immense. Even in the heart of winter, it doesn't matter how cold the air might be: When you're in the sun, you're climbing. On warmer days, on the other hand, you'll seek the shade. Intense sun can ruin your hopes of ever grasping the measly grips of your chosen project, yet the moment the inevitable happens, and the sun drops behind the Sierra... Boom! It's cold, it's dry: You're sending.

THE TOWN OF BISHOP

Bishop is a small town of about 9,000 people, situated at an altitude of about 4100 feet (1250m) at the north end of the remote, overwhelmingly empty Owens Valley, one of the biggest and deepest valleys in the United States. Between the 14,000ft (4270m) peaks of the Sierra Nevada mountains to the west, the equally high White Mountains to the east, and the intervening plateau of the Volcanic Tableland to the north, the town's vicinity is an oasis greened by fast-running creeks and the meandering Owens River.

The melt water pouring from the mountains provides for cattle farming, crop production, and the natural growth of giant cottonwood trees. In late spring, the edge-of-town view of wet green meadows, golden granite foothills, and snowcapped mountains, is a wonder that puts a smile on every face—especially those of local sales people at the many photography galleries who sell prints of the surrounding scenery by the score.

Bishop's 9,000 or so lucky inhabitants do not all live within the incorporated city limits. This explains why the sign at the edge of town lists the population at around 3,500. Small outlying communities, such as Wilkerson, Mustang Mesa, the lush Round Valley, and arid Chalfont, plus the town of Big Pine, 15 miles to the south, bring the total number for the entire area, including Bishop, to around 12,000.

The town itself is dominated by Highway395 that runs the length of Owens Valley. During ski season, the highway is busy with skiers heading to the ski resort of Mammoth Mountain about 40 miles northwest of Bishop.

Year round interest for many different outdoor enthusiasts is to be found here: rock climbing, hiking, back-country skiing, backpacking, and mountain biking are some of the options. Plentiful fishing and hunting are also available when in season, while bird watching is always in season, and simply relaxing by some water for a family camping trip is a popular pastime at the higher elevations during summer. With stable weather and wide open expanses of breathtaking scenery, road biking is also becoming increasingly popular. The truth is, that living here, you get the impression that there is untapped potential in almost every way. Without doubt, Bishop is located in one of the best environments for outdoor sports and adventure in North America.

Views like this are typical on the outskirts of Bishop. Mount Humphrey's (approx 14,000 feet), at left, and Basin Mountain (approx 13,000 feet) at right, form the backdrop.

Bishop Amenities

Despite the fact that the principal source of income in the area is tourism, there sure ain't a hell of a lot going on in the town of Bishop. This, in brief, is Small-town, U.S.A. If you're someone who enjoys night-life, or even just city life, you know you are in trouble when the defining symbol, the emblem, the *icon* of your chosen home town is ... wait for it ... a *mule*. Yes, Bishop, California, is proud, and I mean *proud*, to call itself The Mule Capital of the World.

Which is all well and good, as I'm sure you'll agree, because with scenery and weather, and an environment this good, what more could you need other than a supermarket, a gas station, and, well ... as a stop-gap ... a mule. I mean, really? The Mule is celebrated in the annual Mule Days Festival on Memorial Day in late May enjoyed by up to 30,000 spectators. I'm not making this up.

Tourist Information

The Bishop Area Chamber of Commerce and Visitor's Bureau is located on the east side of Main Street in front of City Park, opposite Schat's Bakery. Open all year during normal business hours. You can pick up a vacation booklet. Web site: www.bishopvisitor.com. Call free (888) 395-3952 from USA or 760-873-8405.

The White Mountain Ranger Station (760-873-2500) is located a block north of the Bishop Area Chamber of Commerce and Visitor Bureau, opposite the Cottonwood Plaza. Here you can pick up or ask for information on the many Forest Service campgrounds.

Groceries

There are three main choices: Vons, Josephs Bi-rite, and Manor Market. The Vons is found at the north end of Main Street, to the east of the junction with Hwy6, next to K-Mart. Joseph's is found in the center of town just north of the Line Street (Hwy168) junction on Main, across the street from Wilson's Eastside Sports, while Manor Market (not shown on the map) is west of the town center about 2.5 miles along West Line Street from the junction with Main Street, toward the Buttermilks. I can recommend the latter for its outstanding beer and wine, plus a good collection of imported items. Also of note is Smart and Final, which does a lot of bulk items, though not exclusively, and often has the best prices in town. It's near Vons, just off Main Street.

Gas stations

These are found along Main Street, Sierra Highway, and Line Street, with the cheapest gas usually being found on Sierra Highway on the northeast edge of town adjacent to the Paiute Palace Casino, or at the Vons supermarket.

Climbing supplies

Just north of Line Street on the east side of Main Street in downtown Bishop, find: Wilson's Eastside Sports (760-873-7520), which is the most fully-equipped; Mammoth Mountaineering Supply and Gear Exchange (760-873-4300), and Sage to Summit (760-872-1756). All are within one hundred yards. In downtown Lone Pine, find Elevation (760-876-4560).

Restaurants & Cafes

1. Astorgas, Mexican
2. Dominos, Pizza
3. Mahogany Smoked Meats
4. Petite Pantry
5. Village Café
6. Upper Crust Pizza
7. Dennys
8. Kentucky Fried Chicken
9. Starbucks, also Quiznos
10. The Pizza Factory
11. Taco Bell
12. Town and Country Buffet
13. The Loco Frijole
14. Schat's Bakery
15. Carl's Junior
16. Yamatani Sushi
17. McDonalds
18. Jack's Waffle Shop
19. Whiskey Creek Pub and Restaurant
20. The Looney Bean, coffee shop
21. Amigos Mexican
22. Bishop Grill, mexican and american
23. Raymond's Deli
24. Nick-n-Willie's Pizza
25. Las Palmas, Mexican
26. Black Sheep Café (behind Spellbinder's)
27. La Casita, Mexican
28. Bill's Barbecue
29. Great Basin Bakery and Cafe
30. Jack in the Box
31. Imperial Gourmet, Chinese

BISHOP TOWN MAP

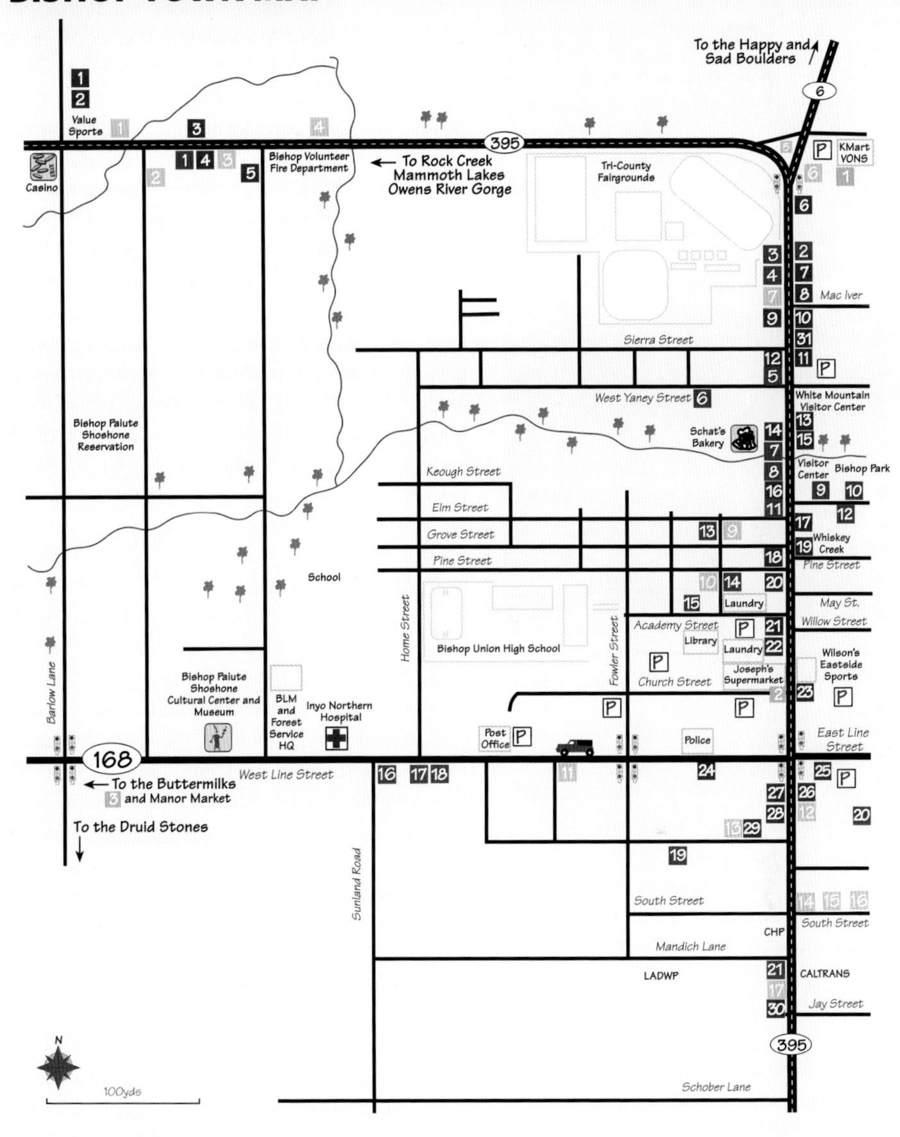

Mechanics & Auto Supply

1. Kragen, 760-872-2587
2. Bishop Automotive Center, 760-873-4430
3. A1 Radiator/John's Muffler & Auto, 760-873-7026
4. Sierra German Auto, 760-873-8923
5. Symmons Tire, 760-873-3528
6. Bob's Auto Parts, 760-873-6385
7. Our Water Works, Oil and Wash, 760-872-2070
8. Napa Auto Parts, 760-872-4281
9. Mr. K's Auto Repair and Towing, 760-873-7149
10. Inyo Mono Auto Body, 760-873-4271
11. Bishop Glass, Auto Glass, 760-872-1191
12. Warren's Auto Repair, 760-873-8284
13. Jim Allen's Auto-Matics, 760-873-7262
14. Perry Motors, Honda/Toyota, 760-872-4141
15. Craig's Auto Repair, 760-873-3235
16. Sierra Auto Body, 760-873-6005
17. Sierra Auto Parts, Beck's Auto Repair, 873-8339

Hotels/Motels

All area codes are 760. Many of these motels also have an online website, and toll-free numbers.

1. Lakeview Motel, 760-873-4019
2. Vagabond Inn, 760-873-6351
3. Best Western, 760-873-3543
4. Motel 6, 760-873-8426
5. Comfort Inn, 760-873-4284
6. Joseph House Inn 760-872-3389
7. Creekside Inn, 760-872-3044
8. La Quinta Inn, 760-873-6380
9. Ramada Inn, 760-872-1771
10. Elms Motel, 760-873-8118
11. Town House Motel, 760-872-4541
12. Rodeway Inn, 760-873-3564
13. The Bishop Village Motel, 760-872-8155
14. Bishop Thunderbird Motel, 760-873-4215
15. Chalfant House B+B, 760-872-1790
16. The Trees Motel, 760-873-6391
17. Mountain View Motel, 760-873-4242
18. Days Inn, 760-872-1095
19. El Rancho Motel, 760-872-9251
20. Best Value Inn, 760-873-4912
21. Super 8, 760-872-1386

Grocery Stores

1. Vons
2. Joseph's
3. Manor Market

Erik Schat's Bakery on Main Street in Bishop is literally famous around the world. Many people only know of Bishop for its bakery!

Coffee Shops

Along Main Street are:

Starbucks on the west side of Main toward the north end, adjacent to Sierra Street, opposite Taco Bell. Schat's Bakery—Bishop's most famous landmark— exactly half-way down Main Street, opposite Carl's Junior.The Looney Bean, on Main and the corner of Pine Street, opposite Washington Mutual Bank.

The Black Sheep is the locals' choice for the best coffee in town, in the back of the Spellbinder Bookstore, on Main Street just south of Line Street (Hwy168)

Great Basin Bakery just off of Main Street, on Lagoon Street, the first street south of Line (Hwy168) on the west side; a locals' alternative to Schat's.

Shopping needs

If there's anything you need other than food, drink, or climbing gear you may want to look first at K-Mart. This store sells everything you can imagine from clothing to car batteries, home and garden supplies, electronic gadgets, and pharmacological necessities.

Laundry

The Wash Tub (760-873-6627) is on Warren Street behind the cinema and Joseph's Bi-Rite Market. Sierra Suds (760-873-8338) is very nearby on Academy Street, just off of Main, across from the Union Bank of California.

Showers

The Wash Tub (above) has public showers for $5. Another option is Keough's Hot Springs Resort, where you can pay $8 to take a shower and enjoy a naturally-fed hot pool and a swimming pool. In summer, Bishop Park Swimming Pool, midway along Main Street, opposite Schat's Bakery is open. The local campgrounds of Brown's Town and Millpond do NOT allow showering for drop-in visitors; showers are available only for paying guests who are staying at the campsite.

Keough's Hot Springs

Keough's Hot Springs is a small resort with camping, tent-style cabins and more. The hot spring itself feeds a large hot pool and a swimming pool with natural hot water. This is an amazing place to relax and soak away the aches and pains from a day's climbing. Open 11am to 7pm on Monday, Wednesday, Thursday and Friday; 9am to 8pm Saturday and Sunday; closed Tuesday. Note: Jun-Aug hours are generally longer and open every day (though Sun closing is 7pm). To get there, head south on highway 395 about 7.5 miles to Keough Hot Springs Road; turn right (west) and drive 0.7 miles.

Restaurants

A list of places to eat is given on page 14 beside the Bishop town map. All are decent, though perhaps none are spectacular. Hey, everyone's taste is different, so you have to experiment. If I *had* to choose, I would probably pick Whiskey Creek (the bar, rather than the formal restaurant), due to the half-price entrée specials (during "happy hour" Mon-Fri 5 till 6PM), the draught beer, and the ambiance.

Casino

If you don't like having money in your wallet, or simply have too much, the Paiute Palace Casino is at 2742 N. Sierra Highway, about 2.5 miles from the center of town.

Staying in Bishop

Hotels/Motels

A list of hotels and motels, along with phone numbers is given on page 15 with the Bishop town map. For links and toll-free phone numbers see the Bishop Chamber of Commerce web site: www.bishopvisitor.com, under "lodging," or look elsewhere online.

Some places such as the Best Western Creekside Inn, the Holiday Inn Express, and Mountain View Motel have apartment style rooms with full kitchens for those looking to do their own cooking and dishes, and others, such as Motel 6, Ramada, Village Motel, and Best Value Inn have rooms with kitchenettes. Most (but not all) hotels will supply you with a microwave and refrigerator for their rooms if you ask (check first).

There are a couple of bed and breakfast places too: the Joseph House Inn (which seems very highly recommended by visitors but also relatively pricey), and the historic Chalfont House B&B (prices similar to the better motels in the area, but with full breakfast included).

Camping

There are many options for camping around Bishop, listed below. You can camp at designated sites where you pay a fee from $2 (at the BLM Pleasant Valley Climbers Campground, also known as "The Pit") up to about $25.

If you want to camp rough in the Buttermilk Country (which you are entitled to do, other than on the DWP land such as that just before the main climbing area on the left), **PLEASE, out of respect to other visitors, pitch your tent well away from the boulders and well away from parking spots**. There are secluded areas to be found beyond the bouldering areas. You can camp "rough" for free, though this is not an ideal long-term arrangement. Be extremely careful if leaving anything out: several climbers have been robbed when leaving their sites to head into town, or even to go climbing. Hoodlums from town sometimes drive this road looking to party or to rip off the climbers. You are not allowed to camp at the Happy and Sad parking areas.

The Galen Rowell gallery and Spellbinder book store (with The Black Sheep coffee shop) at the junction of Main and Line in downtown Bishop.

In the interests of cleanliness of the environment, and of the enjoyment of the fragile desert by all, the Bureau of Land Management (BLM) Pleasant Valley Climbers' Campground ("The Pit") is the best place to stay for those on a tight budget. It is also a great place to meet other climbers and share a lively scene during the prime winter season.

Be advised that, despite the well-known sunny aspect of the weather here, night-time temperatures can be exceedingly low. In winter, -8F (-22C) has been recorded in Bishop, though the average lows are about 21F (-6C). At higher elevations those numbers will be considerably lower: Wrap up warm. It is also worth noting that the winds can be very strong here, so make sure you put some stakes into the ground to hold down your tent (rocks that you can easily pick up generally do not cut it).

BLM Pleasant Valley Climbers' Campground ("The Pit"), 760-873-2500. Elevation 4500 feet. An ultra-low-cost but safe option, with large fire pits including a large communal pit providing a great social scene for visiting climbers. Open Nov 1 to May 1, but also possibly earlier and possibly later. Maximum stay: 60 days. $2/vehicle. Pit toilet block but NO WATER or other amenities. A campground host is typically on site. Northwest of Bishop, near the west end of Chalk Bluff Road (past the Happy and Sad Boulders). From Bishop center, go about 6.5 miles north/west on Hwy395 to Pleasant Valley Dam Road. Turn right and go 0.9 miles. Make a left onto a dirt road, and go up hill a little less than 0.5 miles to the campground.

Pleasant Valley Campground. Elevation 4200 feet. Open all year. Northwest and slightly north of Bishop at the west end of Chalk Bluff Road (past the Happy and Sad Boulders), near the Climber's Campground (previous listing). From Bishop center, go about 6.5 miles north/west on Hwy 395 to Pleasant Valley Dam Road. Turn right and go about 2 miles. $10 per site. Water. Toilets. Next to Owens River.

BLM Horton Creek Campground, 760-872-5000. Elevation 5000 feet. Open approximately early May to the end of October: confirm by phone. West of Bishop on the flank of the Sierra overlooking Round Valley. From Bishop center, go about 6.5 miles north/west on Hwy395. Take Sawmill Road south (left, opposite Pleasant Valley Dam Road) and then an immediate right onto Round Valley Road. Go about 3 more miles and follow signs. $5 per site. No water. Pit toilets. Good view.

Brown's Town Campground, 760-873-8522. Elevation 4000 feet (1220 m). Fully open March 1 to Oct 31, and partially open Oct-Nov. At the south edge of Bishop on Hwy395, beside the golf course and Schober Lane. $20 per standard tent site (based on two people) or $25 RV hook-up (includes electricity and water); small charge for extra people. Token operated showers for paying guests only (no drop-ins); coin-op laundry, general store, bathrooms, TV room; nice environment.

Millpond Campground, (760) 937-6775. Elevation 4000 feet (1220 m). Open March 1 to Nov 31. A few miles northwest of Bishop on Sawmill Road adjacent to the Millpond Recreation Area. Drive 6.5 miles from Bishop center (less from the edge) north/west on Hwy395 and turn south on Sawmill Road. $20 per standard tent site (good for four people) or $25 RV hook-up (includes electricity and water); small charge for extra people. Token operated showers for paying guests only (no drop-ins); coin-op laundry, electric outlets in laundry room, fire pits.

USFS Campgrounds, (760) 873-2500 press "0" to speak to someone. 12 campgrounds in the Bishop Creek valley. Elevation 7500 to 9500 feet (2300 to 2900 m). Only one of the grounds (Intake-2 Walk-In, 8200 feet) is open all year; the rest open around late April and close some time in October. They are located down one or the other of two forks, toward the end of Hwy168 that leads west from Bishop beyond the Buttermilk Road turn-off. $20 at campgrounds with no water, otherwise $21 per site. Pit toilets. For more information see www.fs.fed.us (enter Inyo Campgrounds into the search bar at left).

NATURAL AND HUMAN HISTORY

Geology of the Bishop Region

The Bishop region has a great diversity of scenery due to its dramatic topography. Here you'll find semi-deserts, rocky foothills, forested plateaus, rivers, lakes, hot springs, tall rugged peaks, and even small glaciers.

The massive Owens Valley is a geologic wonder. As a result of text-book block-faulting on an enormous scale, the center is dropping ever deeper while the mountains at either side rise higher along its 100-mile length. The process has been on-going for five million years and is part of a continental-scale stretching across much of western North America, an area known as the Basin and Range Geologic Province. The Sierra Nevada Mountains, at the Basin and Range's western extremity, are creeping skyward at a rate of a little over 1 inch per century.

South and west of Bishop, the displacement of the Owens Valley relative to the Sierra mountain block is accommodated by the warping of the earth's crust, known as the Coyote Warp. This effect is pushing up both the foothills southwest of Bishop, including the Druid Stones, and also the Tungsten Hills. The Tungsten Hills extend from Grouse Mountain high in the Buttermilk Country almost to Hwy395 on the outskirts of town. The rock across the region is quartz monzonite, a rock similar to granite.

Bishop is in a very active geological area. We need only look back 550 years to the last volcanic eruption, just north of Mammoth Lakes, and back to 135 years to the last big earthquake 60 miles south, at Lone Pine—a quake that left a horizontal displacement of 20 feet and leveled almost every building in the Owens Valley.

But that recent quake was nothing compared to what happened 740,000 years ago, when one of the planet's greatest ever pyroclastic events took place: The Long Valley Caldera 30 miles north of Bishop erupted with force equivalent to 500 times that of the 1980 Mount St Helens eruption. This explosion filled the entire north end of the Owens Valley with hundreds of cubic miles of frothy molten rock topped off with volcanic ash, some of which fell as a thin layer across eastern Kansas.

The rock cooled, and depending how deep it was, became more or less dense, later faulting and eroding to become the delicate desert scenery of the Volcanic Tablelands just to Bishop's north. At its lower elevation, this rock, called tuff extends thinly beneath the present day valley bottom. The Chalk Bluff (running beside the approach road to the Happy and Sad Boulders) may look like the edge of that original pyroclastic flow, but is in fact a water-cut cliff. Traveling up Hwy395's Sherwin Grade to the north, the Volcanic Tableland gains thickness and elevation to become the beautiful jeffery- and pinyon pine-covered Sherwin Plateau (see page 70).

Since the caldera explosion, the upper Owens Valley's western edge continued to undergo periods of glaciation, with glaciers grinding down from the Sierras into the Owens Valley, dragging with them huge amounts of debris and boulders. As the glaciers finally retreated, they left enormous long piles of rock—moraines. An excellent example of one of these is crossed by Hwy168 shortly after the turn off for the Buttermilks.

Petroglyphs on the tableland.

Bishop History

The Paiute-Shoshone tribe of Native Americans living in Bishop today describe themselves as descendants of the people who first settled the Owens Valley thousands of years ago. These aboriginal Americans survived into the 1850s largely undisturbed, with no significant contact outside of their ethnic group or region, living in the Bishop area, hunting, gathering, and irrigating the valley.

There are some superb petroglyph sites in the area—rocks on which light-colored symbols and drawings have been etched into a dark patina. These sites are scattered across the tableland. The precise dates of their creation have so far eluded anthropologists.

It is known that the first non-indigenous European Americans made homesteads in the area from about 1850, and after this, life in the valley for the original inhabitants changed forever. The Native Americans' opposition to domination by the settlers didn't last for long. After an intermittent two-year war, the settlers gained the upper hand. A town was established and named after one of its original pioneering cattle-farmers, the corpulent Samuel A. Bishop who had arrived with several hundred cattle in 1861. Through the late 1800s, Bishop established itself as a meat- and crop-producing center for booming mining areas of California and Nevada.

In 1873, a railroad opened in Owens Valley, eventually connecting to Carson City. After riding the line with California's then Senator, soon after it opened, an eminent local banker, perhaps disenchanted with the vast expanses of wilderness, cuttingly quipped, "We either built it 300 miles too long or 300 years too soon!" Hindsight indicates he was right. The line is long gone today, but you can visit the Laws Railway Museum at Laws, northeast of Bishop.

As the mining boom ended, another major change was in store for the area. From 1905 onward, the City of Los Angeles Department of Water and Power (LADWP) began a campaign to surreptitiously buy up lands in order to own the water rights along the entire length of the Owens River and its tributaries. This accomplished, the construction of the 223-mile-long Los Angeles aqueduct—a massive engineering feat—was undertaken, and finally completed in 1913.

With the water pulled out from under the agriculture industry, and with the LADWP, now the major Bishop landowner having no interest in seeing population growth in the area, the City of Bishop became locked in a strange slow-growth time-warp. Meanwhile, disputes about the legalities of numerous LADWP deals, sleights-of-hand, and about government mishandling of Native American land-claims have raged for decades and show no signs of abating.

Vegetation

When arriving at the Volcanic Tablelands or Buttermilks mid-winter, climbers might be forgiven for thinking that this is a barren land of rock, gravel, and half-dead bushes. This is a mistake. First, those bushes are definitely not dead. Even though they sometimes look like firewood, please do not disturb them nor allow your dog to rip them up! Also, in the spring and early summer a rich array of flowers from tall blue lupines and yellow blazing star to delicate carpets of the miniscule forget-me-nots, wooly daisy and evening snow, sprout out of the sand up and down the Happy and Sad Canyons, across the vast expanse of the Tableland, and up to the highest valleys of the Sierra Nevada Mountains.

On the Tableland, these plants survive on the extremely porous soil, with no flowing water, living only by direct precipitation, with annuals waiting to burst forth after a suitable number of warm spring rains. Up in the Buttermilk Country, plants again have to deal with porous soil, but due to the altitude, greater precipitation, and late snow melt, there is a surprisingly moist under-base to the dry gravelly surface through to mid summer. Plants are widely but thinly distributed here, and explode into bloom with abundance when conditions are right.

The permanent low-growing shrubs across both bouldering areas are the sages, including the ubiquitous soft and fragrant-leaved big sagebrush. The common rabbit brush is another: it is richly yellow-flowered in fall. Other attractive displays in the Buttermilk Country in early spring are made by the pink blossoming desert peach, and the miniature yellow roses of the bitterbrush, both sweet-smelling bee-attracters that draw a loud buzz in May, the latter also a staple food of the deer.

Summer is the greenest time in the Buttermilk Country.

The Wildlife

The lower Volcanic Tableland—if you include the adjacent Owens River floodplain below the Chalk Bluff, and spring-fed ponds along Fish Slough Road—has an abundance of wildlife. Mountain lions follow deer across the Owens Valley during winter and early spring but your chance of seeing one in the Happies or Sads is pretty much nil; mule deer are commonly seen; coyotes are here, as are foxes; huge-eared black-tailed jackrabbits (Californian hares) are extremely common; cotton-tailed bunnies too; antelope ground squirrels are also frequently seen, popularly mistaken for chipmunks (which are smaller and fluffier). Another interesting rodent is the cute and tiny kangaroo rat, which hops about on oversized hind legs with its long tufted tail and is seen at night or dusk just before you run it over.

In the Happies and Sads, you will occasionally notice massive nests of sticks under boulders, but primarily in crevices, covered by a dark, shiny resin-like material. These are the so-called middens, of pack rats (a.k.a. desert wood rats). Pack rats build these homes from whatever they can scrape together from nearby. They cover the entire mess with urine, which crystalizes and after many years creates the hard dark shiny solid. Interestingly, the contents of these middens can survive up to 40,000 years and are widely studied for information about past flora, fauna, and climate.

With so many rats and mice about, it is no surprise that the Volcanic Tableland is also a raptor's paradise. There is plenty of open country here for the biggest of North America's birds of prey, the golden eagle, and keen birders have an okay chance of seeing one. Commonly seen are the ubiquitous red-tailed hawks, a huge hawk with a distinctive red-brown tail often seen soaring alone or sitting on a telephone pole around the outskirts of town. The most common giant bird is the turkey vulture. This red-necked carrion-eater is notable for soaring with a tipsy motion and wings in a V. They are often in groups, and have a distinctively black and white underside. A low-flying medium-sized greyish hawk with a white rump is the Northern Harrier.

Up at the Buttermilks, mule deer are seen frequently in late fall and spring. Coyotes are around, as always, though not that often seen around the Buttermilks in my experience. Cattle are around during late spring and summer. Mountain lions are present too following the deer, and are very occasionally seen. This is a wild habitat and it is perhaps not wise to let small children wander off on their own at dusk (they'll probably fall off a rock, anyway). A likely hazard, however, are rattlesnakes, which emerge by the hundreds in late April or early May—be very careful at this time of year because they seem to be everywhere. They become scarce toward fall and are not seen during winter.

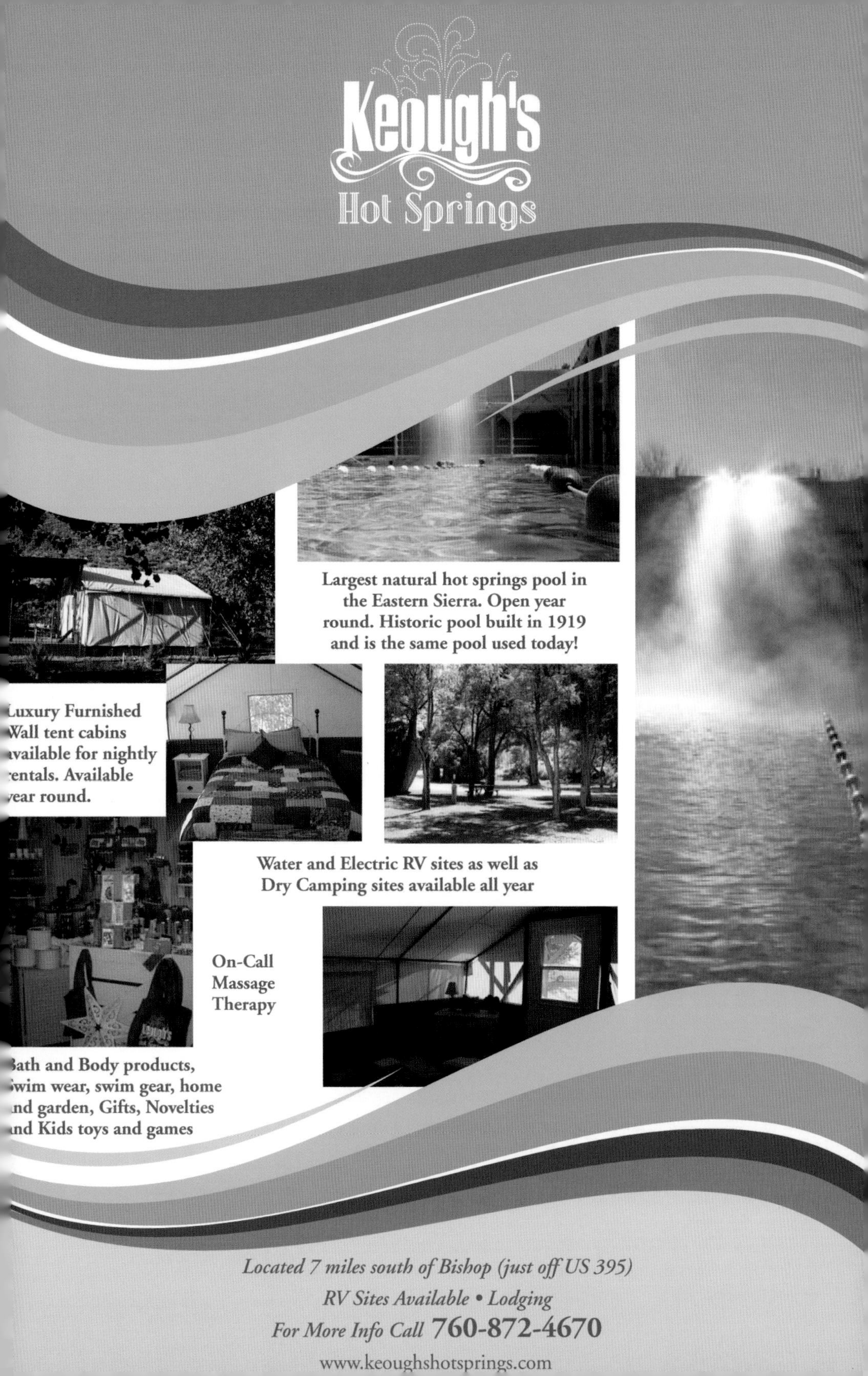

Keough's
Hot Springs
Largest natural hot springs pool in the Eastern Sierra. Open year round. Historic pool built in 1919 and is the same pool used today!
Luxury Furnished Wall tent cabins available for nightly rentals. Available year round.
Water and Electric RV sites as well as Dry Camping sites available all year
On-Call Massage Therapy
Bath and Body products, Swim wear, swim gear, home and garden, Gifts, Novelties and Kids toys and games
Located 7 miles south of Bishop (just off US 395)
RV Sites Available • Lodging
For More Info Call 760-872-4670
www.keoughshotsprings.com

HOW TO USE THIS BOOK

Grades/Ratings

Problems are given ratings using the well-known V system first devised explicitly for bouldering at Hueco Tanks, Texas. This is most effectively used for rating short, sustained bursts of climbing, usually three to ten moves long. The ratings assume that a climber does not jump off the ground to gain holds out of reach, unless instructed to do so, and that the climber begins at the commonly accepted starting point of the problem, or an equivalent place. The V scale is open-ended, and in this book runs from v0 through v14, with the vB (B for "basic") being used to denote a problem easier than v0. Note that even a v0 will have moves equivalent to those found on a crux sequence of a 5.10 climb.

All ratings are open to debate and one must expect most problems to feel a grade or so to either side of the rating given – *that is normal* (unless you really are Mr. Perfectly Average).

Color coding for the problem numbers in the text, on the topos, and on the photo-diagrams is used to denote V-grade ranges as indicated here:

- vB — v2
- v3 — v5
- v6 — v9
- v10 — v14
- = unclimbed or unknown

Grade Comparison Chart

V Rating	Fontainebleau
vB	3 or under
v0	3 to 4
v1	4 to 5
v2	5 to 6
v3	6a to 6b
v4	6b to 6c
v5	6c to 7a
v6	7a+
v7	7b
v8	7b+
v9	7c
v10	7c+
v11	8a
v12	8a+
v13	8b
v14	8b+
v15	8c

Symbols and Stars

 = Scary And/or Highball Problems

Problems that have particularly high cruxes and/or bad landings, are indicated by up to three symbols. The symbol represents a heart flutter, a shot of adrenaline, or a heart attack! The more fluttering hearts, the more brave, or stupid you have to be to attempt the line, and the more spotters and pads you are likely to want. The heart rating assumes the line is near your physical limit, and influenced by likelihood of a big fall. In other words, if the climbing is hard for the overall grade high on the line it gets a higher highball rating than a hard climb with easy moves to finish.

 = Star Ratings

This book uses a simple three-star system. The more stars, the better the climbing.

★ = locally a good line (within its section of the guidebook

★★ = one of the best in the entire Bishop area

★★★ = a world-class problem

BISHOP BOULDERING HISTORY

"There is no way that I know of, to pass on paper the feeling that permeates the person who steps out of the shower with epidermis cleaned and tingling from crystal scrapes, muscles pleasantly tired, joints well oiled, and mind and spirit glowing from a full day of Buttermilking." — **William "Smoke" Blanchard, recollecting experiences of the 1940s to 1980s in his autobiography**

The Chouinard catalog and *Summit* magazine of 1973 heralded both piton-free "clean climbing," and a new era of bouldering.

Smoke Blanchard, a gifted raconteur and renowned mountain guide, is likely the first person to have climbed for fun at the Buttermilks. He moved to Bishop in 1942, and immediately recognized the untapped potential of the Buttermilk Country as a playground for what he came to call his "rock course" involving what he describes as "Buttermilking" – a scramble-climb-hike up chimneys, up slabs, and over summits of the Buttermilk Mountain – north of the main Peabodies area.

Blanchard passed on his love of the Buttermilks to Doug Robinson, John Fisher, Galen Rowell, and Don Jensen among others. Of the boulders, the largest ones were the targets of the early pioneers. They sought tall free-climbing opportunities or first ascents of summits rather than boulder problems in the modern sense. Toproping was the norm for taller lines, but in the case of the giant monolith of the Grandpa Peabody, Doug Robinson placed a bolt on the east face.

The latter line was shown in a Chouinard Catalog in the early 1970s in a piece written by Robinson to herald the new concept of clean, hammerless, climbing. Ironically, the rope runs through a sling clipped to a hammer-drilled bolt. "Locals laugh because the rope in the Grandpa clean-climbing photo runs through a bolt," writes Smoke Blanchard in his autobiography *Walking Up and Down in the World.* "But that's okay because all agree that Doug is certified pure, and the editor needed the picture."

On Grandma Peabody, bolts were also placed on the top. These were then used as toprope anchors. In 1973 Summit magazine printed an article by Galen Rowell about the vast climbing possibilities on the East Side. This included four pages of images showcasing bouldering at the Buttermilks, though the area is deliberately never named. "In one region," states Rowell, "even ropes are not often used." Clearly, bouldering was becoming more and more an end in itself, even though it was rarely the prime focus of top climbers. Certainly by the mid 1970s climbers on the East Side introduced their friends to the area primarily as a bouldering destination. Toproping was still popular, but *Birthday Direct* (v3), *Good Morning Sunshine* (v1), *Green Wall Essential* (v2), *King Tut* (v3), and the *Monkey Dihedral* (v2), among others, were standard bouldering fare for that era.

Dozens of climbers began gravitating to Yosemite Valley during this period, and hot summers moved these same climbers up the hill to the nearby Tuolumne Meadows, where they were just a short drive from the East Side. The

pumice cliffs north of Mammoth Lakes became a diversion to the Tuolumne climbers, offering excellent bouldering opportunities at areas such as Deadman's Summit and the Bachar Boulders. At these areas, an exchange of information took place between the Valley devotees and the Mammoth/Bishop climbing community.

Dale Bard, a long-time Yosemite climber and pioneer, recalls his first visit to Bishop around 1974 or 1975. Arriving at the invite of a friend, the Bishop locals ribbed Bard that he would have to stay back at the house because they were going climbing at "a secret area." This turned out to be the Buttermilk Boulders, an area Bard had heard little of and had never seen.

Some time soon after that first visit, Bard was likely the first person to climb the *Green Wall Center* (v6), up the middle of the immaculate polished rock of the Green Wall Boulder's pretty north face. This achievement becomes ever more impressive the more we modern boulderers neglect our footwork. It is still hard, and superb. *Pope's Prow* (v6) was another wicked old-school line likely done in the mid to late 1970s and still very hard, bouting many top boulderers even today. Precisely who did the first ascent is unclear. The problem is named after a local boulderer Mike Pope, but Pope never climbed the line.

Bard took to the Buttermilks with such enthusiasm that in 1978 he moved there. I don't mean he moved to Bishop, he actually moved to the Buttermilk Country itself. He set up home at the end of a long dirt road, hiding his converted delivery van behind some rocks where he lived like a hermit for about two years. The camp was visible from the Peabodies if you knew where to look, and resulting in the naming of the bouldering area Dale's Camp, many years later.

Around 1979 Bard established *Change of Heart* (v6) and *High Plains Drifter* (v7). Both are solid at the grade (shorter climbers will likely find the first one just as hard as the second). Both are punchy and high and (in an era with no crashpads) remained the most sought-after testpieces in the area for nearly twenty years. Confusion as to which problem was which was compounded by errors in a 1988 East Side Climbs guidebook — a confusion finally laid to rest by Bard himself. *High Plains Drifter* remains to this day one of the greatest prizes of the area.

It was also around the late 1970s that John Bachar began bouldering here, and he was impressed with what he saw. Bachar, on his way to becoming a legendary climber and free-soloist, was also turned on to bouldering.

"Bard took to the Buttermilks with such enthusiasm that in 1978 he set up home at the end of a long dirt road, hiding his converted delivery van behind some rocks where he lived like a hermit for about two years."

Bachar made infrequent visits to the Buttermilk area, but made quick repeats of Bard's Drifter problems. He also added two fine hard problems on the eponymous Bachar Boulder: *Bachar's Wall Left* and *Bachar's Wall Right* (both around v5). By means of a "cheat-stone" and then by clipping into a hanging toprope, Bachar was able to ascend *Rastaman Vibration* from after the crux first move, though he never "claimed," far less named the line (which was eventually done from a ground start in 2002).

Bard, who was relatively short at 5-foot-6, seems to have introduced the use of cheat stones to the area as, for some odd reason, many problems he tried were virtually blank in their lower ten feet. A two-feet high block was used by Bard to ascend the excellent *Scenic Crank* (v6 or v7 from this start), and this block remained under the problem for a generation before finally disappearing.

Bard was basically King of the Buttermilks through the end of the 1970s and into the early 1980s, pulling ascents of most of the area's then-testpieces. His contribution to the bouldering and popularization of this outstanding area is immense. Attention, even from Bard, however, was focused almost exclusively on the Main Buttermilks area – aka The Peabody Boulders.

At the end of the 1970s word had spread far and wide regarding the quality and quantity of climbing at the 'Milks. Amazingly though, keen boulderers were still being shut out by the isolation of the local community, and few people actually knew where the place was. As images of the area seeped into catalogs, magazines and instructional booklets, the sweet-sounding name of "The Buttermilk Country" came to symbolize a kind of Shangri La.

Gary Slate, a devotee of East Side climbing through the 1980s, explains that after moving to Mammoth around 1979, he had to find the area by literally driving around. Having discovered Buttermilk Road on a map, it was only a matter of following the bumpy dirt track far enough. After investigating several less-than-impressive stops along the way, he eventually turned the corner below the humongous Peabody Boulders and his jaw dropped.

The 1980s brought a slow but steady rate of development at the Buttermilks, with seemingly countless climbers all saying they were bouldering there "all the time" but without seeing anybody else. The same comment has been made by so many that it seems they must all have been blind. Kevin Leary – who lends his name to the tall and excellent *Leary/Bard Arete* – was one of the strongest boulderers of the time, as was Roy McClenahan.

Above: Scott Burke looks stylish as he climbs the Sunshine boulder around 1984. Photo: Roy McClenahan.

Tony Pupo, of the world famous Rubber Room resoling business, may have made the first ascent of *The Iron Man* (v4) around 1981. It is probably the most popular climb at the Buttermilks, and for good reason: It is so simple and yet so incredibly good. Route climbers pulling down into the high 5.12 range considered it a sound achievement during the 1980s. It wasn't until the early 1990s that people started regularly campusing it!

Some climbers say that they bouldered a lot during the 1980s but not in any competitive way, as drinking beer and imbibing other toxins were typical of bouldering sessions during this era. Whatever the reason, Bard's "Drifter" problems, *The Leary/Bard Arete* (v5) and *Pope's Prow* (v6) remained the big ticks of the decade, with Tommy Herbert's *Junior's Achievement* (v7) also getting a look-in as a possible contender for having the hardest moves, or at least the thinnest holds. It is worth noting, however, that with the Buttermilks having so many super-highball lines, there were plenty of problems in the relatively low end of the v-scale that were nevertheless top end, highly respected climbs of the day, sans crash-pad.

Dale Bard was King of the Buttermilks during the 1980s, and his testpieces set the standard for twenty years. Photo: Ken Yager.

It is also worth noting a couple of women who contributed to the area's development in the

Lidija Painkiher set high standards for women on the East Side in the mid to late 1980s. Photo: Dennis Jensen.

1980s: Lidija Painkiher and Bobbi Bensman. During a brief few visits, Bensman made several ascents including perhaps a first, the Original Line on the Bowling Pin. Painkiher (nicknamed Lulu) was a regular at the Buttermilks, and pulled off the first ascent of *Lululator* (v4) on the Tut Boulder. After being given a tour of the Pollen Grains area (as it is now most commonly known), her friends joked about how she had been unable to even reach the first holds on the boulders and problems the guys were showing her. As a laugh these same friends named the area the Lidija Boulders in her honor.

Back then, climbers clearly weren't looking for the steep-patina sit-starts and lie-down-starts that are to be had at the Pollen Grains. Proud lines and straight-forward standing starts were what caught the eye. Longtime East Side local Dennis Jensen recalls how he and a friend first investigated the Lidija Boulders and climbed one tall proud line – the northeast arete of the Beekeeper Boulder. It turned out, though, that there was no easy way off the block (downclimbing is at least as hard as getting up!), and they were forced to put in a bolt to descend.

The Bouldering Boom

The early to mid 1990s saw a big explosion in bouldering across the USA and the world. Tommy Klinefelter, a strong young climber living in Bishop, realized that things were beginning to change. Chalk was appearing in unfamiliar places. Tall, strong, and with a ton of natural talent, Klinefelter stepped up and soon added some amazing gems to the Buttermilk circuit, including *Soul Slinger* (v9) around 1996/7, and the amazing *Saigon* (v6) around 1999-2000. How that latter one slipped through the cracks is hard to imagine as it is one of the most sought-after problems at the 'Milks today.

But Klinefelter's biggest claim to fame came in early 1995, when he climbed the striking overhanging groove of *Stained Glass* (v10). The problem involves precarious moves up a gently overhanging glassy dihedral to gain a micro-crimp for the left hand. There follows a giant leap, or massive span, for an incut at the summit of the block.

Another strong climber also completed Stained Glass early in 1995. His name was Fred Nicole. Nicole was—and is still—a Swiss powerhouse who led the world in the development of hard bouldering throughout the 1990s. He also thought he was making a first ascent of the line, and named the problem *Le Livre Ouvert* (which is French for The Open Book). It is worth noting, however, that Nicole pulled his ascent from a sit-start. His assessment … about v12, one of the hardest lines around. Today, some will suggest the sit-start is worth 11 duckets, but that is debatable. My guess is that for Nicole conditions weren't so good on the line.

Around the same time, Nicole also solved a long-standing problem by climbing *Babure* (v12), a very long traverse across the lowest section of the Grandma Peabody's golden patina face. Top boulderers, and any top route climber visiting the area would have been aghast at the size of the holds and the spans needed on this immaculate testpiece – actually they still are. It's "only" a traverse, but it's a pretty darn challenging one.

Nineteen-ninety-five was a big year for Bishop bouldering for another reason as it saw the rediscovery and beginning of new development at an area previously little-visited and generally discarded. This was the year that Mammoth locals started to climb at the Happy Boulders in earnest. Peter Croft, Kevin Calder, Marty Lewis, Rob Stockstill, Scott Sedersom and Kris Carpenter were all part of the frenetic development. Peter Croft's *Hulk* (v6), climbed at that time, is one of the most popular at its grade in Bishop, an intriguing, world-class problem. The focus, however, was as much on running laps on the long but excellent traverses on the rim, as developing pure bouldering problems on the boulders.

The canyon was clearly replete with rock. But to those used to climbing granite trad routes, or even long sport routes, it just didn't look particularly inviting. It had been dubbed Lost Camel Canyon by one group of climbers. Squaw Canyon and Cali Canyon were names used by other groups, while Marty Lewis, in his Bishop Area Climbs guidebook of 1995, used yet another term, The Boulder Farm – a name that might well have become standard. Yet none of these names quite captured the spirit of the age. None of these names told what needed to be told about the area. None of these names summed up the essence of the place with one simple word.

It turned out that Rob Stockstill, an early pioneer of the area, had already hit upon the perfect name. Taking a hint from the nearby Pleasant Valley Dam, he called the place The Happy Boulders. The name stuck, and for one main reason: Mick Ryan.

Mick Ryan was a major force for development on the East Side from 1996 to 2005, documenting all he found and spreading the joy. Photo: Wills Young.

"Within a year, the Happy Boulders were the most talked-about boulders on the planet, and within two years there was hardly a person alive who didn't want to go there, who hadn't already been there, or who wasn't at that moment on his or her way there."

Ryan's arrival in Bishop heralded a whole new era. When Ryan walked up the trail into the Happy Boulders for the first time in 1996, he was beaming from ear to ear. Ryan instantly saw a world of bouldering; a world of first ascent possibilities; a world of fun. This was what Ryan lived for: This was happiness!

Mick Ryan's passion for climbing, for the development and cataloging of boulder problems, and for sharing his excitement was virtually boundless, barely tempered by his fiercely competitive nature. Within a year, the Happy Boulders were the most talked-about boulders on the planet, and within two years there was hardly a person alive who didn't want to go there, who hadn't already been there, or who wasn't at that moment on his or her way there.

Closures and later restrictions on access at Hueco Tanks, Texas, during 1997, accompanied by a flood of magazine articles or cover images of Bishop, served to increase the demand, and climbers poured in from all over the world. Significant ascents from this period include the Happy Boulders' first v10, *Slow Dance*, put up by Tim Clifford of Burley in Wharfedale, England. Clifford also added *Disco Diva* (v8) in the winter of 1996/7. Ryan himself pulled off the first ascent of the exceptional *Morning Dove White* (v7), not to mention a host of other lines, often reluctantly sharing spoils with Greg Haverstock, another of

Tommy Klinefelter back in his heyday on *Change of Heart* (v6) circa 1988. At 6-foot-3 and 135lbs there was little that could stop him – even in a cut-down pair of Resin Roses with the pink blacked out! Photo: Jeff Schoen.

Chris Sharma eyes *The Checkerboard* minutes before the first ascent. Sharma's contribution to bouldering in the Buttermilks was huge, and his influence on the bouldering trend even greater.

the most prolific developers of new lines across the Bishop region.

By the late 1990s, the drive for first ascents was in full swing, not just at the Happies, but at the newly emerging Sad Boulders. It was at this time that Tim Steele began to exert his low-key influence here, steadily becoming a major player both on the boulders and as a mover behind the 'scene,' so to speak. While adding such neo-classics as *Cholos* (v9) at the Happies and *Pow Pow* (v8) at the Sads, Steele was also instrumental in filming and creating West Coast Pimp, a video largely featuring his band of friends and acquaintances pulling down FAs and area testpieces both on the Tablelands, and elsewhere. The vid quickly became a hit with the fast-growing California bouldering community. Memorable moments from the footage include Byron Schumpert working *Rorschach Test*, the short version of which he later climbed at v10, and Michi Tresch's ascent of the Happies' testpiece *Swordfish Trombone* (v11).

Michi Tresch (one of the pair of very strong Tresch brothers) came over from Switzerland two seasons in a row, and was instrumental in pushing the level of bouldering and forcing American climbers to respond with testpieces of their own. Victor Copeland, another 'star' introduced by the West Coast Pimp footage, was one of the Americans who stepped up to the plate. Copeland's contribution was enormous. He not only cranked off some stubborn lines, such as *Shizaam Sit Start* (hard v10, at the Sad Boulders) and *Golden Child* (v9, at the Druids), but he was a master of the highball, revelling in off-the-deck dicey lines that were crying out to be climbed ... just not by you or me. He's another of those modern-era climbers whose major additions are just too numerous to mention. Standouts include *Atari* (v6, at the

"That *The Mandala* (v12) was not climbed until this same time, however, is understandable. Sharma's ascent of this conspicuous prow was hailed at the time as perhaps the finest achievement in American bouldering."

Sam Edwards came over from Tasmania and established what has become today one of the hardest lines on the East Side, *Goldfish Trombone* (v14).

The effervescent Dave Graham, who established The *Spectre* (v13) and several v12s in the Buttermilk Country, checks out the holds on the *Mandala Sit Start,* prior to its first ascent by Tony Lamiche, who looks on. Photo: Wills Young.

Happy Boulders) and his likely first ascent of *Saigon Direct* (v9 highball) at the Buttermilks.

All those climbers were good, and their additions were plentiful and often brilliant. But even more impressive things were around the corner. At the dawn of the new millennium, the most significant visitor to the Buttermilks was Santa Cruz, California, prodigy Chris Sharma. Sharma, if you don't already know, has been perhaps the world's most influential climber of the past ten years. His passion for bouldering, his ability to break new ground everywhere he went, and his facility for releasing well-timed screams while sending his projects rocketed bouldering to a level of public attention it had never before known. For Sharma, and the new generation of boulderers who followed quickly on his heels, a problem like *Stained Glass* (v10) or even his own *Plain High Drifter* (v11) was merely an appetizer to be enjoyed while warming up. In 1999, Sharma's ascent of *The Buttermilker* (v13) pushed bouldering to a new level. The name is even more appropriate when you learn that he climbed it from a sitting start in the warmth of late May!

Sharma also climbed the first ascent of *The Checkerboard* (v7/8), on one of the most amazing pieces of rock on the East Side, adding the "direct" (or left-hand variation) the same day. It is just incredible to think that this spectacular line was not done until February 2000 as without a doubt it is up there with the best of its grade in the world.

That *The Mandala* (v12) was not climbed until this same time, however, is understandable. Sharma's ascent of this conspicuous prow is already legendary. It was hailed at the time as perhaps the finest achievement in American bouldering. Even after Dave Graham (of Portland, Maine) chanced upon an easier sequence and quickly pulled the second ascent early in October 2000, its stature remained supreme (see page 292).

For Sharma, *The Mandala* was but one of many fine achievements in the area. *Sharma's Traverse* (v10) on the boulder of the same name at the Peabodies, is obviously another of Sharma's lines; *The Zen Flute* (v10) and *The Hueco Wall* (v9), both at Dale's Camp are two other outstanding firsts that he checked off with ease. He dispatched *Redrum Sit Start* (v10, though harder today) without fanfare, and added *Sharma's Traverse* (v12) to the Action Figure Cave at the Happy Boulders. It seems clear, however, that *The Mandala* has stood the test of time as his finest contribution. Undoubtedly his ascent of that legendary line did close a chapter in his life as he soon moved on to even bigger and more impressive achievements elsewhere.

Left in Bishop, however, were many hard lines that eluded even Sharma. While most of the

Likely the best boulderer of all time, Anthony (Tony or "Tonio") Lamiche rocked Bishop with his flash of *The Mandala* (v12), and first ascent of *Evilution Direct* (v11). Here he pulls through the opening sequence of *Mandala Sit Start* (v14). Photo: Wills Young.

attention of top boulderers was focused on the Buttermilk region, Sam Edwards, a relatively unknown, but devilishly burly climber from Tasmania, took it upon himself to make a five-week project of a Happy Boulders roof. When finally completed, this became the hardest line in Bishop. The problem was *Goldfish Trombone* (v13/14). With minor breakages, *Goldfish Trombone* has evolved into one of Bishop's hardest lines. It must certainly be acknowledged as the hardest in America established by a Tasmanian.

Dave Graham's return that same winter placed his name into the first ascents register, cranking off the well-known project, *Spectre* (v13) early in 2001. This outrageous-looking glassy roof with widely spaced holds had been shrugging off serious attempts from the world's best. Both Sharma and Fred Nicole had session-ed the line. Graham consumed it in a matter of days. A month or so later, Nicole repeated the feat.

April 2001 brought a historical moment in women's climbing when Lisa Rands pulled off an American female first with her ascent of *Plain High Drifter* (v11), having previously made the first female flash of *High Plains Drifter* (v7) in 2000. She had also pulled off such classic tuff testpieces as *Beefcake* (v10), *Beautiful Gecko* (then v10, now harder) and *Acid Wash* (v10) to name a few. Prior to Rands' time, other women had also climbed some hard problems in the area with France's Stephanie Bodet (World Cup bouldering champion) coming away from a short visit with ascents of *Slow Dance* (v10), *Center Direct* (then v9), *Redrum* (v7), and *Cholos* (v9). In 2000, this was a very impressive tick list. Simona Ulmanova also managed an ascent of *Slow Dance* around that time and Josune Bereziartu cranked off *Center Direct* during an extended visit in February 2001.

One of the biggest, baddest challenges at the Buttermilks today is the front face of the Grandpa Peabody. While Sharma had climbed to the lip in 1999, he never threw a rope down the line or seriously attempted to push on past the dicey-looking moves above the good rail at the top of the glassy patina shield. This amazing overhang, despite being occasionally climbed over the next few years, led nowhere. In 2002, Jason Kehl arrived. Kehl, from Maryland, was beginning to make a name for himself as a performance-artist-cum-climber with a penchant for daring ascents. The Grandpa Peabody simply called his name. It was perfect: Bullet hard, smooth edges led by burly aggressive deadpoints to a physical and mental ordeal high off the deck. A flat landing meant falling was an option, but only with a virtual mountain of crashpads. After initially scoping the direct exit, Kehl settled on the left option where the crux, though desperate, would be five feet closer to the ground! After checking the moves from a toprope, and after falling a couple of times onto pads from the

"Kehl screamed his way past the lip and once safely on the low-angle run to the summit, unleashed a roaring, ear-splitting series of yells, the likes of which had not been heard at the Buttermilks since the extinction of dinosaurs."

Lisa Rands took women's bouldering to a new level with her inspiring ascent of *Plain High Drifter* (v11), a feat she repeated twice for the cameras in late March 2001. Photo: Wills Young.

upper crux, Kehl screamed his way past the lip and once safely on the low-angle run to the summit, unleashed a roaring, ear-splitting series of yells, the likes of which had not been heard at the Buttermilks since the extinction of dinosaurs. Kehl's *Evilution* (v12) was undoubtedly one of the proudest, if not the proudest achievement in East Side bouldering at the time.

But there was much more to come: 2002 was a huge year in Bishop bouldering. The Petzl "Roc Trip" brought a slew of top international climbers to town. Among the group was one of the greatest climbers ever to step up to a boulder – Antony Lamiche from L'Argentière La Bessé, France. At the end of November 2002, Lamiche was planning a rest day, and was out spotting friends who were attempting the first move on *The Mandala*. Having watched them fail one too many times, he jumped on to feel for himself what that initial long stab was like – he stuck it. Then, incredibly, he stuck the next heinous move, and so on to the top … *The Mandala*, flashed! Though planning a rest day, Lamiche ended up making one of the most impressive ascents in climbing history. A week or so later he added a sit start to the problem. A hold subsequently broke, so just before leaving, he re-climbed it. Lamiche originally rated the sit start to *The Mandala* v13. Others, including Dave Graham (with the second ascent in December 2005) and third ascensionist Daniel Woods (April 2006) have suggested v14. Lamiche also added the spectacular *Evilution Direct* (v11).

Dave Graham was back too. Full of energy and positive vibes, Graham added *A Scanner Darkly* (v12, Get Carter Boulder), *Form Destroyer* (v12, Windy Wall Area) and *A Maze of Death* (v12, Bardini Boulders). Indeed, Graham was on a roll, climbing stronger than ever; twisting, torquing, and snaking his way up lines with his unfathomable yet comprehensively effective style. The line that Graham really set his sights on was "The Brown Wall" at the Secrets area. Having warmed up by busting out the first ascent of *Form Destroyer*, he hiked across the hillside and set to work on the Brown Wall. Within an hour he was connecting the moves together and it looked like it might go down. Unfortunately, Graham's skin was cashed and there was no way to continue. Looking sorry for himself, he declared that there was always, "another day." He could return shortly, he explained, so long as no unexpected apocalypse arrived. Sadly for Dave, a huge storm moved in and dumped about two feet of snow across the Buttermilk Country.

Ethan Pringle makes the second ascent of Kevin Jorgeson's extraordinary highball *The Beautiful and Damned* at the Bardini Boulders in January 2007. The climb's name, like that of its amazing companion *This Side of Paradise* (on the other side of the boulder) is taken from a novel by F. Scott Fitzgerald. Photo: John Dickey.

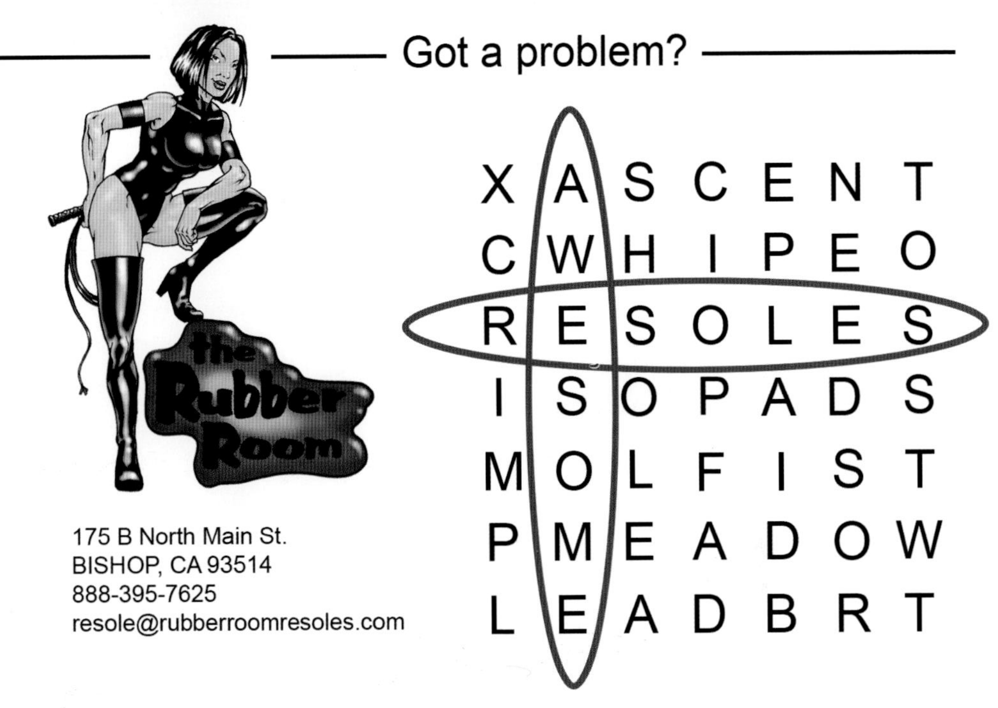

The following season, Matt Birch came from Otley, England, to try his luck on the Brown Wall project. He had visited Hueco earlier in 2003, and crushed some hard lines, including *Slashface* (v13/14 for its third ascent). Birch began working the Brown Wall in 2003 and was still working it in 2004, disabled by bouts of enervating illness. Snapping him out of this depressive state of affairs was fellow Brit, Ben Moon, whose quick send of the problem from the second move to the top provided the necessary impetus to sharpen Birch's focus. Just moments after Moon's near-ascent, Birch walked the problem from the low start. He named it *The Swarm* (v14, see page 322), and it is likely the hardest problem in Bishop.

So where will the future of Bishop Bouldering take us? Matt Wilder showed the way with *This Side of Paradise* (v10) at the Bardini Boulders. The big scary arete had been tried ground-up in the past, but Wilder adopted a Yosemite "headpoint" tactic to complete the first ascent. After his experience working big walls on El Cap, checking off a few highballs by scoping them from above seemed a pretty low-energy-investment by comparison. Wilder also managed to snag a striking square-cut arete above The Pollen Grains, *The Ninth* (v6). There are more of such excellent highballs all over the Buttermilk Country, many of which may require some cleaning, if not actual toproping. Finally, it is worth mentioning another incredible line, *The Fall Guy* (v9, FA James Pearson) and its low start, *Haroun and the Sea of Stories* (v11/12, FA Matt Wilder). This amazing wall of golden patina went unclimbed until 2005 despite being one of the most incredible pieces of climbing in Bishop: big bold moves on immaculate positive holds, right there on the Fly Boy Boulder at the main Buttermilks area. A sea of pads made the ascents possible.

No doubt, with the increasing use of pads, and increasing standards, more such spectacular lines will be revealed and climbed in the coming years. Some of these are already listed as projects in this guidebook.

HISTORY UPDATE

Monster problems lure boulderers to new heights

Pad-pooling and oversized pads are redefining "bouldering." Photo: Wills Young.

Looking back now over the last few years, it is clear that the bouldering development around Bishop has focused on the tall lines of the Buttermilk Country. Indeed Bishop has well and truly come to the fore as the undisputed world capital of highballs.

Kevin Jorgeson from Santa Rosa, California, had been honing his Buttermilk skills over the previous few years, completing such finger-bending test pieces as *The Mandala* (v12), *A Maze of Death* (v12), *Evilution* (v12), and *The Swarm* (v14) among others. As 2007 opened, he turned his attention to some of the more mind-bending possibilities. Within the first week of the New Year, Jorgeson had completed an extraordinary double with two new highballs the equal or the better of all that had gone before.

Arriving early in January 2007, he completed *The Beautiful and Damned* (v13), on the west side of the Bardini Boulder, a highball that took things to a new level. After big moves on crimps and a crux slap for a sloper, the climbing moves into extreme territory with dicey high-steps on poor footholds and big insecure presses between sloping edges. Judging by the combined difficulty and highball factor, this was, at the time, Bishop's hardest challenge. Given Jorgeson's first ascent of another striking and photogenic highball, *The Flight of the Bumblebee* (v8) at the Secrets Area within a few days, it seemed that in the space of a week, he had crowned himself the new king of the 'Milks.

Though narrowly missing out on the first ascent of *The Beautiful and Damned*, Ethan Pringle nevertheless gained notoriety for its second ascent, shown in the movie *King Lines* (by Big Up Productions). The film primarily focused on Chris Sharma, but when the filmmakers stopped in Bishop they captured Pringle's ascent with Sharma nervously spotting. Sharma himself quickly completed the lower section of the line, but chose to drop from the large hold at half way, rather than risk all for the third ascent. Though claiming to be out of shape for bouldering, he

Kevin Daniels climbing the John Bachar Memorial Problem (v1 solo) on the immaculate *White Slab* at the Upper Area of the Pollen Grains. Photo: Wills Young.

nevertheless popped out to the Happy Boulders to dispatch *Goldfish Trombone* (v14) in the space of a couple of hours for its fastest ascent to date.

While Sharma has been able to resist it, the buzz for highballing is a strong drug to those visiting Buttermilk Country, with first ascent mania overcoming peoples' better judgment at times. One climber, a devotee of first ascents, Kevin Daniels, having moved to Bishop in October 2006, soon began scanning the area for new gems on which to test his resolve. In April 2008, Daniels climbed *The KD Factor* (v5-ish) on the Hive Boulder at the Pollen Grains, which he named for the flak he received after chalking his initials on the rock at the base of his prior climbs in a somewhat overzealous desire to alert the world. After John Bachar's memorial in 2009, Daniels went out to the Pollen Grains to add the *John Bachar Memorial Problem* (a v1 solo) up a beautiful white slab, a fitting tribute to the lost master.

However, the most impressive "first" ascent Daniels made turned out to be a second! After the guide came out, he noted a line described there as "an awesome highball/headpoint project" and went out to the Secrets Area to take a look. Rapping the line, he could see that it would go, and if there was any trace of chalk on the holds, he didn't notice it. Daniels certainly felt that inexplicable thrill of being first. In his enthusiasm, he took a serious spill from high on *The Flight of the Bumblebee*, hitting the large rock at the base so hard that his knee slammed into his face to split his cheek. It could have been far worse. Undeterred, however, Daniels went back at the end of November 2007 and with a pit of pads ticked the line, unwittingly making its second "first ascent!"

Lisa Rands is another climber who has always relished the headier challenges. Like many, she was enamored with *This Side of Paradise* (v10), the soaring ship's prow at the Bardini Boulders. Due to the overhang, the lower moves are hard to work on rappel, but Rands was able to lower down and feel the holds just above the crux. With this limited knowledge, and having climbed only the slab topout, she set off from the ground with as many pads under the line as she could convince her friends to carry, plus any others she had taken up the day before! Rands took a couple of huge diggers before making an inspired ascent by a very tricky sequence.

Left: Tony Lamiche visited during a heatwave, but nevertheless left his mark with a re-ascent of *Xavier's Roof* (v11), which he did by a truly heinous method shown here. He also added the excellent *Tony's Dyno* at Rock Creek among others. Photo: Wills Young.

The ascent was documented in the movie *The Sharp End* (by Sender Films).

After Jeff Sillcox completed *The Mandala Direct* (v12) a straightening of the top part of *The Mandala* and harder than the original, Paul Robinson stepped in to complete the sit start to that direct version, *The Mandala Direct Assis*, in the spring of 2007. Robinson considered this to be hard v14 and it may well be physically the hardest problem in the area.

Winters in Bishop can be harsh, and when the snow falls, the only upside is the intense development that is paid to the more sheltered lines. One of climbing's greatest over-achievers, Sean McColl arrived from Vancouver, Canada, at the beginning of 2008. With about a month in the area, then-20-year-old McColl's options were reduced by repeated snow falls, but he made best use of the situation, repeating *The Mandala Sit Start* (v14), *Goldfish Trombone* (v14 at the Happies), and other hard lines before looking around for new options. McColl's efforts culminated in link-ups on the Grandma Peabody's northwest face, including *The Oracle* (v13: *Baburre* into *The Mystery*), and *True North* (v13: *Baburre* into *Direction*). He also added *Water Hazard* (v10) at the Sad Boulders, so named after the lake that had formed at the back of the Ice Caves, and the obvious *Kill On Sight* (v12), in the Slow Dance Cave at The Happy Boulders.

McColl repeated the *Bubba* series of traverses at the Smoking Joe's Area of the Happies too, falling five times at the heartbreaker finish of Dan Mills' recent *Bubba Lobotomy* (v12). We have the elusive Dan Mills to thank for the numerous "Bubba" lines on the Tableland, which appeared just before and just after the last guide came out, and which are allegedly a reference to some shady Bishop drug dealer, though it might also be argued that Bubba is Mills' own alter ego... Who knows? Whatever the reason, thanks to Mills, Bubba is immortalized in the guidebook today.

While the bad weather continued, Lisa Rands started 2008 off with a bang by making the first female ascent of *The Mandala* (v12). When it was first climbed, Rands had considered *The Mandala* the ultimate boulder problem, falling in love with the purity of the line, and its beautiful setting. The first move is a huge one for someone her size, but Rands knew she could complete it if she could stick that one powerful move. She had to be patient as injuries and conditions reduced opportunities, but in the middle of January, after Matt Birch and McColl had helped clear the top of snow, she crushed it convincingly.

One boulder that came to the fore much more recently is the massive block in the gully between the Windy Wall and the Secrets of the Beehive area. Particularly noteworthy was Shawn Diamond's ascent of *Luminance* (v10) in late December 2008. *Luminance* takes on the striking west-facing overhang that glows golden in the afternoon light, drawing people in with widely spaced deep incuts running up the 55-degree overhang. This steep line, though not particularly long for a Buttermilk super-highball,

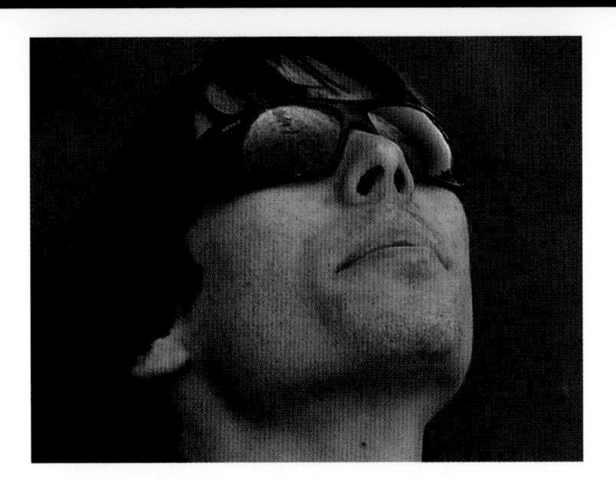

Above: Kevin Jorgeson contemplates *Ambrosia*. Right: Sean McColl sends *True North* (v13). Below right: Matt Wilder climbing *Evilution Direct* (v11).
Photos: Tim Kemple, McColl Collection, Wills Young.

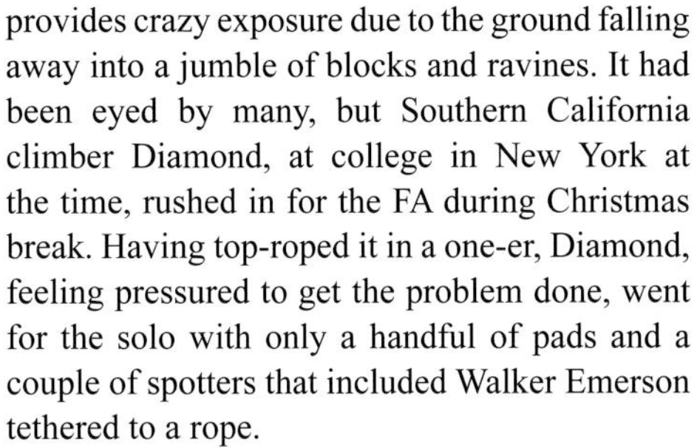

provides crazy exposure due to the ground falling away into a jumble of blocks and ravines. It had been eyed by many, but Southern California climber Diamond, at college in New York at the time, rushed in for the FA during Christmas break. Having top-roped it in a one-er, Diamond, feeling pressured to get the problem done, went for the solo with only a handful of pads and a couple of spotters that included Walker Emerson tethered to a rope.

After one scary spill, all went well, Diamond topped out, and the ascent was bigged up online and in the press with more hyperbole than any Buttermilk climb since *The Mandala* was touted as the world's first v16. The achievment was almost surpassed by the heights of poetic revelry attained in its exaltation. Regardless, this is truly a magnificent line, with some of the most exciting climbing in Bishop.

Kevin Jorgeson arrived early in January 2009, hot on the heels of Diamond to find the scene abuzz with the *Luminance* news. But Jorgeson had yet bigger, badder things on his mind. Just as one crazy ascent pushes the bounds of our credibility, and uses up every known superlative in the thesaurus, another comes along to take things yet further and test our tolerance to the max. Can we take more? Are we all highballed out? Not at all! Jorgeson was in town hoping to succeed on what he considered would be Bishop's new ultimate highball, the real ultimate highball: *Ambrosia.*

The Grandpa Peabody is a massive boulder by any standards and its east face is its most

unrelenting. Sure, there are bigger free standing boulders in the world… but not many. The well-featured, steadily overhanging east face of this monster was once a top-rope project that Tom (formerly Tommy) Herbert had been working back in the early 1990s. Recognizing its beauty, he even named the line *Ambrosia*, food of the immortals, fitting with the Buttermilk theme. Herbert wrestled with the idea of bolting the face, knowing it would make a fine sport route. However, he had already set a precedent for the area: he had removed bolts once placed on the neighboring *Transporter Room* (5.12), as a point of protest against the sport-bolting of Buttermilk climbs. Bolting was not an option. Moreover, the Buttermilks was a lonely, surreal backwater at the time. No place to be seen. Or unseen. Consequently, Herbert moved on to cliffs elsewhere. He left the spectacular wall chalked but unclimbed. In a sense then, we have Herbert to thank for steering the Buttermilks to its current path, one that left the great unclimbed lines for future generations, sparing these climbs the humiliation of a one-way trip to rap-bolted obscurity.

Jorgeson first noticed the line in 2006 and it became his secret goal. He already had well-established highball credentials in Bishop, as noted earlier, but only in late 2008, after returning from a trip to England's gritstone, did he feel ready to take on the super-project.

But he wasn't the first: A young British climber, George Ullrich, had been on the line too, during that previous summer. Indeed Ullrich had climbed the top two-thirds of the line solo, after stepping off a ladder to avoid the lower crux! This in itself was an impressive achievement and made for a fine photo-op: "Although I knew that it wouldn't really 'count' as an ascent, I wasn't bothered," wrote Ullrich in a blog: "The climbing on the rest of the route was bloody awesome so I wanted to do it anyway." Ullrich, with little fanfare, had pulled off a couple of fine feats during a brief trip to the eastside, including his daring ground-up second ascent of Jorgeson's *Footprints* (super-highball v9) and the likely first ascent of *Saigon Superdirect* (v10): Pretty bold stuff from the then-19-year-old British youngster.

Jorgeson, however, was determined to complete the full challenge on the Grandpa's east face, and was training for his ascent during December 2008. After breaking a hold on the lower section, Jorgeson found a new, but extremely hard, sequence starting more directly beneath the gold-streaked line. In early January Jorgeson arrived to attempt the climb, accompanied by a film crew from *Big Up Productions*. Following a dawn start on January 8th, all went well, and with a nod to history, Jorgeson named the 31-move, 45-foot, v12-start, 5.14 highball, *Ambrosia*.

So, until the next "last great problem" comes to the fore, that's that for the highballing insanity. But there's still a lot more to report: for one thing, the women are starting to crank off some of the hard problems. Where Rands led the way with *The Mandala* (v12) and the superhighball *This Side of Paradise* (v10) others are following. Of particular note was the first female ascent of *Stained Glass* (v10) by visiting Australian Tilly Parkins in November 2008. This was all the more impressive for the fact she was on a brief visit at the time and had to dedicate to the effort and conserve strength, and crucially fingertips, for the send — which she managed on the very last day of her US trip!

That same month, Alex Puccio stopped by and worked the picturesque crimps of *A Maze of Death* (v12) for a few days, finally succeeding with style using an extremely powerful sequence. The taller Alex Johnson later completed the same in just a few goes, and also added *The Mystery* (v11/12) to her tick list, after a couple of short trips. Rands followed up with ascents of the incredible *Haroun and the Sea of Stories* (v11/12) and newly popular *Xavier's Roof* (v11).

There simply isn't space to cover all the amazing new lines and ascents, but a few special mentions are in order, one being to Jeff Sillcox who produced *Magnetic North* (v8), on the Grandma North face which is a superb line. This then provided the finish to Shawn Diamond's super-hard sit-starts that begin on *Center Direct*, or *Direction* to give *North of Center* (v11) and *Direct North* (v14). Jeff also found *Aquatic Hitchhiker* (v11), a solution of sorts to the hanging prow project at the back of the Ice Caves. Hats off to Jesse Bonin too, for his link-up of the latter line into

In a sense then, we have Herbert to thank for steering the Buttermilks to its current path, one that left the great unclimbed lines for future generations, sparing these climbs the humiliation of a one-way trip to rap-bolted obscurity.

the finish of *Beefcake*, a version he called *In the Aquarium* (v12).

No doubt there are a lot of unclimbed lines still to be done in Bishop, including many really good ones. Add to this the potential for flash or onsight attempts on the harder highballs, and you have a whole world of possibilities. George Ullrich set the bar pretty high with his ground-up ascent of *Footprints*, already mentioned. Other lines have also fallen to ground-up style, with local hero Charlie Barrett (first), and later Canadian Jerremy Smith making short work of *This Side of Paradise*.

Evilution, ground-up was inevitable, given the scene under that line in early 2009. There were so many pads set out beneath it that on some days the spotters too were in danger of injury—from falling off the back of the stack! The rear layer was four pads deep on one occasion (and we're talking big pads). Successes ground up went to Carlo Traversi (first) and his brother Geovanni, on the original line, and to Austrian Tobias Haller on *Evilution Direct*.

At the very start of the Fall '09 season, even *Luminance* received its first ground-up ascent, from So Cal's Dan Beall, a student at University of California San Diego. One day *Luminance* is the most death-defying climb on planet earth and just a few months later it's another boulder problem, no ropes required: "Even though you feel like you're going to die, I think that the climb is actually fairly safe with just a few pads," wrote Beall of the experience.

With more pads and ever stronger climbers, there is simply no end to the potential!

Right: Lisa Rands makes the first female ascent of the spectacular *This Side of Paradise* (v10). Photos: Wills Young.

MEMORIES OF A GOLDEN AGE

By Vic Copeland

Dustin Sabo and I first met Mick Ryan in the Happy Boulders in 1998. It was during the winter break of my sophomore year in high school. We had already spent some time bouldering in the Happies before that trip: following Ryan's topos from a climbing magazine we had sought out the better-known problems, and word of mouth had led us to a v10 called *Cholos* [since down-rated by a grade] put up by a mythic climbing god called Steele. The day Dustin and I had climbed *Cholos* felt like a kind of graduation day for us. We sat in a booth at Carl's Junior in virtual disbelief. Climbing a problem that hard seemed like one of the most amazing things any young guy could ever hope for.

My obsession with climbing was already well developed when we had planned our winter break that year. I'd spent hours rewinding *The Real Thing* (a video with Ben Moon and Jerry Moffatt) memorizing quotes and sequences. Before we had left home, I had gone to Big 5, a large sporting goods store, to purchase a pair of Adidas shorts that were exactly like the ones Obe Carrion wore in *Free Hueco* (a video by Big Up Productions). I must have watched that movie a thousand times. We had planned a sport climbing trip to the Virgin River Gorge near Las Vegas, intending to stop in Bishop to do some bouldering on our way to becoming bolt-clipping superstars. But we never got there, and to this day I still haven't seen the VRG. We stayed in Bishop instead.

Rumors of Hueco-esque roof climbs completed by Seth Carter led us to an exploration of the Sad Boulders. A frigid wind howled as Dustin and I set out down the deserted canyon. I remember being captivated by a tall, vertical wall covered in moss and lichen and speckled with small finger pockets. There was a terrifying pit landing to one side. We wandered further, awestruck by the potential.

There was a cow skull near a massive boulder wedged like a chockstone to expose a steep featured belly. I pawed at the holds on what I would later call *Cow Skull* [sadly now broken and not as good as it once was]. Dustin crawled through a narrow hole into a cave to find bullet-hard rock, riddled with big pinches, incut crimps, and positive footholds on a roof climb he would call *Enter the Dragon*. Our VRG plans out the window, we headed to Smart & Final to buy a painter's pole and some brushes.

We were two 16-year-olds with nothing but climbing on our minds and the entire sparsely-developed area at our mercy. Other than the essentials, like climbing shoes and chalk, we weren't well prepared. Our nights were miserable. With no tent, we loitered in a booth at Carl's Junior to stay warm while geeking out on climbing trivia. We slept reclined in front seats of an Oldsmobile Cutlass Supreme that my grandpa had given me for my 16th birthday.

One sunny day, about a week into the trip, we bumped into Mick Ryan at the Happy Boulders. Mick was full of vigor and psyched to meet us. When we described what we had been up to, his enthusiasm knew no bounds. He had already mapped the features and rocks we'd climbed on, and immediately recognized the problems we'd completed. To Mick every climb was a masterpiece and no piece of climbing was ever left unrecorded: he even showed us a little four foot tall boulder his son Xavier had chalked up. In the world according to Mick Ryan, our ascents were big news.

As we drove up to Mick and his wife Gabriella's home later that day, following directions on a scrap of paper Mick gave us, we found the neighborhood quiet, dark, and cold. But a gold-yellow glow emanated from the windows of Mick's place. Talk and laughter from a crowd of visitors could be heard as we bashfully knocked at the door. An aroma of orange and curry powder met us as we were ushered in and introduced to a houseful of guests. Mick soon handed me a big solid mug, heavy with tea. I grabbed it by its giant handle. The tea was like nothing I had ever tasted: not scalding hot, but perfect, it was richly flavored and sweetened with milk and honey.

Amid the crowd, we sat around a huge solid oak table that was strewn with black and white photos. One photo showed Wills Young on the first move of the ship's prow that would become the *Mandala* a couple of years down the road. Another was of Hidetaka Suzuki doing the first ascent of the awesome highball *Secrets of the Beehive*. A few bottles of red wine in dark green bottles were comfortably spaced about the table. And then there were all the topographical maps of the boulders on which Mick began recording our contributions, taking careful note of every new climb we did — the name, the date, the rating.

During the rest of the trip, we would make a stop at Mick's each evening for tea, good company, and to give and to hear the latest bouldering news. We met a slew of characters like Russ "Fish" Walling, Hidetaka Suzuki, a fellow by the name of "Hippy Nick," Bruce "Kinneloa" Pottinger, Tony Puppo (of The Rubber Room), Kevin Thaw, Hallie Lee, Marty "Sleek and Gazelle Like" Roberts and numerous others. We steadily learned of a long list of local and visiting boulderers and became friends with many. All these characters were, like us, a part of the burgeoning Bishop scene, for which Mick's bustling home was the de facto headquarters.

Winter break came and went and some time passed during which we lived double lives, Dustin and I. Then, on yet another weekend trip during high school, we found ourselves stranded in Bishop when my Oldsmobile threw its transmission. The mechanic told me he would need at least a week to fix it. I secretly thought: Yes! Then I called my parents to explain the predicament. Mick came to our rescue, letting us pitch tents in his backyard, and soon recruited us to check out a new area he had just found and called the Druid Stones. The idea of an hour-long hike seemed like a monumental ordeal. Mick easily convinced us we should hike up there during the cool of the night. It just made sense.

Vic Copeland made an enormous contribution to the development of bouldering on the East Side, especially with his penchant for highball lines. Here he pulls through for the first ascent of *René* (v5, page 108) a crimpy testpiece on the Happy Boulders' west rim. Photo: Jim Thornburg.

So we headed out into the moonless dark. Mick, Dustin, and I piled into Mick's beater, a little white Mitsubushi pickup full of dents, and headed down Barlow Lane toward the power lines. Mick prohibited the use of headlamps so as to preserve the mysterious quality of the hike. I remember being utterly winded as I struggled up the path. I stared up into blackness surrounded by the sound of footprints crunching in monzonite sand. Switchback by switchback we approached the Druids.

After we arrived I remember Mick dousing a hollow in a rock with a bit of white gas and lighting it aflame, albeit for a few purple-blue-orange-and-red seconds. The flames lit up the underside of a boulder and Mick raved about the enormous potential for hard problems. Being there, that weekday night skipping out on my other life, I felt I was exactly where I needed to be. The next day we scrubbed and worked some amazing unclimbed lines before returning by the same winding path, worn out but incredibly energized.

It was the summer of 1999 that I really got to know the Buttermilk Country and truly fell in love. Dustin, Mick, and I would spend hours wandering the hillsides. Mick would show us what he thought would be the next *Hale Bopp* or *Karma* (problems in Fontainebleau that he knew almost nothing about, but which he believed the Bishop lines would one day need to measure themselves against). We walked back into Dale's Camp, into the Hall of Mirrors, and crossed through a little pass to the Bardini Boulders.

I saw immediately that the Buttermilks were special. The boulders had a grandeur not encountered elsewhere. We were all obsessed back then. We really were. And once the lines became more dangerous, there was a sense of importance to what we were doing that I felt was missing from some of our earlier exploits. Back home, we had been obsessing over the footage in *Hard Grit* (the movie by Slackjaw Films), and had a newfound yearning to terrify ourselves with death-defying ascents.

The area that inspired me most was the Pollen Grains. Just as with the Druids, Mick first took us up there at night and I remember eating cold beans from a can. The next morning the boulders floored me. Mick showed us *Jedi Mind Tricks:* Incredible! He showed us his two standout problems, *Suspended in Silence* and *The Beekeeper's Apprentice*, and pushed us to complete other lines in the area like *Drone Militia, Valentino Traverse* and *Honey Bear Bong*. He showed us the perfect project that would become *The Spectre*, and the wonderland of surreal boulders on up the hillside.

One day, with a tangerine sunset blasting a fiery glow from a triangle shaped cloud expanding from Mount Tom's summit, I blitzed through a flurry of problems, giving rise to *Timothy Leary Presents, Dot Dot Dot Insanity, On the Cusp,* and many others.

Everyday, I sought to climb new problems. I became more and more comfortable wandering onsight, high above the deck. I lived climbing in those days. For me, this was a time before college, before love, before work. Many days were spent just wandering the Buttermilk Country and the Volcanic Tableland. Ask anyone who was a part of that scene, and they will give you a mysterious joyful look. It was a time of unadulterated freedom and reckless youth. Many hilarious stories were told, and long bantering sessions covered every climbing topic, but repeatedly returned to the latest new finds in the local deserts and hills. I am sure some would call it a Golden Age of sorts, sandwiched between the padless hardmen of old and the modern standard bearers streaming from the climbing gyms. I love thinking about those days.

—***Vic***

CHAPTER 1

Rock Creek and the Sherwin Plateau

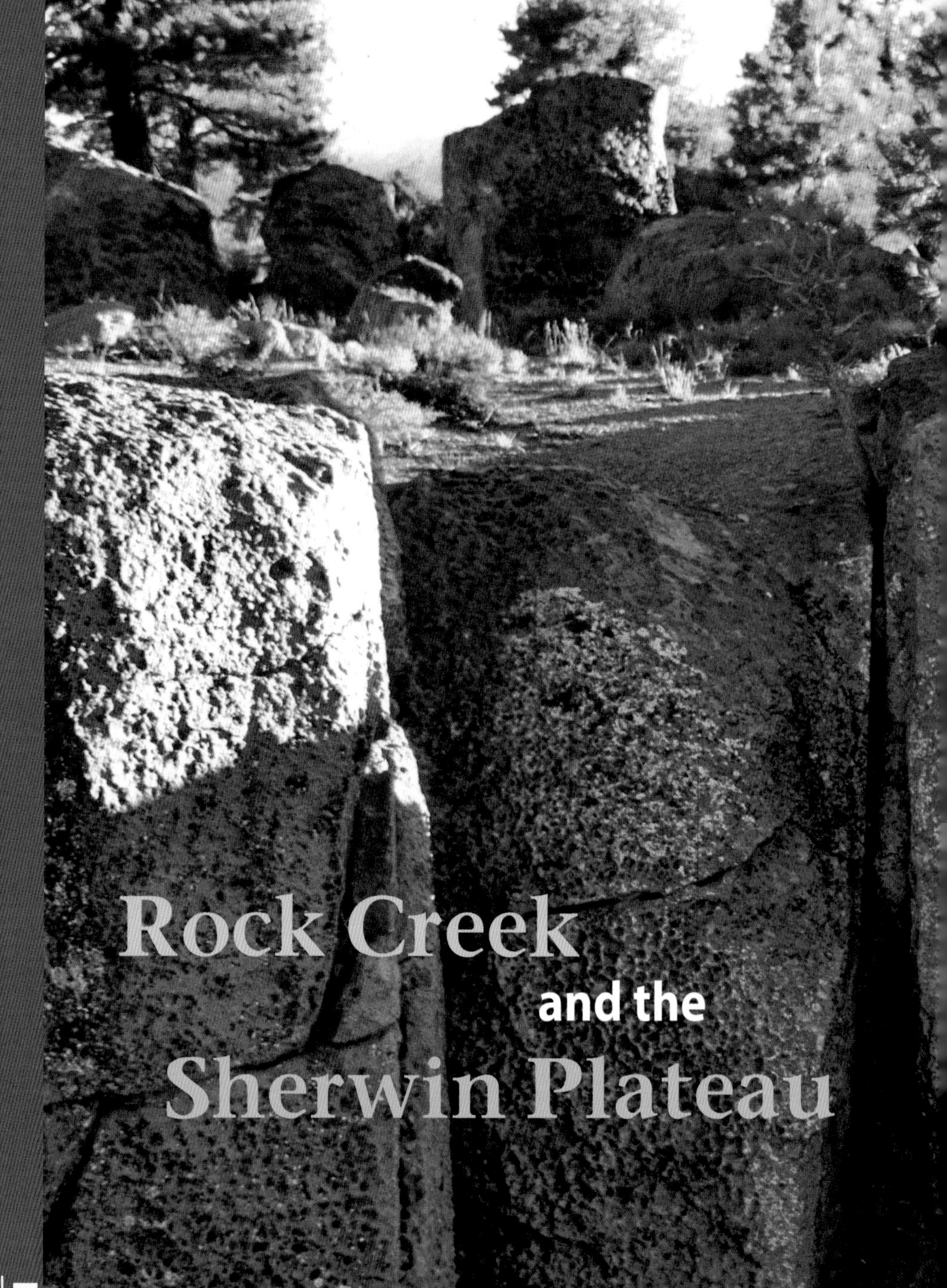

The Catacombs area is scenically so striking that bouldering is merely an excuse to make the drive. Rock addicts, however, will be well rewarded by the amazing *Church of the Lost and Found* (right side v1, left v3, page 94). Photo: Wills Young.

ROCK CREEK AND THE SHERWIN PLATEAU

Driving north/northwest from Bishop on Highway 395, you head up a long and fairly steep hill known as the Sherwin Grade. The road gains altitude providing views back down the Owens Valley to Bishop, out to the southeast across the lower end of the Owens River Gorge, and west across Round Valley to the dominant pyramid of Mount Tom (13,652 ft, 4161m). You are heading up onto the Sherwin Plateau, an area lying around 3000 feet (915m) higher than Bishop. The first communities you come to on the plateau are the tiny Tom's Place to the west, and the scattered Sunnyslopes to the east, both situated near the base of Rock Creek Canyon.

East of Tom's Place is the extensive Sherwin Plateau with its plethora of low-key volcanic tuff bouldering spots (including the few relatively extensive areas mentioned here), while southwest of Tom's Place is Rock Creek Canyon, home to the remarkable Big Meadow Campground boulders.

The drive up is quick, but the changes in the environment are intriguing. While there may be no beating the Buttermilks for its picturesque beauty and variety of granite/monzonite climbing, or the Happy and Sad Boulders for the extensive volcanic-tuff pocket-pulling, there can come a time when a change of scene is welcomed. There is certainly no shortage of stunning views or splitter lines at Rock Creek and the Sherwin Plateau. Those making the short drive north will be well rewarded.

Camping

While clearly you can stay in and around Bishop (see page 17), there are also options for those looking for a quieter time, or perhaps seeking escape from the valley heat. Camping is easy to find in the Rock Creek area as there are a number of campgrounds that hug the river, from Tuff Campground at the lowest elevation (7000 feet, 2130m) just across Highway 395 from Tom's Place, to Rock Creek Lake Campground (9600 feet, 2930m) high up in Rock Creek. These campgrounds close during winter, though usually there is at least one that is open all year. Prices vary, starting at around $20 per site. Call the National Forest for more information at 760-873-2500 (press 0 to speak to someone) or see www.fs.fed.us/r5/inyo/recreation/campgrounds.shtml for pricing and typical season. Another very useful website is www.rockcreeklake.com/camping.

Rooms

Besides the Bishop options (page 17) there are several local places to stay:

Tom's Place Resort (760-935-4239, www.tomsplaceresort.com) signposted on Highway 395 as "Tom's Place" is across the road from the turn-off for Pocketopia and the Catacombs (also the small community of Sunnyslopes). Tom's Place offers cabin accommodation, a store, a bar and a restaurant. Rates are upwards of $65/night for a room in the lodge or $30 per person in the dorm room, though cabins could be a good choice for a group, e.g. 3 bedrooms and 6 beds for $135/night.

Rock Creek Lodge (toll-free 877-935-4170, www.rockcreeklodge.com) is a seasonal resort lodge (summer is the end of May thru late Oct, and winter is Christmas thru early April), about 8 miles up Rock Creek Road from Tom's Place. Cabins are from about $100/night.

Rock Creek Lakes Resort (760-935-4311, www.rockcreeklake.com/resort) is a seasonal resort open in the summers thru the end of October that has cabins from $160 per night. It is about 8.5 miles up from Tom's Place.

Groceries Food and Gas

Tom's Place Resort (year-round. See "Rooms" above) has a grocery store, restaurant and bar. Rock Creek Lodge (seasonal, see "Rooms" above) has a small grocery store and a restaurant (reservations before 3pm are required for evening dinner). Rock Creek Resort (seasonal, see "Rooms" above) has a small store and restaurant/cafe with a reputation for exceedingly good fruit pies.

The nearest gas to Tom's Place is at Crowley Lake, 4 miles to the north. It is probably less pricey to fill up in Bishop.

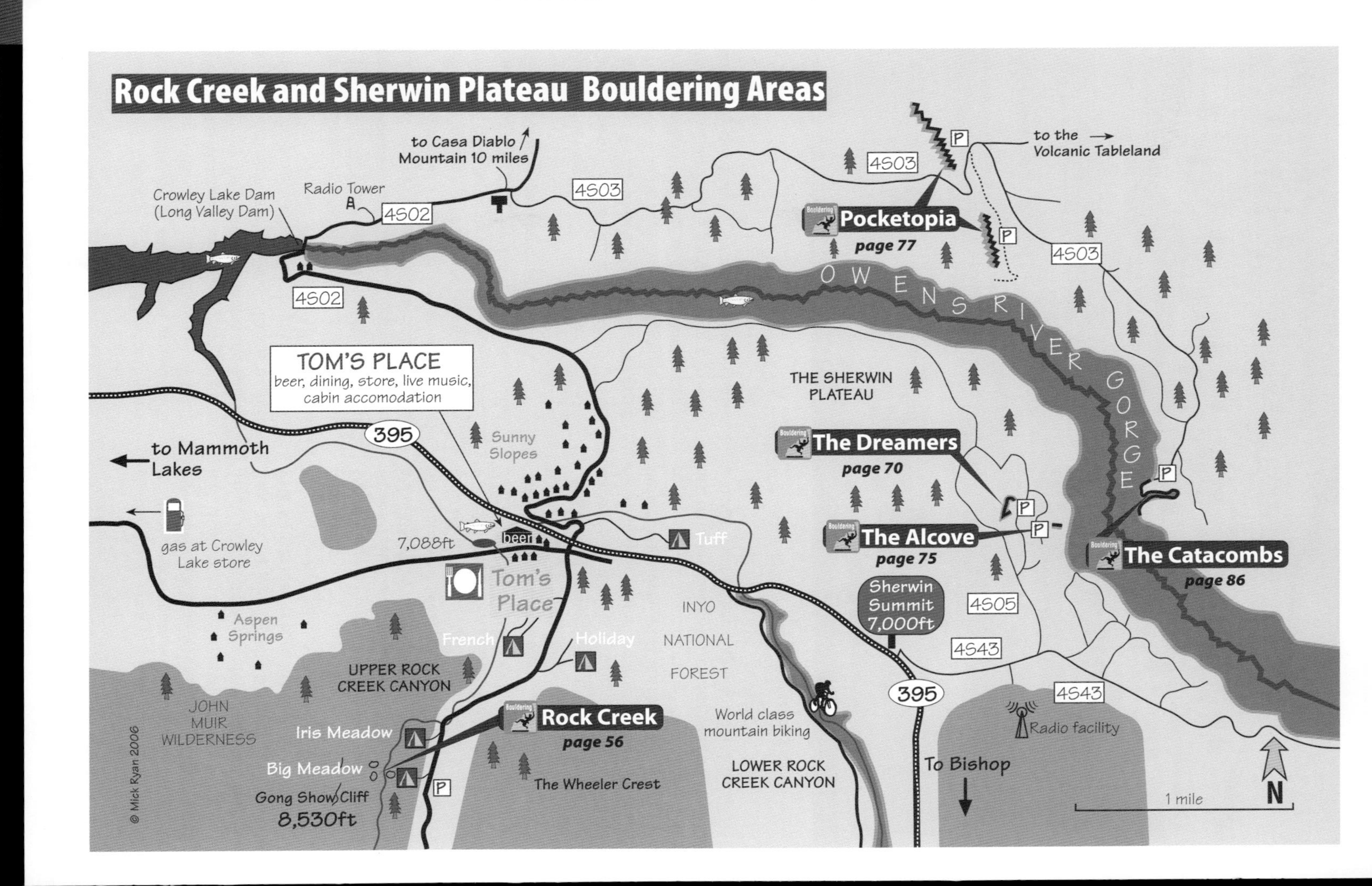
Rock Creek and Sherwin Plateau Bouldering Areas
to Casa Diablo Mountain 10 miles
Radio Tower
Crowley Lake Dam (Long Valley Dam)
4S02
4S03
4S03
to the Volcanic Tableland
Pocketopia
page 77
4S03
4S02
O W E N S R I V E R G O R G E
TOM'S PLACE
beer, dining, store, live music, cabin accomodation
THE SHERWIN PLATEAU
395
Sunny Slopes
to Mammoth Lakes
The Dreamers
page 70
gas at Crowley Lake store
7,088ft
beer
Tuff
The Alcove
page 75
The Catacombs
page 86
Tom's Place
Sherwin Summit 7,000ft
4S05
Aspen Springs
INYO NATIONAL FOREST
French
Holiday
4S43
UPPER ROCK CREEK CANYON
395
4S43
JOHN MUIR WILDERNESS
Rock Creek
page 56
World class mountain biking
Radio facility
Iris Meadow
Big Meadow
Gong Show Cliff
8,530ft
The Wheeler Crest
LOWER ROCK CREEK CANYON
To Bishop
1 mile
N
P
Bouldering
© Mick Ryan 2006

Rock Creek

Shaded by a canopy of giant pines and shimmering aspens, at an altitude of about 8500 feet (2620m), the fine granite boulders at Rock Creek's Big Meadow Campground stay relatively cool during the warmer months, and can be buried under snow in the winter. This is a great place to climb when other areas begin to feel too hot, or when seeking cold temps to maximize hard cranking.

The rock is near-perfect—a fine-textured Yosemite-quality monolithic granite—and on quiet days when the campground traffic is slow, or the campground is closed for the season, the setting is pristine. During the spring, summer and early fall, the beauty of the riverside environment is enhanced by the aspens, while the water bubbling over cobbles adds charm.

The Bouldering

Though many of the problems are of a safe height, and the landings are generally very good, Rock Creek is not a beginner area because most of the problems are thin and hard. Intermediate climbers, while finding plenty to aspire to, will have to try extra-hard here too. This is a granite connoisseur's area, a testing ground for the aspiring technical master. On this vertical and just beyond vertical granite, crimping, keen footwork and dynamics are required in equal measure. There is nothing aggressively steep or thuggish here, yet for high-density bouldering from v6 to v10, Rock Creek is hard to beat.

Directions

Drive: Approximately, 30 minutes from Bishop, Rock Creek Canyon lies west of Highway 395, about 25 miles north of Bishop (15 miles south of Mammoth Lakes) (see map on previous page). Exit Hwy. 395 at Tom's Place at a sign saying Crowley Lake Drive/Rock Creek Lake. Drive about 4.5 miles up Rock Creek Road, signposted "Snow Park" and pull in just after the entrance to Big Meadow Campground.

Hike: Two minutes down the gravel road into the campground. The Campground Boulder is on the right, just behind the first campsite. To reach the other boulders, cross the creek by a large fallen tree just upstream from the Campground Boulder, follow a trail upstream alongside the river for a hundred yards. See map below for details.

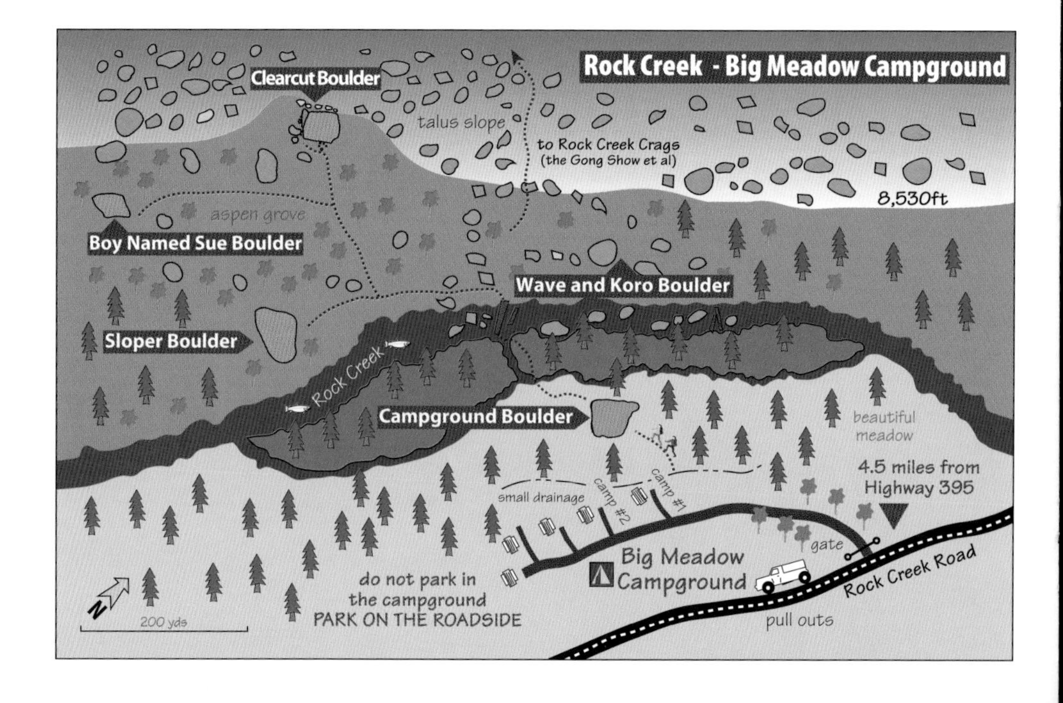

Charlie Barrett, *Groove and Arete* (v3/4), on the small but amazing Boy Named Sue Boulder, page 66. Photo: Wills Young.

THE CAMPGROUND BOULDER

This boulder is the first that you will see when you arrive at the area. It is behind the first campground when approached from the main road. The view above is what you will see when you arrive.

1 Slap Wallick v6 ★ ☐
Sit start with opposing sidepulls. Slap a move, then grapple up the arete to gain the jug. Pulling the arete on its right side is easiest.

2 Unnamed v0 ★ ☐
Climb up past the obvious big flat hold.

3 Unnamed v7 ☐
Start as for *Pull Down Like De Jesus* with both hands at the large triangular hold. Traverse left and up following a faint seam with some very sharp crimps.

4 Pull Down Like De Jesus v4 ★★ ☐
From the large triangular hold, make a big move to a sloper and balance up using the diagonal off-set. Avoiding the crimps out left will add spice to the topout for shorter folks. Add a sit start directly below, or, at a grade harder, from the right. Beware of the block landing.

5 Osama v6 ★★ ☐
A slightly contrived line that climbs beautifully. From the large triangular hold, pull out right using a small crimp at the very edge of the overhang, and make a long cross through to crimps on the right facet (left toe-hook, or heel). Match, then move the left hand up the left arete or to other small crimps as needed, and step up onto that tiny crimp on the edge. Finish by a hard slap to the sloping top (and a hidden crimp beyond the lip).

6 Osama Sit-start Eliminate v10 ★ ☐
A sit start that eliminates the large triangular hold on the left. Begin at the pinch/sidepull and climb directly up the arete. The large triangular feature is off for hands and for feet, but underclings on the left face, and the left arete are on as for *Osama*.

7 Choice of Weapons v4 ★★ ☐
Sit start on the obvious large hold left of the tree. Climb to good holds via crimps out right or by a lunge.

8 River Face Arete v10 ★★★ ☐
Stay on the left side of the Campground Arete: Begin with an obvious left hand hold and pull onto the arete's left side using very high feet. Finish with a long pull with your left hand to stick a shallow divot fortuitously located on the slopey lip.

9 River Face Arete Sit v10 ★★ ☐
This is the sit start to the previous line: left on sloper, right on low sidepull right of the arete. Perhaps a grade harder than the stand.

10 Campground Arete v9 ★★★ ☐
A reachy dynamic lunge from a high pinch, or a technical and powerful press onto a foothold out right gains the sweet spike/edge high in the right face. A fun big move to the top of the arete caps this stellar line.

⓫ Campground Arete Sit v10 ★★ ☐
Sit start with the left hand on a sloper and the right hand on the low sidepull right of the arete. Find the standing start too easy? This should make you feel better about yourself.

⓬ Run-and-Jump v? ☐
A run-and-jump to the spike/pinch on the right side of the campground arete is fun.

⓭ Off the Couch v6 ★ ☐
The middle of the face is climbed starting at a crimp high off the ground. Some may need to stack pads to start this one, spoiling it slightly as the less stretched you are, the easier it is—so it could be really hard, or really easy, depending how high you start. Beginning at the right arete is v1.

⓮ Arete to Arete v3 ★ ☐
Begin at the right, step onto the ledge, then move left and finish as for *The Campground Arete*—a big reach.

The Campground Arete (v9 opposite page): Jeff Sillcox reaches for the pinch. Photo Wills Young

WEST SIDE AND TALUS BOULDERS

These boulders lie on the west side of the river opposite the Campground Boulder, as do all the other boulders described in this guide. To reach the boulders by the river and in the talus, cross the river upstream from the Campground Boulder on a large fallen tree. Alternatively, if the water is low, and you're heading to the first boulders listed here, you can cross just downstream.

WAVE BOULDER

Though obscured by small aspens and other rocks, this boulder is found pretty easily at the base of the talus. Here's how to locate it: Next to the Campground Boulder, on its downstream side, is a felled tree, which points across the river almost directly at this boulder. When just below the boulder (which is hard to identify), approach the last ten yards by walking up a low-angle slab to the boulder's right.

1 Wave O' Babies v5 ★ ☐
Begin on the ground in the slot between the boulders. Step onto the low-angle ramp at the base of the boulder using a flat undercling for the right, and a small sidepull for the left. Move up to a good sidepull for the left hand; set your feet, and dyno to the incut lip. Over.

HAREM BOULDER

This boulder is just up and right from the Wave Boulder about 15 yards away and, like the wave boulder, faces the river.

2 Camel Love v4 ★★ ☐
Sit start with a good sidepull with the left hand and a crimp for the right. Pull onto the sloping ledge to start and then climb up past good edges and pinches to a tricky move to the lip.

3 Harem v9 ★ ☐
Sit start at a big jug under the overlap. A long hard move left to gain a good sidepull is the crux. Slightly spoiled by the close proximity of a tree.

KORO BOULDER

This 25-foot tall boulder has a fine-looking square-cut arete pointing toward the river. It is about 40 yards downstream from The Wave boulder. You can't miss it.

4 Koro v5 ★★ ☐
The very tall face is climbed easily to a double-clutch snatch for the lip from standing high in good underclings. Done on a rope, but not done ropeless at time of press A left version may also be possible.

5 Unknown/Project ☐
Climb the face, move right, and then up the exceedingly tall arete.

6 Project ☐
Sit start around to the right of the tall square-cut arete and move left up the very sloping lip.

7 The Crack v0 ★ ☐
Right of the arete is this fine climb that is not really a boulder problem. The crux is up high where the overlap from the right meets the crack.

SEAM BOULDER

This boulder sits above the Koro Boulder.

8 Project ☐
Follow the seam around the corner above the heinous landing which may be okay with enough pads.

9 Project ☐
As above, but follow the seam up left to the arete and climb up the arete or just to the right of the arete?

10 Project ☐
Grab the good crimp in the seam (just before it goes under the overlap) with the left hand, and press up for the top.

11 Unnamed v2 ☐
Start at the right on the good edge; step up and stretch for the top.

SAPSUCKER BOULDER

This boulder is just a few yards farther north (downstream) from the previous two boulders and has this line facing upstream next to a tree:

12 Sapsucker v7 ☐
Just to the right of the tree, begin with the left hand on a high sidepull/pinch and the right also on a sidepull, but lower. Step on carefully and move up past slopers to a deep crimp for the left and then stretch for a tiny crimp. Pull through to the top. Spoiled somewhat by the tree at left.

Ian Cotter-Brown criss-crosses his way up *Camel Love* (v4), an excellent addition to the area, just across the stream, and slightly downstream from the Campground Boulder at the base of the talus. Photo: Wills Young.

Along with the boulders along the base of the talus, there are some good-sized blocks up in the midst of the talus field. These include:

PROW BOULDER

This boulder is in the talus field a couple of hundred yards steeply uphill of the giant Koro Boulder. It is easily located immediately right of a large juniper tree, which is the only large tree in the vicinity.

13 Compression Session v9 ★★ ❑

Start standing with the right hand on the hanging arete holding a sloper (this is just right of a small crimp on the overhanging face), and the left hand on a glass-smooth undercling far to the left (thumb pinch). Pull on, place a right heel, and slap a very big and intimidating move up with the right hand; set feet and launch carefully up left to good hold, hidden high and left. Several pads needed.

14 Compression Aversion v9 ★ ❑

Start with right hand as above, but with left hand on the small crimp near the arete. Pull on, and climb up the hanging arete using thin crimps on its right side.

15 Project ❑

The ultimate prow project: Sit start on the embedded block with the left hand in a low sidepull/undercling and the right hand at a low crimp on the arete. Climb up the underside of the arête, using sidepull/underclings for the left hand as for *Compression Session* (above).

16 Project ❑

The compression-avoidance version: Sit start as for the previous line, but finish on *Aversion* (above).

LARGE TALONS BOULDER

The Large Talons Boulder is quite high in the talus field, higher than the Prow Boulder, but across left (as you look uphill). It is roughly straight up from the Clearcut Boulder, listed over page and shown on the map on page 56.

17 Unnamed Crack v1 ❑

The crack with a couple of different exits.

18 Large Talons v9 ★ ❑

Start with both hands on a flat edge left of the xenolith. Begin by moving the right hand into a gaston, then left to a sidepull. Make a very hard move up right and top out.

Charlie Barrett climbs *Compression Session* (v9) on the Prow Boulder. The low sit start remains an amazing project at time of press. Photo: Wills Young

Andrew Stevens trying to control *The Batter Effect* (v6, next page). Photo: Wills Young.

SLOPER BOULDER

This boulder is actually one of the first boulders you will find after crossing from the Campground and heading upstream. As you hike upstream (toward the Clearcut Boulder or Boy Named Sue Boulder), it is on the left near the river after about 120 yards. See map, page 56.

1 Blue Ribbon v11 ★ ☐

Left of the top out for *Eric in an Easy Chair* (see below): Sit start under the roof with feet on the large ledge and hands on poor slopey underclings. Climb straight up to topout where the next line finishes. Long moves with micro crimps!

2 Eric in an Easy Chair v7 ★ ☐

Hang/sit start with hands at right side of sloping groove. Move left and up to a sweet mantel finish.

CLEARCUT (FORMERLY TALUS) BOULDER

After crossing the river by the fallen tree, follow a path alongside the river (hugging close to the river) for a hundred yards or so. Where the river cuts left (you can see the low Sloper Boulder in front of you), head right toward the talus.

1 Aspen v2 ★ ☐
Sit start at a large sidepull. Mantel the ledge, then make an awkward move to gain the flake above.

2 Blunder Sit, Left v7 ☐
Sit start down and left with a right heel hook. Avoiding holds (and cobble) up and left, press up right to cobbles and join *One Move Blunder* or (slightly harder) *The Blunder Bus.*

3 One Move Blunder v4 ★★ ☐
Start standing with your right hand on a sidepull four feet off the ground and your left on a knob far to the left. Climb via knobs to the diagonal crimp rail, then make a long scary move to a huge black inclusion up and right. A slightly easier version involves using crimps beyond the blunt rib and pulling a similar move to an even higher flat ledge that is easier to grab.

4 Blunder Sit, Right v8 ☐
Sit start at the right-facing sidepulls.

5 Unnamed v3 ★★ ☐
Start as for *One Move Blunder*, but instead of topping out direct, follow the flake line left.

6 The Blunder Bus v6 ★ ☐
Start as for *One Move Blunder.* After gaining the crimp rail, immediately make a hard move horizontally rightward and continue right to top out as for *Clearcut* (see next page).

7 Clearcut v7 ★★ ☐
Sit start at the sidepull. Follow the crack up and around to the left. Take care not to dismember your fingers as you stab into the sharp V-slot on the left side of the arete.

8 Overzealous v9 ★★ ☐
Sit start at the sidepull. Make one move up with the left hand, then move right to a parallel seam and sidepulls. Top out rightward.

9 Unnamed v6 ★★ ☐
The standing start is a very short but fun v6, which can also be done as a dyno to the horn far right.

10 Unnamed v5 ★ ☐
Start at the right and traverse the lip of the boulder leftward, topping out at the top of *Clearcut*, or (perhaps harder) into the V-notch just before the left arete.

Left: Sweet cobbles on the Clearcut Boulder. Photo: Wills Young.

CLEARCUT BOULDER (SOUTH SIDE)

BATTER EFFECT BOULDER

Just up and left from the Clearcut Boulder, this has a rippled pinkish face on its north (up-valley) side.

Beginning around the back *of this boulder (see photo diagram), and moving right, find:*

11 Jump Start v4 ★ ☐

Jump start to grab the right sidepull-jug, throw a heel and grope over onto the top. More frightening than hard. Bad landing.

12 Scrambler v7 ★ ☐

Great slopers on this: Sit start at the right side of the west face with both hands on a sloping shelf. Cross the slopers and reach left for a sidepull. Roll into the good hold and top out as for the *Jump Start* at left. Serious pad skills needed, or a neck-breaking fall could ensue.

13 The Batter Effect v6 ★★ ☐

See action photo on previous page. This is a great problem other than the weird sloping boulder under the landing. You have to wedge yourself in to start the line: Begin at an obvious left hand horn/sidepull and right hand on a good sidepull around the same height. Pads needed.

BATTER EFFECT BOULDER WEST SIDE (BACK)

14 Ham to Ham Combat v7 ☐

Sit start under the east side of the boulder (the side you approach from the Clearcut Boulder). Climb around onto the slab and head up the middle of this. Line/rating unconfirmed.

THE BOY NAMED SUE BOULDER

This is a smallish boulder with some amazingly good problems. Follow a path west less than a minute from the Clearcut Boulder to find this wonder. To descend the boulder, climb down the southeast arete, which is a little tricky until you get used to it.

1 Dude v9 ★★★ ☐
The clean arete using some tiny footholds and a very big move. Reachy or what? But surprisingly do-able when you find the technique.

2 Dude Sit Start v10 ★★ ☐
Start sitting, with the left on the slopey arete, and right on a nothing nubbin. Start by pulling in and reach high right to a small edge. Continue up the arete to the dyno finish.

3 Tony's Dyno v11 ★★ ☐
A fun problem on perfect rock: Begin as for *The Fluke* (described below), but from the crimp gained after the first move, stall left hand at the slopey crimp just above the angle-change, then leap for the top up and left. **Adam's Variation:** Same idea, but from the good edge of The Fluke, lean left to grab a micro-crimp sidepull and jump for the lip with your right hand.

4 The Fluke, a.k.a. Drunken Master v8 ★★★ ☐
A beautiful piece of rock originally climbed "Fontainebleau-style"with one foot on the rock, one on the ground, and jumping to the edge up high. Flashed on the first ascent. Now done as a standing start (no jump), pulling onto poor feet and making a hard move to gain the same high edge. Match this, then top out.

5 Blood Brothers v7 ★★★ ☐
The left side of the arete. Sit start to the right of the arete (left hand on the arete). Pull up to a good edge on the arete, then around left and up to the big meat-wrap hold for the right hand. Some trickery then gains you the hidden hold far up and left with a lot less effort than at first appears necessary. Photo overleaf.

6 Groove and Arete v4 ★★★ ☐
The fine groove and arete can be climbed as a sit start beginning left hand on the arete. Beautiful moves.

7 A Boy Named Sue v7 ★★★ ☐
The proud blunt rib/arete. Tall people can reel in the points for this and chuckle. Shorter folks, finding this no pushover, will gain extra joy from the bonus moves, the extra stretch, and a damn hard high-step.

8 Life Ain't Easy v9 ★★★ ☐
A sit start to *A Boy Named Sue*, beginning at the left-facing diagonal rail right of the usual start.

9 Twisted Sister v3 ★★ ☐
The flakes in the wall are used to gain an inset flat hold, then the top. Begin standing to the left, with the left hand on the arete of *Boy Named Sue*, or as needed.

10 Seriously Twisted v10 ☐
An eliminate sit-start to *Twisted Sister*, starting as for *Life Ain't Easy* but avoiding all hand holds to the left of the start and pulling directly up into the sidepulls (it's really not so contrived as it might sound, but is certainly awkward).

11 More Twisted v7 ☐
Sit start as for *Life Ain't Easy* and lean across right via small crimps to the right arete, then pull up onto this.

12 Downclimb v0 ☐
The descent is via the southeast face and/or arete.

There are a few fun link-ups on this boulder for those who've done everything! These are the ones I know have been done. All are good:

13 Groovy Sue v10 ☐
Groove and Arete into *A Boy Named Sue.*

14 Groovy Sister v9 ☐
Groove and Arete into *Twisted Sister.*

15 Sue's Groove v8 ☐
A Boy Named Sue into *Groove and Arete*.

16 Sue's Groovy Blood v10 ☐
A Boy Named Sue into *Blood Brothers.*

17 Blood Sport v11 ★ ☐
Life Ain't Easy into *Blood Brothers.*

Ian Cotter-Brown sticks the big move on *Dude* (v9). Photo: Wills Young.

STARLA BOULDER

This boulder is in the talus a couple of hundred yards directly uphill from the Boy Named Sue Boulder. You can even follow a faint trail to start with and look out for a jutting overhang. Climb up behind this overhang on its left side. See the directional photo on this page. Both problems have a slightly reachy start, with the first move pretty much determining the grade for most people.

STARLA BOULDER LOCATION

1 Starla v8 ★ ☐

Sit start with the right hand on a flat crimp about 3 feet up from the rock you sit on and the left hand really low, about a foot and a half up, in the orange streak. Begin with a huge move (which is the crux) to gain the good edge up and left. From here the problem is a nice v3!

2 Rex Kwon Do v8 ★★ ☐

Sit start exactly the same as for Starla (above), but head straight up past a slopey rib to a good edge with the left hand. Reach right to a sidepull and then throw for the lip! Fun.

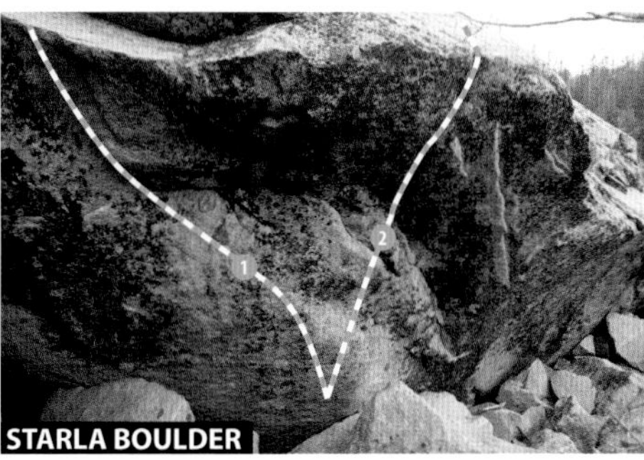

STARLA BOULDER

Below: Detail of hold on *Blood Brothers* (v7, previous page). Photo: Wills Young.

Ryan Olson dispatches the *River Arete Sit Start* (v10) on the Campground Boulder, page 58 . Photo: Wills Young.

The Dreamers

Certainly a dreamy spot. The afternoon sunlight seems even more golden here than elsewhere on the Eastern Sierra. The generally level, but rocky plateau is lightly forested and dirt roads criss-cross the area, wandering between endless scattered outcrops of Bishop tuff, often leading out to the gorge edge where short stretches of tall cliff offer spectacular views. At the Dreamers you get the feeling you are in a surreal world, a quiet world, untroubled. The views to east and west are expansive with clouds often gathering on the mountain ranges or drifting across the blue space between. Tall Jeffrey pines, widely spaced, throw down a little shade, and some of the corridors will offer some respite from the summer heat. The wind-sheltered nature of the walls will also allow climbing on cooler days in fall, winter and early spring.

For an overview map of the area see page 55.

The Bouldering

The rock is highly pocketed volcanic tuff. Many of the lines are perfectly solid, providing reassuring pulls on good holds, while some have fragile holds and are best avoided for all but the most adventurous.

This is a great area for v0 to v4 climbers looking for some good testpieces with flat landings, plus a couple of stiffer challenges for those with stronger fingers. There is an interesting mix of powerful pocket-pulling on gently overhanging rock to heady highballing on vertical faces. The best of the aggressive lines are on the right side of the Crippler Boulder while tall solid lines like the amazing *Bourbon IV* (v0) and *Psychopath* (v2) are scattered around the canyon, the latter is frighteningly high, but manageable for those who are solid at the grade. There are even more scary lines such as *The Thimble of*

Sarah Schneider on the popular v0 classic, *Bourbon IV* (page 73), named in honour of the Yosemite climber, the late Bruce Hawkins who was one of the first climbers to explore the Dreamers. Photo: Mick Ryan.

the High Sierra (v3) with its smattering of friable rock for the highly adventurous—or plain crazy. *Sweet Dreams* (v7) is the area's testpiece involving a move off a mono undercling and a rather bad landing.

Directions

Map page 55. From Bishop center drive about 22 miles toward Mammoth. Climb the long hill of the Sherwin grade, where the roads north and south are separated (two lanes each way). When the hill eases, the north and south lanes join to make a single four-lane road, and after about one mile beyond this point, on a long left curve, you will see a sign saying Sherwin Summit. Immediately before this sign, turn right onto dirt road 4S43. If you are coming from the opposite direction (e.g. from Mammoth), this turn is about 1.1 miles south of Tom's Place. However, it is illegal to make a left turn onto the dirt road here; instead, continue toward Bishop for 1.5 miles and make a legal U-turn by a connecting road.

From the Sherwin Summit sign, drive along unpaved road 4S43 for one mile, then make a left turn at road 4S05. Go 0.4 miles to a fork in the road. From here, you have two options; the first is shorter, but a little rough – fine for cars with good clearance. Turn right and drive 0.5 miles keeping left at the start. After that first rise you can park at the left and walk out to the west or south edge of the Dreamers. Or, you can wind over the next rise (rocky) descend to the flats, and park at the original large pullout on the left where a faint trail heads slightly downhill to the bouldering. Another option is to approach a longer way around on a less bumpy road: from the fork on road 4S05, stay straight and go one mile, keeping straight near the start, staying right after 0.5 miles, and right again shortly after. This gets you to that same last pullout, which is now on your right. Map page 55.

THIMBLE BOULDERS

1 The Thimble of the High Sierra v3 ★★ ☐
The center of the tall prow. Take care as some holds seem less than secure.

2 Yorkshire VS ☐
The tall arete seems to have lost most of its holds and those remaining seem pretty loose. Maybe it will clean up and be a beauty!

3 Zygote v0 ☐
The wavy wall to the crack.

4 Mytoesis v0 ★ ☐
The crack.

5 Performance Anxiety v0 ☐
The flakey arete.

6 Unnamed v2 ★ ☐
Small sharp pockets up the wall above a foot ledge, starting with the right hand in a low pocket and stretching up and right to start. Hard start for the short.

7 Thumby v0 ★ ☐
The bulging arete pulling to the left side at the upper bulge.

8 Hawkman v2 ☐
The steep pocketed wall just right of the arete to dangerously fragile flakes at the top.

MONDO WALL BOULDER

9 Mondo Wall v4 ☐
Face just right of the boulder in the gully, with hard moves through the center to a high pumpy exit. Top out high to the right, or move left risking a worse landing.

10 Psychopath v2 ★★ ☐
The wall just left of the arete finishing with big moves to large round pockets.

11 DSB v0 ☐
The wall above the ledge.

12 Chappy v0 ☐
Climb the short wall passing the slot to a ledge.

13 Unnamed v0 ☐
Another short wall.

14 Marcus Garvey v0 ☐
Thin pockets with some bad rock.

15 Robert Nesta Marley v0 ☐
The wavy wall, which soon eases.

16 Unnamed v0 ★ ☐
Various generic pocket pulling lines up the solid honeycombed wall.

17 Geriatric Burns Off Young Guns v3 ☐
Bulge to slab. Step up and right on slopers avoiding pockets to the left.

WAILING BOULDERS

18 Unnamed v0- ☐
Pockets to slab.

19 Unnamed v0 ☐
The wavy wall.

20 Unnamed v0- ★ ☐
Wavy rock right of the scoop. Nice moves.

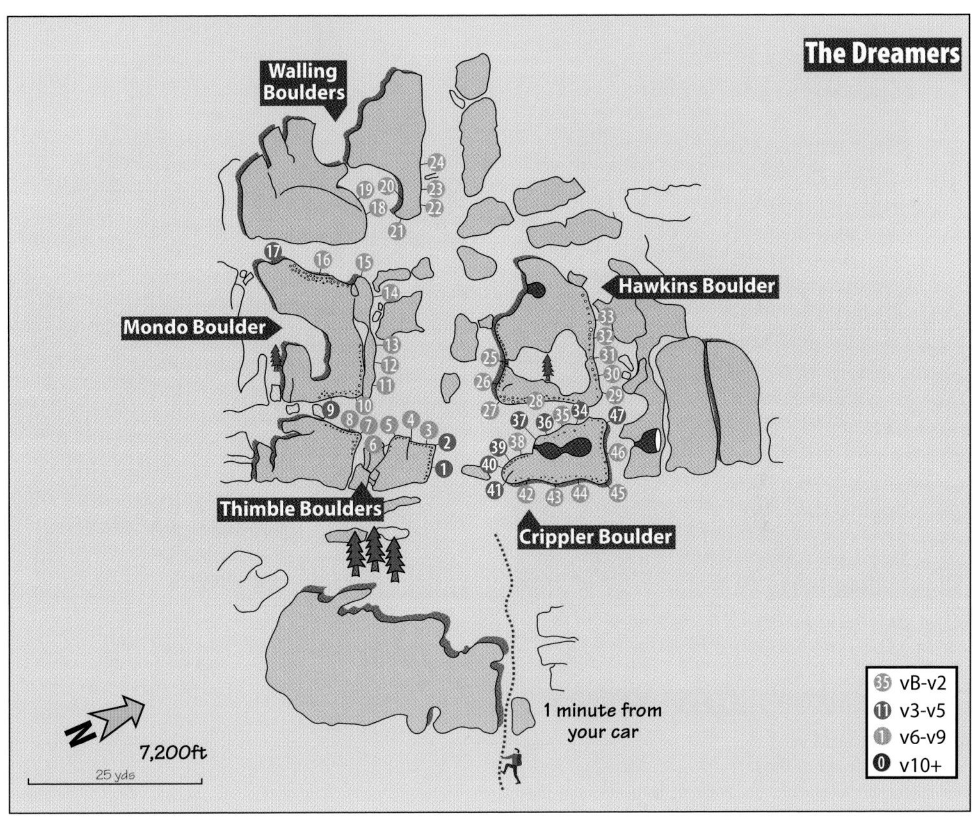

21 Sweet Thing v1 ☐
Fragile rock up prow.

22 Bag of Knackers v0 ☐
The edge of the wall on slots and pockets.

23 Rhythm Stick v0 ☐
Pockets to a big hueco and a testy top-out.

24 Flaggelate Rush v0 ☐
Climb up using the curious inclusion.

HAWKINS BOULDER

25 Bourbon IV v0- ★★★ ☐
(a.k.a. The Black Streak)
Long pulls on perfect pockets to the U-notch. Classic.

26 Pocket Pool v1 ☐
The very tall prow taken at its apex via a fragile flake. Off the deck and dangerous.

27 Chili Chip v0 ☐
The slab to the crack

28 Leather Pant Disco v0 ☐
Various generic pocket-pulling lines are on this wall.

29 Chapman's Dream v0 ☐
The thin crack right of the arete.

30 Blow-Bee v0 ☐
The tiny pocketed wall.

31 Flow-Bee v0 ☐
The wall of bigger pockets.

32 Descent v0 ☐
The way down.

33 Deli Lama v0 ☐
The short wall.

THE CRIPPLER BOULDER

THE CRIPPLER BOULDER

THE CRIPPLER BOULDER

34 Da Chan v4 ★ ☐
Sit start, left hand in the large pocket. Move up and left through the undulating wall, with the crux at the start. Beware the rock at your back.

35 Sweet Dreams v7 ★★ ☐
Sit start, left hand in the large pocket. Move right and pull around the first bulge as for *Too Many Locals,* then move horizontally left into a set of pockets. Make a hard move diagonally up left to a slopey pocket, then a scary move to a pinch at the lip. Continue diagonally left to finish as for *Da Chan.* Beware the rock at your back.

36 Too Many Locals v5 ★ ☐
Sit start, left hand in the large pocket. Move right and up, then directly over the lip past a right-facing flake.

37 The Crippler is Busted ☐
It's busted. The holds on this seem to have disappeared! The line once went from left to right to gain a big jug, followed by a pull over the undercut nose.

38 Three Men and a Crippler v2 ★★★ ☐
Sit start the left side of the wall. Climb on pockets to a flatty at the lip and rock over.

39 Super Crippler v4 ★★★ ☐
Sit start on pockets on the left of a blunt arete and climb directly up the nose.

40 Cripplers v3 ★ ☐
Steep sharp pockets four feet left of the arete to a careful step onto the slab. Sit start, right hand in low pocket, left on small pockets, v5.

41 Exit Planet Dreamer v3 ★ ☐
Climb the left side of the arete beginning at a right-facing flake.

42 Mystery Machine v0 ☐
The steep slab right of the arete.

43 Various v0 ☐
The slab, via many routes.

44 Planet Plush v0- ☐
The slabby arete.

45 Hawkin's Tooth v1 ☐
The pocketed prow.

46 Madman v1 ☐
The center of the wall.

47 Dimitri's Revenge v3 ★ ☐
The arete of the boulder, finishing at a high thin crack.

THE ALCOVE

THE ALCOVE

The astonishing Alcove is a sheltered 30-feet-long, 12-feet-high concave wall of solid volcanic tuff, which curls like a wave up and over a flat landing.

The wall is smattered with pockets large and small, some leading to tricky mantel encounters above the undercut lip. Great bouldering from about v1 to v4 can be had, with any number of eliminates possible, plus a pumpy traverse for the real masochists. The deep pockets are somewhat sharp on the base of the fingers.

Directions: Follow the directions to the Dreamers parking spot (page 71). From that parking spot drive north (either backtracking if following the second set of directions, or continuing if following the first) for another 0.1 miles approx to the first right turn. Take this road 0.4 miles and park at a pullout on the right—the road starts to head downhill about here. Cross the road to the east and walk 50 yards or so down a wash between rocks. The Alcove is on the left.

Clearly, you could climb virtually anywhere, but here are six lines to get you started.

❶ v0+ ❑
The left side of the steep wall.

❷ v3 ❑
Left of a white streak to a hard finish.

❸ v4 ❑
Big move to a jug.

❹ v1 ❑
Small pockets to a slopey, soapy white hold, then mantel avoiding the crack (kind of).

❺ v0+ ❑
The very short wall.

❻ v4 ❑
The full painful traverse.

Kevin Daniels gets his *Welcome to the Pleasure Dome* (v1, page 80), Pocketopia. Photo: Wills Young.

Pocketopia

Pocketopia is a discontinuous band of highly pocketed volcanic tuff on the undulating plateau just north of the Owens River about 5 miles downstream of the Crowley Lake Dam. Its east-facing orientation and 7300 feet of altitude make it a chilly place on winter afternoons, but these features keep the bouldering pleasant during late spring and fall. In winter, you will get sun here early in the mornings.

The Bouldering

With good flat landings and copious pockets, this area of compact volcanic tuff has plenty of enjoyable bouldering in the easier grades (v0 to v3). The Wedge Boulder at the Maximum Joy Area is a great place to start: perfect rock and short routes over flat sand (page 80). In addition, there are some outstanding mid-grade testpieces, including the area's finest contribution, the powerful roof *Everything and Nothing* (v5-v7, page 83). At the excellent Goldenrod Wall (page 85) you will find a couple of tall problems on immaculate tuff and widely spaced pockets, including the world-class *Goldenrod* (v5)—well worth seeking out.

Directions

Map page 55. From Bishop center, take Highway 395 north for about 24 miles (15 miles south, if coming from Mammoth Lakes). Exit Highway 395 opposite Tom's Place and turn right toward Sunnyslopes, signposted "Owens River Gorge Rd." Follow the road for about 4 miles to the Crowley Lake Dam (initially the road takes a sharp left turn, then curves back right leading past houses). From the dam, continue along the road which first narrows, then turns to dirt. At 1.3 miles from the dam, turn right onto road 4S03, signposted "Casa Diablo Mountain."

Follow road 4S03 for about 3.5 miles. After a little over 3 miles, you will head down a hill, and make a sharp hairpin turn to the left, where the road cuts through the Pocketopia escarpment. At the bottom of the hill, the outcrops of Pocketopia lie behind to either side. Look out for a right turn hidden by bushes about 0.3 miles beyond the hairpin before a curve right. Pocketopia South is reached by this right turn. Follow this road for about half a mile until the Maximum Joy Area is visible at right (see photo), and another 0.2 miles to reach the Pocket Rocket Area, along the same cliff band.

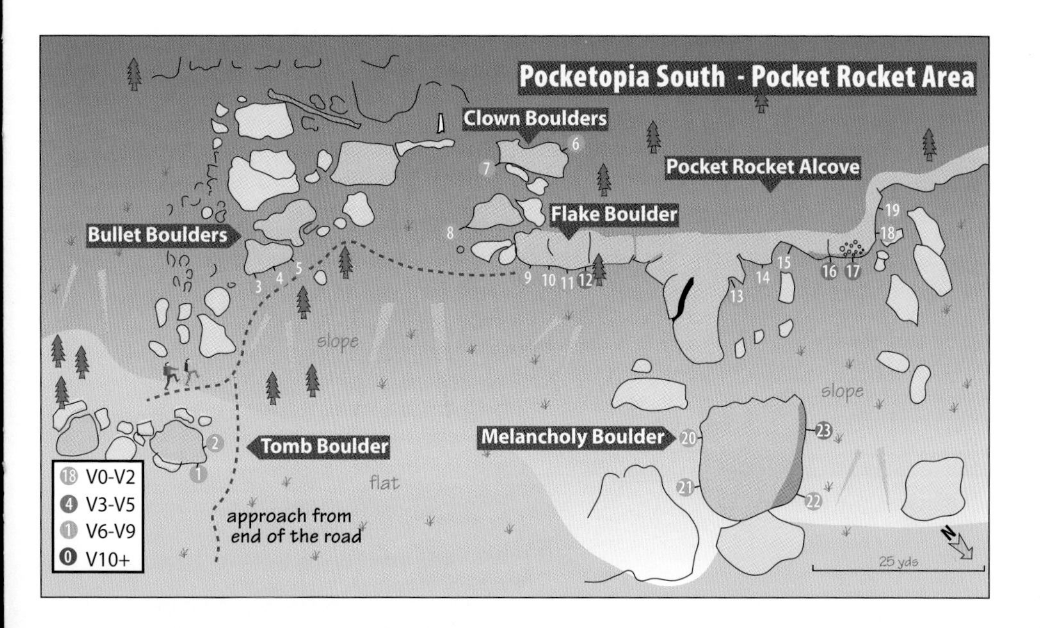

POCKET ROCKET AREA

The Pocket Rocket Area is at the end of the approach road, approximately 0.7 miles from the turn off from road 4S03.

TOMB BOULDER

1 Tombstone v1 ☐
Start from the horizontal crack then over the low roof on pockets.

2 Voodoo Doll v2 ★ ☐
The dog-legged crack and pocket.

BULLET BOULDER

3 Once the Bullet Leaves ... v0+ ☐
Left side of face.

4 There's a Bullet in My Heart v0 ☐
Right side of face.

5 Fire in My Heart v0+ ☐
The pocketed nose/arete.

CLOWN BOULDERS

6 Nemesis v2 ☐
Start on the horizontal, then climb the arete above.

7 Repoman v1 ☐
The undercut prow to loose holds.

8 Rodeo Clown v0 ★★ ☐
The blunt arete requires careful spotting off the boulders to the left and right. Climb as directly as possible up the nose.

FLAKE BOULDER

9 Defcon 5 v0 ★★ ☐
The excellent face is climbed via a flake and one hard move.

10 Merciless Whippin' v0 ★★ ☐
The hairline crack is climbed on good pockets.

11 Unnamed v0 ★★ ☐
The blunt rib has good pockets.

12 Dr. Mofesto v3 ★ ☐
Just right of the black streak is a crimpy wall, climbed without using the pockets at left. Tricky, with small holds.

THE POCKET ROCKET ALCOVE

13 Battered Men Shelter v0 ☐
The crack.

FLAKE BOULDER

14 The Magic Word v0-v1 ☐
The arete is climbable on the left or (harder) right.

15 Unnamed v1 ☐
The face.

16 Blue Steel Heat v5 ★★ ☐
Sit start at the obvious shelf, and climb the crack line via crimps, some sharp pockets and even a sidepull or two if needed!

17 Pocket Rocket v4 ★ ☐
Sit start and make a vicious two-finger pull to gain better holds that lead relatively easily up. Finish slightly left.

18 Pocket Rib v1 ★★ ☐
The excellent blunt arete over a sketchy landing, with a fun hard move down low. Bold, but with sound rock.

19 Pocket Wall v6 ★ ☐
Your aim is to gain the tiny black pocket about 10 feet up near the center of this wall with the right hand. Begin at the crack on the right (right wall off). Step up and lean out left to small pockets using hard-to-see footholds. Make a hard cross-through to gain the tiny but good two-finger hole and pull across left to join *Pocket Rib*.

MELANCHOLY BOULDER

20 Amen for Strange Young Men v0 ☐
The slab on its left edge.

21 Hallelujah for Sad Sweet Songs v0 ☐
The slab on its right.

22 Home is Where You Hang Yourself v2 ☐
Sit start on hollow holds. Climb up to the break then over to the slab. Steep.

23 Transcendent Melancholia v4 ★ ☐
Sit start on small edges. Grab the sidepull and make a hard move to the lip, then over. Steep.

Dink (v3, next page) is one of the excellent Wedge Boulder's short, solid pocket-pulling classics. Photo: Wills Young.

MAXIMUM JOY AREA

About 0.2 miles along the ridge right of the Pocket Rocket area is the Maximum Joy Area. This is about 0.5 miles along the approach track from road 4S03.

BOULDER 1

1 The Professional v0 ☐
The left side of the wall, behind the tree.

2 The Real McCoy v0 ★ ☐
The blunt prow is steep at first, with one hard move.

3 Groundhog Day v0 ☐
The right side of the wall at a white streak.

4 Satan's Little Helper v1 ☐
The yellow wall in the corridor. Bold.

MAXIMUM JOY BOULDER

5 The World is my Oyster v1 ☐
Climb the wall starting up the scoop.

6 Relax v2 ☐
Start on the right wall and traverse left on pockets to a flake low on the left side of the arete, turn the corner and climb the face.

7 Welcome to the Pleasure Dome v1 ★★ ☐
Climb the tall pocketed face left of the nose of the boulder. Very high, but steady.

8 When Two Tribes Go To War v4 ★★ ☐
Sit start with the left hand in a pocket about three feet up. Climb the prow's right side via hard moves on small pockets. Very high, but with the crux low.

9 Maximum Joy v2 ★★ ☐
Start at the right end of the slanting rail and traverse up leftward to good pockets and a biggish move to gain a large hueco, then up carefully but easily. Sit start as for *When Two Tribes ...* for an extended v3 that feels like a route! Very high.

10 Frankie Says v5 ★★ ☐
Sit start as for *Two Tribes* and traverse right and up to the right end of the slanting rail. Continue right to the arete, pull around to gain a crack, and top out via the slab.

THE WEDGE BOULDER

11 Unnamed v0+ ★★ ☐
Sit start at the large hueco, then climb up left past an embedded pebble.

12 Kevin Cauldron v2 ★★ ☐
Sit start at the diagonal feature. Follow this feature left on pockets to a large hueco undercling, then up left past an embedded pebble to the top.

13 Dink v3 ★★ ☐
Sit start at the diagonal feature and pull up and right, then direct past a large shallow hueco by a couple of hard moves. The lip is turned with some difficulty locating the best holds! Excellent and solid.

14 Freedom Gone v0+ ★★ ☐
Sit-start the right side of the wall. Up on big holds to a fun mantel.

15 The Todd Daniels Low Traverse v5 ★ ☐
Start at the very right side of the boulder and climb leftwards, staying low past the blank section to finish as for *Kevin Cauldron.*

BALTIC C BOULDER

16 Molly Heitz's Baltic C v0 ☐
On the road-side face, sit start on pockets and climb the short wall to the slab.

17 Salty C v0 ☐
The crack then right up the small ramp.

18 Middle C v0 ☐
Climb up past the sloping ledge.

MAXIMUM JOY BOULDER

WEDGE BOULDER

Everything and Nothing Boulder
Maximum Joy
The Wedge
Baltic C
POCKETOPIA SOUTH– MAXIMUM JOY AREA

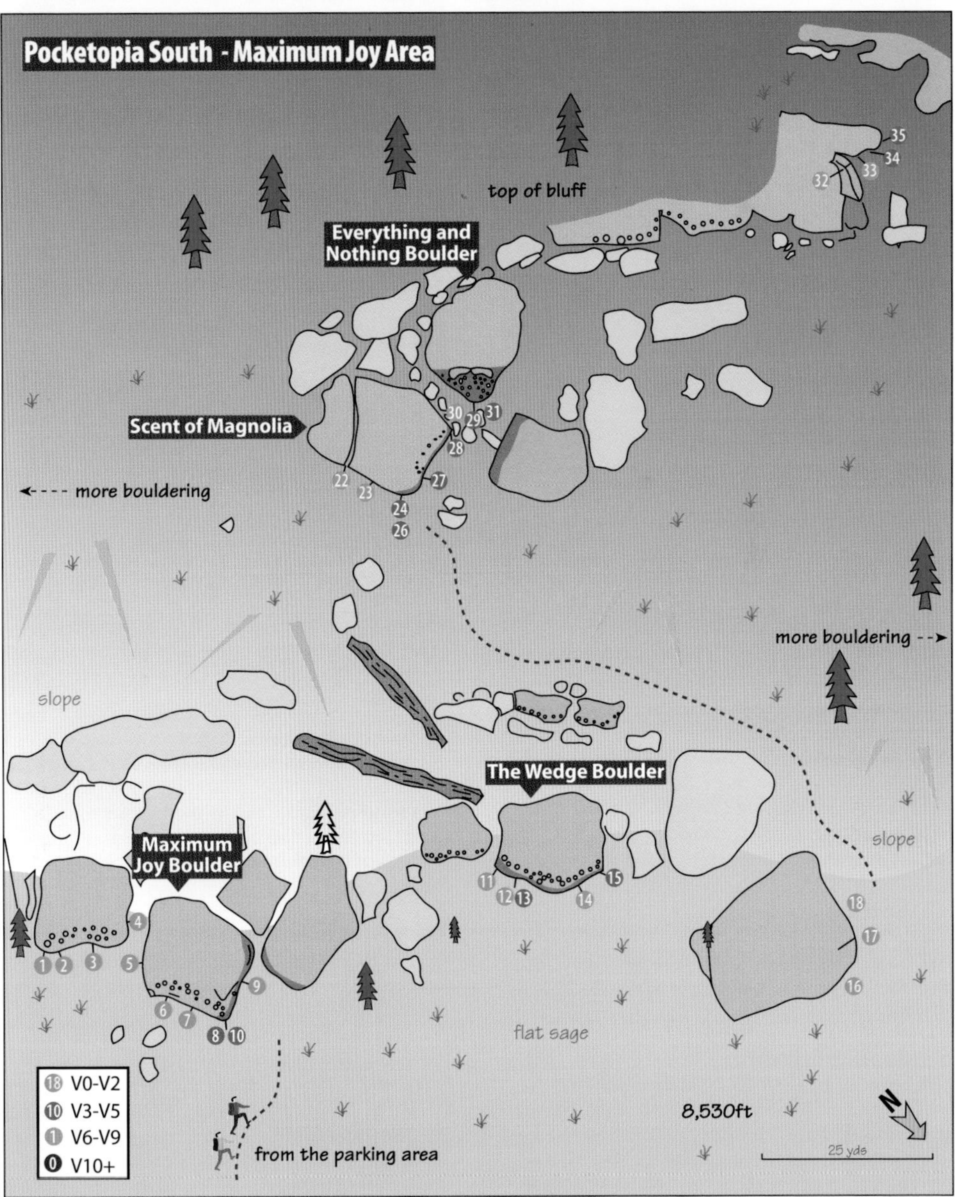
Pocketopia South - Maximum Joy Area
top of bluff
Everything and Nothing Boulder
Scent of Magnolia
more bouldering
more bouldering
slope
slope
The Wedge Boulder
Maximum Joy Boulder
flat sage
from the parking area
8,530ft
25 yds
N
V0-V2
V3-V5
V6-V9
V10+

BOULDERS ON THE SLOPE

19 Unnamed ☐
From a crack, move up to the arete and top out. A fallen tree may be obscuring the top.

20 The Dead C v1 ☐
The orange colored arete.

21 Vitamin C v0- ☐
The orange streak.

THE MAGNOLIA BOULDER

22 F-Squared v0- ☐
The crack on the left facing the road.

23 Ganja Slab v0+ ☐
The middle of the slab facing the road.

24 Outer Galaxy Exile v3 ★ ☐
Sit start on the low small pockets below and left of the arete of *Rhapsody in White* (below). Climb up to pockets over the lip on the slab. Pull over by a big reach to a pocket up left.

25 Rhapsody in White v3 ★ ☐
The left arete of the boulder starting with the right hand on a large slot at about 7-8 feet up. Hard to start if short, using a tiny right crimp (v4?). Pull on with a bad pinch for the left hand and make a hard move to grab a better pinch. Layback the arete to the summit.

Giving it *Everything and Nothing*: Mike Brady on the amazing steep pockets at Pocketopia South. Photo: Wills Young

26 Amber's The World v5 ★ ☐
Sit start on pockets below the arete on the left. Climb up and turn the arete at the good pinch to join *Scent of Magnolia* at its good pockets. Finish along the line of pockets in the wall. It is sustained, but avoids the crux moves at the start of Scent of Magnolia.

27 Scent of Magnolia v5 ★ ☐
Pull on by grabbing opposing vertical slots at 7-8 feet up. Climb the wall right of the arete diagonally rightwards to the apex of the boulder (arete off). You can also pull on with the left hand lower at a tiny crimp-slot and bust a hard move to get started at about v7.

28 The Right Arete ☐
The right arete has been done. Could be good, but needs some cleaning.

EVERYTHING AND NOTHING BOULDER

29 Everything and Nothing v5 ★★★ ☐
The dramatic pocketed roof is the gem of the area: a sustained and powerful climb on excellent rock, requiring hard lock-offs on good holds, and a positive approach. Begin at the horizontal crack formed between the roof and a boulder at the base. Using the crack/lower boulder for your feet, climb directly out on improving holds. **The boulder out left is off**, otherwise v3. Two or three pads could be useful. **Bonus v7**: Avoid both lower blocks. Start on the lowest pocket (5-6 feet off the ground), and climb *Everything and Nothing* avoiding the crack and both large boulders at the base.

30 Native Hymn v6 ★ ☐
As for *Everything and Nothing*, but pull leftward and make a long move to a big flat hold in a shallow hueco. Top out the scoop on the boulder's left side.

31 Shiva Rising v4 ★★ ☐
As for *Everything and Nothing*, using the lower block, but go right to a pocket over the right edge of the boulder, pull around rightward and finish up a small corner. **Bonus v6**: Use the left lower block, but *not* the right one.

GRINDRITE ALCOVE

Follow the walls right of *Everything and Nothing* to an alcove where there are a few worthwhile problems. See topo.

32 Separate Grindrite v2 ★ ☐
An indistinct start somewhere in the horizontal crack leads to a fun encounter at the lip. Named after a local bouldering pioneer and former ski-tuner, this roof crack is virtually a replica for Yosemite's esteemed *Separate Reality*—only in this case without the view, the exposure, the scale ... or the difficulty.

33 **Moving** v2 ☐
Start low at the line of pockets. Climb directly up the wall.

34 **Keep the Afterbirth, Throw the Child Away** v3 ★ ☐
Start low at the line of pockets. Climb rightward up the steep flake.

35 **There Goes a Supernova** v3 ☐
Sit start and climb the edge of the arete to finish pulling right.

ROUND TWO BOULDER

About 200 yards right of The Maximum Joy Area, in a cluster of boulders, is a large boulder facing the road—see photo.

36 **Unnamed** v1 ☐
Sit start the arete which is climbed on sharp pockets on either side over a bad landing.

37 **Round Two** v2 ★★ ☐
Sit start and climb the center of the face via a two-finger undercling pocket.

38 **Bump** v4 ★ ☐
Sit start the center of the face, but avoid the two-finger undercling by moving right and making a hard move to a pocket hidden on the upper facet of the boulder.

39 **Unnamed** v2 ☐
Sit start at the right arete, but pull around to the right immediately on tiny pockets to gain the slab.

HIDDEN CLIFF

The Hidden Cliff is obscured by trees about 0.2 miles along the ridge right of the Maximum Joy Area. It has some long climbs and a tall jutting prow that makes for a couple of good problems. It is about 0.35 miles down the turn off for Pocketopia South from road 4S03.

40 **Unnamed** v1 ☐
The slab up the center.

41 **The Hidden Arete** v4 ★ ☐
Start at small pockets on the left side, and climb the hanging arete. Purists and lovers of stupid human tricks will avoid the boulder below by making a hanging start. Make some hard locks between excellent pockets to good jugs over the lip. The large flake and pocket holds in the cement-like rock to the left side of the prow's wall are avoided.

42 **The Hidden Prow** v3 ★★ ☐
The front of the jutting prow taken straight on avoiding the jammed block and boulder to the right. Purists can do a harder start by avoiding the lower boulder too. Fun moves on solid positive holds.

GRINDRITE ALCOVE

ROUND TWO BOULDER

HIDDEN CLIFF AREA

Opposite top: Mike Brady gets extended on the tricky start to *Goldenrod* (v6). Photo: Wills Young.

POCKETOPIA NORTH

Although only one boulder is mentioned here, there is clearly scope for exploration along this bluff, much of which is too high for bouldering. The Goldenrod Wall has good solid lines on it that should not be missed.

Directions: Follow the directions for Pocketopia South until the hairpin turn on road 4S03. Continue to the flat ground and make a left turn about 0.3 miles beyond that hairpin, just 50 feet or so beyond the right turn for Pocketopia South. Park at an obvious large pullout on the left a few hundred yards down this approach road. Look out to the cliff band: the Goldenrod Wall will be slightly to the left.

THE GOLDENROD WALL

This is the imaculate, north-facing gold-streaked wall seen to the left as approached via the overgrown approach road running north from road 4S03.

1 Unnamed v3 ★ ☐

Sit start and climb up the groove.

2 The Wave of Hope v4 ★★ ☐

Another glorious Pocketopia line that justifies the visit. Sit start on the left of the blunt arete or stand-start the right side, and climb up, moving rightward. Make a heady finish using slopers and hidden holds beyond the lip.

3 Goldenrod v6 ★★★ ☐

Tall and outstanding, this is one of the best tuff lines on the Sierra's East Side. Climb the blank-looking face following the golden streak to the apex of the boulder. Crimp on a small square inclusion, a mono, and some good pockets. The flake at right is off.

4 Doubletree v0 ★★ ☐

Pockets to the juggy flake on the right.

THE GOLDENROD WALL

The Catacombs

Gigantor (v3) is an excellent highball not described here. Photo: Mick Ryan.

The catacombs area is in such a beautiful location, and the jumble of rock formations so intriguing, that the climbing is almost immaterial to enjoying a day out there. Bouldering could be just an excuse to make the drive. Here, a flood of water once cascaded into the Owens River, cutting channels into the volcanic plateau to create towers of rock tightly stacked together at the rim of the present-day gorge. Now we can walk through chasms, displacing soft pumice, and marvelling at the massive monoliths. Backing away from the gorge edge, the ground rises, while the rocks remain roughly of the same elevation, leaving smaller towers, perfect for bouldering, usually above flat pumice landings.

Backing off further still from the gorge, the rock architecture continues to shrink until the scenery resembles a child's adventure playground of miniature cliffs and boulders with fascinating shapes: a perfect family picnic spot, and kiddies bouldering area!

At the gorge rim a cliff band is breaking up and tumbling down the slope. To the south, along the rim about four hundred yards and five minutes' walk from the Catacombs main wash is another bouldering area with some potential.

At around 7200 feet altitude, as with all the Sherwin Plateau areas, the air is reasonably cool compared to that in Bishop. Shade is easily found within the wash, as the curving chambers of rock and myriad towers present walls facing all directions. Tall Jeffrey pines grow sparsely across the plateau all the way to the rim, creating a forested feel, but without obscuring the spectacular views or the winter sun. This is good, because winters can be cold and sometimes snowy, making the approach a bind—occasionally requiring four wheel drive. Along the rim of the gorge itself, the west-facing cliffs and tumbled-down boulders soak in the afternoon sun and the evening's rays until the sun drops behind the Sierras and the sky turns pink.

The Bouldering

Within the Catacombs' main wash, most of the problems involve relatively easy pocket pulling up to v2. These are often fun, sometimes on wonderfully sculpted features: walls that curve and curl in waves of pockets, polyp-like protrusions and giant mushrooms. There are some moderate testpieces of reasonable quality, the standout being the tall and plucky *Looks Like We're One Horse Shy Partner* on the Devil Boulder (page 88). The hardest lines are found on the Beautiful Man Boulder, with a couple at about v9 (page 92) including the excellent sit-start to *I Am a Beautiful Man*. But the real gem of the area—one of the finest little problems on the entire Sherwin Plateau—is an arete, found by a five-minute walk along the gorge rim to the south. Dubbed by Mick Ryan, *The Church of the Lost and Found* (v1 and v3, page 94), this arete provides both left and right options, each superb.

It will be clear to any visitor that there is vastly more bouldering in this area than is documented here. Some excellent problems are easily found by walking about beyond the Catacombs Main Wash, the principal area covered by this guide.

Directions

From Bishop center, take Highway 395 north for about 24 miles (15 miles south, if coming from Mammoth Lakes). Exit Highway 395 opposite Tom's Place and turn right toward Sunnyslopes, signposted

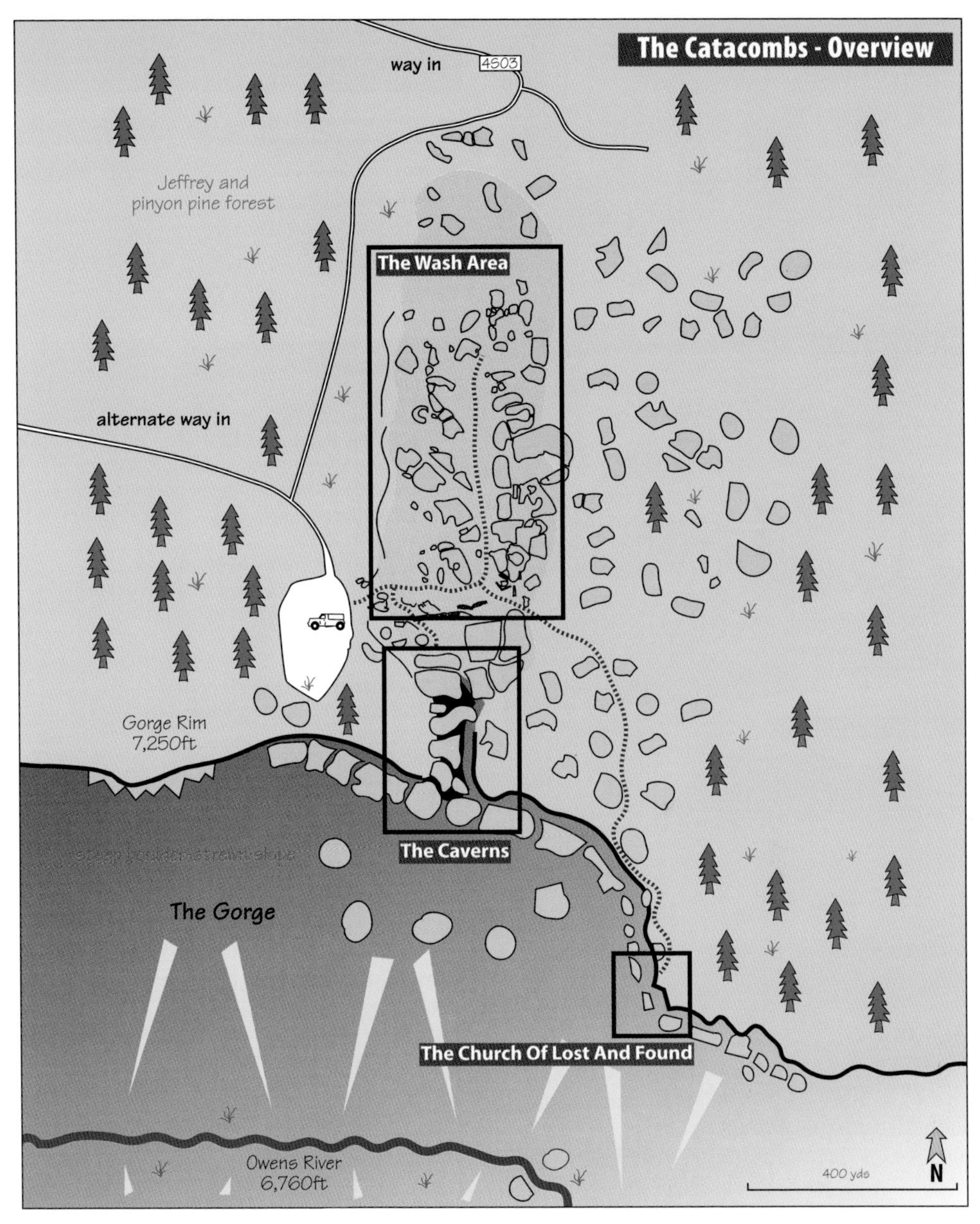

"Owens River Gorge Rd" follow the road for about 4 miles to the Crowley Lake Dam(initially the road takes a sharp left turn, then curves back right leading past houses). From the dam, continue along the road which first narrows, then turns to dirt. At 1.3 miles from the dam, turn right onto road 4S03, sign-posted "Casa Diablo Mountain."

Follow road 4S03 for about 4 miles to a fork/right turn—this is 0.5 miles beyond the turn-off to Pocketopia South. Turn right and head down the road—which is still labelled 4S03—passing a faint left fork after 50 feet. Continue straight to a major fork after about 0.9 miles. You have two options. Stay right and continue staying right until the road ends at the Catacombs turn-around (slightly bumpy); OR fork left for a marginally less bumpy drive, continuing on for about 1.2 miles to another fork right, then about 0.2 miles to a junction where you go left down to the Catacombs turn-around. Take care over rocks near the end of this road.

MAIN WASH AREA

The wash is approached by a 30-second hike from the turnaround at the end of the road.

THE DEVIL BOULDER

1 Monkey On My Back v0- ❑
The left side of the wall.

2 Pokehoedown v0 ❑
Climb the wall moving right.

3 A Deal with the Devil v3 ★ ❑
Sit start on pockets and climb up and around the left side of the arete.

4 Looks Like We're One Horse Shy Partner v5 ★★ ❑
Sit start on pockets. Climb up, slightly right via a hard crank on a small two-finger pocket to gain a good jug up high. Friable rock—care needed on exit.

5 The Alabama Frame of Mind v3 ★ ❑
Sit start and climb via a deep mono (crux) to gain better holds, staying slightly left at the top. Friable rock—care needed on exit.

6 The Mississippi Line v2 ❑
The wall using thin flakes right and left.

7 The Regulator v0 ❑
The shortest wall.

SHOOTER BOULDER

Opposite the Devil Boulder.

8 Unnamed v0 ★ ❑
The tall shaded, north-facing wall.

9 The Shooter v0 ❑
The wall left to the scoop.

10 Leprechaun v0 ★ ❑
Climb the wall moving right to the peak of the boulder.

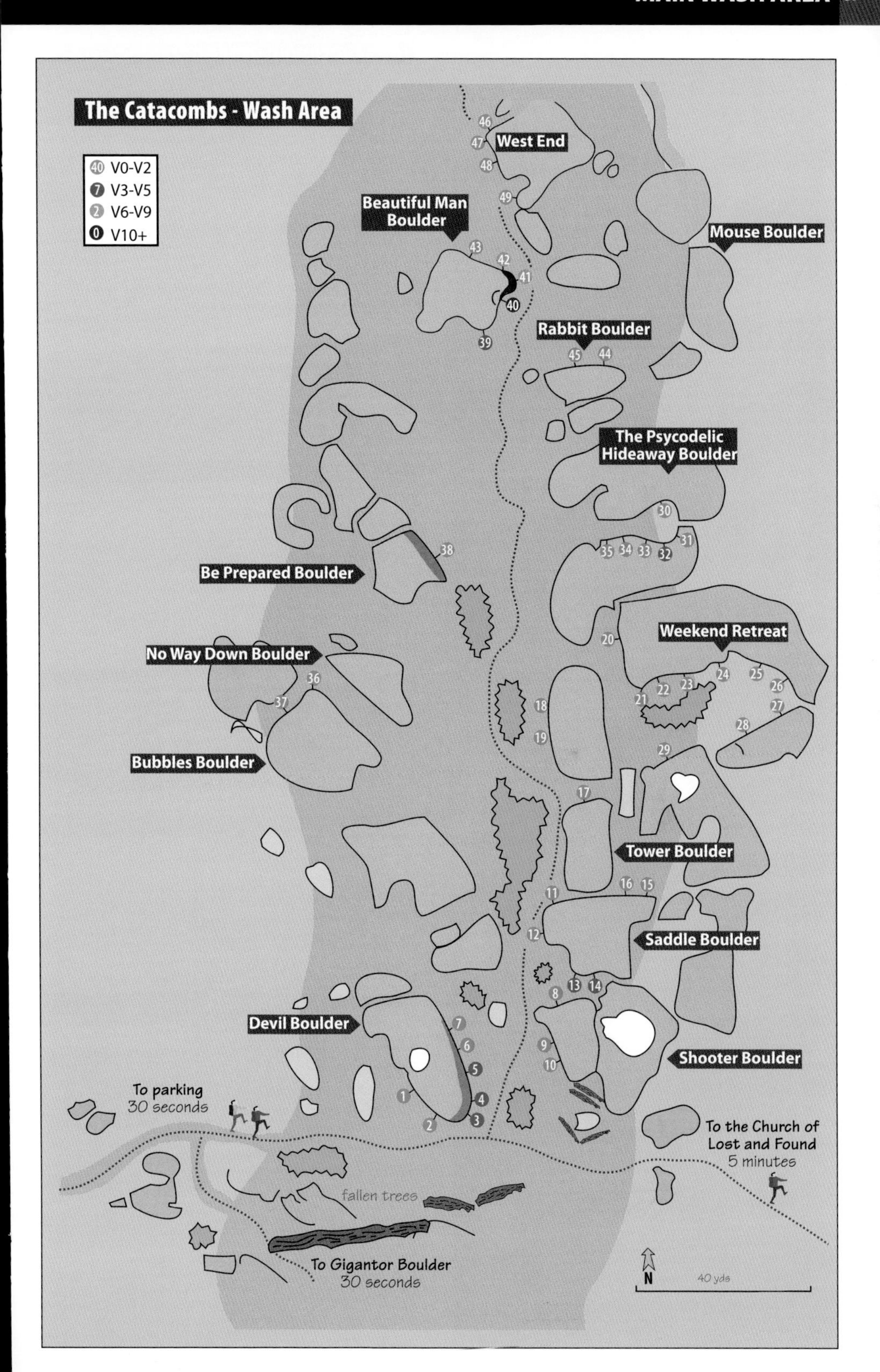

The Catacombs - Wash Area
40 V0-V2
7 V3-V5
2 V6-V9
0 V10+
West End
Beautiful Man Boulder
Mouse Boulder
Rabbit Boulder
The Psycodelic Hideaway Boulder
Be Prepared Boulder
Weekend Retreat
No Way Down Boulder
Bubbles Boulder
Tower Boulder
Saddle Boulder
Devil Boulder
Shooter Boulder
To parking
30 seconds
To the Church of Lost and Found
5 minutes
fallen trees
To Gigantor Boulder
30 seconds
N
40 yds

GROTTO WALL

SADDLE AND TOWER BOULDERS

BOULDER 5

THE SADDLE BOULDER

On the right side of the wash heading north.

11 Unnamed v0 ★ ☐
Begin on the left edge of the lower slab and climb left around the arete and up the north-facing wall.

12 Unnamed v0 ☐
The face.

13 Monster Zero v3 ★ ☐
Climb the wall and continue directly through the triangular roof by good pockets.

14 Saddle Up Your Thoughts and Rope Them In v5 ★ ☐
Climb the wall just right of *Monster Zero,* avoiding the triangular roof by employing some finger bending small holds.

GROTTO WALL

On the back of the Saddle Boulder is the little grotto, with Grotto Wall facing north.

15 Grotto Left v0 ☐
Arete and mantel.

16 Grotto Wall v0 ★ ☐
The wall.

TOWER BOULDER

This boulder is identified by the crusty slab facing the wash and a fine spire facing north.

17 The Tower v0 ★ ☐
Climb the tall tower direct on good edges.

BOULDER 5

18 Unnamed v0 ☐
Climb the right nose. Not the best landing and not the most secure holds.

19 Unnamed v0 ☐
The left side of the face is shorter and unexciting.

THE WEEKEND RETREAT

The first alcove on the east side of the wash.

20 Unnamed v0 ☐
The slab at the entrance to The Retreat can be climbed virtually anywhere at the same grade. See topo (page 89) for location.

21 Unnamed v1 ☐
The arete. Not great.

22 Unnamed v2 ★ ☐
From the right, climb up into the funnel.

23 Unnamed v1 ☐
Climb the face left of the right scoop using some friable rock.

THE WEEKEND RETREAT

24 Unnamed v1 ★ ☐
Climb the right scoop, exiting slightly right using a shallow pocket, avoiding the arete to the left.

25 Unnamed v0 ★ ☐
The thin crack requires no crack technique.

26 Unnamed v0- ★ ☐
The wide crack requires little or no crack technique and also serves as a good down-climb.

27 Unnamed v2 ★ ☐
The undercut wall immediately right of the corner, is climbed via shallow pockets and a tricky move. Watch your back.

28 Unnamed v1 ★ ☐
Starting at a large flat pocket, climb directly through the bulge, making a hard move up and left around the lip to a good jug.

29 Unnamed v0 ☐
The undulating face. See topo (page 89) for location.

THE PSYCHADELIC HIDEAWAY

The second, smaller alcove in the east side of the wash.

30 Psychadelic v0 ★ ☐
The left scoop provides an excellent little flexibility problem.

THE PSYCHADELIC HIDEAWAY

31 Unnamed v0 ★ ☐
The left side of the black scoop at the back right.

32 Unnamed v3 ★ ☐
Start at an obvious large pocket on the right of the black scoop, and climb directly up to the crack at the lip and over.

33 Unnamed v0 ☐
Start at the obvious large pocket on the right of the black scoop, and move rightward then up on good holds.

34 Unnamed v0 ☐
Begin at the right on a slab and move across left to finish as for problem number 4, or just right.

35 Unnamed v0 ☐

THE BUBBLES BOULDER

THE BE PREPARED BOULDER

THE BEAUTIFUL MAN BOULDER

THE NO-WAY DOWN BOULDER

You can climb some problems on this if you like. The south overhanging arete for example. But don't say I didn't warn you .... Central and to the left as you walk up the wash.

THE BUBBLES BOULDER

On the west side of the wash.

36 Bubbles v0 ★ ☐

The undercut nose is climbed direct.

37 Unnamed v0 ☐

The black streak.

THE BE PREPARED BOULDER

In the middle of the wash.

38 Be Prepared: Always Bring a Condom v1 ★ ☐

The wall, climbed on positive edges.

THE BEAUTIFUL MAN BOULDER

The strange mushroom-like boulder with three flying prows in the center of the wash.

39 I Am a Pathetic Bastard v3 ★ ☐

The prow is climbed using some friable flakes then some good pockets, pulling left to a questionable jug before topping out. Fun, but care needed.

40 Funnel Man v9 ★ ☐

Sit start down and left at the base of the black streak (right hand just below the deep two-finger pocket), and climb via some hard pulls, and interesting moves, directly up the funnel. A nasty mono at the lip may help. Good, but painful.

41 I Am a Beautiful Man v7 ★★ ☐

Start standing at the base of the arete with a big pocket for the left hand. Climb the arete and wall to its right by a powerful start and sustained pulls on pockets and edges.

42 I Am a Beautiful Man, Sit v9 ★★★ ☐

Start sitting as for *Funnel Man.* Move up right, match the crimp and pull around and up *I Am a Beautiful Man.* Beautiful, man!

43 I Was Beautiful 'Till I Woke Up v8 ★ ☐

The thin orange wall. Begin with the left hand on the initial holds of *Beautiful Man* and move up and slightly right to a mono and crimps then more pockets and a twisted mono, staying direct to the top. Lots of options on small painful holds. Not so pretty.

44 I Was Beautiful 'Till I Woke Up, Sit v9 ★ ☐

Start sitting as for I am a Beautiful Man, Sit, but finish with *I Was Beautiful 'Till I Woke Up.*

45 The Sniper v1 ★★ ☐

The steep orange wall with big positive holds is excellent.

Looking across The Sherwin Plateau to the Wheeler Crest. Photo: Mick Ryan.

RABIT BOULDER

This boulder is to the right of the Beautiful Man Boulder as you walk up the wash.

44 **Rabit** v0 ☐
Climb the very left side of the wall.

45 **Unnamed** v0 ☐
Climb past deep pockets up the face.

MOUSE BOULDER

This boulder is to the left of Rabit Boulder. Two very short v0 faces are found here, facing west.

THE WEST END BOULDERS

These are on the west side just beyond the distinct mushroom-like Beautiful Man Boulder.

46 **West End** v0 ★ ☐
The pleasant little wall.

47 **Todd's New Standard** v4 ★ ☐
Climb the arete from low pockets, moving to a good hold at right.

48 **Unnamed** v0 ☐
The face.

49 **Unnamed** v0 ☐
The prow.

THE BEAUTIFUL MAN BOULDER

THE WEST END BOULDERS

Carl Harrington on the delicate *Ride The Very Thought to The Ground (v1)*. Photo Mick Ryan.

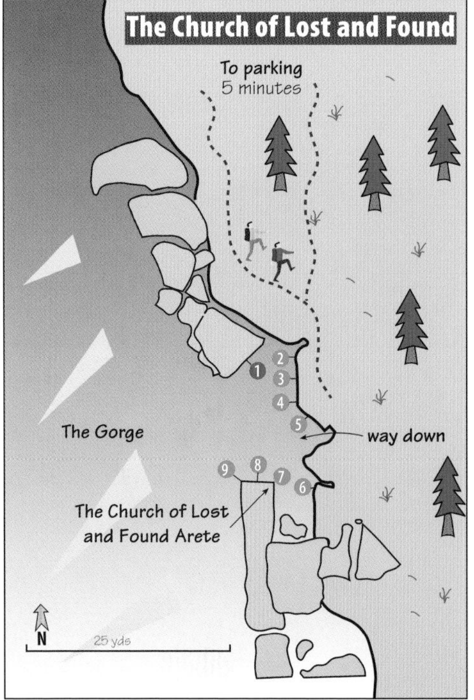

LOST AND FOUND AREA

Approach this pretty area from the main wash by walking from the Devil Boulder southeast across flat ground to the rim, and following this (staying up on the plateau) until the Church of the Lost and Found Boulder is seen from above (photo opposite). The walk will take just two or three minutes.

THE WALL OF THE LOST AND FOUND

1 Amazing Cragging Cuisine v3 ❏
Climb the pocketed wall to a dusty exit.

2 In Thick of the Woods v0- ❏
Climb the honeycombed pockets at the very left edge of the wall.

3 Pocket Wall v1 ★★ ❏
Climb directly up the wall just left of center using some shallow pockets, monos and confident footwork.

4 Ride the Very Thought to the Ground v1 ★ ❏
Easy pockets lead to a delicate step up through the black streak.

5 The Open Sky v0- ❏
More honeycombed pockets. Apparently a hold broke on this line at about four feet up. Hopefully it still goes ...

6 Cossaboom Bang Bang v0 ★★ ❏
The excellent arete.

THE CHURCH OF THE LOST AND FOUND

7 The Church of the Lost and Found
v3 **(left) and** v1 **(right)** ★★★ ❏
Left: The left side of the arete is climbed with a tricky start (especially if you begin low and don't jump) and a relatively easy finish. Smooth rock and fluid moves make this a rare beauty.
Right: The right side is also tricky at the start, but easy to finish. For any bouldering devotee, finding this arete will be a near-religious experience.

8 Unnamed v2 ❏
The center of the wall between the two aretes. There is a long stretch for the summit that shorter people will struggle to make.

9 The Two-Dimensional Tucker v0 ❏
The right arete is frightening but not hard.

VERVE
www.verveclimbing.com

Volcanic Tableland

CHAPTER 2

Josh Huckaby catches some evening rays on one of the most distinctive features at the Happy Boulders: *Atari* (v6). Photo: Kevin Calder.

VOLCANIC TABLELAND

Storm clouds gather across the tableland delivering a sprinkling of snow on the White Mountains.

The Volcanic Tableland is an area to the north of Bishop. It is called 'volcanic' because the bedrock is volcanic, a kind of ash and tuff, the result of a cataclysmic eruption that took place about 740,000 years ago (see page 20 for more about the area's geology). This volcanic rock spilled down from its source to the north, around Crowley Lake, filling the valley southward. Today the area slopes down steadily and is cut through by the Owens River Gorge. Other than this deep sheer-sided canyon, there are only small, shallow valleys across the region and the terrain is raised up above the Owens Valley's edges, and above the town of Bishop, hence, the term 'tableland.'

As for this guidebook, the Volcanic Tableland chapter covers the area closest to Bishop, and includes both the Happy Boulders and the Sad Boulders. The rest of the lower-elevation tableland is considered by the Bureau of Land Management, which manages the area, to be a fragile environment best left for climbers to explore for themselves, and it is with respect to their wishes that some other good sectors are not included in this guide. (The Sherwin Plateau, also part of the tableland, page 70, is described in the previous chapter due to its more distant location from Bishop and its higher elevation and weather conditions.)

The 4500 feet altitude (1370m) tableland of the Happy and Sad Boulders sits in a rain shadow and receives very little precipitation. It is a hot, dry and dusty place during much of the year, but in the cooler seasons it comes into its own for bouldering, with November to March being prime. There are no trees here, only low-lying shrubs. The views are extensive, and when the mountains to east and west are covered with snow, the vistas are breathtaking.

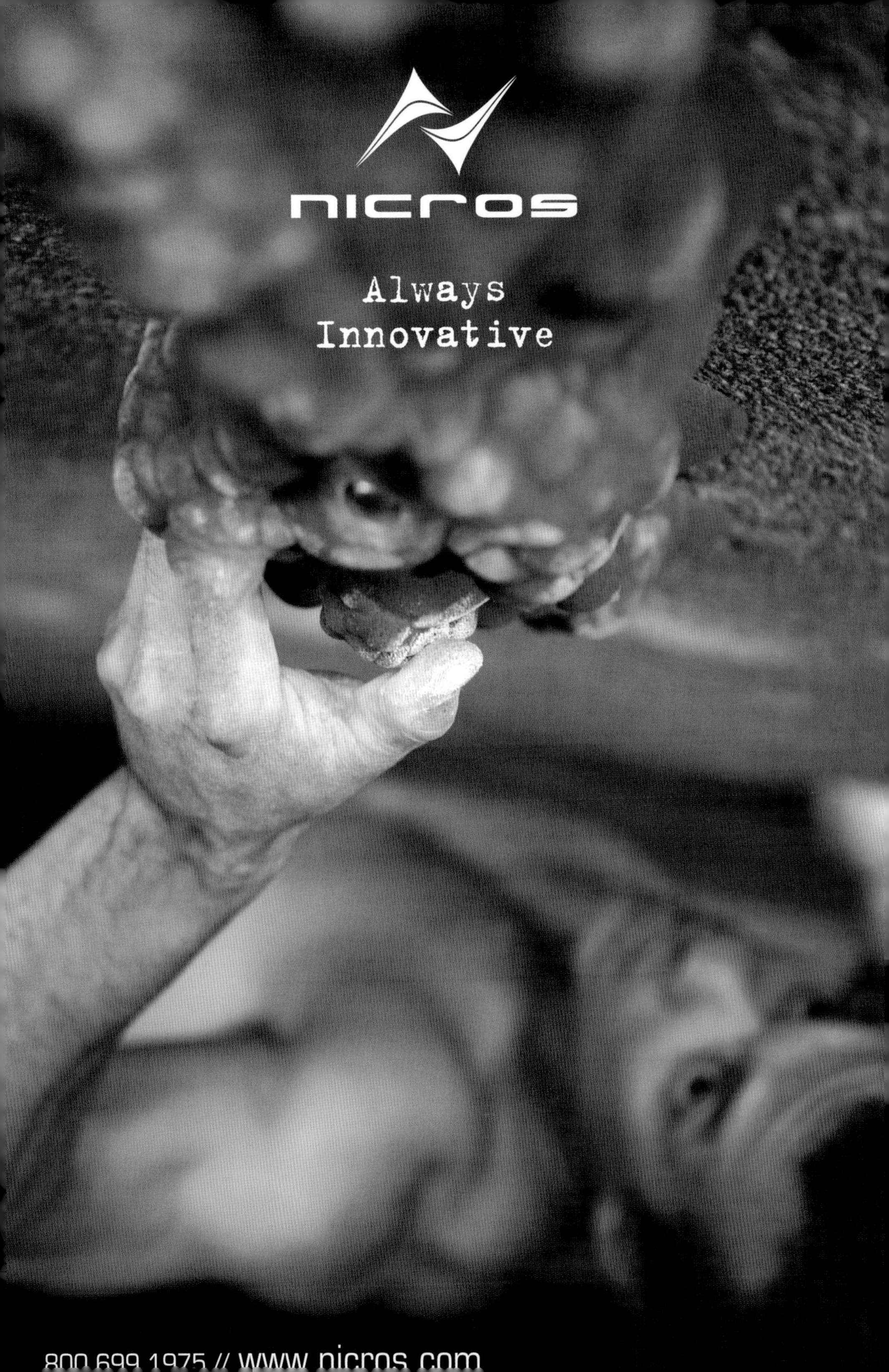

The Happy Boulders

Jen Chee Penrod pulls perfect gold-brown patina on the *Solarium* V3, page 151.

The Happy Boulders is a 3/4-mile-long shallow canyon that cuts into the southern end of the volcanic plateau north of Bishop. The rock is the volcanic Bishop tuff typical of this area. The canyon is at about 4500 feet in altitude (1370m). From the Chalk Bluff Road, where you park, it cuts up into the tableland in a northwest direction. This means that the cliff-band forming the western rim of the canyon (facing northeast) gets a lot of shade during the day making it a great place for climbing on warmer days, while the east rim (facing southwest) takes a lot of sun. Situated like the rest of the tableland in an area of rain-shadow between the great ranges of the White Mountains to the east and the Sierra Nevada Mountains to the west, this drainage receives minimal rainfall. Even while snow is falling on the Buttermilk region, the Happy Boulders will often remain dry. The bigger storms will, of course, make their mark felt here too but few climbing areas on earth will have as many climbable days as this one.

The Happy Boulders canyon has tall, intermittent cliff-lines running along both sides, which sometimes break up into boulder-like buttresses. The valley sides and the center are strewn with blocks of rock with larger boulders appearing with increasing frequency toward the lower end. Though the boulders here are replete with overhangs, there are few real caves, and few accumulations of boulders on top of each other. This makes the area comfortable and easy to walk around, with a lot of space to enjoy the views of the Owens Valley, the cameraderie of other climbers, and the sunshine that is usually abundant.

The Bouldering

The aptly named Happy Boulders is an extraordinarily rich bouldering area with over 500 problems all within about 10 minutes walk of each other. Many of the problems here are world class and have great level landings and open viewing areas. Regardless of the grade, the climbing tends to be physical and steep using good-sized holds of aggressively textured volcanic tuff, very often deep pockets (from mono to full-hand), but also huecos, large blobs and various pinches. There are, however, a few spots where the rock is smooth, and others where the climbing is more technical. In short: there's way too much to describe, and you've no time for lazing around, so have at it!

Directions

From the center of Bishop: Drive north on Main Street (Highway 395) to the junction of Highway 6 (The "Y") signposted to Tonopah. This is the point where Highway 395 makes a long left turn to the west and becomes Sierra Highway. Highway 6 is the straight on option, so don't take the long left turn: Instead, signal right and head directly out of Bishop. Drive along Highway 6 for about 1.3 miles to where the highway begins a long right curve. Turn left on Five Bridges Road. Follow Five Bridges Road for about 2.4 miles, going past the gravel works (at left) to where the road becomes a dirt road. Here, at the crossroads, turn left onto Chalk Bluff Road. Follow Chalk Bluff Road for about 2.3 miles, looking out

For ease of navigation, use your guide's left cover flap to mark this map. Find the boulders you want by the page references here.

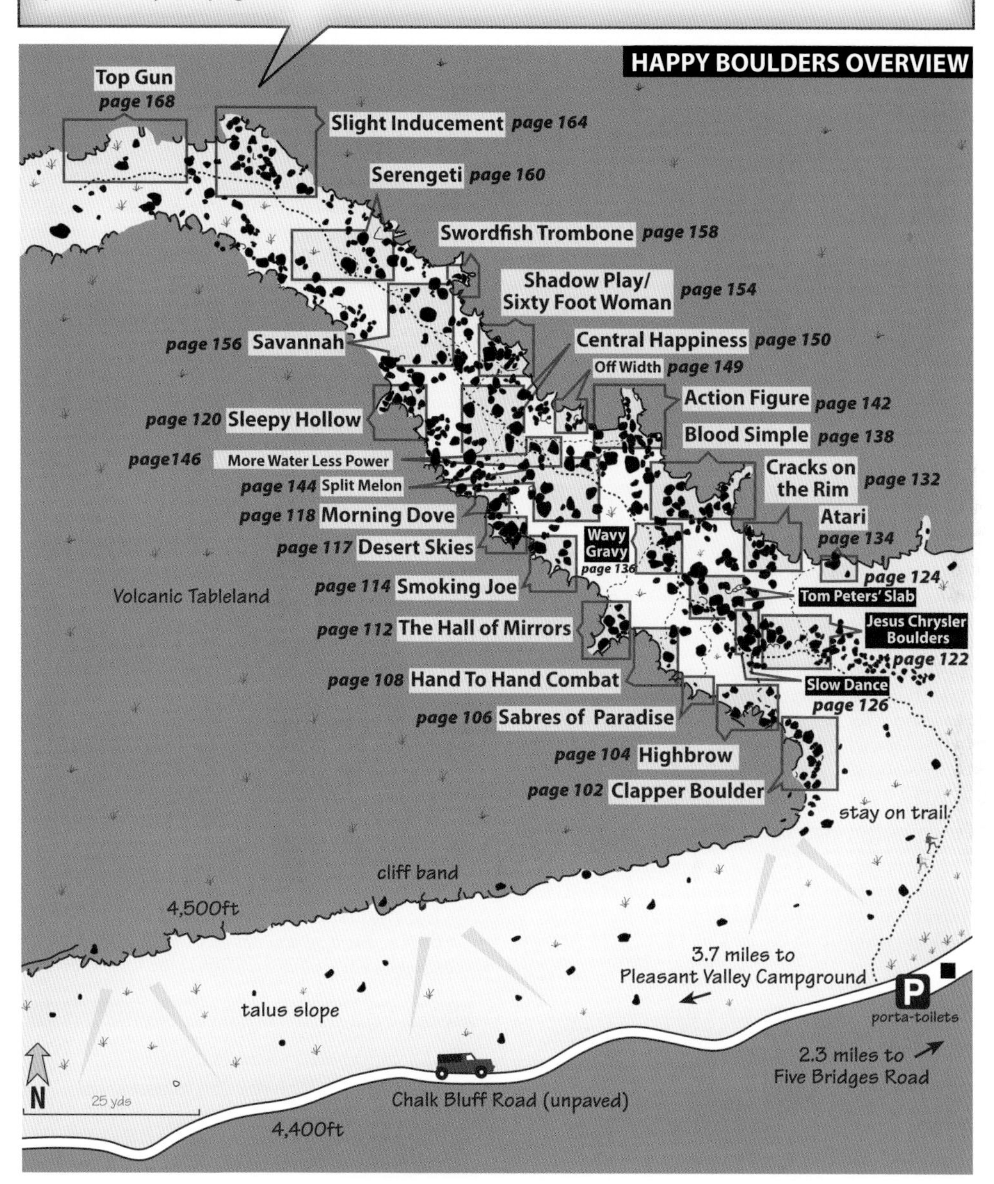

for the long layby parking lot at the left side. There is a large wooden notice board at the right end of the parking lot opposite the trail up to the Happy Boulders.

From Mammoth: Drive in toward the center of Bishop to the long right-hand bend where Sierra Highway becomes Main Street. Instead of making the bend to the right, take Highway 6, by a left turn and drive out of Bishop about 1.3 miles to Five Bridges Road. Turn left at Five Bridges Road, and follow the remaining directions above.

From The Pit campground: Turn left at the bottom of the hill onto Pleasant Valley Dam Road. Follow this road past the Pleasant Valley Dam Campsite, taking a bend to the right after about 0.7 miles that puts you on Chalk Bluff Road. Follow Chalk Bluff Road below the cliff line for about 3.6 miles to a long pullout on the right side.

CLAPPER AREA/ PIG PEN

The Clapper Area is the first area on the West Rim of the canyon, when looking into the Happy Boulders Canyon from the road. It is at the edge of the canyon mouth. At this point, the cliff-line forming the canyon rim takes a turn west and north to become the Chalk Bluff above Chalk Bluff Road. The Clapper Area has some of the best rock at the Happies and some of the best problems too. The problems on the Clapper Boulder itself take full sun in the afternoons, making them a good choice on cloudy or cooler days. The problems are listed from the nearest to the canyon mouth, from left to right.

Approach: Hike up the main Happy Boulders approach trail, and then turn left up the hillside at the Grindrite Boulder, which is a large boulder on the right where the trail passes close between large boulders left and right (see the Tom Peters' Slab Area on page 124 and the overview map on page 101).

TIM'S PROBLEM BOULDER

A lowish boulder that tilts downslope with smooth rock on its uphill side. It is near the end of the Happy Boulders Canyon, but it is not the last boulder along here. Some lines are unrecorded on boulders at the very mouth of the canyon.

1 **Tim's Problem** v6 ★ ☐

Sit start below the arete with the left hand on a shallow pocket and the right on a tiny crimp. Pull up to the sloping hold on the arete, then surmount the arete on its right side using a very shallow pocket and a bit of a trick move if you have long enough legs.

BIG ARETE BOULDER

The big boulder with an overhanging face, and impressive jutting arete, overlooking the lower end of the canyon. It is the right one of two similarly large boulders visible from the parking lot.

2 **Unnamed** v3 ★ ☐

Sit start at a big flat ledge down in the hole at the base of the arete. Watch your head. Climb the arete.

3 **Unnamed** v1 ★ ☐

Stand start at the base of the wall and climb up using the left side of the blunt arete and a shallow groove. Slightly contrived as you can escape rightward, if you prefer.

4 **Unnamed** v6 ★★ ☐

Using a left toe hook in the deep pocket, make scary moves up right and over. Variation: Cross throughto the pocket with right hand and climb direst at v3.

5 **Unnamed** v4 ☐

On the left of the downhill side: Start at right on pockets, and move up to a thin crimp rail, then left to a pocket and up over the top of the boulder on holds of questionable integrity. If you're heavier than average, this is probably not for you!

CLAPPER BOULDER

The first three problems have common sit starts at a horizontal break three-and-a-half feet off the ground.

6 **Needle Across The Groove** v2 ★ ☐

Sit start and launch across the groove to a big pocket. Continue left and up. A reachy start.

7 **Pig Pen** v2 ★★★ ☐

Sit start, and pull up into the groove with some difficulty. Climb the groove to gain a big hidden pocket on the upper slab. From here, finish boldly rightward on ripply holds. A real gem. Starting by climbing the arete (one hand each side at the lower section) is perhaps a grade harder.

8 **The Clapper** v6 ★★★ ☐

A forced but excellent problem. From a sitting start at the horizontal break (with your feet either side of the arete), go right immediately to an undercling. Use the wide pinch, then make hard moves up the arete. Mantel over with good crimps.

9 **Standing Ovation** v7 ★★ ☐

Slightly contrived, but super-good. Sit start at the arete, but move right, then up across the face using sweet crimps and bad footholds to top out via the good holds on the boulder's right side. Use the large rail holds for your feet but not your hands.

10 **A Big Round Of Applause** v8 ★★ ☐

Another slightly forced, but great line: Sit start down and right on big holds. Follow the rails up and left, but off-route the slot at the boulder's lip and all the holds right of this by moving further left via crimps beneath the lip. Hard moves gain a hard-to-find shallow divot on the slab right of the left arete.

11 **Not The Clapper** v1 ★★★ ☐

Sit start on the diagonal ramps. Climb these up and left, then reach for hidden holds at the lip and over.

PIG PEN SLAB

12 **Unnamed** v1 ★★ ☐

The left side of the slab on small flakes. Subtle.

13 **Unnamed** v2 ★★ ☐

Right side of slab on tiny pockets and edges. Precarious.

POKEMON BOULDER

14 **Pokemon** v4 ☐

Sit start up pockets then climb small sharp edges, staying to the right (hard), or moving left (easier).

15 **Paper Crane** v8 ★★ ☐

Sit start on pockets. Move up and right to the arete and the top. Excellent moves.

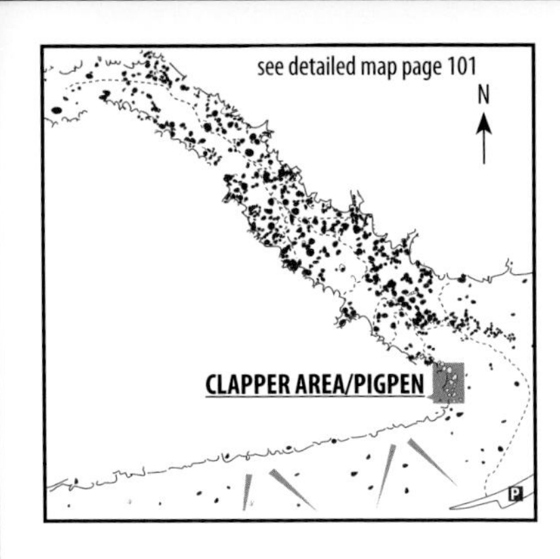

OVERVIEW

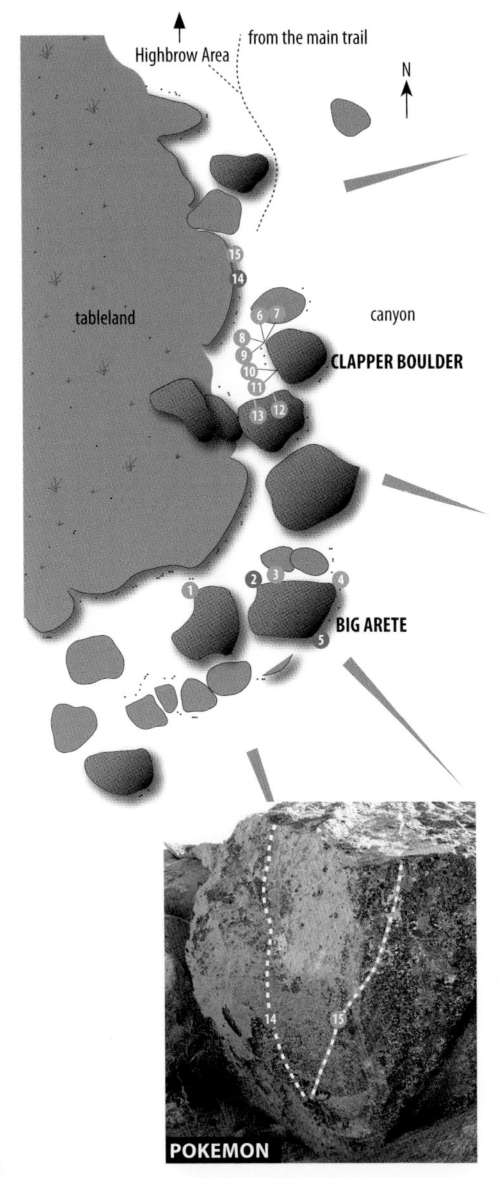

TIM'S PROBLEM

BIG ARETE

POKEMON

CLAPPER BOULDER / PIG PEN

HIGHBROW AREA/FRONTIERLAND

The Highbrow Area is named for a spectacular problem on a prow that juts out over a small flat landing zone just big enough to make it boulderable with care and pads. It is jammed into a corner along the rim, so not easily visible from below. This area is located on the west rim to the right (looking at the cliff) of the Clapper Area (see previous pages). It has some superb problems on immaculate tuff that stay in the shade pretty much all day. The problems are listed from left to right along the rim, starting just to the right of the Clapper Area and Pokemon rock, listed in the previous section. **Approach:** Follow the main trail into the canyon and take a path left up the hillside from the Corridor Boulder. The Corridor boulder has a distinctive brown wall that faces the trail as you approach, and forms the left side of a corridor between two large boulders (see the Slow Dance Area, page 126). Overview map: page 101.

To the right of the Pokemon problems (previous page) is:

1 Sorry About That (East Side) v3 ☐
Sit start and make a hard move to a pocket. Then up and over on more sharpish pockets. Steve made me do it.

Downslope under the above problem is a slab.

2 Lichen Slab v0+ ★ ☐
Climb the pretty slab's left side past a good, but sharp pocket up high.

The cliff forms a tall, slightly undercut buttress that faces up canyon.

3 There's Nothing You Can Do That Can't Be Done v5 ☐
Sit start under the left side of the arete on two very small pockets. Make a hard snatch to the lip at right, then around and up. Top out with care.

4 Unnamed v3 ☐
Climb the wall, starting with opposing sidepulls or pockets and a big move to a high crimp. Then more easily up and left. Top out with care.

Down and left of the prominent prow of Highbrow, *the base of the cliff leans out over an adjacent low boulder.*

5 Orange Crush v7 ★ ☐
Sit start at pockets with the rock slab at your back: beware the rock. Move up to a sidepull crimp, then up and right to gain a jug with difficulty.

HIGHBROW AREA

6 Unnamed v4 ☐
Sit start at an undercling and pocket and, with a tricky start move left to a higher pocket then up to a sloper.

7 Highbrow v8 ★★★ ☐
Sit start and climb the incredible overhanging fin on good holds and heel hooks to an exhilarating finish. Needs pads and spotters. World class. Photo overleaf.

8 Frontierland v0- ★★ ☐
Sit start and climb the beautiful blunt arete. A fun beginning and perfect rock all the way to the top.

HAIR TRIGGER WALL

9 Unnamed v8 ☐
Sit start with a low pocket/sidepull for the right hand, a crimp in the crack for the left, and a heel hook. Make exacting moves up and right past dreadful holds to join the top of *Hair Trigger*.

10 Hair Trigger v5 ★★ ☐
Sit start with a high two-finger pocket for the right hand; make a hard move to gain good holds, and then climb slightly left and over.

11 Hair Trigger Variation v5 ★★ ☐
As above, but starting at right.

12 Western Motif v2 ★★ ☐
Sit start and climb the overhang with big moves on good pockets.

13 Merriweather v0 ★ ☐
Sit start and climb the pockets.

14 Westward Expansion v6 ★★ ☐
Sit start way over on the right side of the overhanging pocketed wall. Traverse the wall left, finishing at *Hair Trigger*.

WORK WALL

This is a tall wall right of the Hair Trigger Wall. At its right side is a bulge next to a high corner formed by the cliff.

15 Wall v0 ☐
Sit start and climb the wall.

16 WORK is a Four Letter Word v6 ★ ☐
Start low on pockets: slap to a sloping divot, then up and over the bulge, topping out on decent holds.

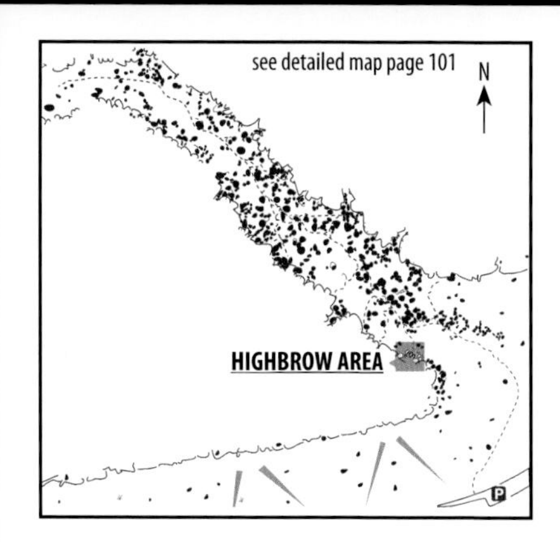

OVERVIEW

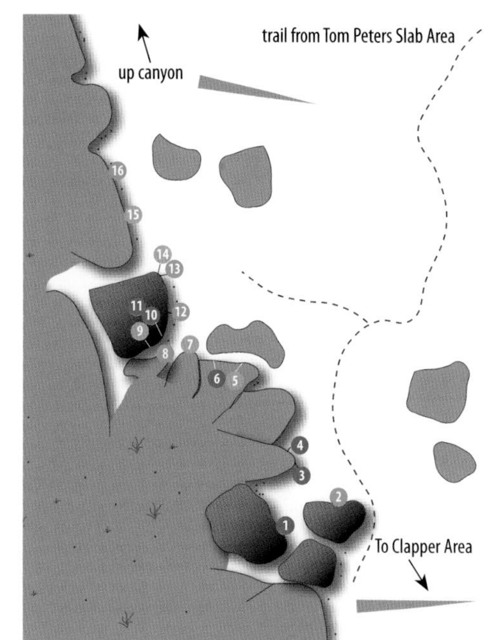

THERE'S NOTHING YOU CAN DO ...

HAIR TRIGGER

HIGHBROW

WORK WALL

SABRES OF PARADISE

This area is around the corner to the right of *WORK is a Four Letter Word* (basically right of the HighbrowArea/Frontierland). It is known for its extraordinary traverses: the warm up being *Little Fluffy Clouds* (v2), and the big one, *Sabres Of Paradise* (hard v7). Both are great for gaining power-endurance. There are also some excellent up problems that climb through the big traverse. Shaded nearly all day.

Approach: Take a short trail up from opposite the Corridor Boulder as for the Highbrow Area/ Frontierland (see previous page). Overview map: page 101.

1 Youth v0 ★ ☐
Avoid the off-width by stemming, though jamming it is possible and a little harder.

2 Unnamed v1 ★ ☐
Sit start. Climb the left side of the pocketed wall.

3 Unnamed v6 ★ ☐
An eliminate: Sit start and climb up to a pair of terrible pockets for the left hand—the big undercling out right and pockets above this are off. Somehow gain the good flat hold up high right.

4 Unnamed v4 ★ ☐
Sit start and move right to a good undercling, then past a pocket to the good flat hold above.

5 Unnamed v2 ★ ☐
Sit start and climb up and left.

6 Unnamed v0 ★ ☐
Sit start and climb up and right.

7 Unnamed v1 ★ ☐
Sit start and climb the prow.

8 Sabresonic v7 ★ ☐
Climbs the leaning face direct, avoiding the big flake hold at left. Sit start in low pockets under the bulge, pull up to more pockets, then make a huge move to a crimp and up.

9 Jack of Swords v9 ★ ☐
Sit start at the pockets under the bulge, move up to more pockets, then make a hard move right to crimps on the left side of the blunt prow, and finally the jug on the prow, then up. v8 + pain = v9?

10 Stroking the Walrus v7 ★ ☐
Sit start at two pockets at the bottom left of the hanging prow with your feet on the back wall. Climb the prow to a jug on its upper right side.

11 Sabres of Paradise v7 ★★★ ☐
A monster traverse: hard for the grade, but the most powerful moves are all done in the initial sequence. Sit start on the starting block, go left using the "keel" to horizontal moves past pockets (crux). Go around the corner on the front face all the way to the small recess/roof. Move down at the left side of the rock scar (second crux), and then up at the end.

12 Supernova at the End of the Universe v4 ★ ☐
Sit start on the starting block: go right on pockets then immediately up the left side of the nose with the neighboring block at your back.

13 Alex Patterson v5 ★★ ☐
Sit start on the starting block: go right on pockets, staying low around the corner, then up.

14 The Orb v7 ★ ☐
Sit start on the starting block, go rightward low around the corner, and continue across the right wall, making a long move to gain a sharp pocket near flakes. From here, climb up using an obvious "gaston" hold (a good thumb-down sidepull) for the left hand, pressing up and right from this to crimps.

15 Orb Short v4 ★ ☐
Sit start below the topout of *The Orb,* and climb it.

16 Little Fluffy Clouds v2 ★★ ☐
On the buttress just right of *The Orb.* Make a right-to-left traverse on good pockets.

Sweden's Said Belhaj climbs *Highbrow* (v8). Bring plenty of pads for this beauty, and get a good spot! One of Bishop's best. Photo: Wills Young.

HAND TO HAND COMBAT AREA

This is the next area along the west rim from the Sabres of Paradise Area. It is directly above *The Gleaner* (page 131). Here, the wall forming the rim of the canyon has several up problems including one of the best highballs, *René* (v5), and the superb pocketed traverse that gives the area its name. There is also the excellent Powis Boulder, with a smooth, hard surface providing something a little different to the typical thuggish Happy Boulders fare.

Approach: At the Gleaner Boulder is a crossroads in the trail. If you're heading up canyon, the left trail runs uphill to the Hand To Hand Combat Area, the right leads down to *The Gleaner.* Overview map: page 101.

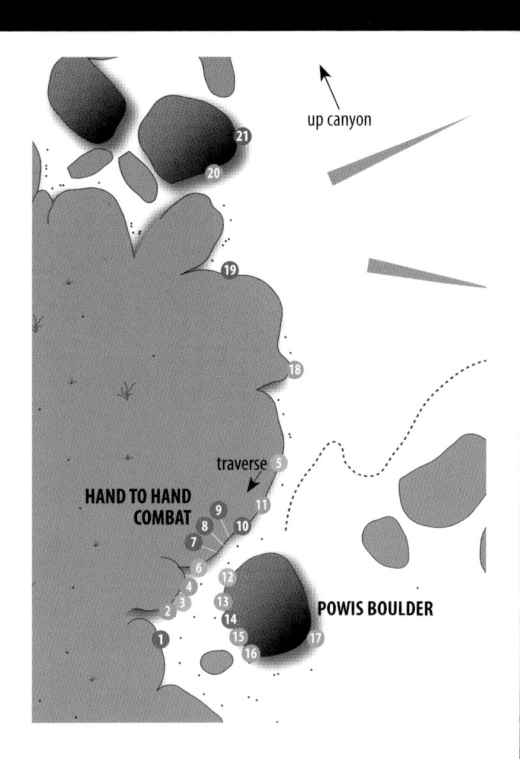

The cliff line at the back of the alcove has a couple of good problems.

1 René v5 ★★★ ☐
An exacting highball. Climb the center of the back wall to the deep hueco then commit to tiny pockets on the headwall, and a frightening move to the lip. One of the best. A few pads can make this fairly safe.

2 Dirty Hooker v1 ☐
Sit start in the corner and climb up using the right wall only. Not hard and not very good either.

3 Not Another Brit In Bishop v7 ★ ☐
Sit start at a horizontal break. Move up right to a slopey sidepull then left to very poor holds in a left-facing groove. Make a couple of short adjustments with opposing bad sidepulls, and then snatch for better crimps higher up. A little crusty, but with some good movement.

4 No Sleepy Yet v1 ☐
Use the crusty undercling to reach a crusty jug. Crusty.

To the right is an bulging pocketed overhang.

5 Hand To Hand Combat Traverse v7 ★★ ☐
Traverse the long pocketed wall in either direction at about the same grade. Stay below the lip. Either start at the crack way right, or just right of the crack on the left. Countless link-ups from the traverse into the various up-problems can be contrived.

The up problems along the line of this traverse are as follows:

6 Hamtaro v8 ★ ☐
Sit start on the lowest pockets below the left start of *Hand To Hand Combat.* Climb up the prow to gain a smallish good pocket on the right, then use hidden edges to reach the ledge. The crack and the wall to the left are not used.

7 Sidepull Problem v5 ★ ☐
Kind of a one-move wonder, so it may seem easy for some: Sit start and climb the overhanging wall past an obvious left-hand sidepull. The crux is grabbing the huge hold at the lip. Tricky, especially if you're short. Pull over.

8 Pocket Problem v3 ★ ☐
Sit start and climb the wall past a baffling collection of pockets to a good hold over the lip right of the target flake of the *Sidepull Problem*. Mantel over.

9 Crack Problem v3 ★ ☐
Sit start and climb the honeycombed pockets through the overhang to a crack. Mantel over.

10 Pinch Problem v4 ★ ☐
Sit start and climb through the overhang to the lip via a hard move from a sweet pinch. Improvise over with difficulty and stand up.

11 Unnamed v1 ★ ☐
The right side of the blunt prow on good pockets.

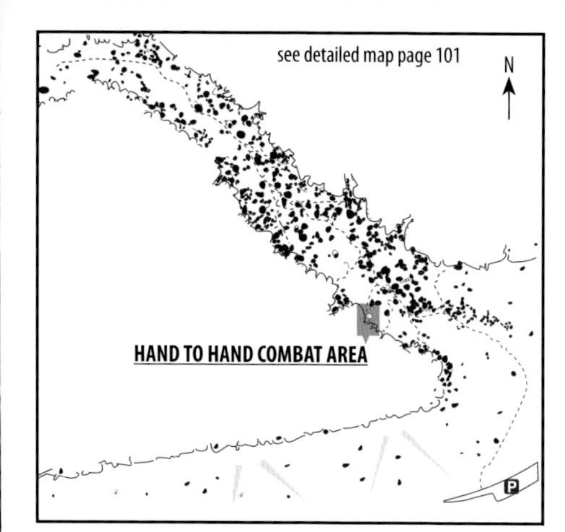
see detailed map page 101
N
HAND TO HAND COMBAT AREA
P

1
2
RENE

Not Another Brit
Hand to Hand
3
4
6
7
Powis
NOT ANOTHER BRIT/HAND TO HAND

7
8
9
10
11
5
HAND TO HAND COMBAT

POWIS BOULDER

CAPTAIN HOOK

IF BISHOP WERE FRANCE

POWIS BOULDER

This is the large, smooth, pale-brown boulder that sits in the alcove next to *Hand To Hand Combat.* Smooth holds and great moves characterize the bouldering on this exceptional rock.

12 Powis Traverse v6 ★★ ☐
Sit start at a hueco and slap up and right across the slopey lip to get established on the face. Continue right on small edges and hidden feet then up the *Number One* problem. Perfect rock and good moves.

13 Tao v2 ☐
An up problem through the middle of the *Powis Traverse*—standing start.

14 Number One v3 ★★ ☐
The finish to the *Powis Traverse*: Best get this wired before you do the *Powis Traverse*, unless you're going for the flash! Stand start on edges and climb up and right by some tricky moves.

15 Not A Number v1 ★★ ☐
The subtle wall with bad holds requires a lot of confidence. There is a crimper for the right hand to start, and you end up standing on it.

16 Powis Arete v0 ★ ☐
The arete. Great fun.

17 Son Of Paul Arete v2 ☐
The exposed southeast arete.

Just a few yards beyond the right end of the Hand to Hand Combat Traverse *is a short overhanging prow that appears a little taller from its right side.*

18 Bear Hug v2 ★ ☐
Start on the right at a good lay-away down and right, and climb up and left using heel hooks and bear-hug moves. Quite exposed for such a short problem and well worth doing.

There is a V-shaped bay, further right still, and just south of the Hall of Mirrors area.

19 Captain Hook v5 ★ ☐
On the left wall of the alcove, sit start on the lowest pockets. Use a trick move to gain jugs up and left, then make a couple more easy moves to the ledge. The clue is in the name. Have fun!

On the boulder right of the Captain Hook *alcove, is a steep overhang that faces into the canyon.*

20 If Bishop Were France v1 ☐
And the Happies were Font, then this would be an awesome solid line ... running with water. Climb the just-under-vertical face using good pockets, staying direct and avoiding the loose-looking rock to the right. Cleaned up, this could be worth climbing!

21 Unnamed v3 ★ ☐
Climb the overhang from pinches. A little scary, but good. Spotter useful.

Lisa Rands anticipates the joy of *Captain Hook* (v5) opposite page. Photo: Wills Young.

THE HALL OF MIRRORS AREA

This is a cluster of boulders packed into a hidden alcove on the west rim between The Hand To Hand Combat Area and the Smoking Joe Area, and directly above the Slap Happy Boulder (Wavy Gravy Area). It has the amazingly sheer slab of *The Hall of Mirrors* with a beautiful traverse on pockets. You will also find a couple of testy high face climbs, plus a host of short mini-problems that are perfect for those who like their bouldering very close to the ground!

Approach: Hike along the cliff rightward from the Hand To Hand Combat Area (previous pages) past Captain Hook (in the V-shaped alcove) and a large boulder with a jutting roof. Just beyond this roof, scramble over two low boulders to find the entrance to the Hall of Mirrors Area. You can also easily approach left along the cliff from the Smoking Joe Area (page 114) or from a trail up from just behind the Slap Happy Boulder in the Wavy Gravy Area down by the Happy Boulders Canyon's main trail. Overview map: page 101.

FRONT BLOCK

Hiding the Hall of Mirror's alcove from view are:

1 Latona Basin v0- ★ ☐
Up pockets to the top, go right to finish with a mantel.

2 Sacré Coeur v3 ★★ ☐
Start at a cluster of pockets. Make a hard long move up left to an isolated pocket, then pull through to the top. Beautiful gymnastic moves.

3 Grand Trianon v0+ ☐
Stand start at a small pocket and a sloping pocket. Go up and right to sharp holds on a small shelf, then the top.

MAXIMILIEN BUTTRESS

Behind the Front Block are:

4 Maximilien v5 ★ ☐
Sit start down and right, climb up and left to gain the left side of the undercut face using slightly painful pockets. A mono can be useful to gain a good crimp from which the top is easily reached.

5 The French Connection v6 ★★ ☐
A memorable face climb. The center of the wall on pockets then very small edges. If you like this, check out the *Mr Witty* and the *Grotesque Old Woman* lines of the Desert Skies Area (page 117).

BAROQUE BUTTRESS

Further into the hillside, 20 yards past the Maximilien Buttress, another low pocketed buttress is on the right. It has three diminutive, but nevertheless good problems. Left to right are:

6 Let Them Eat Cake v2 ☐
Sit start as low as you can. Small but fun.

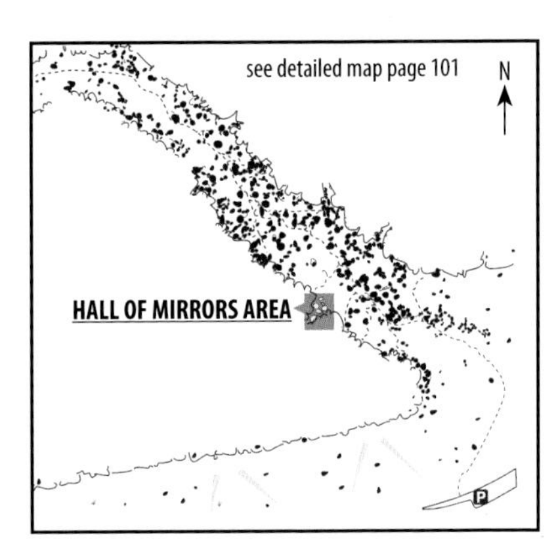

7 Size Matters v3 ★ ☐
Sit start as low as possible. Climb up with a move to grab a hold on the left side of the shallow scoop above the lip. Mantel: an extremely small, but excellent problem.

8 Baroque v3 ★ ☐
Sit start on the lowest pockets. Move up and left on pockets then a long reach to the top and the crux mantel. Surprisingly good.

KING LUIS

The tiny arete facing the former problems is:

9 King Louis v1 ★ ☐
Sit start on the lowest pockets with your feet on the back wall. Climb the pocketed prow. More short fun.

THE HALL OF MIRRORS

The long smooth slab is hidden on the south side of this area.

10 Galerie des Glaces v2 ★★★ ☐
The mid-height traverse on pockets. A classic, and a bit of a frightener if you start to get tired. Top out at a slot when the pockets vanish. If you pump out, grab for the top!

11 Pompidou v0 ☐
Start off cheater stones to reach pockets. Pull up, then climb to the top by more pockets.

12 The Salon of Hercules v0+ ☐
Start off a two-finger pocket and a thumb sprag, move up past pockets to the top.

13 Napoleon's Bedroom v0+ ☐
A hard move off the ground using shallow pockets to gain a slot and the finish of the traverse.

14 Unnamed v3 ☐
Make tricky moves off the ground to climb this small wall on tiny, almost non-existent holds.

15 Sharp and Short v1 ☐
The smooth wall from a high edge.

Adam gets *Slap Happy* (v3), page 136

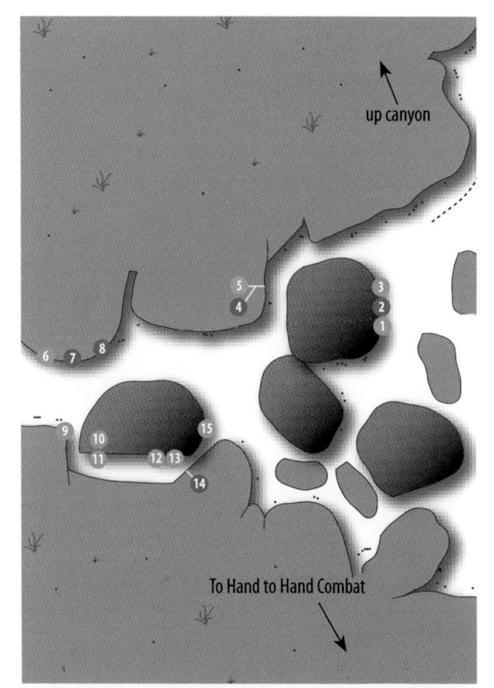

SMOKING JOE AREA

This is a "bay" in the cliff-line up on the west rim (left as you look up canyon), above the Split Mellon Area. It is down canyon from the Desert Skies Area (*Wills' Arete* etc.) and up canyon from the Hand to Hand Combat and the Hall of Mirrors Areas. This area has the most bullet-hard piece of rock in the area in the form of *Toxic Avenger* (v9), *Mr Happy* (v5) and *Hit the High Hard One* (v3). There are several other superb lines too, mostly steep.
Approach: Hike up from the Wavy Gravy Area or back-track up from the Central Happiness (page 150) or Split Mellon (page 144).

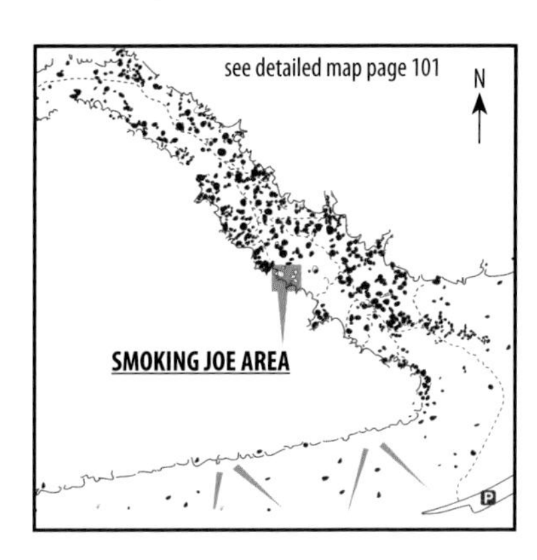

PISS AND VINEGAR

Left of the main Smoking Joe Area is a small 20-feet deep slot in the cliff, where someone once built a wall to conceal the entrance.

1 Piss and Vinegar v6 ❑
Sit start and climb the center of the left wall of the alcove, using a gaston for the left hand and some very small crimps.

THE TOXIC AVENGER/MR HAPPY WALL

On the left side of the main Smoking Joe Bay is:

2 Toxic Roof v4 ★ ❑
Crawl in, climb out. Fun climbing in a slightly toxic environment.

3 Resolution v2 ❑
The right of two short aretes.

4 Toxic Avenger v9 ★★★ ❑
Sit start as low as you can on the off-set rail. Move up the rail and throw for the top. Mantel. Bullet hard rock and a really superb movement make this one of the best in the area for a quick hit!

5 Mr. Happy Extended v7 ★ ❑
Sit start on the off-set rail, as for *Toxic Avenger.* Stretch right to pockets leading into *Mr. Happy.*

6 Mr. Happy v5 ★★ ❑
Start on the lowest pockets and climb up and over the prow using the crack as needed. Another good clean line with powerful moves.

7 Hit The High Hard One v3 ★★ ❑
The overhanging arete from a stand-up start using pockets to a throw for the top.

8 Hit the High Hard One, Sit v9 ★★ ❑
Sit start way down at the back with shallow pockets/pinch. Avoid touching the rock at right. Bust a very hard move to the lip, then up the arete.

There are also some amazing hard traverses possible here:

9 The Bubba Butt Buster v11 ★★★ ❑
Left to right. Begin at *Toxic Avenger* (sitting) and climb right, crossing *Mr. Happy* to finish up *Hit the High Hard One.*

10 Bubba Lobotomy v12 ★★ ❑
Right to left. Sit start as for *Hit the High Hard One, Sit,* and make a sustained pocket traverse left across the wall to a potentially heart-breaking finish on Toxic Avenger.

And two shorter right to left traverses are:

11 Bubba: The Legend v11 ★ ❑
Sit start as for *Mr. Happy* and follow pockets left to finish as for *Toxic Avenger.*

12 Bubba Gets Committed v10 ★ ❑
Sit start as for *Hit the High Hard One*, Sit, and climb left across pockets to top out on *Mr. Happy.*

To the right of Hit the High Hard One *are:*

13 Hippy Bishop v4 ❑
Traverse small low pockets and mantel the slab.

14 Cheap New Age Fix v2 ★★ ❑
Sit start and climb the pocketed nose.

Opposite: Sean McColl finishing up *Toxic Avenger* during his second ascent of *Bubba Lobotomy* (v12), this page.

OVERVIEW

TOXIC AVENGER/MR. HAPPY WALL

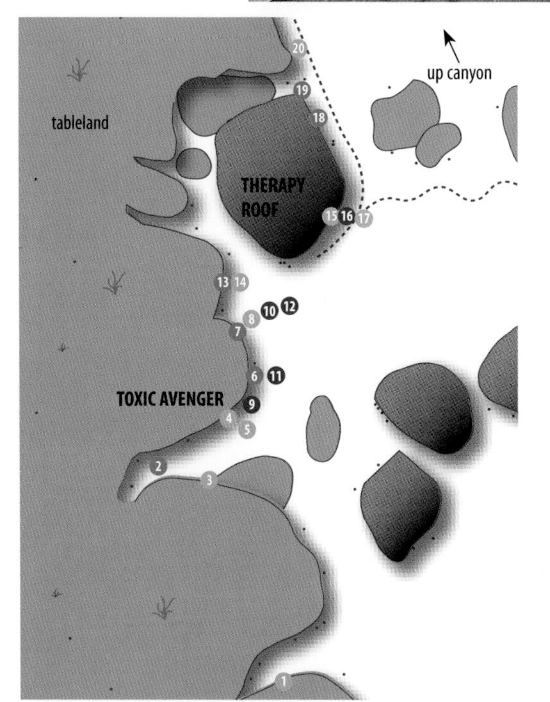

HIT THE HIGH HARD ONE / HIPPY BISHOP

Korni Obleitner tries to keep his fee dry on *Every Color You Are*. Photo: Zlu Haller.

THERAPY ROOF

A giant boulder forms the cliff edge below and right of the Toxic Avenger/Mr. Happy wall. It overhangs on its lower side. See the topo on the previous page.

15 Pappachubby v7 ★ ☐
Sit start and climb up left to small edges; make a couple of hard moves around the corner leftward on poor pockets to gain the upper headwall.

16 He Got Game v12 ★★ ☐
Sit start as for *Pappachubby* and climb out the roof directly to a hard lip move and a big pull on the short headwall using a poor pocket. A lot harder than it once was, this rating is unconfirmed.

17 Therapy v8 ★★ ☐
Sit start as for *Pappachubby* and climb out the ceiling on good pockets. When they run out, swing a toe-hook or make a hard snatch to the lip. Struggle around and finish leftward up the crack. Rewarding!

Further right on the same buttress are:

18 If All Else Fails, I'll Raise Pigs v4 ☐
Climb the thin seam left of the arete, then the face and arete, moving up to an undercling at the top.

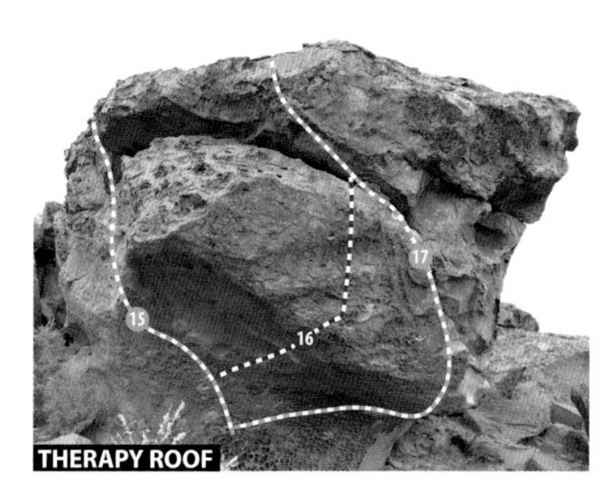

19 Unnamed v3 ☐
The arete can be climbed direct from off the block.

Just across the gap to the right is:

20 Since I Lost My Head It's Awright v0 ☐
Climb up to the ramp. Traverse this right and up.

DESERT SKIES AREA

This area is up on the west rim between the Smoking Joe Area and Morning Dove White, and directly above the More Water Less Power Area (see the overview image, previous page). The Mr. Witty wall is shaded all day and the rest of the problems only get a small amount of sun. Nearly all the problems are hard. They include a long pocketed traverse, some superb thin faces, and some good steep mid-grade classics.

RUSSIAN WALL

1 This Is How We Do It ... v8 ★ ☐
... At the Russian Space Station. Left of the arete, climb the tall wall past pockets with a very balancey crux up high.

2 Russian Arete v0 ★ ☐
Climb the well featured arete on solid holds.

3 Russian Arete Sit v5 ★ ☐
Sit start with a good sidepull out left and climb the solid nicely cut arete on good rock. First couple of moves are the crux.

EVERY COLOR BOULDER

A ship's prow of bullet-hard rock; steep on the downhill side, and just less than vertical on the right.

4 Every Color Left v8 ★ ☐
Start low on pinches. Cross the small roof to a jug. Go up and left on tiny holds and a scrunchy move.

5 Every Color You Are v6 ★★★ ☐
Start low on pinches and cross the small roof to a jug (hard move). Go right to a crack, then move with difficulty up right to edges, and finally decent sidepulls in a left-leaning crack. Classic.

6 Tie Me Up With Kindness v7 ★ ☐
Start on a cluster of pockets, go left to a poor, shallow two-finger pocket, throw for the arete and climb it. Better still, start the problem on the far right side of the face at about the same grade, maybe harder.

7 Grotesque Old Woman v7 ★★ ☐
Start on a cluster of pockets and climb the thin wall by moving up left to an obvious ear sidepull, which is up and left from the obvious small lower sidepull. Great moves, though slightly forced.

8 Mister Witty v6 ★★★ ☐
From a cluster of pockets or just right, climb the wall with a long reach/jump to the top from a shallow pocket. Excellent! Just tall enough to add spice. Another great problem similar to this *The French Connection* on page 112.

DESERT SKIES

The wide undercut buttress with a line of pockets running along its base has:

EVERY COLOR/DESERT SKIES

EVERY COLOR / MISTER WITTY

9 Chimney v? ☐
Behind the left side of the Desert Skies buttress is a chimney, which has even been done from a sit start!

10 Wills's Arete v5 ★★★ ☐
Start on pockets down and right of the arete. Climb up to the arete and climb the arete with a punchy move to gain a good left sidepull up high. Needs a strong nerve. The upper rock is a little insecure.

11 Witty Indeed v6 ★ ☐
Climb the wall left of the big hueco, avoiding the hueco, by using hard-to-see holds. Slightly contrived.

12 My Heart Grew Wings ... v3 ★★ ☐
... Under Desert Skies. Climb direct to the big hueco using pockets. Treat the big hueco gently, passing it to gain the horizontal that is not as good as you'd like. Make a leg-shaking top out. A character-building highball. Care needed!

13 Unnamed v6 ☐
Start on pockets and climb the wall using a mono and then edges to the break. Finish direct.

14 Rice Crispies v1 ☐
The right edge of the face is a bit crispy. Snap, Crackle, Pop! Take care!

15 Less Poetry Please v8 ★★★ ☐
A superb right-to-left traverse along the good, sometimes full-hand pockets and up *Wills's Arete.* Begin around the right side of the right arete. This supersedes the original *Shattered Dreams on a Bed of Lies* (v6), a traverse to nowhere, which stopped at the left arete. An even more complete version (slightly contrived across the first section), beginning with a sit start at the far right side of the right wall has been dubbed *Nick 'n' Willie's.*

MORNING DOVE AREA

Home to one of the best problems in Bishop, this area is on the West Rim (left as you look up canyon) directly up from the Happy Boulder, and right of the Desert Skies Area. It basks in the happiness emanating from the Center of Happiness and is a wonderful spot to hang out and try some hard steep moves in the shade.

Approach: Walk up a trail from the Central Happiness Area (see page 150). Or, from the Desert Skies Area, simply walk along the rim 50 yards to the right. Overview map: page 101.

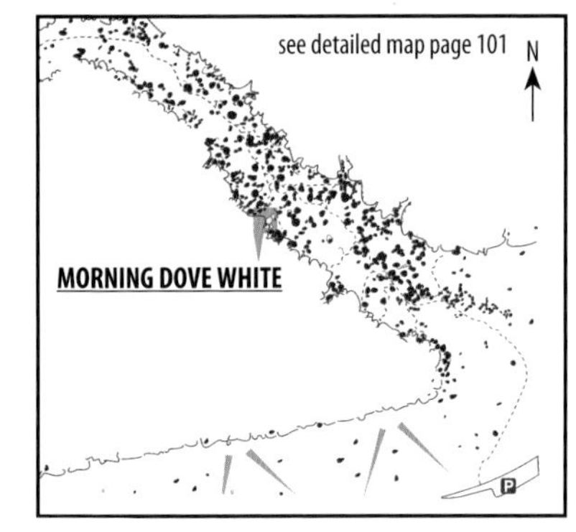

On the left, and below the main pocketed buttress of Morning Dove White are:

1 Slab v3 ☐
Climb the left side of the slab.

2 Flabmaster v9 ★★ ☐
Sit start at two small crimps and make a couple of very hard moves to get both hands above the lip, then over. This is very short, but with really cool movement.

MORNING DOVE WALL

On the main boulder/cliff itself are:

3 Take The Force Of The Blow v6 ★ ☐
Around the left side of the wall, stand start and climb up and right with a tricky move.

4 Dove Direct v9 ★ ☐
Stand start, with the right hand on a good crimp. First: Pull off the ground (don't jump). Then: Reach to the mono and make a big move from this out right to join *Morning Dove White.*

5 Morning Dove White v7 ★★★ ☐
Sit start on the right side of the overhanging face. Climb leftwards on deep pockets to a hard move to good horizontal above the lip. Top out with a couple of long lockoffs on the face, and with care on good but perhaps fragile holds at the top.

6 Happy Hardcore v6 ☐
Climb the loose face right of *Morning Dove White* over a shockingly bad landing.

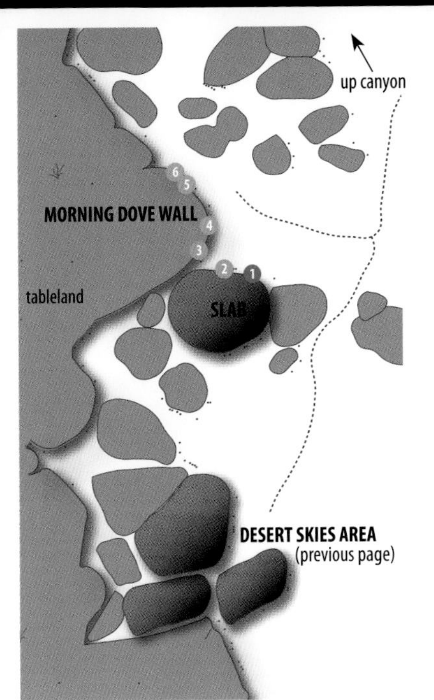

Said Belhaj keeping it real on the pumpy classic: *Less Poetry Please* (v8). Photo (and FA): Wills Young.

TALL WALL AREA

This is an undeveloped area on the West Rim located above a rocky slope on the left side as you walk up canyon from the Happy Boulder. Only two problems are recorded, although there could be some potential for more.

THE TALL WALL

THE TALL WALL

1 Tall Wall Left v1 ★ ☐
At the left side.

2 Tall Wall Middle v3 ★ ☐
Up the middle with a hard move low and climbing pretty close to the left line higher up.

SLEEPY HOLLOW AREA

This dark, cramped cave is on the west rim, above the Savannah Boulder. This is a cool place but the problems are a little squeezed in. *Gobble, Gobble* is a pretty good hard little problem on bullet rock. **Approach:** Walk to the Savannah Boulder and use the photo-locater (opposite).

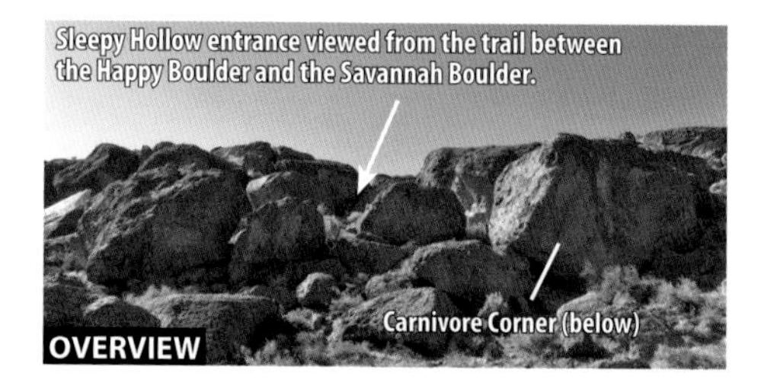

OVERVIEW

1 Colin's Traverse v5 ☐
A low-level leftward traverse on the right wall as you enter the cave.

2 Gobble, Gobble v7 ★ ☐
A stand up start on widely spaced holds. The left hand is in a small shallow pocket, the right on a good sidepull. Make a couple of hard moves up into daylight. Beware the rock at your back.

3 The Original ... v2 ☐
Climb the crack in the corner. A sit start on hand stacks is reported at about v4.

4 Erik's Arete ☐
Sit start the arete with a good right pinch on the arete, and a pocket on the left. Make a couple of hard moves to better holds above.

5 Edge Of Reason ☐
Reportedly a very low start up the crimpy wall hidden on the left side of a coridor.

6 That Traverse v9 ☐
Start with double hand jams in the crack then traverse left moving onto the left wall, and out the cave.

7 Pirate Booty v4 ☐
The pocketed arete.

8 Tim's Obscurity v7 ★ ☐
Sit start at the pocketed arete. Move your right hand up to a pinch, swing left to crimps and, with a hard move, gain the left arete. Pull the slab to finish.

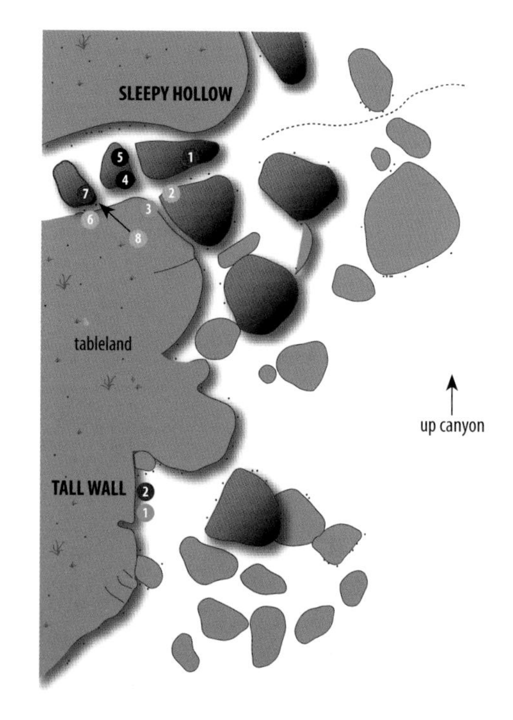

9 Carnivore Corner v0 ☐
Climb the conspicuous dihedral in the photo above.

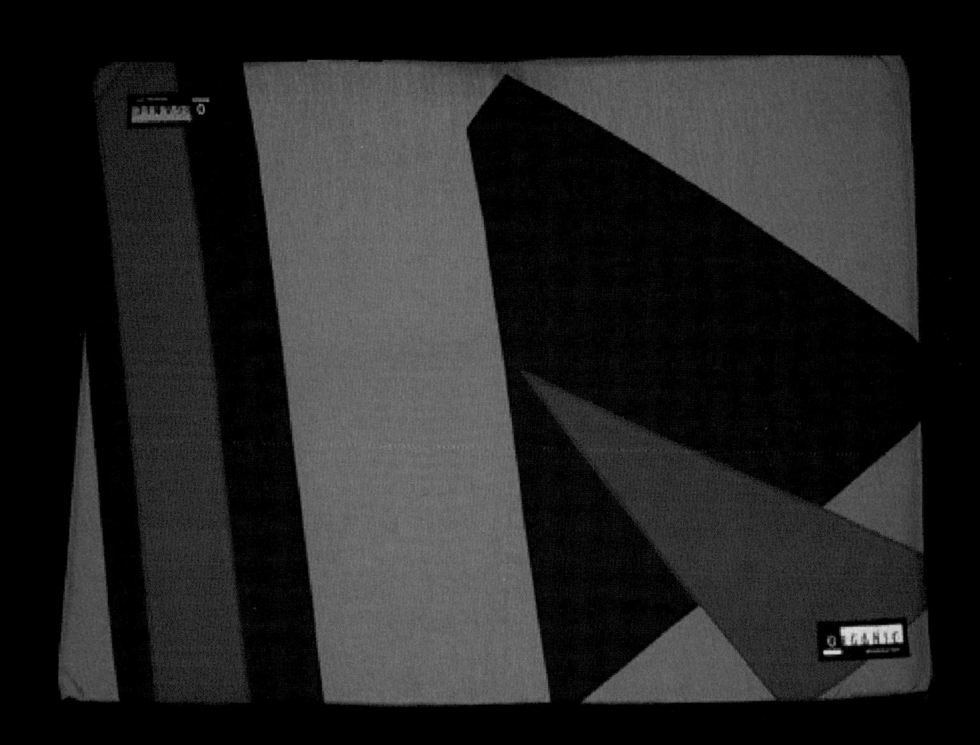

THE CENTRAL CANYON

In this section of the guide, the problems in the canyon and on the east rim (right as you look up canyon) are included side by side roughly in order of appearance as you walk up the canyon. This means that areas on the east rim that are along the rim from each other will not always be adjacent each other in the text, but rather placed next to the areas within the central canyon nearby. Problems on the west rim (the left side as you look up-canyon) are in the previous section of the guide, beginning on page 102.

JESUS CHRYSLER BOULDERS

This area has some good short problems that are never high. The Headbangers Cave is a must-visit for those seeking short gymnastic moderates on great rock.

Approach: Walk up the main trail. As it levels out, look to the right for a boulder with a traverse facing toward the trail (about 10 yards to the right). See the photo of the Jesus Chrysler Boulder, opposite. Overview map: page 101.

JESUS CHRYSLER BOULDER

This is the first boulder with the traverse almost adjacent to, and facing the main trail.

1 **Auto-gedden** v2 ★ ☐
Start on the far right at a good ledge and make low, leftwards traverse on pockets, rising when you reach a big flake and some small boulders that bar progress.

2 **Paranormal in the West Country** v1 ☐
Sit start and climb the short face.

Around the back, facing up canyon is:

3 **Ain't But the One Way** v0+ ☐
Sit start and climb the rib, staying to the right until sense dictates rolling onto the slab at left.

GET AROUND BOULDER

A boulder a little further from the main trail has:

4 **You Can't Get Around Getting Around** v0 ★ ☐
Sit start and climb up and left, or more interestingly, and a bit harder, move up right and traverse the lip for a couple of moves before topping out.

5 **Chrysler Crack** vB ★ ☐
On the back of the boulder is a nice crack.

ZERO BOULDERS

Tiny boulders just up from the Jesus Chrysler Boulder.

6 **Zero** v0 ☐
From the pocket to the top.

7 **Zero Roof** v0 ☐
Sit start in the tiny cave and climb out the incredibly low roof to a low mantel.

SUPERSTAR BOULDER

On a small boulder adjacent to the main trail, facing away from the trail are:

8 **Superstar** v0 ☐
The very short face climb on good holds.

9 **Project** ☐
A short sit start looks possible here on rough crimps.

DUSTY CAVE BOULDER

This forms the right side of a corridor leading to the distinctive overhang of the Headbangers Cave.

10 **Unnamed** v4 ☐
Sit start at an undercling to the left and move up and right past some sharp crimps and a sharp pocket!

11 **Unnamed** v5 ☐
Stand start with side-by-side pinches. Make one hard move up and left, then easily over.

12 **Unnamed** v1 ☐
Sit start at big holds at the back of the cave at right. Climb out and over.

HEADBANGERS CAVE

This cave can be seen from the main trail just up from the Jesus Chrysler Boulder. Well worth a look.

13 **Pimp Trick Gangsta Chicks** v9 ★ ☐
A low traverse of the cave from the left side to the far right, or (easier) finish at *Beer Tumor Right.*

14 **Headbangers Ball** v1 ☐
Sit start the left side of the cave.

15 **Beer Tumor** v3 ★★ ☐
Crouch start at a good finger jug. Pull up left and out the roof direct with some burly moves.

16 **Beer Tumor Right** v4 ★★ ☐
Crouch start at the same good finger jug. Pull up left, then move right with difficulty past an undercling, and over.

17 **Masterbeat** v1 ☐
Start at protruding holds; yard up and over.

18 **Dance Mix** v2 ★ ☐
Start as for *Masterbeat*, but climb diagonally up left just past the center and top out on the last moves of *Beer Tumor.*

19 **Extended Mix** v2 ★ ☐
From sitting at the right side (left hand on small horn/protrusion; right foot heel-hook), pull up and around left to traverse the lip as for *Dance Mix.*

20 **Reggae Chillin'** v1 ☐
Sit start at the right side of the cave, as above. Pull up and over.

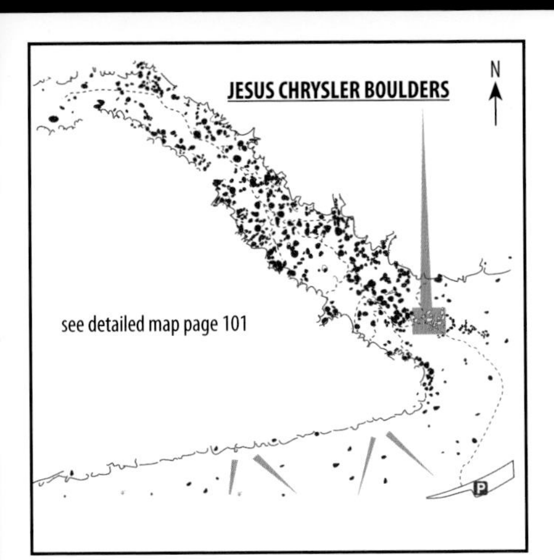

JESUS CHRYSLER

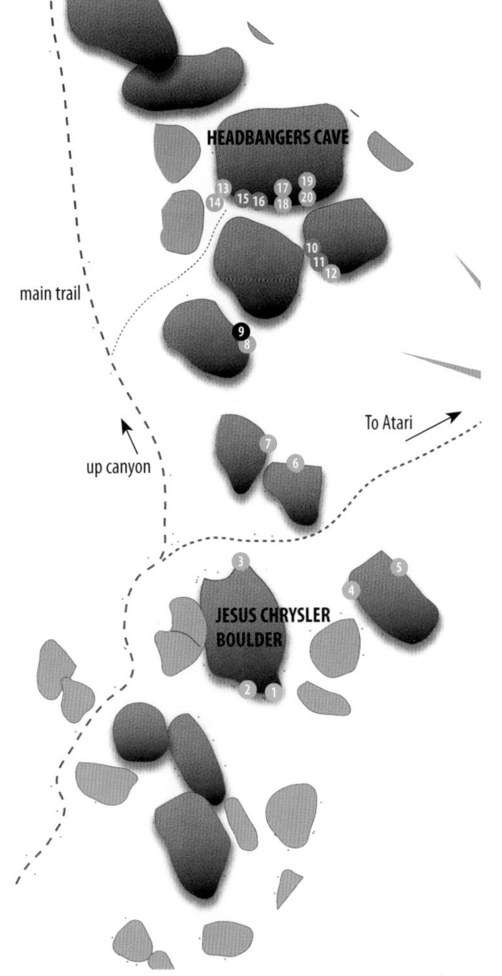

GET AROUND

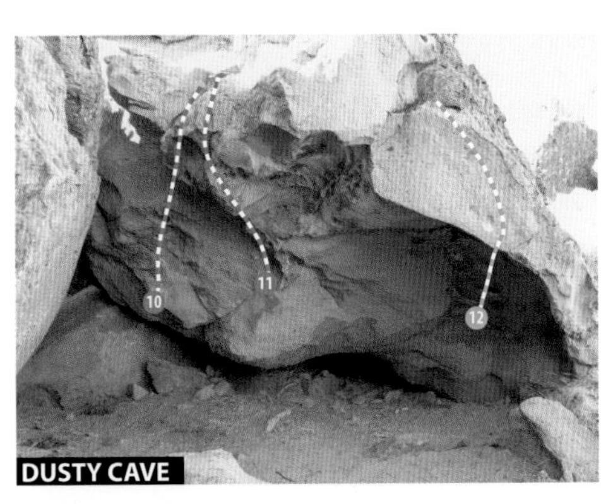

DUSTY CAVE

HEADBANGERS CAVE

TOM PETERS' SLAB AREA

This is a large area distinctive for some superb vertical and off-vertical highball moderates on excellent rock, plus a few good steeper climbs.

Approach: Hike up the main trail passing a constriction where small boulders hug the trail and the path levels out a little (the Jesus Chrysler Area). Walk on a few yards and down below at right you should see the Headbangers' Cave, which is a large boulder with a roof facing down canyon in an alcove, sheltered by a cluster of boulders around it. Beyond, more or less adjacent, but uphill from this cave, are some large boulders hugging the trail: These boulders form the Tom Peters' Area. Overview map: page 101.

TOM PETERS' SLAB

This excellent slab faces away from the main trail.

1 Liberation Management v1 ★★ ☐
Start on the block. Pull onto the tall wall and make a big move left to a slot pocket. Reach high to another pocket, and up. The flake at right is avoided.

2 The Pursuit Of Wow v0 ★★★ ☐
Start on the block and climb the tall wall left of center up a flake to the slab. Deep pockets to a good diagonal crack. Excellent.

3 Topsy-Turvy Times v0 ☐
Climb easy flakes to big underclings up high. Finish on the slab using hidden pockets to gain the very apex of the boulder.

WOW IS ME BOULDER

On the boulder below Tom Peters' Slab is:

4 Wow Is Me v0- ★ ☐
Sit start and climb flakes up and right.

NONSUCH BOULDER

The corridor between the Nonsuch and the Classique boulders has a problem on its left side as you squeeze through the gap from the Tom Peter's Slab side:

5 Nonsuch v3 ☐
Sit start at a low hueco. Climb to another hueco. Grab a crimp and pull up left to good holds.

CLASSIQUE BOULDER

This is the boulder on the right if you face out from the Tom Peters' Slab. The problems are on the east side (right as you look up canyon).

6 Too Hard For Bob Harrington v0+ ☐
Short-lived thin pulls. Finish up the high wall right of the arete.

7 Too Much For Mike Pope v0+ ★ ☐
Climb the wall above the low flake on good pockets merging toward *Classique* at the top.

8 Classique v0+ ★★ ☐
The center of the wall on tennis-ball sized pockets.

9 It's The Altitude v2 ★★ ☐
Thin sharp pulls to a good pocket. Finish excitingly by moving up and left from the big slot/pocket at 10 feet.

10 Not High Enough v1 ★ ☐
The right side of the wall (the left side of a blunt arete), has nice moves on shallow pockets.

11 It's The Add-itude v3 ★ ☐
A traverse on solid holds from the back of the corridor. Start on a good edge. Make a couple of hard moves left across the crimps and follow these to join *Not High Enough* (previous line).

SUNBURST BOULDER

Adjacent to the Classique Boulder, at right.

12 Sunburst Seahorse v2 ★★ ☐
Sit start on the rock in the cave and climb towards the light. Top out way up and left, or move right and up.

13 Lack Luster v0- ☐
The wall left of the hueco.

14 Spectral Morning v1 ★ ☐
Sit start at a flake in the cave at right. Climb left and up.

GRINDRITE BOULDER

This boulder is adjacent to the trail just beyond the Tom Peters' Slab Boulder and the problems face up canyon and slightly away from the trail (turn to the right to see them).

15 My Fingers In Your Brain v4 ★ ☐
Sit start in the big hueco down and left. Go right then up to better holds. The best finish is to keep moving right past striations of rock to gain the incredible lava-like rock horn. Then, quite easily gain the top.

16 Grindrite v3 ★★ ☐
The arete: Start with the right hand on a good sidepull at about six feet. Pull on and make a couple of hard moves to gain good holds, and ultimately an incredible lava-like rock horn. Top out more easily. Photo opposite.

STRANGE BOULDER

This boulder faces uphill toward the approach trail. It is just downhill from the Grindrite problems.

17 Another Stranger v0+ ☐
Climb the arete on the left side of the face, staying on it at the top.

18 Strange Quotations v0+ ☐
The creaky wall at right is climbed on good holds. It is even creakier at the top.

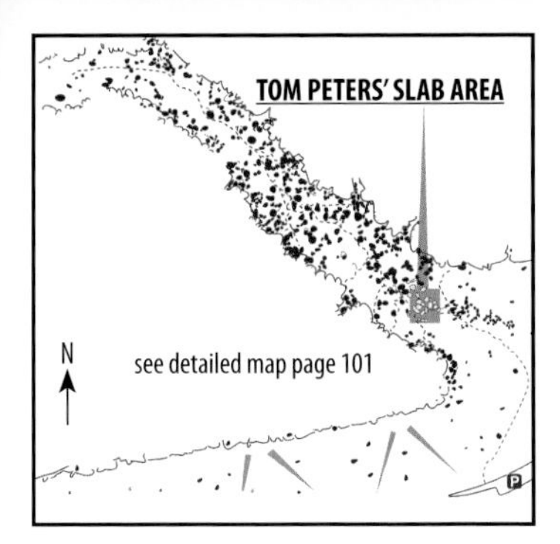

Tim Steele pulls onto *Grindrite* (v3, opposite).

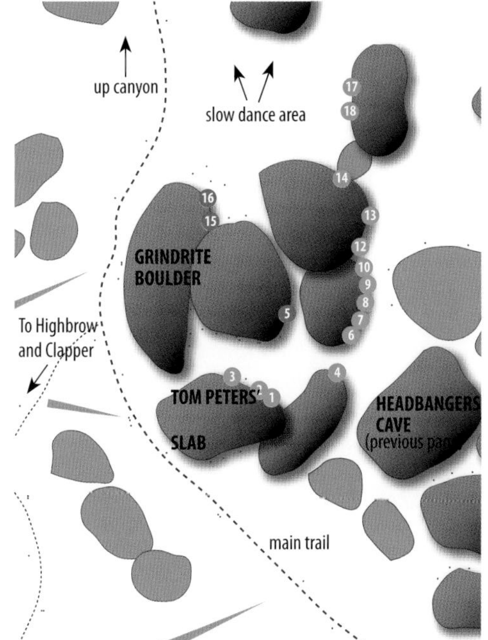

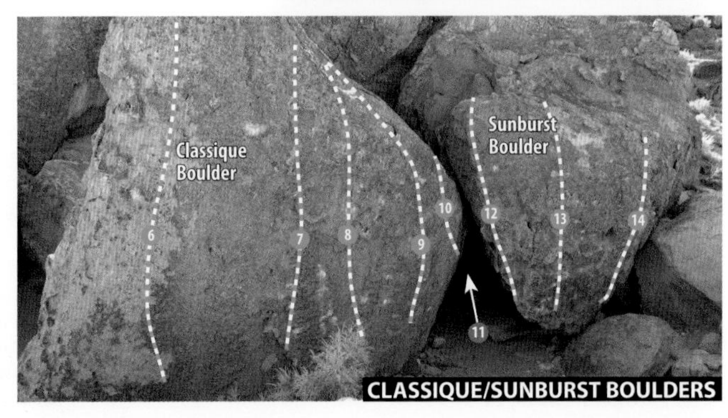

SLOW DANCE AREA

This is one of the most concentrated areas at the Happies, with several big boulders and a variety of bouldering, from classic hard sit starts to some of the best relatively easy highballs. There are low-to-the-ground moderates, traverses, and roofs.

Approach: Follow the main trail up into the canyon until you see at right the chocolate-brown-colored face of the Corridor Boulder (photo opposite). Pass down and through the corridor to find the Monkey Hang Boulder, the Corner Boulder, and the Slow Dance Cave. Continue slightly further up the main trail to find the Prow (at left, almost overhanging the trail) and the Gleaner Boulder (20 yards beyond, at right). Overview map: page 101.

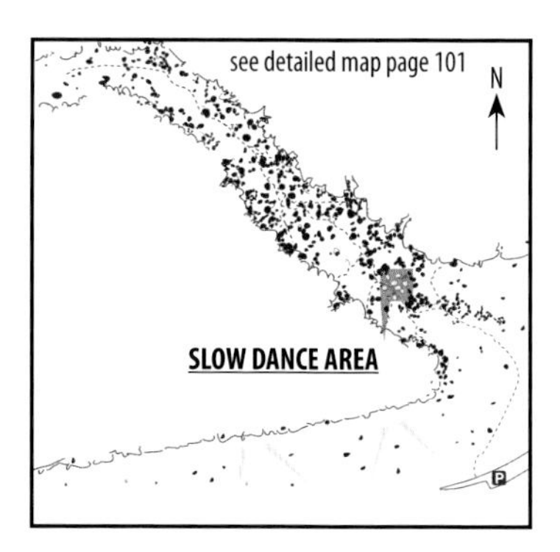

TOTTY BOULDER

A fairly low, wide boulder close to the trail.

1 Totty Traverse v1 ★★ ☐
Start on the northwest arete on the right side of the corridor entrance as you look from the main trail: Circumnavigate the boulder, either circumnavigating to the left, or to the right. If you like circumnavigating, you'll love this!

On the Totty Boulder's east face are a number of good vB problems, making this a great place for warming up.

MONKEY HANG BOULDER

This is the boulder with the large overhang east of the Totty Boulder (right as you look up canyon).

2 Monkey Hang v3 ★ ☐
Sit start in the cave on the left. Reach for the lip. Top out. Or, better, traverse around the lip rightward.

CORRIDOR BOULDER

This is the giant boulder that forms the left side of the corridor as seen from the trail, and also the Rave Wall of the Slow Dance Cave (on its northeast side).

3 Exit The Rat v2 ☐
Sit start in the cave then exit right past sharp crimps.

4 Halloween v1 ☐
The easy wall, then the spooky roof.

5 Blessed v0+ ☐
Either the arete, or wall on the right to a smooth finish.

6 Browning Variation v4 ★ ☐
Eliminate: Begin with both hands in a large pocket. Avoid the flakes and the good ledge to the right (for your hands) and climb using small pockets up the brown wall.

7 Run With Me v2 ★★ ☐
From the giant hueco, climb up left to gain the good holds on *Browning Variation.* A right-facing fingertip sidepull could be useful to make the span.

8 Hair Loss v1 ☐
Scary climbing up the wall right of the big hueco.

9 A Bit Of Fluff v3 ★ ☐
Start low on side-by-side crimps at the back of the corridor. Move up, then traverse left on good holds to join *Run With Me.*

10 Crumpet At The Crag v7 ★ ☐
Start low on side-by-side crimps at the back of the corridor. Traverse low leftwards. The small flake above the starting break is on near the start. Drop into underclings and use a mono for the right hand (about a foot left of the curving seam) to gain the big hueco. Finish up *Run With Me.*

SLOW DANCE CAVE LEFT

The next problems are on the north-facing side of the Corridor Boulder, forming the south side of the Slow Dance Cave:

11 Meth Squealer v2 ★ ☐
Sit start and climb the diagonal seam to slopers and a finish up right.

12 Rave v7 ★★★ ☐
Sit start on the banana hold (more like a squashed banana today since erosion and/or overbrushing has destroyed the patina) and a small crimp just right. Make a couple of hard pulls to gain the sloping ledge, then bust a beautiful tricky move past the dish to better holds. Superb. Stand start this for a fun v5.

13 Fast Dance v9 ★ ☐
Sit start on the banana hold and a small crimp just right. Gain a broken crimp (it's missing a notch in the middle) as a sidepull for the left hand at the left edge of a bulge. Dyno to the juggy break above and right.

14 Last Dance v9 ★ ☐
Sit start at two good crimp sidepulls about four feet off the ground at the base of the bulge. Move the right hand up to a wide slopey crimp then the left to the notched sidepull crimp (as on *Fast Dance*) and so to the jugs above.

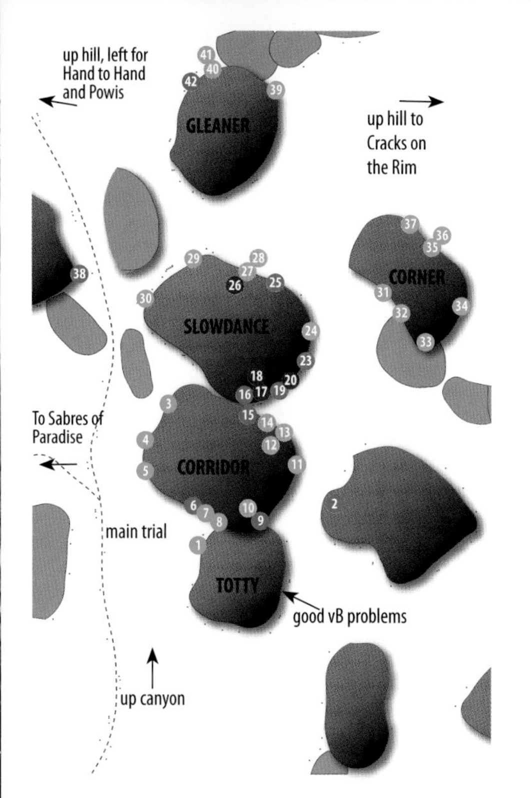

TOTTY BOULDER EAST

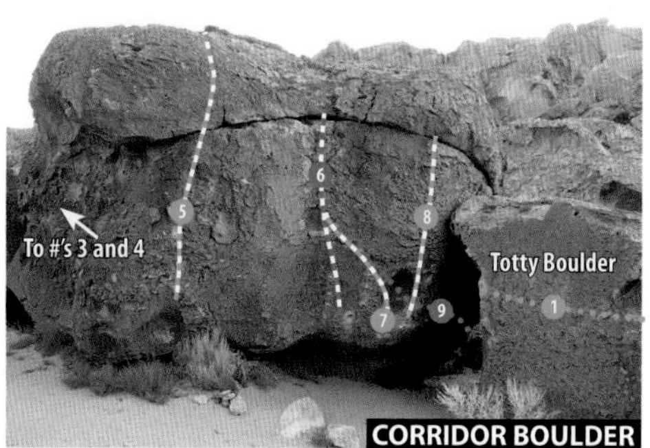

CORRIDOR BOULDER

SLOW DANCE LEFT WALL

SLOW DANCE RIGHT WALL

ACID WASH

15 Morgan's Traverse v3 ☐
Start right of the large bulge. Pull onto the wall and get established over a small bulge. Move left to the rail of jugs, then pull directly through to the top. Please avoid breaking the handholds of the above problems with your feet!

SLOW DANCE CAVE RIGHT

The southeast side of the Slow Dance Boulder forms the northwest side of the Slow Dance Cave:

16 Weekender v4 ★★ ☐
Start at the giant hueco in the back of the cave. Traverse right on good holds until a huge move right gains a deep slot. Follow this break diagonally up all the way to its end where it pulls over onto the slab. A traverse off left is also possible from a rest point, and is slightly less committing. This is very long and high!

17 Slow Dance v10 ★★ ☐
Slide in and sit start deep underneath the *Weekender* traverse at a small double jug. Pull to a razor-like sidepull then make hard moves up and left past the crack to the deep giant hueco. Drop off.

18 Slow Dance Right, a.k.a. Mandance v11 ★★ ☐
Climb as for *Slow Dance*, but continue up the crack rightward. Noticeably harder.

19 All Nighter v3 ★★ ☐
Stand start at a deep slot. Pull up directly into the rising diagonal break shared by Weekender and follow this up. This avoids the big span of *Weekender*.

20 Kill On Sight v12 ★★ ☐
Sit start at the right side of the Slow Dance Cave at a big undercling – right hand in large undercling, left hand in undercling further left, and left heel! Climb directly up the arete with a very hard move to a left-facing sidepull to start. Match the sidepull and then go up over the bulge by a punchy move to sloping crimp. A dirt-dragging link up from *Slow Dance* into *Kill On Sight*, named *The Asset* (v13?) was also climbed (after shoveling the dirt out).

21 Dance the Night Away v11 ☐
Start as for *Kill On Sight*, but after gaining the good left-facing sidepull, make a long move left to a jug and join *All Nighter*.

22 Standing Kill Order v11 ★ ☐
The standing version of *Kill On Sight*, beginning with left hand on the good sidepull, right on an edge.

23 Push It v5 ★ ☐
Start from the rock platform up and right from the cave, beneath a prow. Pull onto the rock using a square-cut edge. Quickly gain a deep sidepull with the left hand. Slap out right and climb the prow's right side. A low start and a left variation look possible.

24 Time To Go v0- ☐
Start off the block and pull into the scoop.

ACID WASH CAVE

Around on the up-canyon side of the Slow Dance boulder is another cave.

25 Azzeed Jiz v3 ★ ☐
From the slab at left, reach up right to gain the good holds at the lip of the roof. Pull through for the top.

26 Acid Wash v10 ★ ☐
Sit start at a crimp in the base of the overhanging groove. Make a desperate lock off to gain a slot, then a big move up right to start. Then, shift into sidepull underclings and launch up and left to the good jugs at the lip of the roof. Extendo-legs would prove very useful to keep the feet on the decent holds while making this massive span. For those without such long legs/arms, pulling across left using tiny underclings is possible at about the same grade (touch easier?), though a better option might be the right exit, described next. The standing start from the highest holds is said to be around v6. Photo opposite.

27 Acid Wash Right v9 ★ ☐
As for *Acid Wash* to the good jug on the right side of the overhanging groove. Grab a crimp above with the left-hand, then press right, make a big move to the lip and turn it.

28 Jug-start to Acid Wash Right v7 ★★ ☐
As above, but missing the first (desperate) move by beginning at the good jug low on the right wall.

oel Ruscher focuses hard on *Acid Wash* (v10, opposite), looking to stick the last really hard move. Photo: Tim Steele.

Trevor Markel seeks the hidden pocket on the Happy classic, *The Gleaner* (v6). Photo: Wills Young.

CORNER BOULDER

29 Benny v1 ☐
Sit start under the nose and climb up the lip leftward, and then into the smooth scoop.

Around to the right on the same boulder is:

30 Ha-Ha v0- ☐
Sit start and climb the featured face to its highest point. Several variations exist.

CORNER BOULDER

This is to the east of the Slow Dance Boulder (right as you look up canyon) and has a distinctive angling open corner on its left side, facing the Slow Dance Boulder. Topo page 127.

31 Corner v0 ★★★ ☐
The corner is climbed on good holds. High and classic.

32 The Tall Wall v1 ★ ☐
Wander up the huecos to a nerve-wracking finish. Crux at top. Sketchy rock and very bad fall.

Around to the right of the high cornered face are:

33 Time To Go v0- ☐
Start up the arete; cross the crack and climb up diagonally right.

34 Wolverine v0- ★ ☐
Climb a nice lava-rock slab, left of a scoop.

CORNER BOULDER'S UPHILL FACE

Topo page 127.

35 Tin Medusa Left v2 ☐
Sit start on the giant patina jugs and pull up left by a hard move.

36 Tin Medusa Right v1 ☐
Sit start on the giant patina jugs and pull out right by a possibly less difficult move.

37 Time To Play v0- ☐
Several nice problems up the corner and wall. For example, start on the pockets at left and traverse up and right across the slab to the high hueco.

CORNER UPHILL SIDE

GLEANER BOULDER

PROW BOULDER

The Prow Boulder is at the left side of the main trail almost overhanging the trail next to the Slow Dance Boulder. Topo page 127.

38 A Happy Slapping v4 ★★ ☐
Start on some crusty edges, but immediately move up left onto the high solid prow on smooth holds. Awesome slopers and a great position.

GLEANER BOULDER

Twenty yards beyond the Prow Boulder, down and right is the Gleaner Boulder. Topo page 127.

39 Portal to the World v0 ☐
From the jug at left, contrive a line by moving right at first, then back up left past the hole.

40 The Gleaner v6 ★★ ☐
Start standing at the pointy undercling. Pull up past sticky-out edges, then make a desperate or tricky move to gain an elusive pocket around the lip. The easy finish still requires a touch of finesse.

41 The Gleaner Sit Start v9 ★★ ☐
Sit start at a low undercling. Pull your butt off the ground. Grab a tiny crimp and make a hard move to gain the pointy undercling. Finish as for *The Gleaner*.

42 Joseph v3 ☐
Start on two good sidepulls down and right. Climb up and left to the arete to a good hold and pocket side-by-side, then up and left again past more good pockets to the top.

CRACKS ON THE RIM AREA

This is an area up on the east rim (the right side as you look up canyon) above the Slow Dance Area. There are many short, fun crack climbs here, and also some excellent tricky aretes and thin vertical and off-vertical faces. To skip this area and continue up the center of the canyon, turn to page 136. **Approach:** Hike uphill from the Corner Boulder or Slow Dance Cave (see Slow Dance Area, page 126). Overview map: page 101.

CHOCOLATE SLAB

There is a cluster of boulders below the cliff. On the up-canyon face of one is a clean smooth slab with:

1 **Chocolate** v0 ★ ☐
Sit start and climb the arete.

2 **Veruca Salt, I Want You** v0- ★★★ ☐
From the right side traverse left up the perfect chocolate-brown slab.

The left side of the slab has a nice vB problem.

More boulders are even closer to the cliff, the right one has a beautiful flake on its right side. The left boulder has a big rotten face with:

3 **Oh Baby, Veruca!** v0+ ☐
Climb the tall wall leftish past the break and big huecos. Or don't as it's a little scary...

MARVELLOUS FLAKE BOULDER

The boulder just up from the Chocolate Slab with the perfect flake on the wall that faces down canyon.

4 **A Flake As Marvellous As You, Veruca** v0- ★★ ☐
The tall flake: Marvelous! A great position, although with so many holds you hardly need the flake itself!

5 **Boy** v2 ★★ ☐
The short wall right of the tall flake does have holds. Start low, not off the block, using a round dish. The key hold to aim for (left hand) is a small crimp five feet directly up from the round dish. Careful footwork makes this seem easy.

6 **Boy-Oh-Boy** v3 ★ ☐
The blunt arete, beginning by stepping off the block up and right of the start to Boy, using a small but good crimp. Delicate and precarious.

7 **Boy-Oh-Boy-Oh-Boy!** v4 ☐
The third in a series. Less precarious this time. Start on a pair of miniature mico crimps. Step on nothing and grab the top. It's that easy.

THE CRACKS ON THE RIM RIGHT SIDE

Along the cliff from **right to left** are:

8 **Veruca, I Will Do Anything** v0- ☐
The right side of the slab to the hueco and the top.

9 **Oompa-Loompa** v6 ☐
Climb the rising arete, avoiding the rock at left. Sit start down and right under the hanging arete. Move up left under the arete, then slap up and gain big blocky holds on the left side of the arete. Pull up and rock over the right foot, then pull around to stand on the arete. One step up from here gains a good hold and the top. A hidden pocket around the left side of the arete makes the final move avoidable, at the cost of bumping into (or nearly) the rock at left.

10 **Veruca, Veruca** v0- ☐
The crack: Veruca being the left finish ... and Veruca being the right finish. You could say someone has Veruca on the brain.

11 **Toffee Crack** vB ☐
Just right of the arete is this fine easy crack.

12 **Matilda** v3 ★ ☐
The arete climbed on its left side. Begin with a high right-hand pinch and a good low dish for the left hand.

THE CRACKS ON THE RIM LEFT SIDE

13 **My Veruca** v0- ★ ☐
The nice hand crack. Only this grade if you are a complete crack novice.

14 **I'll Kick The Butt Of That Mike Teavee** v0- ☐
The diminutive crack. This grade only if you are a complete laybacking novice.

15 **If That Augustus Gloop Looks At You One More Time ...** v0- ☐
The right of the two cracks.

16 **Garbage Chute** v0 ★ ☐
The right arete of the big chimney/crack.

17 **Violet Beauregarde Sucks** v0- ☐
The wide crack is also the descent chimney.

18 **Little Brute** v0 ☐
The left arete of the chimney using holds out left to a junky exit.

THE UNCRACKED WALL

Left of the last crack/descent chimney is a wall with:

19 **OK: I'll Share With Charlie Bucket** v1 ★ ☐
Climb the pockets to a black streak, then up with some difficulty past some slightly iffy holds above a slightly iffy landing.

20 **But Not With Willy Wonka** v1 ☐
Gain the black streak from the sandy rock and big flakes to the left and climb it to a slightly difficult exit with some questionable rock.

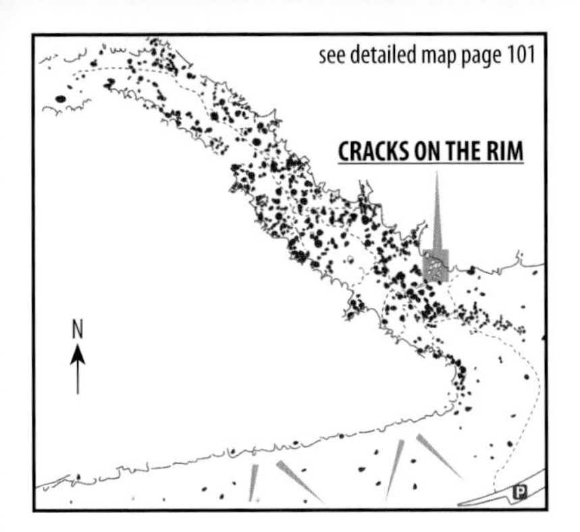

CHOCOLATE SLAB

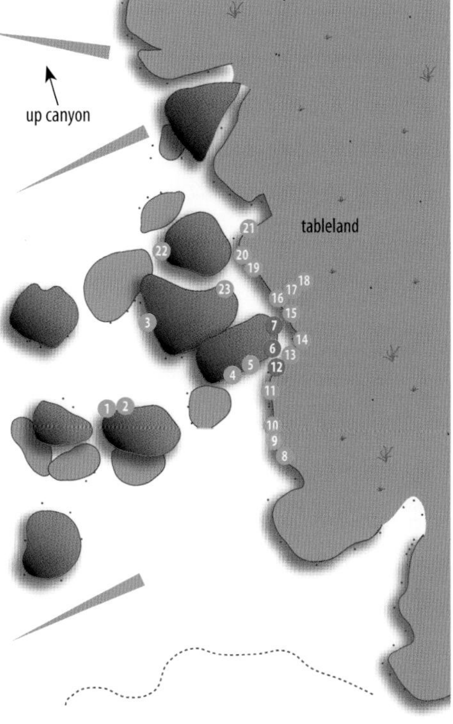
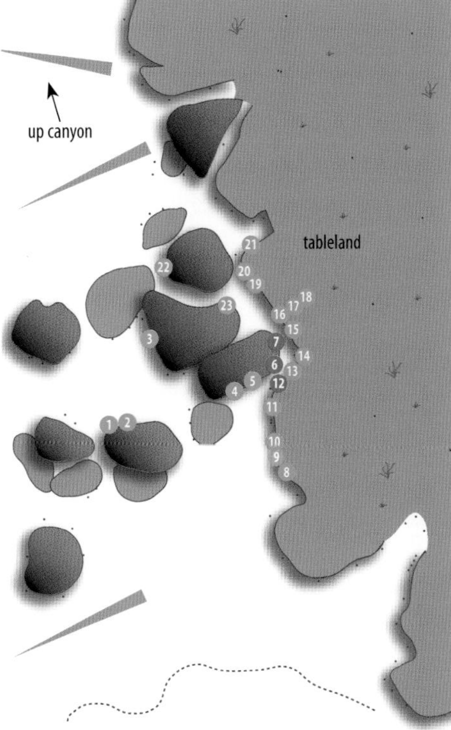

CRACKS ON THE RIM RIGHT/MARVELLOUS FLAKE

CRACKS ON THE RIM LEFT

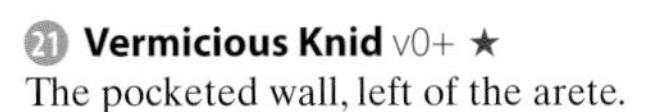

21 Vermicious Knid v0+ ★ ☐
The pocketed wall, left of the arete.

The boulder to the right of Vermicious Knid *has:*

22 Fizzwiggwiggler v0- ☐
The wall facing down slope.

The uphill side of a boulder below Violet Beauregarde Sucks *has:*

23 Unnamed v0 ☐
Sit start and climb the slopey left-leaning prow. Contrive it so you stay left to make it harder.

THE UNCRACKED WALL

ATARI AREA

Site of the beautiful *Atari* (v6) prow and a couple of other problems, including a fine slab (v0).
Approach: Walk along the rim from the Cracks on the Rim Area. Or hike up from directly below. The Atari prow, which faces up canyon, is easily visible on the east rim (right as you look up canyon) as soon as you are level with it. It is more-or-less directly up from the Jesus Chrysler Boulders. Overview map page 101.

THE ATARI BOULDER

1 Atari v6 ★★★ ☐
The outstanding Atari-shaped prow is an amazing line that provides an incredible amount of exposure, standing out at the edge of the canyon, with a slope of talus to its right. Climb it using heel hooks, a thumb-catch, and wide-spans on slopers to a thrilling slap for the summit. Add a low start if you can.

ATARI

ATARI CORRIDOR

No topo. On the Atari Boulder, but in the corridor behind *Atari* are:

2 Unnamed v0 ★★ ☐
The Slab: Climb the right slab with a thin crack to a slopey topout. Nice rock and a cool finish.

3 Unnamed v3 ★ ☐
At the far end: Sit start down in the hollow, left hand on a slopey sidepull and right on an undercling on the right side of the arete. Climb up the arete a little, then move left across the lip. Pull onto the slab using holds out left and top out up and right.

On the left side of the corridor:

4 Unnamed v1 ☐
Climb the right side of the pocketed left wall.

HOLE BOULDER

No topo. Down the slope, below and right of the Atari Buttress, is a nice triangular slab, and lower still a boulder with a hole running through it. On the downhill side of the latter boulder is:

5 Cornholeo v4 ★ ☐
A sweet sloper problem. Start sitting at a sidepull at the right side of the hole and climb up using the right arete.

THE HARD CRACK

THE HARD CRACK

No topo. Along the cliff-line right from Atari (as you face the cliff) you will find many more undocumented climbs, including:

6 The Hard Crack v4 ★★★ ☐
The splitter crack climbed on ringlocks is a beauty for crack lovers who want to try something hard.

Oh, my! Can you imagine a more striking line than this? Spanish ace Pedro Pons grapples with *Atari* (v6, opposite).
©PatitucciPhoto / Aurora Images.

WAVY GRAVY AREA

This is a small area to the west of the trail (left as you walk up canyon), shortly after *The Gleaner* (Slow Dance Area). There are some good problems here on two main boulders, including a short powerful sit start and some rare smooth rock on the back side of the Slap Happy Boulder.

Approach: Walk up canyon from the Slow Dance Area, staying in the canyon bottom. The trail immediately passes large boulders on the left. As you pass these boulders look left to see an alcove formed by boulders and the distinctive Wavy Gravy Boulder; photo this page. Overview map: page 101.

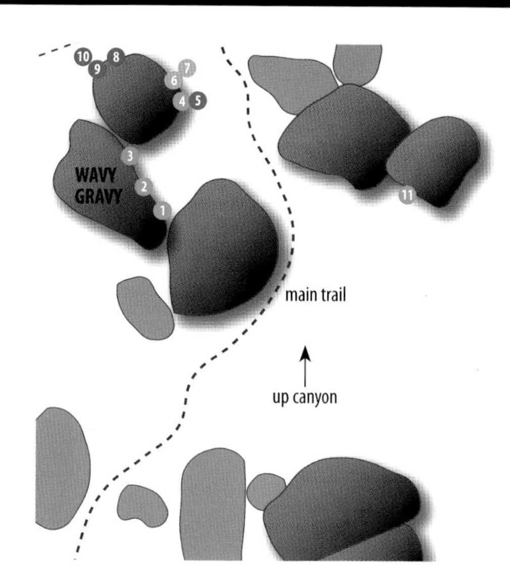

WAVY GRAVY BOULDER

This boulder is set back left of the trail, with boulders either side forming an alcove. It is covered in ripples and striations with positive, but very sharp crimps.

1 Hugh Romney v1 ☐
The left-edge of the wall. Gymnastic to start, balancey to finish. The left boulder is off-limits.

2 Wavy Gravy v2 ★★ ☐
Sit start and climb the center of the wall on solid but very sharp edges.

3 Hog Farm v0+ ☐
Make thin pulls up the right side of the wall.

SLAP HAPPY (A.K.A. BD) BOULDER

This boulder is right of the Wavy Gravy Boulder.

4 Hippie Hyannisport v1 ☐
The blunt nose: Start off good pockets, and climb up to a rock-over/mantel leftward.

5 Ben & Jerry's v3 ★★ ☐
Begin at the blunt nose; gain the lip holds on the prow's top and traverse right and up into the scoop at the top of *The Twilight Zone.*

6 The Twilight Zone v6 ★ ☐
Sit start with the right hand in a shallow pocket four feet off the ground. Climb up into the scoop.

7 Twilight Variation v7 ☐
Sit start with the left in the shallow pocket, right in a pocket low right. Pull on; slap to the good hold at the lip, then over.

SLAP HAPPY BOULDER NORTHEAST

8 Slap Happy v3 ★★ ☐
Start with both hands on hold "a" and climb up moving right, then back left before topping out.

9 Impulse Control v4 ★ ☐
Sit start at "b": go up and diagonally left using everything. If you eliminate the buckets above the slopers used by *Slap Happy*, this is v6 and called *Control Technique.*

10 Pirate Booty v3 ★★ ☐
Sit start at "b" and climb directly up the arete using everything.

Worth a note, just across the trail, to the east of the Wavy Gravy Area (right as you look up canyon) is a funky little cave with a hanging stalactite-like fang on its left.

11 Unnamed v1 ★ ☐
Begin hanging on the fang, launch up right to the good jugs and top out.

WAVY GRAVY AND SLAP HAPPY

SLAP HAPPY NORTHEAST

Melissa Smart follows the *Heavenly Path* (v1) up one of Bishop's most beautiful slabs. Photo: Wills Young.

BLOOD SIMPLE AREA

This section covers an undulating stretch of East Rim (right side as you look up canyon) uphill from the Wavy Gravy Area. The cliff here includes a small sub-canyon with a freaky-looking flying saucer of rock. This area also includes the large Rio Rose Boulder and the tall Black Magic Boulder, named for its testy classic *Black Magic* (v3). The *Blood Simple* (v4) problem has immaculate pockets, while a high-roofed cave has one of the Happy Boulders' most spectacular highball problems, *Water Saps* (v8).
Approach: Walk up the hillside to the east (right as you look up canyon) from just past The Gleaner, or from the Wavy Gravy Area. Overview map: page 101.

BLACK MAGIC BOULDER

The high tower-like boulder up on the right side, as you face up canyon, with a dark face that faces the main trail.

1 Naked v1 ★ ☐
Tall pocketed arete, would get an X if it were a route.

2 Black Magic v3 ★★ ☐
The technical and tenuous brown wall direct to the square-cut top out.

3 Wicca Warrior v2 ★★ ☐
Start off a boulder at the arete. Climb diagonally up the front-face of the brown wall, following the weakness, to the square-cut top out.

4 Unnamed ★ ☐
And while you're at it, why not climb the right arete as well. How hard can it be?

RIO ROSE BOULDER

This is the large boulder immediately down canyon from the Black Magic Boulder. On the down-canyon side, find a small bulge:

5 Does A Rose Lose Its Color In The Rain? v4 ★ ☐
Sit start at two small pockets about three feet off the ground. Climb up on edges and pockets around the bulge.

6 Unnamed v0+ ☐
Climb the arete right of the above problem.

NOTE: *The rest of the Blood Simple area is covered from left to right, beginning far to the left of the Black Magic Boulder, beyond a trio of large boulders. See the overview photo opposite.*

CALIFORNIA BOULDER

This is below the cliff line with a small boulder, adjacent and uphill of it.

7 Take California v0 ★ ☐
Sit start on a fang: climb either to the right or the left.

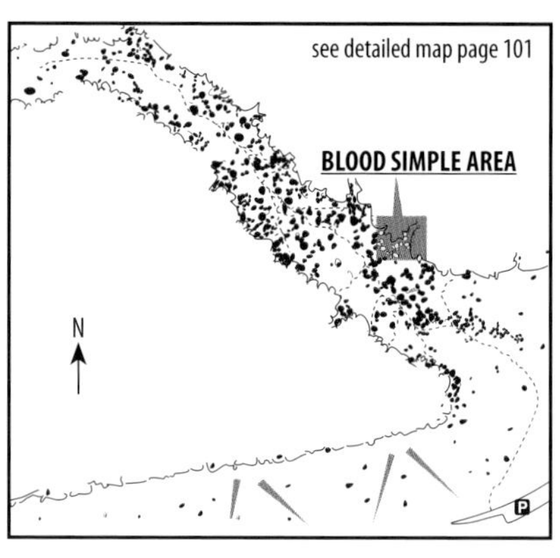

On the cliff itself is:

8 California Über Älles v4 ☐
No topout: You must downclimb. Pocket pulls lead up the smooth overhanging wall to a flake.

On a large boulder downslope of another large boulder is:

9 Unnamed v0- ★ ☐
Climb the smooth solid rock with a crack and pockets.

In a shallow alcove on the rim is a rock forming a corridor. The cliff here offers several generic v0 climbs, and the boulder itself has a small prow at its upper end, with:

10 Unnamed v1 ☐
Start with a heel hook, and climb up and left.

Around on the open cliff to the right, is a curved roofed shallow alcove/cave with a chute above it:

11 Unnamed v1 ☐
Start on the right of the alcove/cave and climb up into the chute where the rock could be better!

BLOOD SIMPLE BUTTRESS

Further right is another jutting section of cliff, which is solid for its lower third. Climbing to the top of this very high wall is possible, but the rock quality is bad.

12 Coen v3 ★★ ☐
Sit start on the big flat hold. Climb pockets up the wall just left of the nose. Downclimb and drop off.

13 Blood Simple v4 ★★ ☐
Superb climbing up the prow avoiding the holds on *Coen*: Sit start just to the right of the blunt prow. Climb pockets with one hand each side of the prow to a testy move to gain a good hold at a small ledge. Downclimb! Tall and pumpy but with a flat landing.

14 Fargo v2 ★ ☐
Sit start: Climb the center of the leaning wall five feet left of the blocks. Find the right sequence of pockets, or this will feel much harder! Downclimb or drop off.

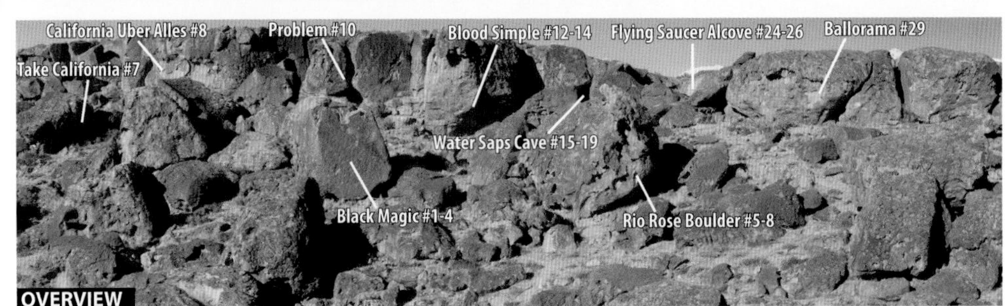
California Uber Alles #8
Problem #10
Blood Simple #12-14
Flying Saucer Alcove #24-26
Ballorama #29
Take California #7
Water Saps Cave #15-19
Black Magic #1-4
Rio Rose Boulder #5-8
OVERVIEW

1
2
3
4
BLACK MAGIC

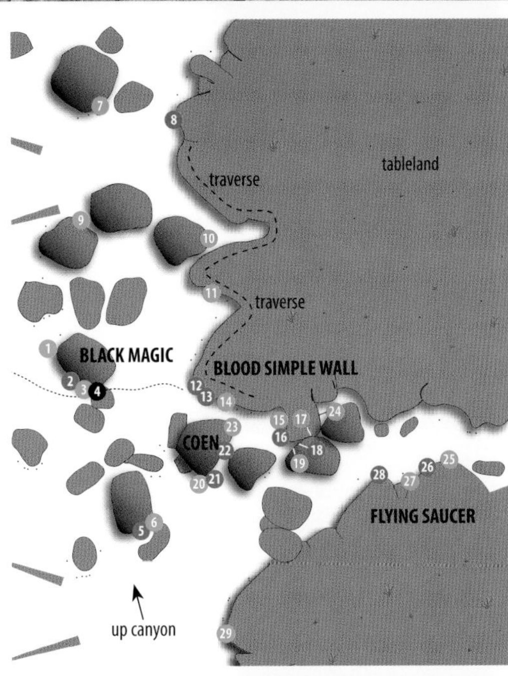
tableland
traverse
traverse
BLACK MAGIC
BLOOD SIMPLE WALL
COEN
FLYING SAUCER
up canyon

Downclimb from here or
press on with total
disregard for your safety
12
13
14
BLOOD SIMPLE WALL

WATER SAPS CAVE

COEN BROTHERS BOULDER

WATER SAPS CAVE

This is the high-roofed cave.

15 Pokeriotous v0- ★ ☐
The arching confederation of pockets that follows the lip of the cave.

16 Done With The South v5 ★★ ☐
Make a move on dusty rock to thin flake crimps. Grab knobs and pockets and climb the steepening overhang. Turn the lip. Several pads could prove useful if you fall. The upper pockets are very positive.

17 Water Saps v8 ★★★ ☐
Impressive and bold: Start at the back of the cave at a flake. Make a long reach left to pockets. Traverse the pockets in the ceiling to join the previous line. A stack of pads could prove useful for the blocky landing.

17a Unnamed v3 ★ ☐
From the flake used at the start of the previous line, at the back of the cave, climb up right through the hole.

On the right wall are:

18 Two-Stroke v4 ★ ☐
The face avoiding the left arete: Leap off small edges to a good hold and top out. Or: From the same edges, make a big span left, then back right to get to the same place.

19 Fluke v2 ★★ ☐
The short technical wall of good polished rock using tiny flakes and pockets.

COEN BROTHERS BOULDER

This boulder forms a corridor with an adjacent, smaller boulder, it is opposite the Blood Simple prow down from the Water Saps Cave.

20 Joel v0 ☐
Climb the high left arete. Big moves; big holds

21 Ethan v3 ☐
Sit start just right of the arete, move right to an undercling and up.

22 Intolerable Cruelty v5 ★ ☐
Sit start with a small but positive left hand sidepull and a very poor right handhold. Pull up and over the bulge, and then up left on very sharp holds.

23 Oh Brother ... v0 ★ ☐
Sit start and climb the low prow.

Walk through the tunnel of the Water Saps Cave (above) and look to the left to see a series of vertical cracks in the rim-rock. These are all vB, except:

24 Unnamed v0+ ☐
The first of two cracks on the left after passing through the Water Saps Cave.

FLYING SAUCER ROCK

After passing through the Water Saps Cave or over the top, you come into a wide alcove where you will see the giant flying-saucer-like rock.

25 Flying Saucer v0+ ★★ ☐
Jump or grab the big holds above the lip and pull over. Fun.

26 Antigravity Geobat v3 ★ ☐
The hard version: Reach out to the lip from a good jug/jam, then pull around to gain a good left pocket and mantel over.

The extraordinary Flying Saucer Rock is up on the East Rim, blocked from view to hikers in the canyon below. Here, Tim Steele attempts an antigravity maneuver on a high gravity day. Photo: Wills Young

27 Frisbee v1 ★ ☐
Reach out relatively easily to the lip from a good flake. Pull around and over.

There is also a nice crack traverse under here.

To the right of the flying saucer is an overhanging arête.

28 Unnamed v4 ★ ☐
Sit start on a sloper pocket with the left hand and a poor double-pocket for the right on the underside of the boulder. Climb the short pocketed prow rightward, with the crux at the start. Avoid touching the rock to the left.

Back on the main cliff-band facing into the Happy Boulders Canyon, up from the Rio Rose Boulder is a band of cliff (see topo and image on the previous spread). The cliff is undercut and pocketed at right:

29 Ballorama v2 ★ ☐
Sit start: Climb the leaning pocketed prow on its left side using the big flake holds.

ACTION FIGURE AREA

This area is on the East Rim of the Happies (the right side as you look up canyon), above the Split Melon Area. From the Split Melon, look to the East Rim, and slightly to the right. The area is famed for the steep problems *Action Figure* (v6) and *Cholos* (v9), both on any hard-climber's tick list, plus a mass of variation traverses.

Approach: From the main trail, take a path up to the rim from the right side of the Split Melon Boulders (page 144). Overview map: page 101.

There are some problems along the rim to the north of the Action Figure Alcove (just to the left, looking up from the canyon). Where a rock leans against the cliff you'll find:

1 Big City Boy v6 ★ ☐
Sit start at underclings on the left, with a sharp rock at your back. Watch your back! Move up left via sharp crimps to the lip and over.

2 Little Country Girl v6 ★ ☐
On the cliff-side wall, sit start awkwardly down on a big flat ledge. Climb right and up via pockets, trending right with difficulty into a scoop. Sadly, an easier version exists where you match hands in pockets on the arete and reach the left through to a good sloper where the boulders almost touch, then pull through higher. This seems more like v5!

3 The Land Of Milk And Honey v5 ★ ☐
A right to left traverse.

4 Traditional Crack v0 ☐
Climb the right crack of the twin cracks.

ONE NOTE BOULDER

These problems face southwest on the boulder at the entrance to the Action Figure alcove.

5 One Note Sample v0- ☐
Climb the polished scoop to good holds.

6 Loop v0- ☐
Climb spooky-looking flakes and threads.

7 Dirty Sound v0- ☐
Climb more spooky-looking rock.

ACTION FIGURE CAVE

This is a popular spot on the left side of the Action Figure Alcove. **Also see variations below.**

8 September's Here Again v3 ★ ☐
Climb the narrow prow from a sit-down start.

9 Cholos v9 ★★★ ☐
Climb the widest part of the overhang from a sitting start at pockets. Several variations exist for sticking the move to the lip. For *Low Rider* variation, see #14.

10 Action Figure v6 ★★★ ☐
Sit start at underclings on the right hand-side of the cave. Move up to the crab hold and then a one/two-finger pocket. Grab the top. Pull over. Great moves.

Filler problems: Taste the Razor Wire *(v9) is 4-5 feet left of* Cholos, *starting with the left hand on a sharp crimp and the right on a poor pinch. A squeezed line to the right of* Action Figure *starts from underclings to climb the very shallow scoop. There are also these:*

VARIATIONS & EXTENSIONS

Any number of traverses and variations can be climbed on the Action Figure Cave. Some have names and grades. The options are virtually limitless.

11 Realization Traverse v13 ☐
Start around the corner from *September's Here Again* (#8, above) at the dihedral. Traverse across the top of the smooth wall and downclimb *September's Here Again* to its starting pinches, then right on pockets all the way past *Action Figure*, through the hole to finish on *Runaway Slave* (#14, above).

12 Sharma's Traverse v12 ☐
Start at *September's Here Again*: Traverse right on pockets with feet on the back wall to finish up *Cholos*. Keeping your feet down low on the footholds could be height-dependent.

13 Dirty Boulevard v11 ★ ☐
Start at the fin of *September's Here Again*: Traverse right on pockets (as above) with feet on the back wall to finish up *Action Figure*. Kinda natural line.

14 Low Rider v10 ☐
Start at the underclings under *Action Figure*, but climb left to finish up *Cholos*. A nice extension.

15 Gang Related v7 ☐
Start at the *Cholos* start, traverse right and finish up *Action Figure*. Bored, much?

16 Action Jackson v10 ☐
Time to kill? Start on the right side of the small block right of *Action Figure*, on *An Artist of Leisure*. Traverse left under the rock and climb *Action Figure*.

17 Human Contra-Ban v10 ☐
Start as for *Action Jackson* and traverse left under the rock and climb the wall about 5 feet right of *Action Figure* via a very shallow scoop using a good undercling for the right hand.

18 Reuniting the Family v11 ☐
Start as for *Action Jackson*, and traverse left under the rock, pass *Action Figure*, and finish on *Cholos*.

19 Project ☐
As above but keep going across to finish on *September's Here Again*. Ridiculous? Come on!

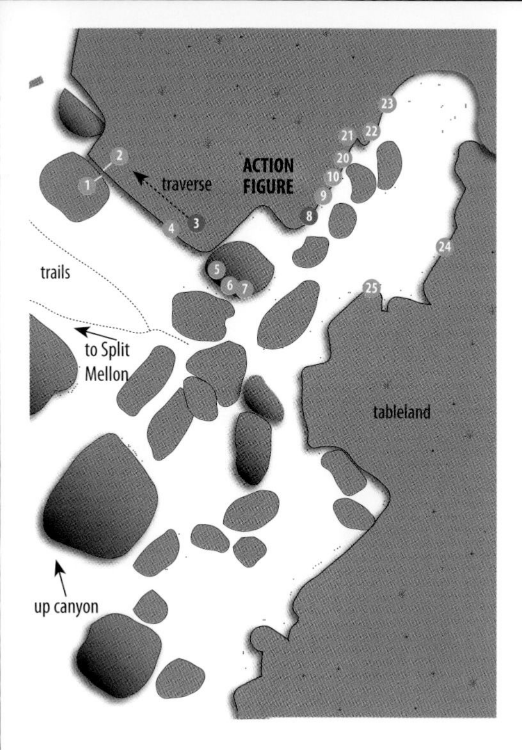

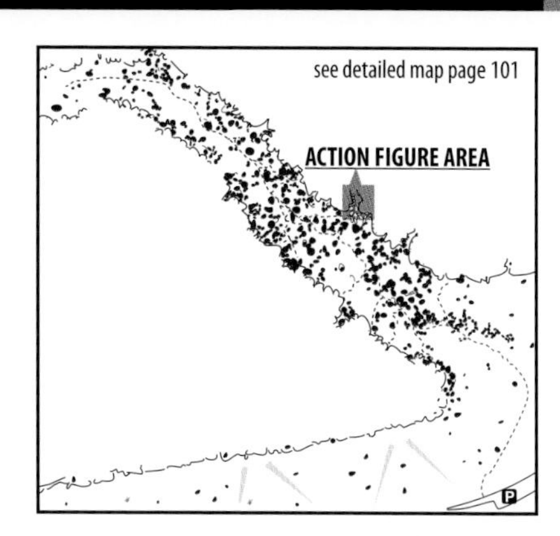

LITTLE COUNTRY GIRL ALCOVE

ACTION FIGURE CAVE

ACTION FIGURE BACK WALL

BACK WALLS

The right side of the Action Figure Cave is blocked by a low embedded boulder. Just right of this constriction are:

20 An Artist Of Leisure v2 ★★ ☐
Sit start on the low flake by the boulder (a bit of a squeeze) and use pockets to gain a good flake and the top.

21 One-Pull v1 ☐
Sit start: Make one pull to an undercling, then up. On the next small buttress to the right:

22 Immigration In The Media ... v1 ☐
... is a Chossy Belly Bulge. Sit start on pockets; go left and up around a bulge.

23 Runaway Slave v0 ☐
Start on some good honeycomb pockets and climb the wall.

On the south side of the Action Figure alcove are:

24 Bark v0 ☐
Climb the black streak.

25 Blue Note Special v0+ ★ ☐
Start at the right side of the smooth wall. Climb into the break, then up past small crimps. Good.

SPLIT MELON AREA

This is a large area located just down canyon from the More Water Less Power area and up canyon from the Wavy Gravy Area. There are many moderates here, and the Safe Surfer Boulder has a couple of low-to-the-ground testpieces.
Approach: Walk up canyon from Wavy Gravy Area, or down canyon from the Happy Boulder (Central Happiness Area), on the east side of the trail (the right side as you walk up the canyon), there are a pair of large boulders beside the trail. The left corner of the right boulder has sheered off and dropped into the gap between the pair: This is the Split Melon, giving the name to the area. Overview map: page 101.

SPLIT MELON BOULDERS

A trio of boulders surrounding the Split Melon.

SPLIT MELON LEFT BOULDER

1 Kirilee's A Problem v4 ❑
On the left boulder: Make some thin pulls up the concave wall.

SPLIT MELON RIGHT BOULDER

2 Split Melon v0- ❑
On the right boulder: Climb the arete between the brown and yellow rock.

3 Fractured Personality v0 ★ ❑
The sweet brown wall starting five feet right of the *Split Melon* arête.

BEHIND SPLIT MELON

4 Bear v2 ★★ ❑
On the boulder behind the above two boulders, climb the overhanging arete on good holds, moving left at the top.

TIMMY TAYLORS' BOULDER

Across the trail from the Split Melon, and to the left, are two boulders; the left one is the Timmy Taylors' Boulder.

5 Best Bitter v2 ★ ❑
Sit start on good holds. Go up right to prominent sidepulls then back left to crusty pockets and jugs around the prow.

6 Old Peculiar v1 ★ ❑
Sit start on two good holds. Move up right to the prominent sidepulls and the top.

7 Landlord v0+ ❑
The grungy wall left of the scoop.

8 Golden v0- ❑
Two problems in one: The scoop, or the juggy fin.

COORS BOULDER

Across the trail from the Split Melon are two boulders; the right one is the Coors Boulder.

9 Weak As Piss v0- ❑
Stand on the flake and pull up the wall.

10 Pottenger's Wish List v3 ★ ❑
The crack and painful holds. Harder than it looks.

11 Coors Is Light v2 ★★ ❑
Climb the wall starting left of the arete on small edges, moving left and up.

SAFE SURFER BOULDER

This boulder sits opposite the Split Melon Boulders a little up canyon from the Coors and Timmy Taylors' Boulders. It is easily distinguished by a low-to-the-ground long slopey lip traverse on its right side.

12 Not Raving But Drowning v1 ❑
Sit start at the the fang, then up.

13 Froz v7 ★ ❑
Sit or hang start at a pair of low pockets, pull up to crimpy shallow pockets and dishes, and make a long move left, then up. A scrunchy heel-hook could prove useful at the start.

14 Safesurfer v3 ★★ ❑
Sit start from the two big low pockets. Go right up the arete to a grovel finish.

15 Son Of Claudius Rufus v5 ★★ ❑
Start down and right and traverse the lip from right to left to mantel at *Safesurfer*.

16 Super-Froz v9 ★★ ❑
Start down and right and traverse the lip from right to left; reverse *Safesurfer* to its starting pocket and then climb *Froz* — all without touching the ground, or the rock below! Also known as *The Dirty Sock Link Up, Surf-Froz,* or mundanely, *The Froz Traverse.*

THE BIG CORNER BOULDER

This boulder is up and left of Safe Surfer Boulder.

17 Big Corner v0 ❑
The obvious big corner.

BIG NOTHING BOULDER

A boulder just up canyon from the big corner boulder, on its up-canyon side has:

18 Double Vegetation v0- ❑
The juggy and isolated arete. An esoteric find.

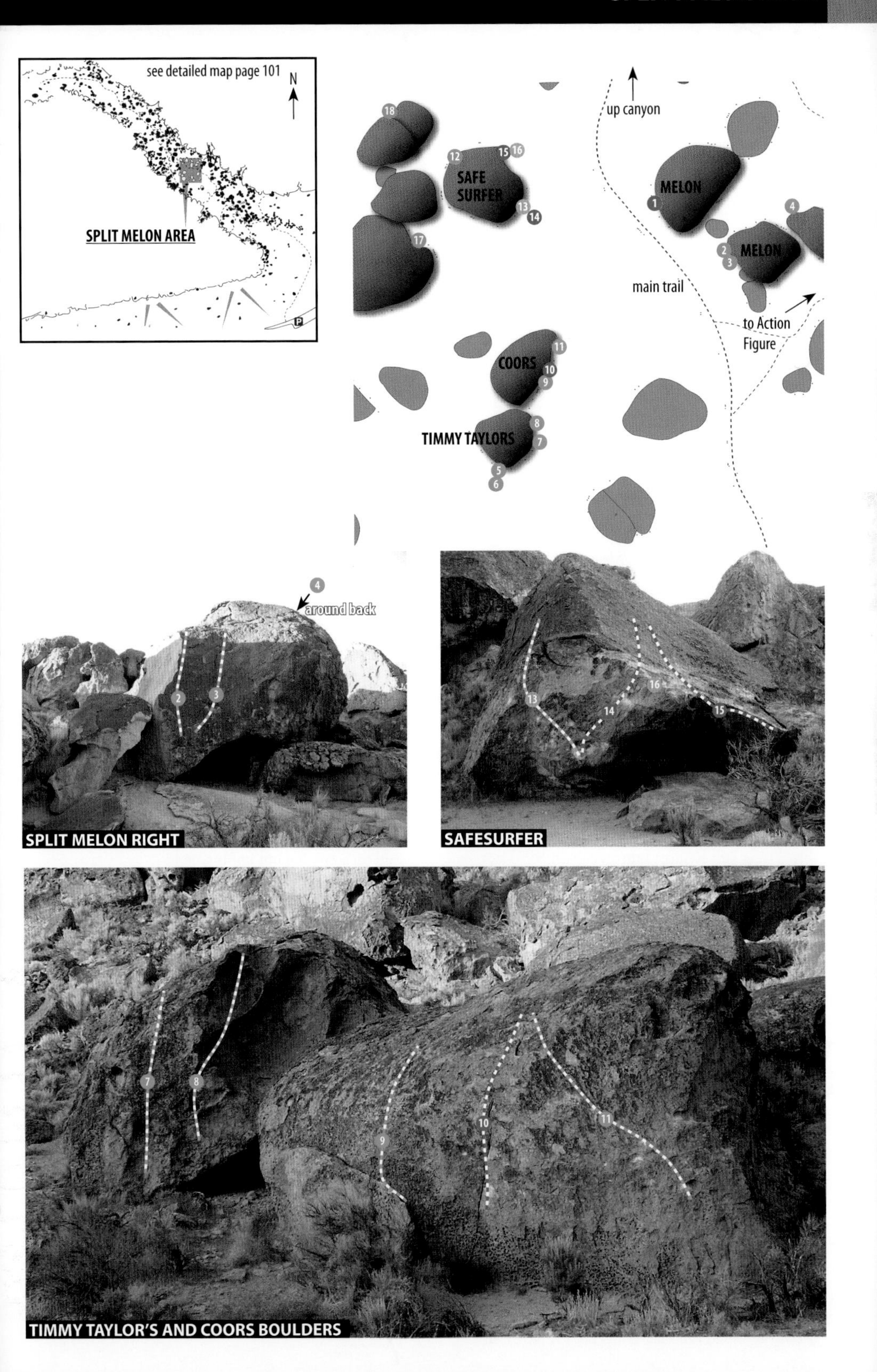
see detailed map page 101
N
SPLIT MELON AREA
P
up canyon
SAFE SURFER
MELON
MELON
main trail
to Action Figure
COORS
TIMMY TAYLORS
18
12
15
16
13
14
17
1
2
3
4
11
10
9
8
7
5
6
around back
SPLIT MELON RIGHT
SAFESURFER
TIMMY TAYLOR'S AND COORS BOULDERS

MORE WATER LESS POWER AREA

This is a smallish area with a stack of popular, low-to-the-ground problems, plus a super-high slab with one of Bishop's finest easy lines, *Heavenly Path* (v1).

Approach: Walking up canyon from the Split Melon Boulder, you can't miss the More Water Less Power Area. After passing the Split Melon (the broken piece of boulder dropped between two others on the right) you pass a beautiful, tall brown slab off the trail to the right (the Heavenly Path Boulder) and then meet a low boulder that has a pointed end that splits the trail. This latter boulder is the More Water Less Power Boulder. It is 20 yards beyond the Split Melon and about the same distance south of the Solarium Boulder. Overview map: page 101.

MORE WATER, LESS POWER BOULDER

This is the low boulder that splits the path, left of and very slightly up canyon from the tall brown slab of the Heavenly Path Boulder.

❶ **More Water, Less Power** v5 ★ ☐
Sit start at a tennis ball-size heuco on the left side of the boulders' pointed end and traverse rightward, following the low lip across the first bulge. Drop down and continue across the northeast face; drop down and stay low around the boulder's overhanging side too. Finish at the slab.

❷ **Corporation Pop** v3 ★ ☐
Sit start on pockets and climb up and left on pockets.

❸ **Groundwater** v5 ★★ ☐
Sit start on pockets and climb directly up and over with a long move. Short but very good.

❹ **All The Way Down** vB ☐
From the good ledge, climb up and left.

❺ **Vision Arete** v1 ★ ☐
From the good ledge low and left, climb up and slightly right to pockets and the arete. Don't use the slab for footholds.

❻ **Hydra Pilferers** vB ☐
Climb up past the small corner.

❼ **Carpenters Arete** v0+ ☐
Climb via pockets to a sloper, then finish left up the corner.

❽ **Any Which Way** v0+ ☐
Climb pockets left of the right arete.

❾ **Comfort of Home** v2 ★ ☐
Sit start on the left side of the boulder's overhanging north side and climb good pockets leftward to the slappy arete. Top out.

❿ **Swing Your Partner** v1 ★ ☐
Sit start as for Comfort of Home, but climb steeply right to the crack/flakes. Top out.

⓫ **Grant's Christmas Present** v1 ★ ☐
Sit start at the right side of this face and follow a rising traverse across the overhang to finish up *Swing Your Partner.*

⓬ **Happy Hooker** v0+ ★ ☐
From the bottom right, climb direct to a thrutchy finish up the slab.

XAV'S BOULDER

⓭ **Xav's Problem** vB ★★★ ☐
One of the best problems for the under-twos takes the south face of the diminutive boulder next to the southern end of the More Water Less Power boulder.

THE WINDOW BOULDER

This boulder is across the main path to the west of the More Water Less Power Boulder, and has a large natural arch or window.

⓮ **Hole In My Heart** v1 ★ ☐
Climb the outside arch of the window. Tons of fun on a unique formation.

⓯ **Mother Earth** v0 ☐
The center of the tall wall with a crux at the top.

HEAVENLY PATH BOULDER

This is the boulder, adjacent to the More Water Less Power Boulder with a striking chocolate-brown slab facing southwest toward the main trail.

⓰ **Which Road** vB ★★ ☐
The left side of the up-canyon face is a good warm-up on some big but knobby holds.

⓱ **Donkey Boy** v0+ ★★ ☐
The thin wall on the right.

⓲ **High Road** v0 ★ ☐
The arete on dodgy rock is still a decent climb in a good position for the adventurous climber.

⓳ **Heavenly Path** v1 ★★★ ☐
Climb easily to a long reach that gains a slot, followed by the committing slab. Photo opposite.

⓴ **Cross Roads** v0+ ★★ ☐
Climb the slab above the large slot, which is hard to start. Make a committing move at half-height to leave a good finger juglet. Trend right at the top.

㉑ **Celestial Trail** v0- ★★ ☐
Climb the slab above a good hueco staying slightly right. Good, but escapable to the right.

㉒ **Path** vB ★★ ☐
Climb the right edge of the face. Airy and fun.

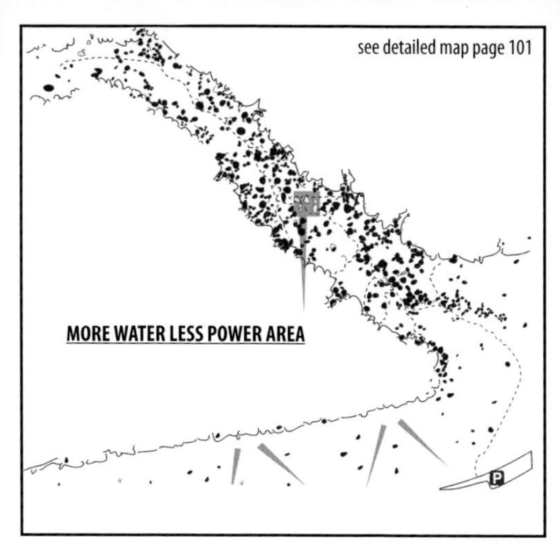

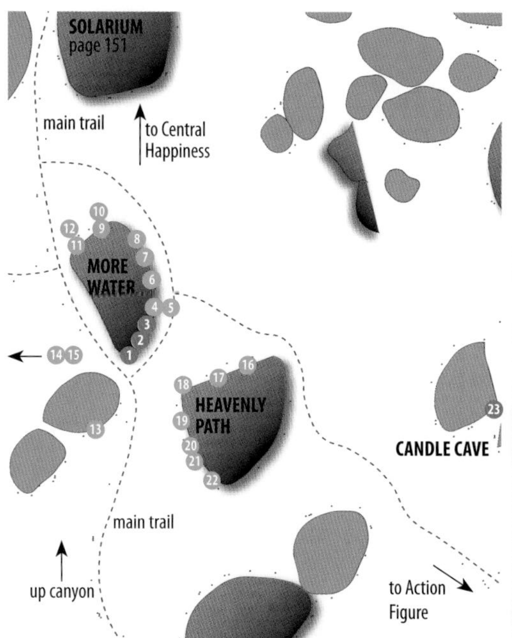

THE CANDLE CAVE

The Candle Cave is on the east side of the Candle Boulder, hidden from view. It is east (right side as you look up canyon) and up toward the rim above the Heavenly Path Boulder.

23 Better To Light A Candle Than To Curse The Darkness V5 ★ ☐

Creep in past the block and sit start at the back of the low cave. Climb the juggy hand rail then make a hard throw to the arete and up.

Todd Daniels throws a dyno on the DWP Boulder.
Photo: Wills Young.

Lisa Rands makes light work of the *Big Chicken* (v2 or v4 sit), page 150. Photo: Wills Young.

OFFWIDTH AREA

This East Rim area (on the right side, as you look up canyon) is distinguished by a massive offwidth in a giant dihedral. The dihedral faces down canyon and is directly above the More Water Less Power Area (previous page). There are some very high climbs here, including the offwidth itself, which goes at v0-, and the superb frightener *I Am Leaving For Constantinople Tonight* (v0+).

Approach: Hike up to the canyon rim directly from the More Water Less Power Area. Overview map: page 101.

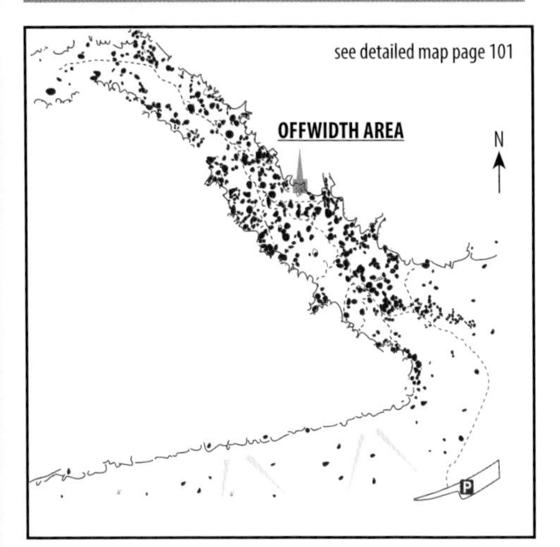

Lupine, Happy Boulders. Photo: Tim Steele.

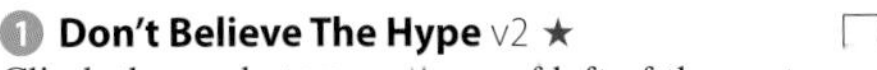

1 Don't Believe The Hype v2 ★ ☐
Climb the pockets over the roof left of the arete.

2 Lay The Candle Lady Later v3 ☐
A low traverse, through the pockets, around the arete, and into the corner.

3 Bouldering.com v0- ☐
The tall wall, ten feet left of the corner crack.

4 The Corner v0- ★ ☐
The offwidth corner crack. Big, but not so bad really. It makes an excellent 5.8 squeeze chimney if you slide inside.

5 Project ☐
Climb the tall wall starting way down and left, and trending right. Kinda sketchy looking.

6 Unknown ☐
Step off the rock platform and climb past a blank section to gain better holds, then on to the top.

7 I Am Leaving For Constantinople, Tonight v0+ ★★★ ☐
Start at the left end of the flake. This time commit left up the wall by using a sidepull hold to gain airy good holds up high. Excellent rock and a true gripper!

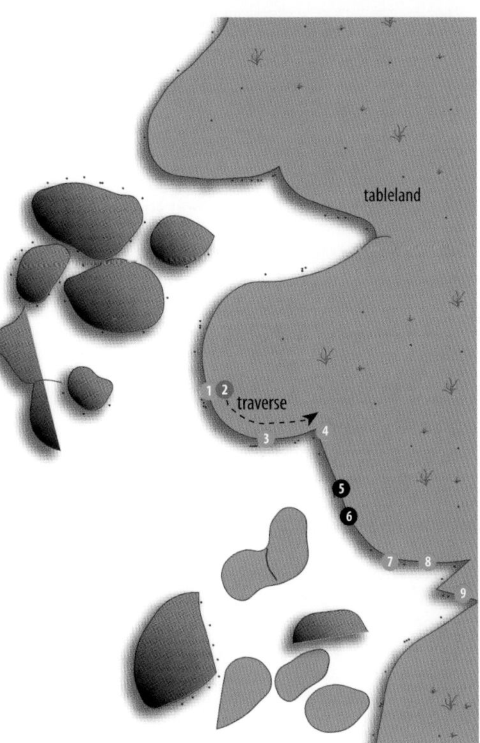

8 Plastic-Bandi-Whoopies v0- ☐
Start at the left end of the flake and climb the crack in the wall above.

9 Rosalie's Chimney v0- ☐
Climb the smooth chimney right of the rock fin.

CENTRAL HAPPINESS AREA

The central area of the canyon has a host of outstanding lines from easy to demanding, including the world-class *Hulk* (v6), the ever-challenging *Solarium* (v3), and superb arete of *Big Chicken* (v2). It's really hard not to be happy here: the Happy Boulder is like an epicenter of happiness, emanating good vibes throughout the area. Commonly, many people will be basking in sunshine at the boulder's south side. Most problems here are on good rock and in an open and pleasant position.

Approach: Walk up the canyon on the main trail until you feel the happy vibe. You are up canyon from the Split Melon and the More Water Less Power Boulders. You are down canyon from the Savannah Boulder. The Solarium is a fairly distinctive tall wall of good brown rock on the right of the trail. Overview map: page 101.

HAPPY BOULDER

HAPPY BOULDER (SOUTH FACE)

❶ **Castrate Your Television** v1 ☐
Sit start down and dirty in the back of the cave and emerge on the west side.

❷ **The Vulcan Traverse** v5 ★★ ☐
Sit start at the back left of the cave and traverse low right finishing up *Big Chicken*. Great climbing.

❸ **Weapons Of Mass Distraction** v5 ★ ☐
Sit start on a big flake and wrestle yourself left and up on edges and dimples, using a ridiculous leg grapple. Pretty hard if you're short, but otherwise fairly simple though painful.

❹ **Disco Diva** v8 ★★ ☐
The original testpiece of the canyon. Sit start with both hands in the thread, undercut to gain the hideous sloping crimp, then climb up steeply via more crimps leading to a long throw to a hand-sized hueco. A knee at the start can be useful.

❺ **Disco Tramp** v7 ★ ☐
Sit start with both hands in the thread, climb up, then move around left into the scoop. Fun and awkward.

❻ **Disco Hulk** v9 ★ ☐
Sit start with both hands in the thread; climb diagonally up and right to join the top of *The Hulk* with some hard shoulder moves. Or (easier) move right first, and then up.

❼ **The Hulk** v6 ★★★★ ☐
World class: Sit start at good jugs; move casually up to a good hueco. Complex steep moves gain the boss—the large square-cut block up and left: Hang on to it! If you're still around, move up right to good holds and a satisfying finish.

❽ **Prozac** v9 ★ ☐
The marginal-looking line up the wall between *The Hulk* and *Big Chicken* with a big move from bad opposition holds.

❾ **Big Chicken** v2 ★★★ ☐
Climb the superb right arete of the Happy Boulder with some great sidepull moves and a highish topout. **Sit start** at v4 immediately below, or to the left, or try *The Vulcan Traverse* (above) at v5. Photo page 148.

On the northeast face, just right of Big Chicken is a short vertical wall with:

❿ **Unnamed** v4 ☐
Start with two opposing crimps and make a hard move to gain a good edge, then up more easily.

Further around on the northwest side, find:

⓫ **X-Static** v0- ☐
Climb the blunt arete, slightly overhanging low down, with some tricky moves at the start.

⓬ **Jugs Of Life** v1 ★ ☐
Climb the tallest part of the boulder on small crimps escaping slightly right near the top. Thin and precarious up high if you don't escape too far right.

⓭ **Indecision** v0+ ☐
Climb the left-leaning diagonal crack, then up.

JOLLY BEGGAR BOULDER

A small boulder on the left of two, that is just east of the Happy Boulder (right as you look up canyon).

⓮ **Jolly Beggar** v0 ★ ☐
Climb the left arete. It has been suggested that you can then leap to the next arete and continue the climbing, making this about v3!

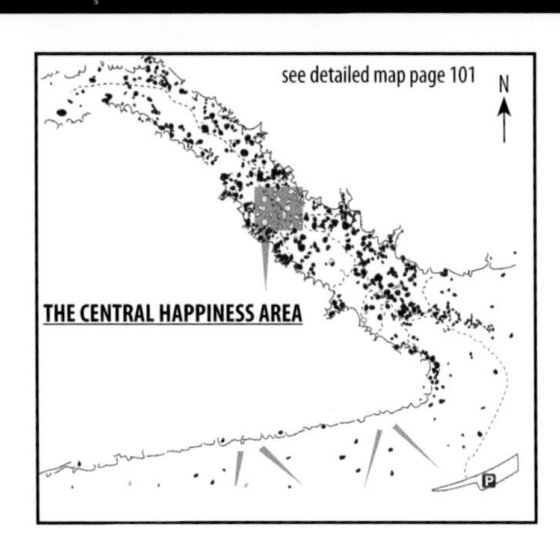

SOLARIUM BOULDER (WEST FACE)

The large boulder with the richly featured deep red-brown face next to the path.

15 Beam Me Up Scottie v2 ☐

The arete staying on the arete with some big moves to pinchy jugs. If you pull around to get both holds on crimps on the left wall, this becomes much easier.

16 Solarium v4 ★★★ ☐

Climb the center of the wall. Starting at good huecos, then move up and slightly right past a trio of pockets. A big move to the lip is the key. Harder since small breaks. Photo: turn the page.

17 Western Round Up v1 ★ ☐

The shorter wall with a pocket pull.

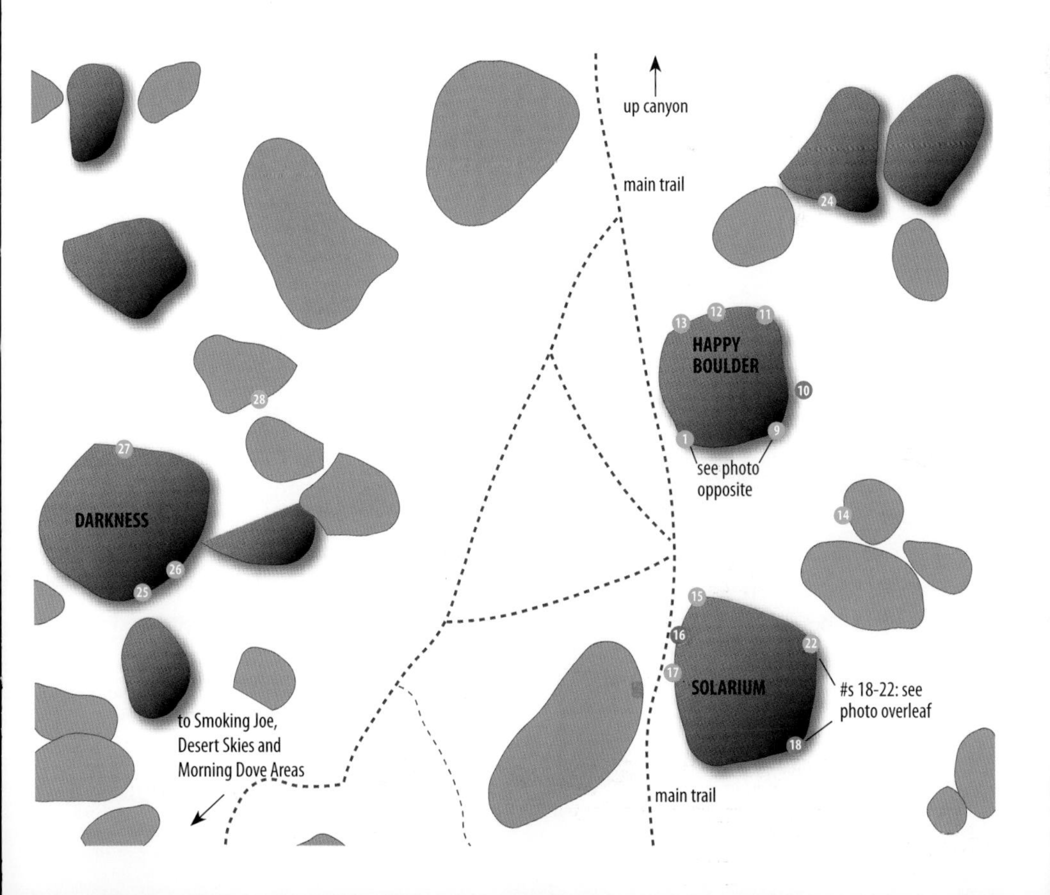

Charlie Barrett skips all the moves from the pocket to the lip on *Prozac* (v9), previous page. Photo: Wills Young.

SOLARIUM (EAST FACE)

18 Rendezvous With An Alien v3 ★ ☐
Sit start at the left side of the cave and traverse right and then up.

19 Redrum v7 ★★ ☐
The original: Start with both hands in the sidepull feature. Pull on, then bust out left to gain ripples, blobs, pinches and hopefully that big hold over the lip. Good rock, and some funky moves.

20 Redrum Sit v10 ★★ ☐
Sit start with a sharp left undercling plus a very low right pocket/crimp, with your butt on the floor. Slap a big hard move to start. Then carefully match hands and move up to finish as for *Redrum* original. This was once a superb problem, but the rock on the underside has deteriorated and the underclings have begun to disappear, making the start ever harder.

21 The Shining v9 ★ ☐
As for *Redrum* standing start, but from the rippled fin, swing left across the underside of the roof using a hidden undercling pocket for the left hand. You stay under the lip, but reach a hold over the lip at the far left side (see photo), before dropping into the underclings and exiting left and over.

22 The Shining Sit v11 ★ ☐
As for *The Shining*, but from the sit start at underclings. The same sit start as *Redrum Sit*.

23 You Said You Wanted Some Space ... v2 ☐
... Is This Enough For You? Climb the overhanging arete on painful holds.

Up canyon from the Happy Boulder, and diagonally right as you look up the canyon, are a couple of side-by-side boulders providing:

24 Fodder v0+ ☐
Sit start on a flake down and left.

THE LEFT HAND OF DARKNESS BOULDER

This is the large boulder up toward the west rim (the left side as you look up canyon) from the Solarium and the Happy Boulder. Topo previous page.

25 Heart of Darkness v1 ☐
The folded, overhanging rock right of the dusty stuff.

26 Undercover Of Darkness v1 ☐
Climb the overhanging face on big but awkward holds.

LH OF DARKNESS BOULDER (NORTH FACE)

27 Barbi On The Rim v1 ★ ☐
On the side that faces up canyon, climb up diagonally right to left with a long move to gain the softball-sized hueco up high.

RIGHT HAND OF DARKNESS BOULDER

28 Unnamed v1 ☐
Sit start and climb the face, just right of center.

The last rays of the sun drench *The Solarium* (v4) in evening light. See previous page. Photo: Wills Young.

SHADOW PLAY/ SIXTY-FOOT WOMAN AREA

This area is situated diagonally right (facing up canyon) from the Happy Boulder, and diagonally left (facing down canyon) from the Savannah Area. The Sixty-Foot Woman Area, on the East Rim, includes the gem *Secret Arete* (v2) and the *Sixty-Foot Woman Traverse* (v2), a great introduction to pumpy pocket pulling and a good place to catch sun late in the day. The Shadow Play area, on the canyon slope, offers great steep problems like the excellent *Cue Ball* (v4) plus one of the best v0's in the canyon, *Althea*.

Approach: From the up-canyon side of the Happy Boulder (Central Happiness Area, see page 150), face up the canyon and walk diagonally right between two boulders and head for another pair of boulders forming a kind of cave. These are the Shadow Play Boulders. Go up right to the rim for the Sixty-Foot Woman Area. If you're coming from up-canyon areas, such as Savanna, head down canyon a short way, then, from Girlfriend Rock (page 156), go left and up toward the rim on a clear trail toward the cave formed by the Shadow Play Boulders. Overview map: page 101.

SHADOW PLAY BOULDERS

On the smaller, lower boulder, facing up canyon is a low roof.

1 Don't Know v7 ★ ☐
Labelled in a former mini-guide as "Don't Know, Hard Though," the roof is now named *Don't Know*, and it is still hard, so not much has changed. Sit start in the cave at a small flake. Positive holds and aggressive moves. A little sharp.

SHADOW PLAY MAIN BOULDER

2 Silence So Red v0- ☐
The wall at the left side of the up-canyon face.

3 Althea v0 ★★ ☐
Climb the tallest part of the up-canyon wall. Nice climbing in a great position, though very high.

4 Brilliant Trees v3 ★ ☐
Sit start and climb the arete. Finish past big huecos.

5 Vampyros Lesbos v6 ★ ☐
Sit start as for *Brilliant Trees*: traverse right and finish up *Cue Ball* (below).

6 Vampyros Rheinstor v7 ★ ☐
As above, but continue further to finish as for *Rheinstor* (below).

7 Spinal Snap v2 ★★ ☐
Start low on a good undercling and climb more or less direct, slightly right at the top where it gets a little pumpy.

8 Spinal Snap Right Start v2 ★★ ☐
A slightly easier version begins sitting at the big sidepull to the right.

9 Carnivore Hate Devil v4 ★ ☐
Sit start at big pockets and climb the concave wall past a pair of good crimps and a blankish section with some painfully small pockets. Good flexibility could prove useful.

10 Cue Ball v4 ★★★ ☐
Sit start at a big pocket and climb up right to the sloping arete. An excellent problem on good rock.

11 Vampyros Lesbos Going Left v4 ★ ☐
Sit start as for Cue Ball; traverse low left to finish up *Brilliant Trees.*

12 Rheinstor v6 ★ ☐
Sit start as for *Cue Ball*; go right around the arete and up on pockets. Kinda trick move getting around the corner. Good climbing though.

13 Unknown ☐
There appears to be a problem that climbs out left from the recess on pockets. Sorry, no more info!

SECRET ARETE BOULDER

This is on the cliff just above the Shadow Play Boulder. The Secret Arete itself is on the back of this triangular boulder that is "fitted" into the canyon rim.

14 What Did The Aliens Say? v0- ☐
Climb the short wall left of *Celebrate The Stars.*

15 Celebrate The Stars v0+ ☐
On the down-canyon end of the boulder, climb the arete using a crack to its left.

16 Flag v4 ★ ☐
On the down-canyon end of the boulder, is a flying arete. Start at right on some good holds and, avoiding the rock at right, pull onto the face and move up left to gain a sidepull way up high, either by a long stretch around, or by using a tiny slot for the right hand. Match and move on up the arête.

17 Rio's Secret Arete v3 ★★★ ☐
The secret arete is clean and pretty. It is also bunchy and balancy and requires finesse. The sit start at the same grade adds a reachy move.

From the Secret Arete Boulder, hop over a small boulder just to the southeast, or slide through a narrow slot to find:

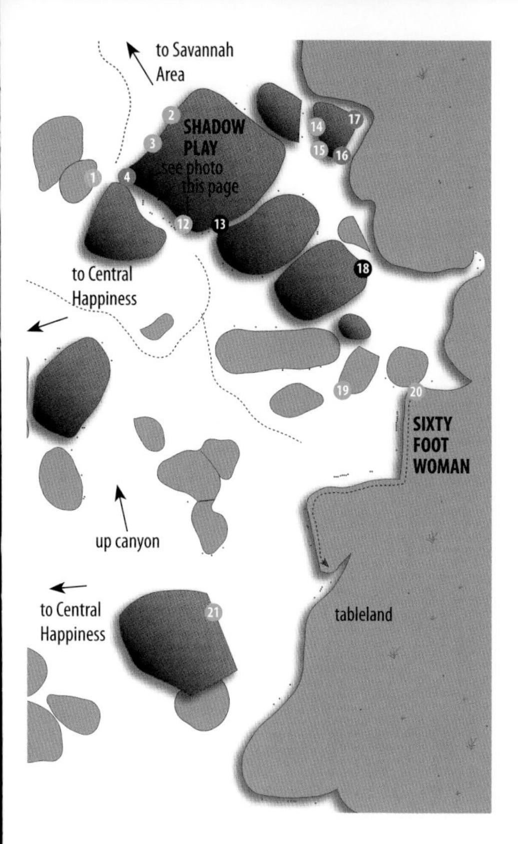

SHADOW PLAY

SHADOW PLAY CAVE

RIO'S SECRET ARETE

THE SIXTY-FOOT WOMAN TRAVERSE

18 Project ☐
The thin seam could be climbable.

On a boulder just left of the Sixty-Foot Woman Traverse in a kind of small cave is:

19 Where's The Curry House? v2 ☐
Sit start on pockets with your feet on the back wall. Climb up with awkward moves on good holds.

THE SIXTY-FOOT WOMAN WALL

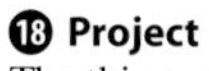

20 The Sixty-Foot Woman Traverse v2 ★★★ ☐
A popular pocket traverse that is one of the last places to lose the sun—which is useful to know when it is late on a cold winter afternoon. Start on the left and traverse right on pockets into a corner. Keep low and continue around the nose and on to some small edges beyond, finishing when the rock deteriorates. A great test for your fingers and excellent practice for your brain in figuring out which pocket to use in the sea of options.

Just down and right from the Sixty-Foot Woman Traverse is a square-cut boulder with a slab facing toward the cliff, which has:

21 Unnamed v0- ★★ ☐
A very nice little slab with good but small pockets and small footholds.

SAVANNAH AREA

Another great area, open and fairly level with good landings. There are many moderate classics on gently overhanging rock, with the Savannah Boulder providing an idyllic hang where you can sit in the sun, and climb in the shade. Does it get any better than this? Deservedly almost as popular as the Central Happiness Area.

Approach: Leave the Happy Boulder and walk up canyon. Don't despair: the Happiness is all pervasive and ever-present. You will pass between two boulders, a large one at left, which is the Girlfriend Rock. A little further, on the right, is the giant flat-topped Savannah Boulder and just beyond this, the Fred Boulder. Overview map: page 101.

The small boulder, left of a large low one, on the east of the trail (right as you walk up canyon) provides:

1 **Please Please Me** v0- ❑
Climb the nice brown wall with some shallow huecos at mid-height.

GIRLFRIEND ROCK

At the west of the trail (left as you walk up canyon):

2 **Mmm... Nice** v0- ★ ❑
The sexy brown patina wall next to the trail is worth a second glance. Climb the middle, starting just right of a low hueco.

3 **Giant** v0 ★ ❑
Sit start at pockets. Climb up by pockets to sidepulls and a stretch up the arete.

4 **Unnamed** v3 ★ ❑
Start at an undercling/sidepull and pull out right, then up using a trick foot move.

5 **Up Your Skirt, Left** v2 ★★ ❑
Sit start at a sidepull and a good pocket. Climb direct up a blunt prow using shallow dishes for the right hand but good huecos for the left.

6 **Up Your Skirt, Right** v2 ★★ ❑
Sit start at the same sidepull as above. Move up right to a big hueco and then the top.

7 **Unnamed** v2 ★ ❑
Sit start at the left side of a small scoop (not the very wide scoop further right) and climb up and left to the big hueco.

8 **Unnamed** v3 ★★ ❑
Sit start left of the very wide scoop and climb up left into the scoop then out the top of the small scoop.

9 **Unnamed** v0 ★ ❑
Climb the large scoop.

SAVANNAH BOULDER

This is the giant flat-topped boulder that is unmistakable when walking up canyon from the Central Happiness Area. It overhangs on its north side, providing a slew of superb lines and endless entertaining eliminates.

10 **Dumb** v0- ❑
Start on a flake and follow flakes to the top.

11 **Beat It** v3 ★ ❑
Sit start low on a small juglet, left of the *Ketron Classic* start. Climb left to shallow pockets and up past edges to the good jug at the top end of the diagonal crack.

12 **Marty Lewis's Ever-Changing Hair** v2 ★★ ❑
Sit start at a low pinch as for *Ketron Classic*, but make a rising leftward traverse, joining a crack system.

13 **Ketron Classic** v4 ★★★ ❑
Sit start on the low pinch: Go up and left to a good undercut, and then diagonally right to rippled sloper. Top out on good holds.

14 **Kling And Smirk** v2 ★★★ ❑
Sit start on undercuts at the right end of the steep wall. Climb up and left by some confusing moves between good holds, following the lip to an easy juggy finish.

15 **Duck Soup** v0- ★ ❑
The smoothish brown wall is climbed at its right side.

16 **Margo's Arete** vB ★ ❑
The arete.

17 **Savannah** v4 ★★ ❑
Traverse the path-side (west) face of the boulder from right to left, turn the arete and continue across the lowest part of the overhanging face to finish at a ledge on the left side.

The boulder to the left of the trail, just up canyon from the Savannah Boulder has:

18 **Echo** v0- ❑
Sit start on big huecos and climb the arete.

FRED BOULDER

If you stand at the Savannah Boulder's overhanging north face and turn around you will see two boulders touching. The right one of these boulders is the Fred Boulder. The problems face up canyon. From left to right:

19 **Sucker Punch** v5 ★★★ ❑
Short, but excellent. Start standing at a good shoulder-height edge. Move left to small edges and punch for the top.

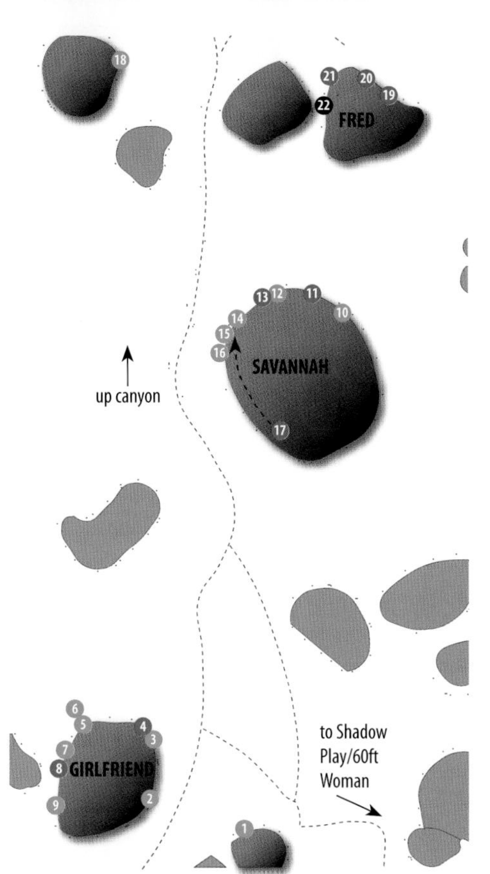

FRED BOULDER

SAVANNAH BOULDER

GIRLFRIEND ROCK

GIRLFRIEND ROCK

20 Carrot Top v3 ★★★ ☐
Stand start from a good flake jug: Go right up the front face to the blunt arete, and a crux getting onto the finishing slab. Delightful.

21 East Easy Rider v5 ★ ☐
Sit start on the low flake and make a huge move to the deep slot. Finish up *Carrot Top.*

22 Pop-A-Tendon ☐
Start low on sharp pockets. Move up to an edge and then one of two huecos. This appears to be broken. The alternative would be a big hard move left from the pockets.

23 Tequila Flange v1 ★ ☐
A mid-height left to right traverse from the start of S*ucker Punch* around the arete, across to the good huecos, then up right.

24 Tim's Fred Traverse v9 ★★ ☐
Start as for *Pop-A-Tendon* and make a hard shouldery stretch left to the start of *East Easy Rider*. Instead of punching the normal move of *East Easy Rider* to the large slot, avoid that slot, using the smaller hold to the left, and stay low around the nose. Continue left to finish as for *Sucker Punch.* Could be harder since breakage to *Sucker Punch*.

SWORDFISH TROMBONE AREA

This area is directly above the Savannah Boulder on the East Rim (right side as you look up canyon). There's not much here other than a big swath of steeply curving overhang, but the two problems that cross this roof are among the best and hardest in the canyon.

Approach: Walk up to the hidden alcove on the East Rim (right as you look up canyon) from the Savannah Boulder.

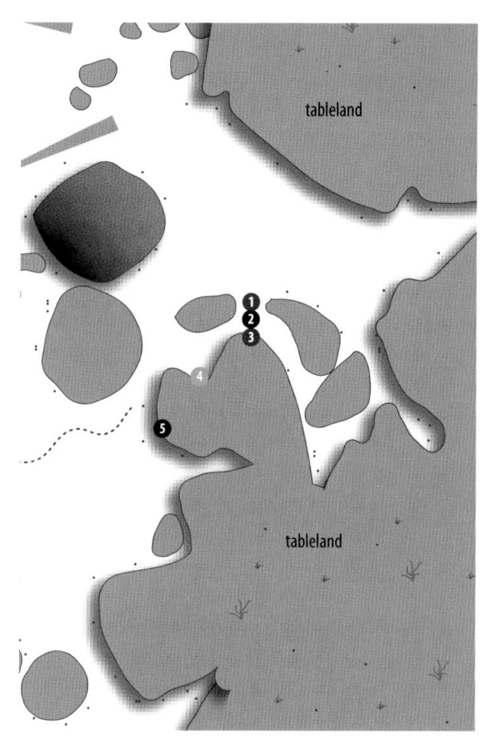

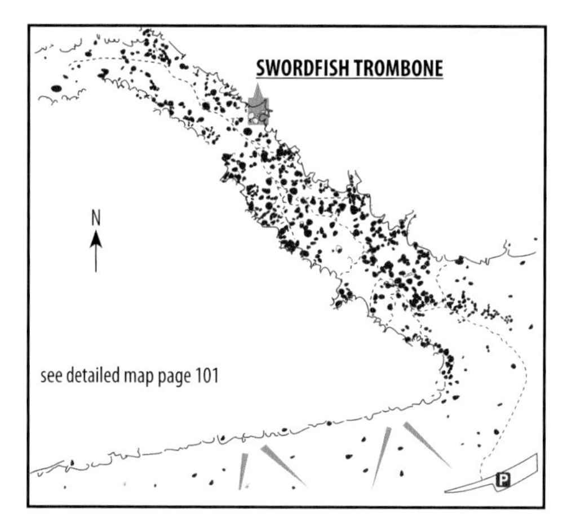

SWORDFISH TROMBONE BOULDER 

1 Goldfish Trombone v14 ★★★ ☐
Sit start at some small underclings at the back of the cave (your left hand is on a pinch undercling with the thumb in a small pocket). Head out and left on pockets to a brutal move to stick a sandy pinch. Then launch leftward with big squeeze moves on slopey dishes to gain a good hold. Finish by climbing an extremely tricky vertical headwall on small crimps. A stunning line and one of America's hardest. The final wall from the good hold is about v9.

2 Project ☐
Start as for *Goldfish Trombone,* but after the crux move to the pinch, and the reach left, instead of heading left up the headwall, throw directly to the lip on the right side of the prow.

3 Swordfish Trombone v12 ★★★ ☐
Start as for *Goldfish* at small underclings and traverse right, and then over the lip on improving pockets. Make a hard move with the left hand to start.

4 Pupfish Souzaphone v1 ☐
Climb the scoop from a standing start.

5 Project ☐
Sit start the prow and make a big move from tiny pockets. Ridiculous.

GOLDFISH/SWORDFISH

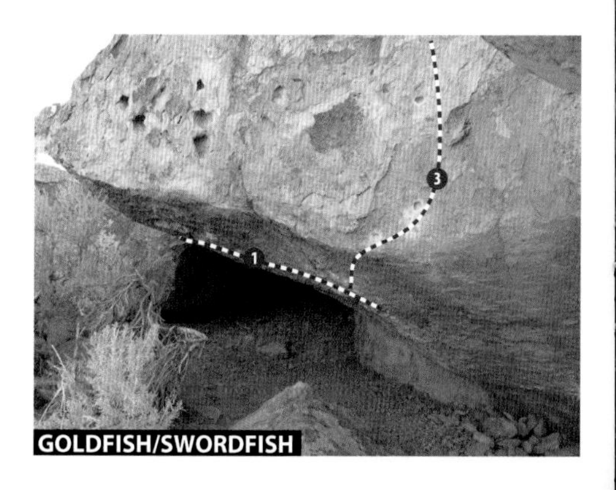
GOLDFISH/SWORDFISH

Daniel Woods looking golden on the crux of "*Goldfish*" (v14 opposite page). Photo: Tim Kemple

SERENGETI AREA

This area is in an open, level setting with lots of great moderates and some excellent easier problems. The *Serengeti* problem itself is always popular. Most of the problems face the afternoon sun, so it can be hot here.

Approach: Walk up canyon from the Savannah Area. The area is distinguished by a tall boulder blocking the path and a row of smaller boulders at right. Overview map: page 101.

SERENGETI WEST

SOWETO BOULDER

SERENGETI BOULDER WEST FACE

The left side (as you look up canyon) has a lot of good v0 problems, but the wall is extremely high, making the climbs more like miniature routes than bouldering. Excellent climbing, but not recommended for climbers looking to push themselves at this level!

1 Aerial Surveillance v0- ★ ☐
Sit start and climb big huecos to a deep one at 14 feet; finish up the brown wall as directly as possible.

2 Incoming v0 ★ ☐
Climb the wall passing huecos to a big scoop. Then, either climb the slab above on spaced crimps to questionable platey holds (well scary), or move right more safely and easily.

3 Crash Dive v0- ★ ☐
Climb the ramp and then the crack.

4 Durban Poison v0- ☐
Climb the steep crack to join the finish of *Crash Dive*.

5 I Killed A Man... v1 ★ ☐
...A Man Who Looked Like Me. The center of the vertical wall. Interesting climbing up big flakes and huecos.

6 Weasel Robbers v1 ★ ☐
The left side of the arete.

SERENGETI BOULDER SOUTH FACE

7 You're A Disc Jockey: What's That? v0+ ☐
The right side of the arete.

8 Elephant Graveyard v0- ☐
Left of the small cave, climb huecos and the crack.

9 Serengeti v5 ★★★ ☐
People love this one. Start up the flake on the left-side of the shallow cave. Move right on slopey huecos and pull past crimps to gain the good jug. Make this a bit easier by a long reach right to a pocket, then up. It's basically the same problem!

10 War Drum v4 ☐
Sit start in the hueco three feet off the ground and climb the wall trending left to a pocket and flake to finish. Somewhat painful.

11 Sentimental African v0- ☐
Climb the black streak up the wall.

SERENGETI BOULDER EAST FACE

12 Paco The Weasel ☐
On the east face (right side as you look up canyon), make some short pulls to the arete. Holds appear to have broken.

13 Spear Mint v0 ☐
Sit start and climb huecos at the right end of the east wall.

SOWETO BOULDER

To the right of the Serengeti Boulder (looking up canyon) are some smaller boulders. The furthest left of these is overhanging along its west side, providing:

14 Hector v3 ☐
At the left side of the small cave. Hands on underclings, feet on the dusty back wall. Make a dynamic move up.

15 I'll Never Be A Veteran v4 ★ ☐
Start standing with underclings and poor footholds. Make a couple of hard moves up, then left and over.

16 Soweto v0+ ★ ☐
Sit start on the right side of the small cave: Climb left and then up.

N
see detailed map page 101
SERENGETI AREA
P
up canyon
SERENGETI
SOWETO
to Crimpanzee Area
to Savannah Boulder
to Fred Boulder
1
2
3
4
5
6
7
8
9
10
11
12
13
14
15
16
17
18
19
20
21
22
23
24
25
26
7
8
9
10
11
SERENGETI SOUTH

BLEACHED BONES AND CILLEY BOULDERS

17 Ghetto Justice v0+ ★ ❑
Sit start on the right side of the small cave: Climb directly up.

18 Burning Rubber Necklace v4 ★★ ❑
Starting on the right, traverse the lip of the small cave on pockets and underclings to finish up *I'll Never Be A Veteran.*

BLEACHED BONES BOULDER

This is another steep boulder to the right.

19 Bleached Bones v4 ★★ ❑
Sit start on a good flake. Make a hard move up to pockets then use a heel to stay on as you climb either direct or left (harder), but not right. The stand start is v2.

CILLEY BOULDER

The smaller boulder.

20 Circle Of Life v0+ ★ ❑
Sit start and climb good holds to the arete.

21 Cilley Mantel v0 ★ ❑
Sit start and climb the right line of steepness to the slab. Starting ridiculously low makes it a grade harder.

GIGGLE GIGGLE BOULDER

Behind the Bleached Bones and Circle of Life Boulder is:

22 Giggle, Giggle v2 ❑
Sit start at the back of the low cave.

LAZY LION BOULDER

This large low boulder is the southernmost in the chain.

23 Lazy Lion v3 ❑
Traverse the boulder right to left, staying just below the top.

To the left of the Serengeti Boulder (as you look up canyon) are a few problems:

24 Unnamed v1 ❑
On the nearby rock is a nice slab.

*Up and left of the Serengeti Boulder (as you look up canyon) is a pair of boulders forming a corner alcove. The left boulder has a face that faces **up** canyon with:*

25 Crispin Waddy v6 ★ ❑
Climb the wall with sharp crimps, almost no foot-holds and a good small pocket.

26 Unnamed v1 ❑
Sit start and climb onto the slab.

The cliff-band running along the southwest rim above the aforementioned boulders is comprised of sections of tall vertical faces which look to have some potential not covered in this guide, though they are a little lichened and have some loose flakes. On the left side of one of these blocks/walls is:

CRIMPANZEE AREA

On the southwest rim, above the Serengeti Boulder is a section of the canyon wall that is eroding into boulder-like buttresses. This section of canyon rim is the Crimpanzee Area, where there really isn't a lot to record yet! But perhaps one day the rock will clean up and people will get excited for some first ascents.

27 Crimpanzee v6 ❑
Right of a tower formation is a wall that is undercut at its left side and has a good sidepull-pinch at about 10 feet. Climb this blunt left arete to the face on sharp crimps passing the pinch. Start high on stacked pads, by squeezing on painful holds.

28 Hematoma v6 ★★ ❑
If you like a fine slab, this is one of the best around! You will find it facing up-canyon on the right side of the Crimpanzee Boulder. Nice smooth rock and tiny crimps!

Scott Chandler reaches up for the tiny shallow slot on *Mr. Witty* (v6), page 117. Photo: Wills Young.

SLIGHT INDUCEMENT AREA

Here find more excellent bouldering and the slight inducement of a brace of top quality problems at v1 and v2. The first buttress, which has three of these superb lines, is only 100 yards or so beyond the Serengeti Boulder. On the East Rim above the Slight Inducement and the Cry Baby Boulders are some tall problems for those seeking esoteric highballing at v0 to v2 with some decent rock and memorable lines. With plenty of afternoon sun, the rock here is usually warm!
Approach: Walk up the canyon beyond the Serengeti Boulder. The Slight Inducement Boulder is a hundred yards further, on the right.

CRY BABY BOULDER

THE SLIGHT INDUCEMENT BOULDER

This is a really nice solid piece of rock with a trio of outstanding v1 and v2 problems as good as any in the canyon.

1 Future Planet Of Style v0- ☐
The extremely short wall, and then the slab.

2 Don't Box Me In v1 ☐
The nice wall via a right hand pinch.

3 Amphibian/Junkyard v0+ ★ ☐
Climb the right side of the front face. Start at a giant up-pointing fang; move directly past a pocket, avoiding the flake out right, and top out left of the big incut flakes used at the top of the next problem.

4 Secret to Success v2 ★★★ ☐
Sit start at the good jug right of the arete. Move left around the arete and up the front wall.

5 Slight Inducement v1 ★★★ ☐
Sit start at a good jug as above. Climb the series of great holds directly up the arete finishing at a good flake.

6 Slight Inducement Right v2 ★★ ☐
Sit start at the good jug right of the arete. Climb the series of great holds, but stay right to gain the lip. Move right across the lip of the boulder along a crimpy rail. Mantel over above this rail, or go all the way right on bigger holds: pumpy.

The little perched block above and right has:

7 Unnamed v0+ ☐
Start low on a big hold down and right, and climb up and over. Pretty bad.

The boulder to the right has:

8 Unnamed v3 ☐
Sit start and climb some dreadful rock. Pretty bad.

Twenty yards up-canyon from the Slight Inducement boulder is another boulder with:

9 Nameless v2 ☐
Stand start: Climb the overhanging face of the leaning wedged block. Awkward.

10 Painless v0- ☐
Make an easy start on jugs then a thin pull onto the slab to the underclings.

11 Blameless v0- ☐
Climb the flake and shallow dishes.

12 Shameless v0- ☐
The wall behind the bush.

And yet further along is:

13 Radio, Radio v0- ☐
Start at the big hueco, go left into the scoop and over the short bulge.

CRY BABY BOULDER

14 Bitter Lander Cowboyz v0- ☐
The flake crack up the west wall.

15 Cry Baby v2 ☐
Feeling lucky? Climb the overhanging arete with some insecure holds.

16 Gamekeeper Clifford v4 ★ ☐
Sit start and climb the overhanging face right of *Cry Baby*, staying left to avoid more rotten rock out right. Not quite as good as it looks.

17 Lady Chatterley's Toy Boy v0+ ☐
Contrive a way up the flakes. Not recommended.

18 Unnamed ☐
Slab undercut by a short steep wall looks climbable.

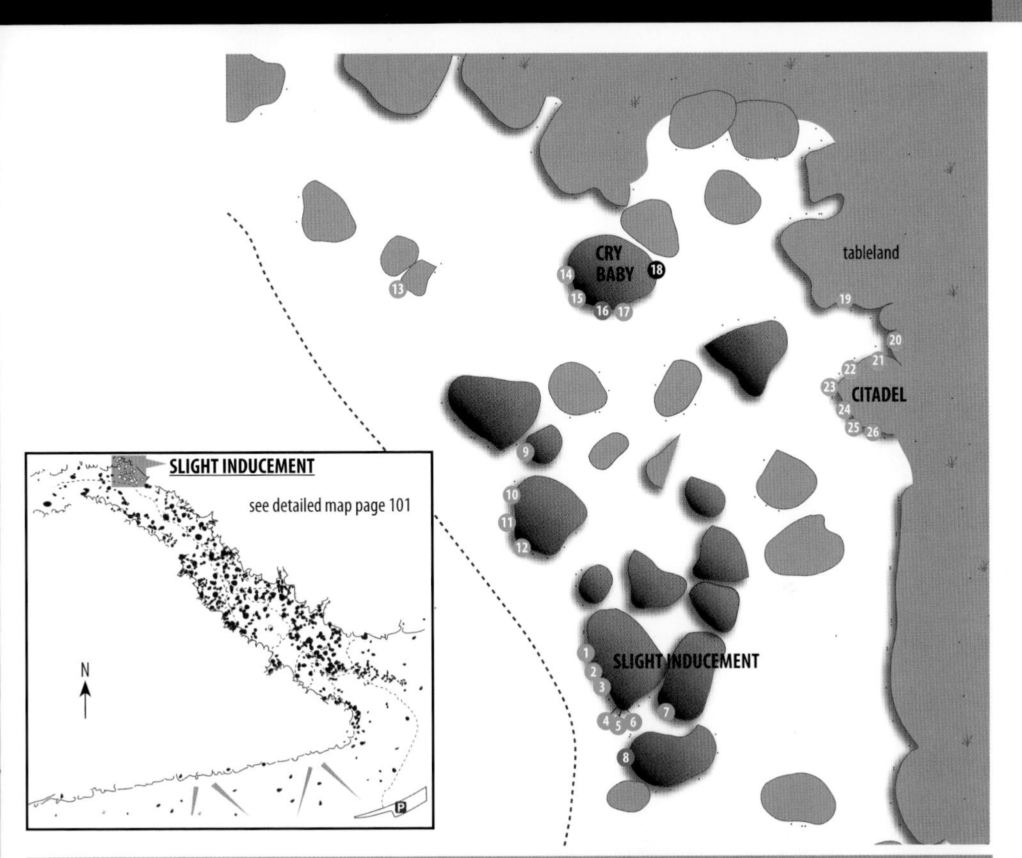
CRY BABY
tableland
CITADEL
SLIGHT INDUCEMENT
SLIGHT INDUCEMENT
see detailed map page 101
N
P
1
2
3
4
5
6
7
8
9
10
11
12
13
14
15
16
17
18
19
20
21
22
23
24
25
26

1
2
3
4
5
6
SLIGHT INDUCEMENT

On the boulder on the cliff up and right from Cry Baby *is:*

⑲ **Future Primitive** v0 ☐
The crozzly wall that faces down canyon.
The undercut boulder to the right has:

⑳ **Foreplay** v0+ ★ ☐
Full title: *When Was the Last Time You Had Foreplay?* Start on the big flat edge. Move up to the pockets and finish direct.

THE CITADEL

THE CITADEL

TAKE IT LIKE A MAN/YOU ARE MORTAL

THE CITADEL

This is the tallish buttress up above the Cry Baby Boulder to the right.

㉑ **Mongol Hordes** v0 ☐
The crozzly, tall wall right of the crack.

㉒ **I Want A Guy ...** v0+ ★ ☐
... Who Appreciates Me And Buys Me Nice Underwear! (That's the full title). Climb the smoothish wall with some good pockets.

㉓ **My Last Boyfriend ...** v0 ★ ☐
Not a bad ride, but over too fast. Now ditch him...

㉔ **Frontal Assault** v1 ☐
The wall with the stuck-on plate.

㉕ **Shaker** v2 ☐
Another intriguing crozzly wall.

㉖ **Killing Fields** v0+ ☐
Start on sandy pockets and climb the right side of the buttress.

Below the cliff, and to the right of The Citadel (left of the Mortal Buttress) is a low boulder with a shallow cave that faces downhill.

㉗ **Take It Like A Man** v2 ☐
A one-move-wonder: Sit start and climb the shallow concave wall at its right side. Once was a different problem, but a hold broke. Not exactly a proud line!

YOU ARE MORTAL BUTTRESS

This is a very high buttress: You *are* mortal. V-grades are used for the problems, but this wall is kinda beyond bouldering.

㉘ **Each Day We Get Closer ...** v2 ★ ☐
... To The Big Bad Fire. Follow the left-edge of this buttress by the arete and holds just right. The crux is at the start.

㉙ **I Want More Life** v0 ☐
Climb to an undercling, then launch up the wall above.

㉚ **Getting Lonely, Getting Old** v0- ★ ☐
Climb up the scoops, then trend slightly right up the dark wall.

㉛ **Make Me Believe I'm Not Going To Die** v1 ★ ☐
On the right edge of the buttress, climb up to a funky pinch in a scoop, then move right and up on better holds.

Got Spotters? Mary Williams, *Wills's Arete*, page 117. Photo: Wills Young

TOP GUN AREA

The Top Gun Area is the last area at the Happy Boulders listed in this guide. It has a few excellent tall problems. It is seldom visited and so provides a more natural and quieter experience than the areas down canyon. It gets plenty of sun.

TOP GUN AREA

N

see detailed map page 101

On the up-canyon side of the boulder by the trail is:

1 Aaarhhhhh v0-
Climb the scoop.

MORE SMACK PLEASE VICAR

2 Brock Bating v0-
The easy wall up the gully.

3 Brock v1
Start low and climb the flakey nose.

4 More Smack Please Vicar v1 ★
The tall brown wall left of the corner crack leads to a bold finish left or an escape right.

5 Wainright v6 ★
Start right of the corner crack. A long reach from pockets to an edge out right. Finish on the next climb.

6 A Brief Conversation Ending in Divorce v2 ★★
Stretch to the small flakes and a pocket three feet right of the lichen streak, then climb up and left.

7 Guidebook Writer's Love-In v1
I guess I wasn't invited. Which is a good thing in this case. Start on underclings and climb directly up.

8 Viva Dead Mules v2
Start at the football-sized dusty hueco and climb directly up.

9 Nagasaki Badger v0-
The right edge of the buttress.

WAYKO BOULDER

10 Tricky Kid v0
Sit start on a jug and pockets. Follow more pockets up the wall.

11 End of the Road v0+
Climb flakes and the scoop to a diagonal crack.

TOP GUN BOULDERS

12 Flyboy v0+
Swing right from the arete to a pocket and up.

13 Top Gun v3 ★
Climb the concave wall on pockets then head straight up the dark wall.

14 Keep on Sending Him Up v0 ★
Also known as: *What Comes Naturally.* Climb the concave wall on pockets; go right to a good hold, and then up the blocky wall.

15 Big Dick American Hero v3 ★
Pull into the big undercut hueco, and then out left to a good slot and up.

16 Even Bigger Big Dick American Hero v4 ★★
Stretch into the big undercut hueco, then head right and up the leaning wall.

17 Marriage-Go-Round v0-
The flakey wall.

18 Cockpit v1
Several pockets lead to a crack-like feature. The sit start from the right is v4-ish.

19 Invisibility Lessons v0+
A chossy undercut wall.

20 Nice Curves v0
The hanging arete.

21 Tom's Cruise v0+ ★
The shallow scoop on the left wall of the alcove.

22 Clifford the Dog v3 ★
The right wall of the alcove. Take the pinch above your head, climb to the flake, and up.

23 Don't Believe v2
The undercut crack.

24 Rude Awakening v2
Take the jug above your head and climb up.

25 Pish v0-
Follow a rising right to left line on good holds.

26 Strangle Hold v0-
The nice brown wall on the right side of the right wall, staying off the slab up right.

Explore more bouldering up the canyon, or leave it as a natural sanctuary.

MORE SMACK PLEASE VICAR

WAYKO AND TOP GUN BOULDERS

The Sad Boulders

Nick Rueff, *Lawnmower Man.*

The Sad Boulders is a half-mile-long shallow canyon, running roughly north-south, cut into the southern end of the volcanic tableland north of Bishop. There are small bands of cliff at either side, some free-standing boulders, and a few areas where the giant blocks create a cave-riddled chaos. At around 4400ft (1340m), the Sads are generally free of snow during the winter, and only get rain during the heaviest mountain storms. During hot days, The Sads is remarkable for offering some cool air within its many caves. There are beautiful views from the canyon's southern end out over the Owens River flood plain with its oxbow lakes and S-bends, and across the valley to the Buttermilks and the mountains beyond. Looking north and east, the view across the volcanic tableland is equally expansive.

The rock is volcanic Bishop tuff, like the neighboring Happy Boulders; often heavily pocketed or roughly featured, but occasionally smooth. There is relatively more water-polished rock here than at the Happies. Climbing within a few days of rain or after a heavy snowfall can be dangerous as water can soften the porous rock.

The Bouldering

The Sads is not only a tuff connoiseur's paradise with a slew of amazing hard lines (high single digits on the V-scale), it is also an explorer's treasure trove of climbing at every level on some of the best rock in the Bishop area. With 250 problems crammed into a small area, and much more to be done, there is plenty to enjoy here no matter what level you climb. There are some double-digit testpieces, sometimes in squeezed situations, but not always, and some stellar open highballs covering a spread of grades. The Prozac Nation Bluff is up in an airy sunny location at the top end of the canyon; the Outer Ice Caves take plenty of sun as do the Strength In Numbers area, the whole Central Joyless area, and the Molly Boulder. But at some other areas the landings can be less even, so a pad and spotter are all the more important. At the lower end of the canyon blocks jumble together to create intriguing nooks and crannies and low-roofed caves for which the area is famed, and for which a taste is innevitably developed. The fun of discovery within the jumble, and the unusual rocky surroundings are a major part of the experience that makes this place so special. Don't miss out!

Directions

From the center of Bishop, drive north on Main Street (Highway 395) to the junction of Highway 6 (The "Y") signposted to Tonopah. This is the point where Highway 395 makes a long left turn to the west and becomes Sierra Highway. Highway 6 is the straight on option, so don't take the long left turn: Instead, signal right and head directly out of Bishop. Drive along Highway 6 for about 1.3 miles to where the highway begins a long right curve. Turn left on Five Bridges Road. Follow Five Bridges Road for about 2.4 miles, going past the gravel works (at left) to where the road becomes a dirt road. Here, at the crossroads, turn left onto Chalk Bluff Road. Follow Chalk Bluff Road for about 1.5 miles, looking out for the layby parking lot at the left side. There is a large notice board set back from the road on the right, next to the trail leading to the Sad Boulders.

Coming from Mammoth, you drive in toward the center of Bishop to the long right-hand bend where Sierra Highway becomes Main Street. Instead of making the bend to the right, take Highway 6, by a left turn and drive out of Bishop about 1.3 miles to Five Bridges Road. Turn left at Five Bridges Road, and follow the remaining directions above.

From the Pit, turn left at the bottom of the hill onto Pleasant Valley Dam Road. Follow this road past the Pleasant Valley Dam Campsite, taking a bend to the right after about 0.7 miles that puts you on Chalk Bluff Road. Follow Chalk Bluff Road below the cliff line for about 4.5 miles to a long pullout on the right side, about 0.9 miles beyond the similar, but larger Happy Boulders' pullout.

For ease of navigation, use your guide's left cover flap to mark this map. Find the boulders you want by the page references here.

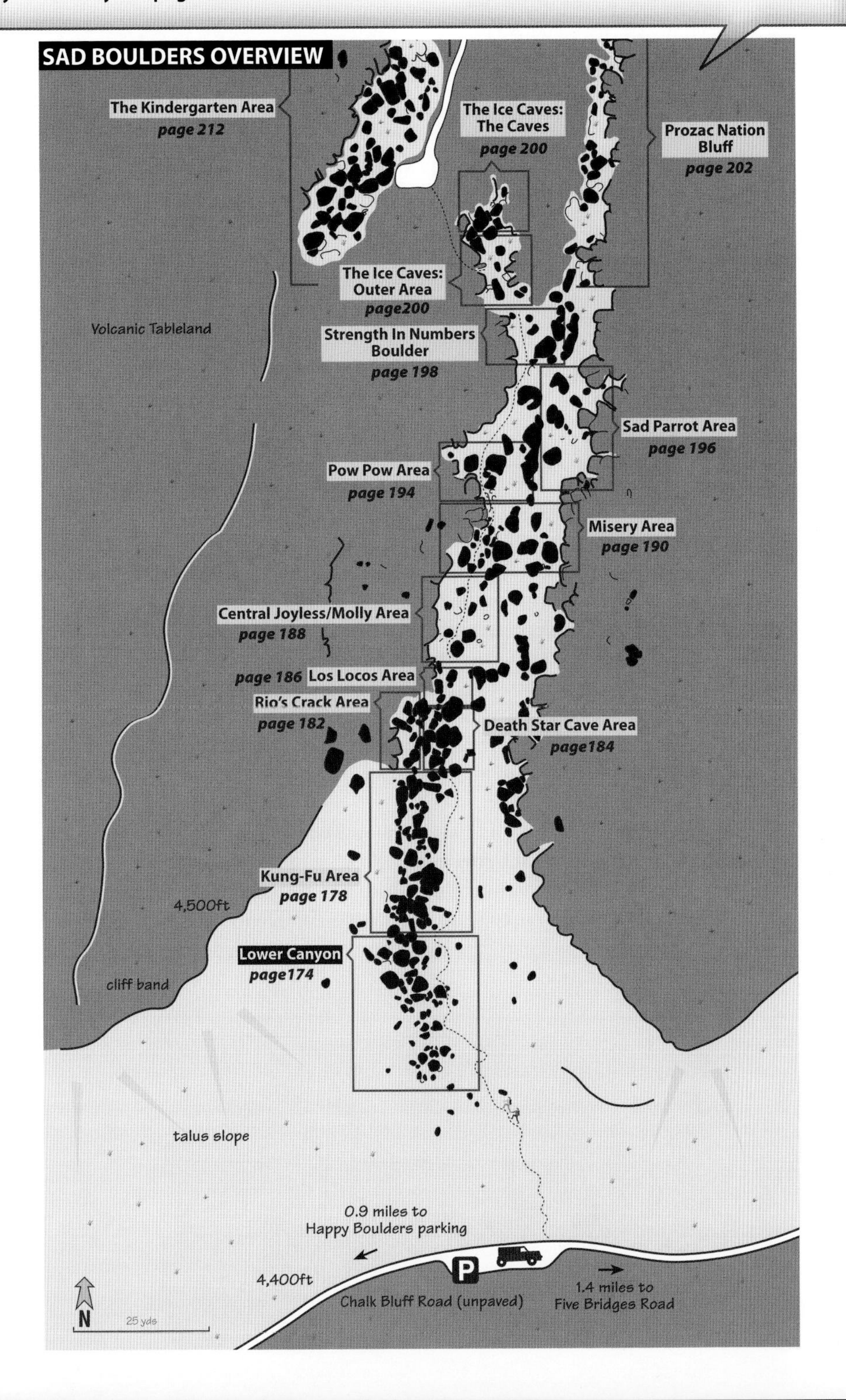

THE GLORY DAYS

Sad Memories of a Tuff Convert

By Tim Steele

Tim Steele: Happy to be sad?

The first time I visited the Volcanic Tableland, I vowed never to return. I couldn't see the attraction of the scrappy looking rock. None the less, two years later I found myself camped outside of Bishop. Originally a Hueco Tanks devotee, the thought of not being able to roam where I liked had motivated me to find a boulderfield in my own backyard.

In the winter of 1999 I started to explore the Sads canyon, and began to realize its huge potential for producing new lines. Many "classics" had already been plucked. The Prozac Nation Bluff was well chalked, as were a few stand-outs like *Strength in Numbers, Rio's Crack, Molly,* and the *Leubering* problems, but for the most part, there seemed to be acres of passageways, caves, and untouched holds.

I don't know if it was the *Sad* name that scared people away, or some kind of pre-Millennial tension, but there were few visitors that winter. None the less, a core group proceeded to attack the canyon in what became a sort of *feeding frenzy* (as the name of one problem done during that time period alludes). In the ensuing orgy of development, problems gushed forth so fast, that even though I knew all the people climbing them, they seemed to have sprung up over night.

In the wide scheme of things, being first to climb a line isn't important. Other than for a few notable ascents nobody cares for the name of the climber, and in many cases there's no way of knowing. But, the process of envisioning a line that hasn't been done before—of coming to terms with it and believing that you can do it – has always had a certain *je ne sais quoi* attraction to me. I have a suspicion that something of the like fueled the others as well.

Is that really a hold up there? Will the hold stay on the wall when I weight it? Is the move possible? Will I break a leg if I fall and get yelled at by my mom?

Guidebook grades say little, usually failing to do justice. The supressed fear, or perhaps hubris required by a first ascensionist to cast out towards the finish on problems like *Los Locos* or *Atari* is not captured in a simple description and number. Once a problem has been done, the doubt is erased... The impossible becomes real... The initial fears are squelched...The adventure is lost.

Wills Young

Tim Steele tries his luck with *Molly* (v5, page 188), one of the sweetest problems at "the Sads."

It seems strange now to ponder the origins of problems. Consider the *The Rorschach Test*: The line originated as a joke; the holds chalked in haste to fool a friend. Hey, check this line out! Try to pull on these crimps, buddy! But, the joke was soon reversed, as a motivated Byron Shumpert ticked the rig a couple of weekends later, inadvertently adding one of the hardest testpieces to the Sads. Now a problem replete with its own check box; *The Rorschach Test* has become real.

I'll always treasure the memories of those days when I would wake at a deserted campsite, head to the boulders, and run around like a lunatic with coffee in hand, spying the lines to attempt later that day. I would never trade the times I had with friends there, each casting forth into the unknown where the rock became a sounding board to our creativity and imagination, allowing us to find ourselves within the vast expanse of this wonderful Volcanic Tableland.

LOWER CANYON

The lower section of the Sads provides a number of great little problems scattered in a kind of talus of large blocks and a fair share of esoteric gems hidden in small caves and passageways. Its southern aspect means it catches a lot of sun, but on cool days this is a great place to stop, being a very short hike from the car. The rock can be pretty much perfect, as found on the Bird Boulder and the Cool Boulder. In contrast, the caves are always shaded, though occasionally cramped. The best problem among these is perhaps Humpty Dumpty (v3), a great little testpiece requiring a couple pads and a close spot.

APPROACH

BIRD BOULDER

FIRST BOULDER

One of the first decent sized boulders left of the trail. It has a horizontal shelf running across the middle.

1 Unnamed v0 ☐
Climb the face to the left, right, or center, or from sitting at left, all at a modest grade.

BIRD BOULDER

This is a little uphill from the First Boulder and has a strange tapering shape, a little like a bird skull or lizard's head.

2 Unnamed v3 ★★ ☐
Start at the base of the arete with the left hand on the slab above, holding a small dish, and the right on a big undercling down below. Slap up and right, then pull onto the upper facet precariously. Nice moves on good rock.

On the west side of the Bird Boulder (left looking up canyon) is a small pit. The pit has a boulder jammed over its west side to create a prow that provides:

3 Unnamed v3 ★ ☐
Sit start and climb the prow with a big move to a good hold over the lip. Then, instead of moving right to easy ground, launch up left to another good hold, then top out. The right exit is v1.

BRUISER BOULDER

Above the Bird Boulder is a nice-looking wall with very blunt arete:

4 Bruiser v6 ★ ☐
Start at a decent two- or three-finger pocket high up for the right hand. Pull to a horizontal and then pockets up right. Take care on the top out.

COOL BOULDER

Found by following a small trail away from the main trail at the first sharp right-hand switchback.

5 Easy Cool v3 ★ ☐
Sit start at crimps beneath the rail. Pull to the rail then climb the left side of the boulder using a layback for the left hand. Excellent rock.

6 Birth of the Cool v6 ★ ☐
A very cool eliminate on perfect rock: Sit start at crimps beneath the rail. Pull to the rail, then climb the right side of the narrow wall via a shallow pocket and a hard move to good holds. The ledge and holds out left are off, as is the arete to the right.

GUANTANAMERA BOULDER

7 Guantanamera v3 ★★ ☐
Sit start and climb the left arete.

8 José v5 ★ ☐
Sit start and climb the face avoiding the left arete. Use pockets and a sidepull to make a big, testing reach to the baseball-sized hueco. Not the best landing.

SUN TRAP BOULDER

This boulder faces down canyon and takes a lot of sun. It's a big boulder with pockets across its base and some flakey rock up its middle. Photo page 176.

9 Project ☐
Sit start near th right side of the boulder under the blunt arete, with left hand on a sidepull, and pockets for the right hand. Climb pockets through the overhang to the lip, and then the blunt arete.

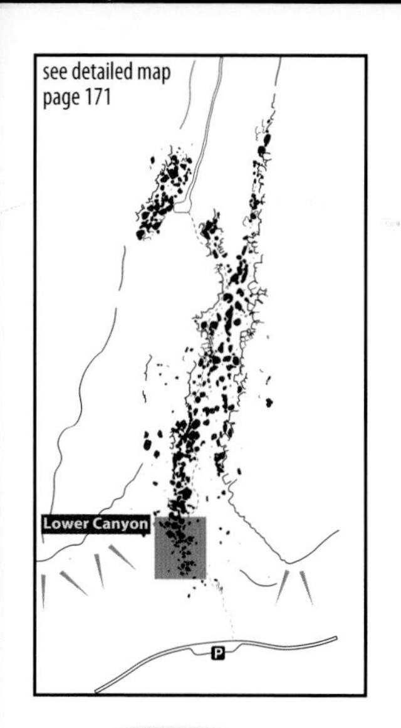

APPROACH

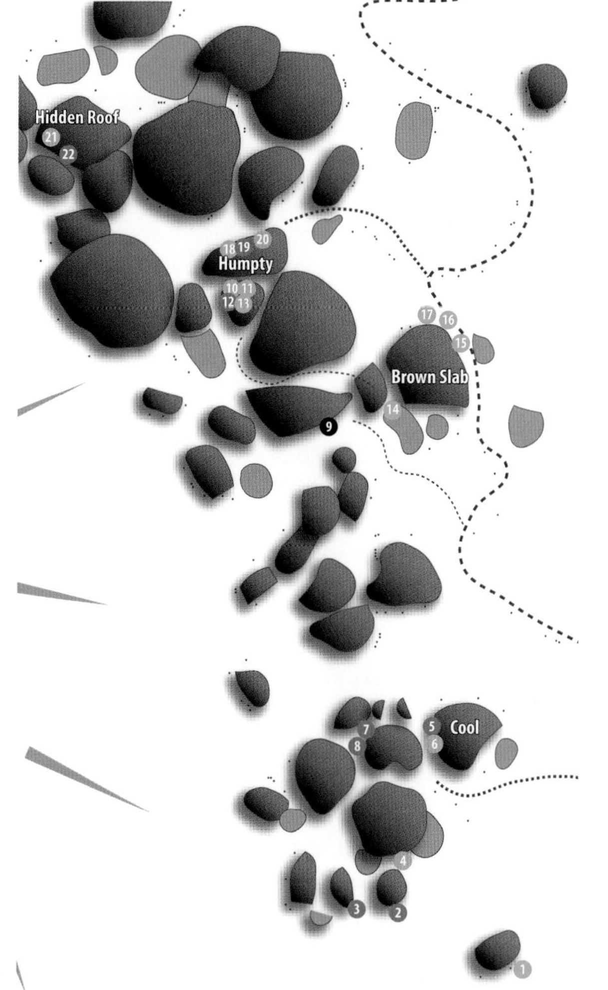

BRUISER BOULDER

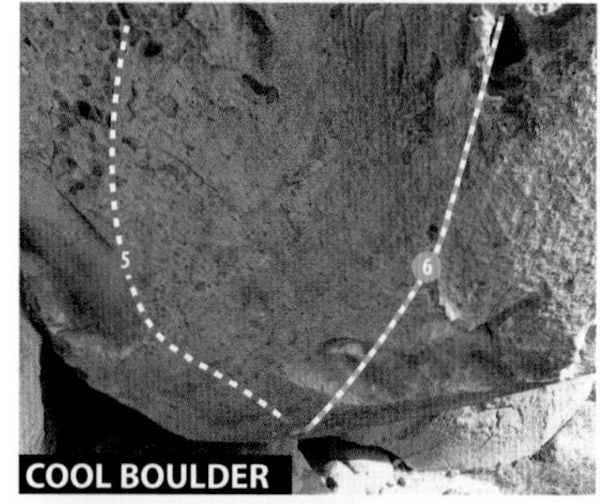

COOL BOULDER

GUANTANAMERA

SMALL CAVE

A small, dim cave is found by walking from the main Sad Boulders access path across the top of the Sun Trap Boulder and then turning right.

10 Pinball v7 ★ ☐

A bit of a squeeze job. Sit start at the base of the keel. Ascend the inside face with a couple of hard moves to gain a good sidepull, followed by a delicate finish.

11 Dumb Luck v2 ★ ☐

From sitting at the base of the keel, climb to the south (outside) of the cave. Pull into the niche, then, if you're feeling very adventurous, exit up and right on frighteningly insecure holds to the top of the boulder. Not one to climb after rain.

12 Fumble in the Dark v3 ☐

On the small boulder at the back of the cave. Sit start at the big holds. Pull up to a good sidepull and make a huge reach to good holds up left.

13 Your Sloper is a Two-Dimensional Dress v1 ☐

On the right side, at the entrance to the small cave, sit start with the right hand high on a sloping hold and the left down to the left. Pull to a hold up and left, then step up right. A nice move.

BROWN SLAB BOULDER

The trail uphill from the Chalk Bluff Road passes adjacent to the Brown Slab Boulder, with the boulder on the left and some small blocks at right. After summiting this boulder, descend a slab by the boulder's northwest side, or climb down the southeast corner (and onto the nearby low boulder).

14 Unnamed v0+ ★★ ☐

Climb from deep huecos to the edge of the slab, follow this left and mantel onto it. Frightening.

15 Unnamed v0 ☐

The face is climbed on good pockets.

16 Double Arete v0+ ★ ☐

Climb the arete, staying right and reaching back to the second arete as necessary.

17 Brown Slab vB ★ ☐

Climb the slab trending right. Unfortunately getting down is only marginally easier than getting up.

HUMPTY DUMPTY BOULDER

Walking up the trail from Chalk Bluff Road, after passing by the east side of the Brown Slab Boulder, turn left and walk to the jumble of boulders to find the Humpty Dumpty boulder suspended above a pit.

18 Humpty Dumpty Left Start v6 ★ ☐

Begin hanging with both hands on a good hold just left of the left arete of the large suspended boulder. Make some hard pulls rightward across the front face of the boulder and finish up the headwall.

SUN TRAP BOULDER

19 Humpty Dumpty v3 ★★ ☐

Climb from a giant hueco on the underside of the boulder's north side past giant holds in the roof to the lip. Reach around to crimps on the right and pull through to a good hold with difficulty above a blocky landing zone.

20 Humpty Dumpty Low Start v7 ★ ☐

Begin with both hands at the lowest point on the underside of the suspended boulder and make one desperate move to gain the giant hueco that represents the starting hold of *Humpty Dumpty*. Continue up *Humpty Dumpty*.

TRUCKER CAVE

The Trucker Cave is just up from the Humpty Dumpty Boulder. To find it, face away from the *Humpty Dumpty* problem duck down and enter a cave; walk back to a room-like space where, on the right you will see this problem:

21 Trucker Fucker v7 ☐

Begin around on the left side of the overhang at a good jug. Traverse right, turning the first arete and across the lip to the right arete, which is climbed up into the light.

HIDDEN ROOF

The Hidden Roof is on the west side of the canyon across from Humpty Dumpty and very slightly up-canyon. The entrance is out of view, facing southwest. See the photo (opposite, bottom) for location.

22 Unnamed v6 ★★ ☐

Sit start on a boulder near the back of the cave with a deep left-hand hold and a good pinch/jug for the right. Pull up to a good pinchy hueco for the right hand and use foot trickery to launch yourself out the extremely steep roof to the lip. From here swing across left to a giant hueco that has incut sidepulls and underclings. Keep moving left to the far left side of the boulder and pull up and over.

23 Unnamed, Right v4 ☐

As above but curtail the journey and exit right on big rough holds.

In this area there are other unrecorded problems. There is also quite a bit of potential around the canyon mouth.

Charlie Harnach steps up on the excellent, but surprisingly bold *Big Slab* (v0, page 178)

HIDDEN ROOF FROM HUMPTY DUMPTY

Hidden Roof under this boulder

View from top of Humpty Dumpty Boulder

KUNG FU AREA

Has a mix of highballs on a few big boulders, plus short steep stuff in caves and tight overhangs. *Kung-Fu Grip* is a classic problem, steep and on perfect rock. The Dragon Cave is one of the Sad's ultimate squeeze-in-squeeze-out experiences, that lends the area a unique feel—steep v8 to v11 problems tight to the ground with rocks at your back. You'll either love it or hate it.

Just a few yards down canyon from the Big Kipper Boulder, in a hollow, is a smooth wall that is home to:

1 Project ☐
On immaculate water-polished rock, begin with the right hand on a really good crimp and left on a good pinch; make an absurdly big pull to a good left-hand sidepull, then launch far right to a decent edge, etc. Two incredibly powerful moves, then easier.

BONELESS HERRING BOULDER

2 Boneless Herring v0 ★ ☐
Climb the rib, which is kinda high.

3 Fish Sticks v2 ☐
Climb the wall on the right side, by a crack, trending left on crimps, and avoiding the junky rock at right.

BIG KIPPER BOULDER

This is a heavily featured giant brown boulder sitting in the center of a flat section of wash about 50 yards downstream from Kung-Fu Grip and 50 yards up from the Hidden Roof. See topo, opposite.

4 Salmon v4 ★ ☐
On the east side of the boulder is a short bulging wall of solid rock. Start with two opposing sidepulls about 5 feet off the ground and just under the small overlap. Climb straight over.

5 Kipper Snapper v1 ★ ☐
Sit start at the south-facing end of the large boulder, and climb up to the right of the niche using big, funky holds.

6 The Sardine Can't v1 ☐
Begin on sloping holds and climb up right to huecos.

BIG CAVE BOULDER

The Big Cave Boulder is immediately next to the main path up the hill and just south of the Big Slab Boulder. On its north side, by the path is:

7 Sit-Down Job v0 ☐
Sit start and climb up to a good ledge that you can then sit on to finish the problem.

BIG SLAB

The Big Slab Boulder is innocuous looking from its east side, but shows a tall, pyramidal slab on its western aspect.

BONELESS HERRING BOULDER

8 Big Slab v0 ★★★ ☐
Start way down low and climb the slab, moving right to the smaller pockets in the middle. Step up to reach the sloping arete and precariously ascend this, pulling onto the lower-angle facet to finish. An engaging enterprise.

SPACE SUIT BOULDER

Below the Big Slab Boulder is:

9 The Space Suit v3 ★ ☐
Slide in and make an absurdly low start on good holds and climb out the underbelly of the suspended boulder on more giant holds. Another constricted pain in the ass, but fun anyway.

REWARD AND TREASON

Uphill on the west side of the canyon are two huge side-by-side boulders forming a barrier. The problems are on the west side, facing up hill.

10 Reward v0 ★ ☐
The tall ramp. More of a route than a boulder problem.

11 Treason v1 ★ ☐
The leaning arete climbed on its left-side. Unlikely looking at the grade.

12 Environmental Masquerade v1 ★ ☐
The blunt arete.

KUNG-FU GRIP

13 Kung-Fu Grip Left v2 ★ ☐
Sit start with both hands on the lowest big undercling. Go left to a hueco. Grab it with a kung-fu-like grip. Pull through to the top. Turn the lip.

14 Kung-Fu Grip v5 ★★ ☐
Sit start with both hands on the lowest big undercling. This time cross the roof to the right, avoiding the left facet of the boulder. Use varying degrees of trickery as necessary to make a huge move to a big right-facing flake. Use of a kung-fu grip to stick the move is optional, but could definitely help. Finish right at a crack. Keeping your feet off the rock at right is a challenge. Shorter climbers will probably be reduced to tears.

BIG KIPPER BOULDER (see descriptions for details)

BIG SLAB

VIEW INTO CANYON FROM BIG CAVE BOULDER

SPACE SUIT BOULDER

REWARD AND TREASON

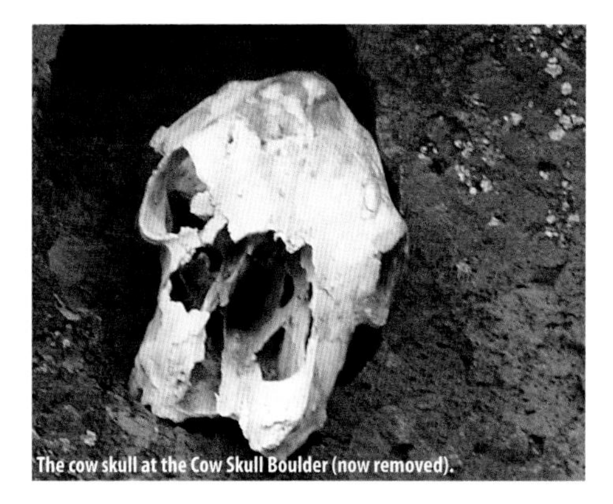
The cow skull at the Cow Skull Boulder (now removed).

VIEW FROM TRAIL

DRAGON CAVE

Find a low cave between boulders on the west side of the canyon just up from Kung-Fu Grip, and enter the Dragon. See the entrance photo, opposite page.

15 Honalee v8 ★ ☐
Start with a good undercling at the base of a heavily featured fin. Climb toward the daylight, exiting the tight hole with dexterity, flexibility, and extraordinary frustration.

16 Enter The Dragon v9 ★ ☐
Start at the two lowest of three hueco-pockets left of the *Honalee* feature. Climb right into the end of *Honalee* (above), topping out through the hole. Great rock and good moves in an absurd location.

17 Exit The Dragon v11 ★ ☐
Sit start far to the left at a left-facing rail and climb rightward joining *Enter the Dragon*. Extricate yourself with much difficulty from the cave through the small hole as for *Honalee* (above).

COW SKULL BOULDER

Walking up or down the base of the canyon between Kung-Fu Grip and the Rio's Crack or Los Locos areas, you come to a boulder hanging suspended above the wash, almost blocking the trail. This is the Cow Skull Boulder.

18 Cow Skull v5 ★ ☐
Since a massive hold came off the underside of this roof, the original version that climbed out the roof is no more. However a variation can be forced where you begin at right and stay under the prow at its end. Start sitting on the boulder in the ground, with your hands at the very deep pocket low on the right side of the upper wall, and climb this vertical side of the roof on edges to deep jugs and out to the big hueco sitting above the nose on the north side.

Just north of Cow Skull are:

19 Unnamed v0 ☐
The short wall next to *Cow Skull* (right as you look up canyon). A couple of moves to a big ledge-hold.

KUNG FU GRIP

20 Unnamed v3 ☐
On the low boulder left of *Cow Skull* as you look up canyon, sit start and climb the slopers and crack.

21 Unknown ☐
On the same boulder, but in a tiny pit over the back, it looks like someone has climbed the ultimate squeeze job.

Above the rock slab (immediately up and left, as you look up canyon form Cow Skull) is:

22 Unnamed v0 ★ ☐
The wall above the block is very nice.

Facing down-canyon toward Cow Skull's topout is:

23 Unknown ☐
I'm sure someone must have climbed this jutting prow from the right side.

On the same boulder, but on the up-canyon side is:

24 Maximum Relaxum v3 ★★ ☐
Sit start at the low block on big holds and climb easily to jugs in the upper boulder. Pull around and launch left to the lip. Top out rightward. Not exactly high, but with pinball potential.

Reaching out on *Maximum Relaxum*, v3 (opposite).

RIO'S CRACK AREA

Named for the three-star classic *Rio's Crack* (v6). Awkward, frustrating, powerful, and technical, it will kick your ass one day, and feel easy the next. Once you've mastered *Rio's Crack*, there are adjacent pocketed and fingery walls to go at, which are different in style, more straight forward pulling; not particularly steep, but with big moves.

RIO'S CRACK LEFT BUTTRESS

1 Ice Cream Against Time v3 ☐
The face just right of the left arete.

2 I Hardly Know Her v1 ☐
Climb the wall past a flake.

3 Strength in Numbness v6 ★ ☐
Begin at the obvious small crimp with the right hand. Move up past a small sharp pinch, and a horrible pocket to grab a good hold at the lip. The arete at right is avoided. Sharp! But if you have steel fingers, you might enjoy it.

4 Strength in Numbness Sit Start v9 ☐
Sit start somewhat awkwardly. Grab a shallow pocket and make a hard pull to gain the small crimp and finish as for the standing start.

RIO'S CRACK WALL

5 Rio's Crack v6 ★★★ ☐
For the full tick, start with both hands (yes both), just up from the base of the rail. Your right hand can be on the slightly better crimp. Follow the line of the crack using all holds available.

6 Chicken Licken v9 ★★ ☐
Start as for *Rio's Crack* (above). Immediately grab a gaston pocket with the left hand in the wall above the rail and make a hard pull right (with the right foot on the base of the rail). Pull through to the top on tiny pockets.

7 Leubering Direct Start v8 ★★ ☐
Short, but good. Start at a small pinch with the right hand, and the left foot stretched out to the rail of *Rio's Crack*. Make a hard pull off the ground to gain a pocket with the left, then pull up the wall via the right sidepull, topping out direct.

8 Leubering With Intent v8 ★★ ☐
An eliminate line, named after the infamous Austrian layabout Chris Leube. Sit start at pockets down and right. Angle up the boulder leftward to top out in the scoop up and left of the prominent sidepull. At the small right-facing sidepull, go straight up to sloping holds above the lip.

9 Leubering Bypass v6 ★ ☐
Moving up right from the sidepull or left-hand "gaston" provides an easier outlet, but avoids the fun topout of the original line.

RIO'S CRACK LEFT BUTTRESS

RIO'S CRACK WALL

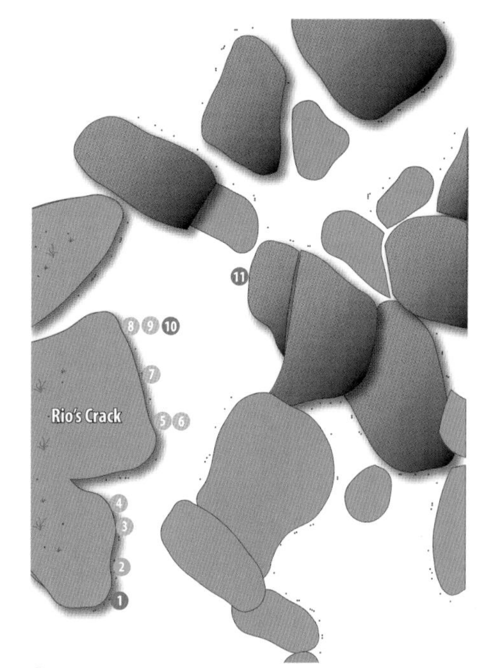

10 Leubering Without v5 ★ ☐
Sit start at the right side of the boulder, but from the pockets, climb direct with a long reach.

On the rock facing the start of Leubering is:

11 Unrio v5 ☐
Sit start down in the pit and climb the short wall on sloping pockets. Unconfirmed rating.

Rio's Crack (v6): impossible one day, easy the next. At least that's what you keep telling yourself as you struggle desperately with the virtually footless opening sequence. Here, Lisa Rands tries a heel-hook. Photo: Wills Young

DEATH STAR CAVE AREA

Now we're talking sad: The Death Star Cave is one of the classic Sads spots, archetype of that pull-your-ass-off-the-ground and slap-a-couple-hard-moves style that was the coolest expression of bouldering in the mid to late 1990s. It demands that special kind of masochistic retrospective climb-anything attitude that the Sads Canyon seems to bring out in people. Yes, you too can be sad and proud. The brilliant *Anti-Hero* (kinda gimme v5) is something of an anomaly here, climbing, in relative terms, like a freaking route up the 45-degree wall.

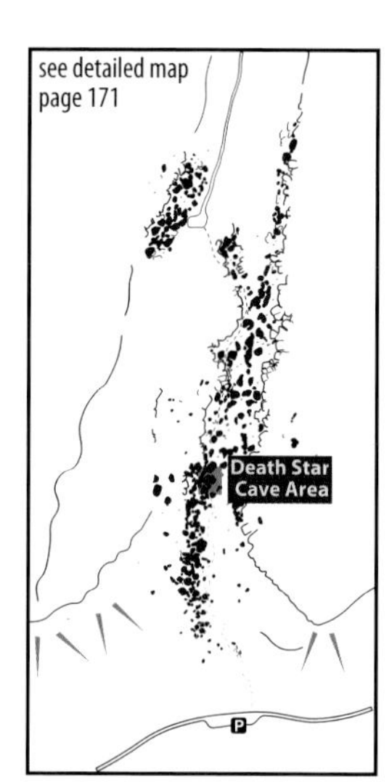

Topo showing Death Star Cave problems: page 187

THE DEATH STAR CAVE

This is a large cave, hidden under a giant capstone boulder, at the east side of the canyon, 50 yards up canyon from the Cow Skull Boulder and across the canyon from the Rio's Crack main area.

1 El Barracho v1 ★ ❑

Sit start and climb the arete on the cave's south end.

2 Anti-Hero v5 ★★★ ❑

Just right of the left arete inside the cave, sit start at the lowest possible holds. No, not those ... the lower ones. The left hand on the left arete, right on a good incut. Climb up via powerful moves between good pockets, flakes and underclings. Easy to work the moves. Pads useful.

3 Evil Eye v5 ❑

On the boulder and to the right of *Anti-Hero*, sit start really low again, this time with one hand in an undercling and one in a pocket. Make a hard move to gain slopers then up more easily.

4 Soma v7 ❑

Squat start with the left hand in a small pocket and the right on a crimp above the hueco to the right. Set a heel-toe lock in the right hueco. Slap around and pull up to better holds above, either left or (better), right to the finish of *Death Star 2000*.

5 Death Star 2000 v8 ★ ❑

Sit start with both hands in the very low shallow huecos. Pull up to sloping crimps and then more sloping crimps. Finally, grab a good hold hidden up and right. A knee bar may help. Brute force may also be useful.

Near the middle of the small boulder on the east side of the cave is:

6 Unnamed v3 ❑

Sit start with two crimps and climb up the short blunt prow opposite *Death Star 2000.*

Just outside the north end of the Death Star Cave is a split boulder that also forms the south end of the Los Locos den:

ANTI-HERO

7 Xingu v6 ★ ❑

Sit start at the undercut nose of the boulder. The right hand is on a shallow pocket, and the left on an undercling. Lock off the pocket and grab a good crimp, then struggle.

Face out from Xingu, and look to the right, here on the northwest side of the Death Star Boulder is:

8 Pitfall v6 ❑

Kinda ridiculous: Sit start deep in the pit on the northwest side of the Death Star Boulder. Both hands begin on tiny crimps (or one hold higher, it doesn't really matter as no-one is looking). Pull up to pockets and then a sloping crimp. Rock up on the left foot to a good crack. Done: Now call your sponsors.

OVERVIEW

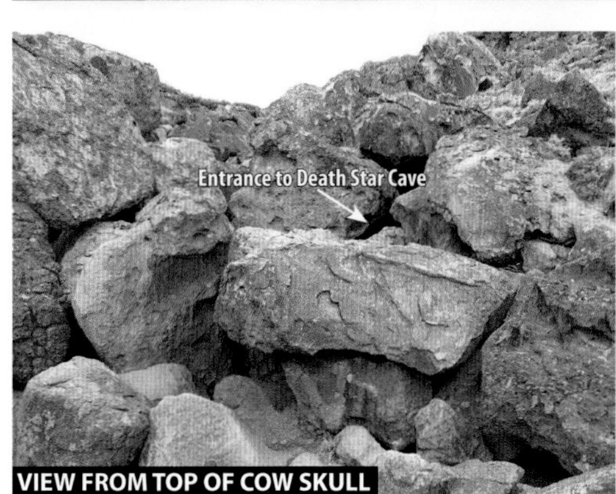

VIEW FROM TOP OF COW SKULL

DEATH STAR

XINGU

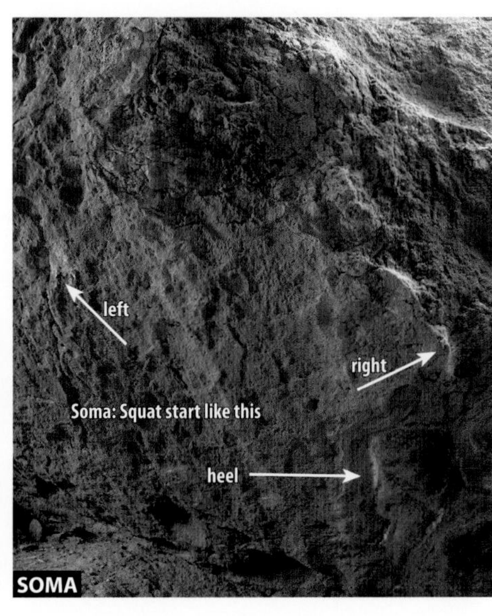

SOMA

LOS LOCOS AREA

In brief, this area comprises a bunch of average problems surrounding two stunning lines, *Lawnmower Man* (v7) and *Los Locos* (v7), both of which are high, hair-raising, and have great moves. Two big lines: take your pick and take pads and spotters too. The excellent *Pocket Traverse* (v3), an outlier line, is also worth the visit.

LAWNMOWER MAN BOULDER

On the west side of the canyon is a prominent tall wall with a radically undercut prow on its left side. This is home to:

1 First the Garden, Next the World v4 ☐

Good first moves, but spoiled by rotten rock up high. From a deep pocket on the left side of the hanging prow swing around with the right hand to opposition holds on the right side. Gain a big sloping jug on the lip of the prow and pull up onto it. Top out with extreme caution.

2 Lawnmower Man v7 ★★★ ☐

Not a gimme, unless you happen to be very tall. Gain the big jug in the middle of the wall by a long move in from the right. Another big and considerably harder move gains a good slot high in the face. With determination, push on for the top. It might help to grow some inches in your arms or legs.

Hidden in a labyrinth just down from the tall wall of Lawnmower Man is:

3 Slick Toe v4 ☐

Start sitting just left of the toe of a slick boulder with a big slopey hold for the right hand. Pull up to crimps and rock up onto the slick toe. You can climb up and out on the same boulder.

LOS LOCOS CAVE

Across the canyon from the proud *Lawnmower Man* is a deep cave formed by a jumble of giant blocks. Climb into it at an entrance between boulders on its west side. The east wall of this cave is the site of one of the Sad Boulders' most amazing problems:

4 Los Locos v7 ★★★ ☐

An intriguing and sustained line seeking its way to daylight from a deep cave. Begin down and right, move up to good holds, then improvise leftward and make some hard locks to gain slopey crimps. Press left and up into the daylight of the upper headwall. The block at left is avoided to the end, and provides excellent incentive not to fall from the final moves. Scary and brilliant.

LAWN EQUIPMENT BOULDER

Just north (up canyon) of the Los Locos Boulder, the wash at the base of the canyon widens and on the west side is a long overhang. At the left end of this overhang is:

5 Vibrating Lawn Equipment v8? ☐

An unpleasant one-move wonder. Considering that the overhang looks like it should offer something special this is disappointing. The name has occasionally been confusingly applied to the fine *Lawnmower Man* on the big boulder around to the left.

COCAINE BOULDER

On the first boulder south of *Molly* (overleaf), and just north of the above problem, are:

6 Lines Of Cocaine v0 ☐

Left side of the south end of the boulder.

7 Brothers and Sisters v0 ☐

Right side of the south end of the boulder.

8 Feel The Vibe v0 ☐

On the up-canyon side, facing toward *Molly*, start down in the hole and climb out.

TRAVERSE BOULDER

Halfway up the slope directly above the Death Star Cave a boulder has a fine traverse on its north side.

9 Pocket Traverse v3 ★★ ☐

From the base of the northwest arete, traverse up and left on pockets with increasing difficulty to the left arete of the boulder. Fun pocket-pulling to rival the Happy Boulders.

EXTRAPOLATOR BOULDER

Further uphill, on the rim, and along toward the mouth of the canyon, are a pair of boulders that conceal east-facing walls. See the photo opposite. Here you will find:

10 The Extrapolator v6 ★ ☐

Start on the good holds low and right: dyno to the sloping lip and top out. Avoid the crack and boulder at right.

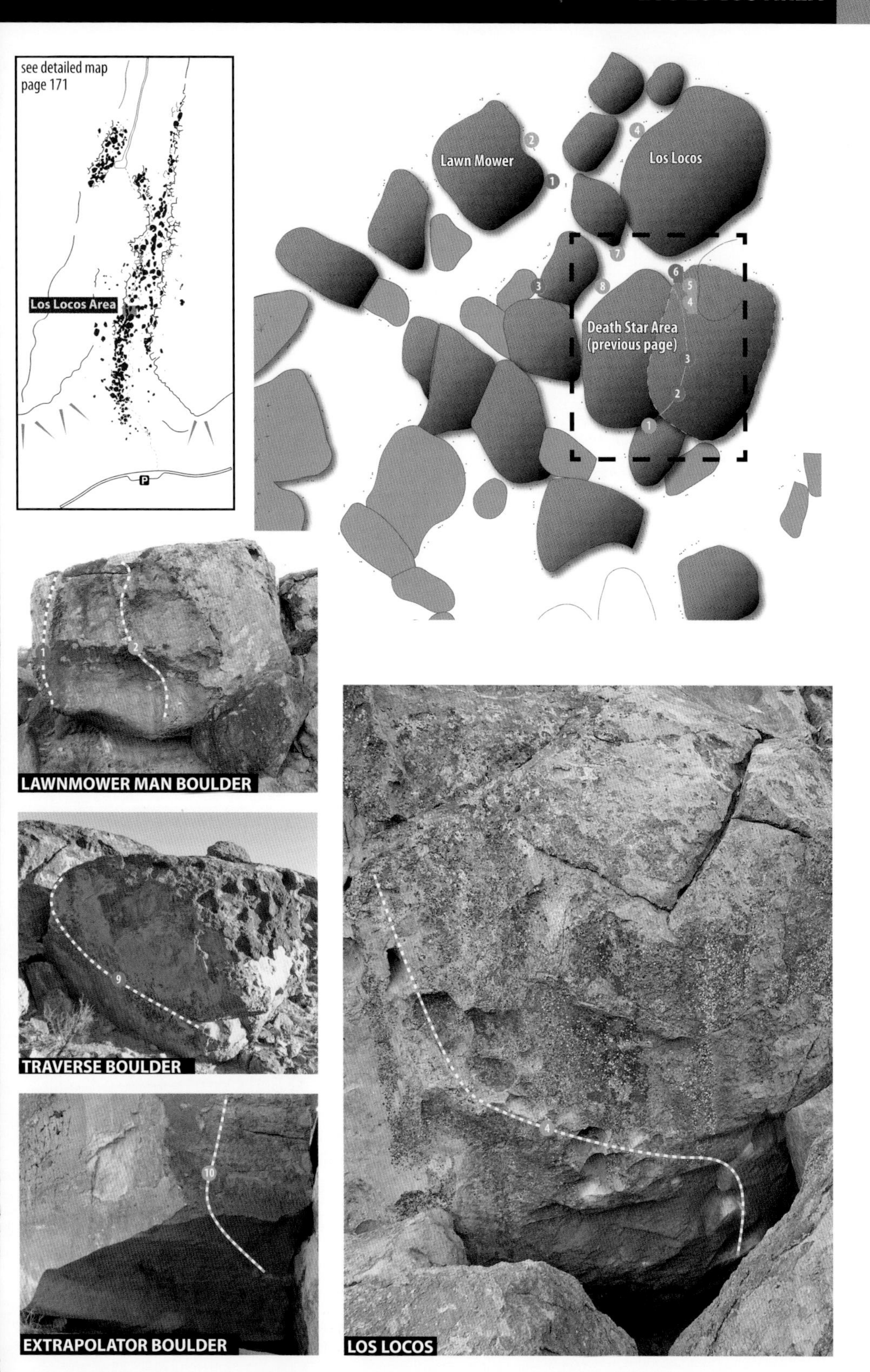
see detailed map page 171
Los Locos Area
P
Lawn Mower
Los Locos
Death Star Area (previous page)
LAWNMOWER MAN BOULDER
TRAVERSE BOULDER
EXTRAPOLATOR BOULDER
LOS LOCOS

CENTRAL JOYLESS/MOLLY AREA

Up-canyon from the Los Locos and Anti-Hero Caves and just down-canyon from the Misery Cave is a relatively open area with a wall of vertical tuff at its west. The Central Joyless—ah, that's a sad sounding name! And misleading, because you'll be glad when you get here. The wider valley catches more sun, and many of the problems have some decent flat ground below them. The Molly Boulder is a splendid boulder with near-perfect rock and a host of great variations to have endless fun on. *Molly* (v5) itself is the must-do line. The rest is gravy.

MOLLY BOULDER

Facing up-canyon is the clean solid wall of the Molly Boulder. From left to right are:

1 The Great Dominions v1 ★ ☐
Sit start at the good low holds, make a hard move to join better holds and follow the ramp diagonally left.

2 Head Heritage v3 ★ ☐
Sit start at the low flake, then climb more-or-less direct using underclings past an ear-like edge to the top. Finding a good sequence is an effort, and the line is not that clear—the further left you move, the easier it becomes.

3 Molly v5 ★★★ ☐
An area classic on perfect rock. Sit start at pockets beside an embedded block. Climb past more pockets and stretch left to a sidepull, moving through to the top with a powerful lock-off or dyno.

4 Molly Left Start v6 ★★ ☐
Sit start at the low good holds on the left side of the boulder. Begin with a traverse right past small pockets, then join *Molly*.

5 Molly Variation v6 ★★ ☐
Avoid all the pockets at right. Stand start, just left of the regular *Molly* start, with the right hand at a small crimpy pinch. Begin with the left hand at (or pull up into) an undercling-sidepull and make a big move to a small edge at the base of the left-facing feature up high. Crimp hard! Pull through for the top.

6 Molly Variation Left Start v7 ★★ ☐
Sit start at the low good holds on the left side of the boulder. Traverse right, then up the *Molly Variation*.

7 Smiths v0+ ★★ ☐
Sit start on the pockets as for *Molly*. Move up and right to the arete, following this up and left to a flying finish. Easier than it looks. Avoid the big foothold out right if you can.

8 Molly Dyno ★ ☐
A superb dyno from the deep pockets of *Molly* and *Smiths* to the big jug at the top of the boulder.

Down at a lower level around to the right, but on the same boulder are:

9 World Shut Your Mouth v2 ☐
Sit-start at an obvious flake and climb directly up.

10 Chewed Out v4 ☐
Sit start on the right side of the boulder. Make a hard move to gain painful holds, then climb the blunt rib, staying right or slightly left, gaining a large slot-undercling with the left hand before topping out.

CHINA DOLL BOULDER

Left of the Molly Boulder is a tall, highly featured wall:

11 China Doll v0 ★★ ☐
The left line of features up the wall. Climbs well.

12 Mothers v0 ★ ☐
The right line is also good.

13 Girl Call v0 ☐
Climb the very right edge by a weird tufa feature, almost squeezed against the Molly Boulder.

14 Sue Me v1 ☐
On the left, down the corridor between the China Doll and the Molly Boulder, is not a bad little arete climbed with opposing good sidepulls.

CENTRAL JOYLESS

On the west side, across from *Molly* are:

15 Have A Cigar v1 ★ ☐
Climb the end of the vertical prow on good pockets.

16 Riding The Gravy Train v1 ☐
From the deep slot/hueco, climb the face.

17 Which One's Pink? v2 ☐
Sit start on sidepulls to the right side of the face.

18 Spacehopper v0 ☐
The slab.

19 Bouncing Babies v0 ☐
Climb the right side of the slab avoiding the cracks.

20 Sleeping Gas v2 ★★ ☐
The left side of the funky shallow groove.

21 Unnamed v4 ☐
The right arete, undercut and hard to start, is climbed with some fear of falling against the rock behind. After getting established, a long reach will prove useful.

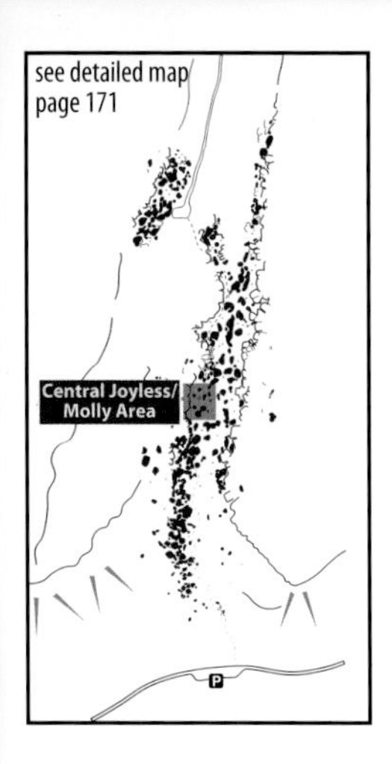

MOLLY BOULDER

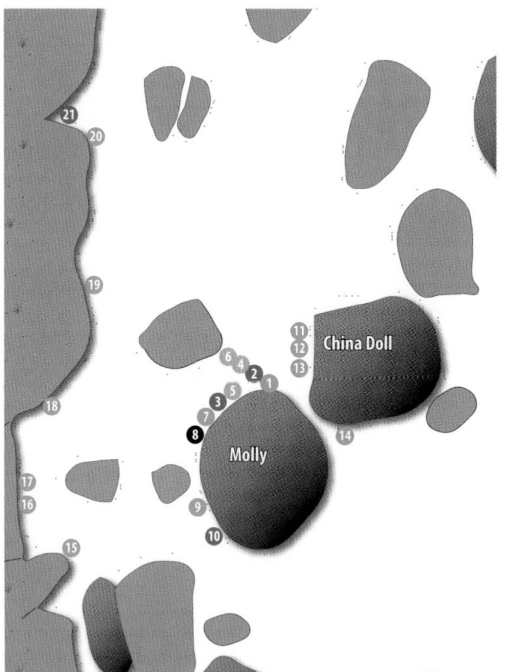

LOWER MOLLY BOULDER

CHINA DOLL BOULDER

CENTRAL JOYLESS

CENTRAL JOYLESS

MISERY AREA

The Misery Area is a jumble of big blocks just south of the Pow Pow Area and just north of the pleasing open expanses of the Central Joyless. As well as some painful dregs, there are some great problems here: *French Press* (v6), *The Black Stuff* (v2, highball); plus up the hillside to the east, the excellent Flake Boulder provides the very pretty side-by-side *The Arete* (v0-) and *The Groove* (v0-) among others. Don't miss the latter boulder.

MISERY CAVE SOUTH ENTRANCE

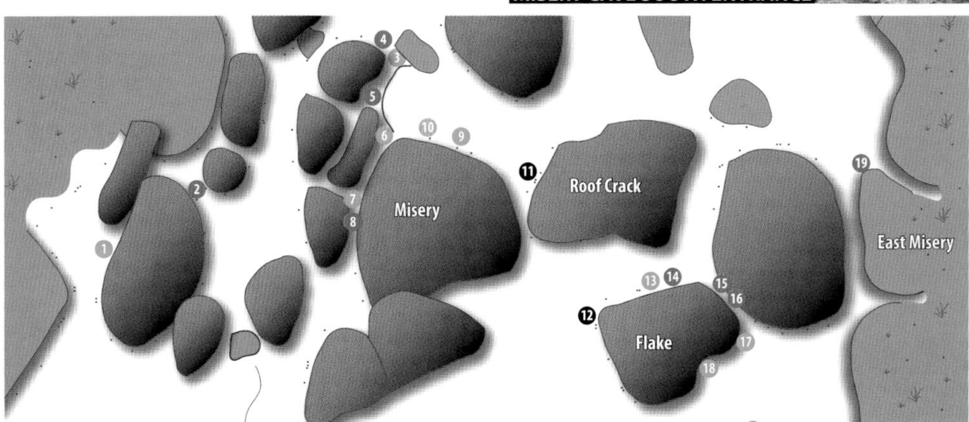

In a jumble of boulders on the west side (left as you look up canyon) opposite the Misery Cave are:

1 Rabies v2 ☐
A hidden roof facing toward the west rim: Sit start at a good hueco and climb up and right, topping out on the right side of the capping stone.

2 Feral Child v3 ☐
A hanging arete just inside a corridor on the right: Sit start and climb the arete past a biggish hold, pulling right to finish. Looks like it should be easier. Maybe it is.

MISERY CAVE NORTH ENTRANCE

3 Any Which Way But Loose v0+ ★ ☐
The hanging prow offers some fun pulling.

4 Oceania v4 ☐
Pull off the ground at the left side of the right boulder using almost no footholds. Grab some painful bumpy crimps and try desperately to reach the top.

MISERY CAVE

5 Hovercraft v3 ☐
An arete faces you as you walk into the north entrance of the Misery Cave. Make a hard move off the ground using sidepulls and bad high feet. The holds feel good, but then it all goes to pieces and the top is kinda junky.

6 French Press v6 ★★★ ☐
A rating of Font 7a+ was originally suggested for this technical slab. With extreme difficulty, or the use of a couple of crash pads, you can pull yourself off the ground. By using some very poor holds, you might even make it to the top.

7 Press That! v7 ★ ☐
Left of *French Press* is a blunt arete. Try to climb it. A small nubbin serves as a foothold. The rock at right is annoying. Good luck.

8 Misery v3 ★ ☐
Climb the flake line through the roof and follow deep jugs to a top-out above the lower boulder. A potentially back-breaking and junky line in a spectacular position.

Leave the Misery cave by its left side, opposite French Press, *or walk over boulders to the left of* Any Which Way But Loose *to find:*

9 The Black Stuff v1 ★★★ ☐
The superb wall, which once grew moss faster than chalk. A tall, exciting climb above a flat-block stage. There are good holds all the way, and the landing is pretty good, so long as you don't fall into that pit at right! Photo: opposite.

10 True Love v7 ★ ☐
Begin down low to the right of *The Black Stuff* with the hands on crimps and the left foot low on a good dish. Climb up past a crimp with a good thumb catch and use some trickery to join *The Black Stuff.*

Julia Krueger fighting for the send on *French Press* (v6), opposite. Photo: Dan Brayack.

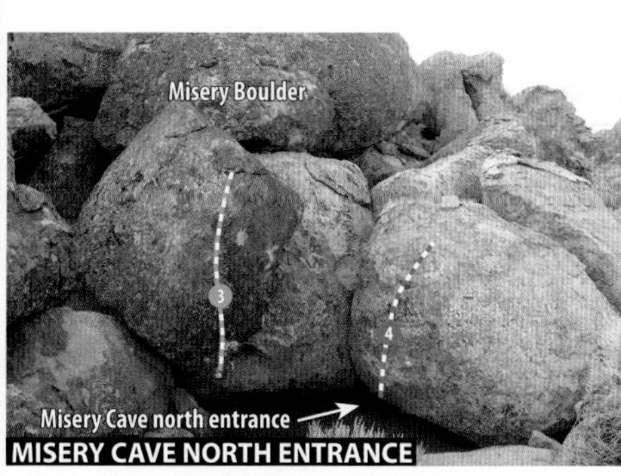

MISERY CAVE NORTH ENTRANCE

FRENCH PRESS MISERY CAVE

⑪ Project ☐
Above the north side of the Misery Cave, left of *The Black Stuff* on a separate boulder facing into the canyon is an unclimbed roof crack.

The Black Stuff (v1) is not so hard if you know where to go. Photo: Wills Young.

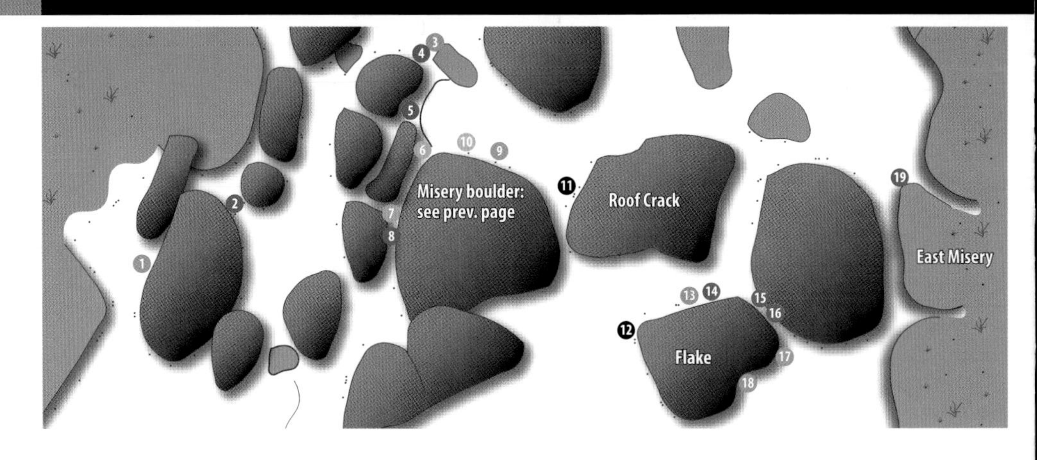

FLAKE BOULDER

Above the Misery Cave and the Unclimbed Roof Crack, near the top of the slope is a large boulder with a fresh-cleaved chalk-colored slab on its uphill side and a dark-brown north-facing side with a large left-facing flake crack.

12 Project/unknown ☐
The overhanging rounded prow facing downhill is just begging to be climbed. It has a very bad landing.

13 The Flake Crack v0 ☐
Climbing the crack is not highly recommended, though alpinists will probably enjoy it.

14 Unnamed v3 ★★ ☐
Gain the northeast arete by a hard pull on sharp underclings. Follow it up right to the apex of the boulder with relatively little incident. The first move seems slightly height-dependent. Add or subtract points as you deem fair! A left start up the arete looks like it might be good too.

15 Unnamed v3 ☐
Start at a deep pocket in the overhang. Pull up and over.

16 Unnamed v4
Start with hands over the lip and mantel.

17 The Arete v0- ★★★ ☐
The excellent arete. The sit start is pretty tricky and technical!

18 The Groove v0- ★★★ ☐
The excellent groove.

EAST ARETE

From the Flake Boulder, walk north (up canyon) past the neighboring boulder (with its pocketed traverse), then up to the rim to find:

19 East Arete v5 ★ ☐
Sit start at the right side of the arete. Gain a good hold on the arete, then move up and right with difficulty. Top out with care.

Reed Harvey is, *Lawnmower Man* (v8), a great highball with a big move to a shallow pocket opposite the Los Locos Cave. Photo: Wills Young.

POW POW AREA

The Pow Pow Area is just down-canyon from Strength in Numbers, and up-canyon from the Misery Cave. This small area is home to one of the Sads' best problems, *Pow Pow* (v8). The innocuous-looking line combines the cool temps and den-like Sad's ambiance with good-length intriguing climbing on immaculate rock. Next to this line are the steep and relatively juggy, *Still Life* (v2), and a few other worthwhile problems, such as the baffling *Water Colors* (v7).

OW OW

POW POW

In an alcove on the west side, just down-canyon from Pow Pow, is a short steep orange wall with a few pockets low and a horizontal break.

1 **Ow Ow** v8 ★ ☐
Sit start with both hands in pockets (now that really would be impressive!). But seriously ... From the pockets, pull up right to a shallow pinch with a good thumb sprag. Up with difficulty past a micro crimp to better holds. Top out slightly left with a big move (or escape right). Short and powerful.

In another alcove, a.k.a. The Meltwater Cave, is the excellent Pow Pow. *Find it by walking up-canyon from the Misery Area until the path rises over bedrock giving a view to the White Mountains and a short juggy roof to the right. Then take a left turn.*

2 **Pow Pow** v8 ★★★ ☐
Awesome! Start at the obvious large holds on the left side of the corridor (or sit below), then cross the roof left to gain miserable holds and make a tricky pull around the lip using whatever form of jessery or sleight-of-hand you can manage: heel hooks, toe hooks, toe drags, cross unders, roll overs, pinches and spraggles ... or just swing and campus it. Only v8 if you find it hard, like me, otherwise it's v7. Be honest!

3 **Still Life** v2 ★★ ☐
Sit/hang start down and left; the block is off. Climb up and right by some stylish moves.

4 **Oil On Canvas** v1 ★ ☐
Sit start at some flakes. Climb the face.

Opposite Pow Pow is a hanging slab, with:

5 **Unnamed** v1 ★ ☐
Start hanging and pull up to gain a sidepull. Then layback and pull over onto the slab.

6 **The Cheese Curd Traverse** v6 ☐
Begin as for the previous line. Grab the high crimp in the small triangular dihedral, throw a heel-hook with your left leg and traverse right precariously, with an awkward couple of moves to start. Finish by pulling around the blunt rib to top out.

WATER COLORS ALCOVE

Just behind and right of *Pow Pow* and up a little is an alcove/corridor with:

7 **Water Colors** v7 ★ ☐
Correct me if I'm wrong, but does this little problem seem desperate, or what? Start with a tiny mono for the right or both hands on the edge just left. Make a hard move to grab small crimps above.

8 **Hands-Free Slab** v0 ★★ ☐
Climb the featured side of the slab without hands, or knees!

9 **Hands-on Slab** vB ☐
Climb the smoother slab to the right with a couple pockets and things.

THE SUN SPOT BOULDER

On the east side across from Pow Pow is a shallow cave facing the afternoon sun:

10 **Sun Spot** v2 ★ ☐
Sit start with the right hand on an undercling, the left on a flat hold or large pocket. The jammed block beneath the boulder is off. Climb directly with some long pulls.

11 **Sun Spot Right** v4 ☐
Sit start as for the previous line. Climb up and across right by a hard move to gain crosley jugs on the lip at right. Continue to the arete and up.

Playing the piano, Jerry Lee Lewis style with fingers and a foot, on *Pow Pow* (v7, or is that v8?). Sticking that next move feels *so* good! Photo: Mick Ryan.

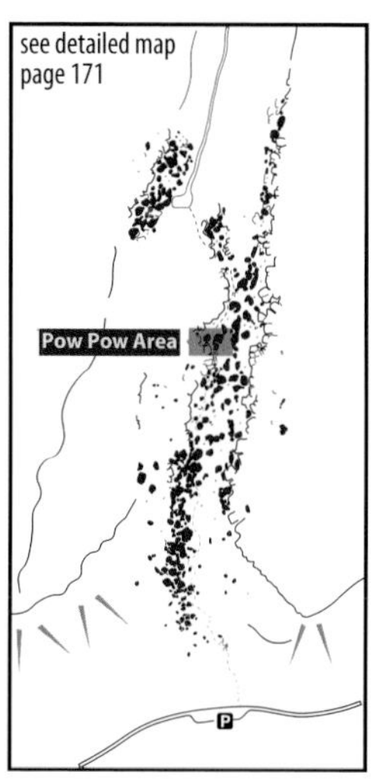

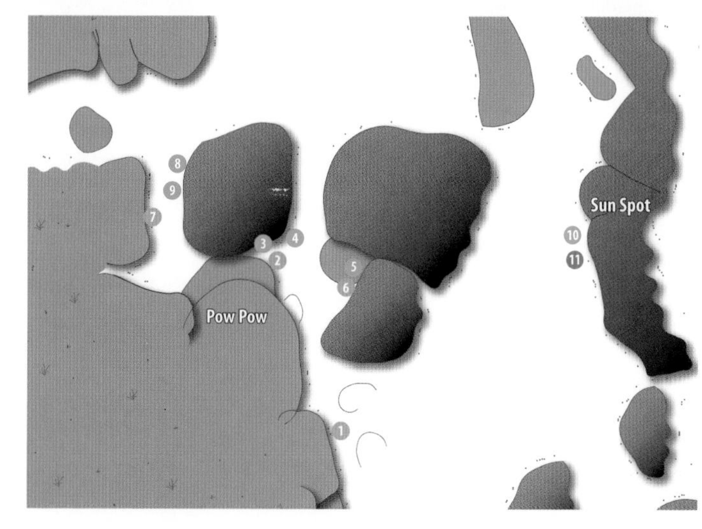

SAD PARROT AREA

This is on the eastern slope of the canyon, just up-canyon from the Pow Pow Area and down-canyon from the Strength in Numbers Boulder. With good landings and a lot of options at the lower grades, there is a bit of every style here, from the steep thuggy roof of the *Bird Cage*, to pockets on the rim, plus crimping testpieces on perfect rock of the excellent Sad Parrot Boulder itself. The slope catches afternoon sun, making it a good area for cold days.

THE BIRD CAGE BOULDER

Between Pow Pow and the Strength in Numbers, and half way up the slope to the west rim of the canyon is a boulder leaning on a lower boulder to create a cave with a fang-like feature at its south end. The next three climbs all begin on the big jug at the back left of the cave. All embedded blocks and rocks below the main wall are off.

1 **Feeding Frenzy** v7 ★ ☐
From the jug at the back left, climb directly out the roof to gain a heel hook on a good jug rail, then pull hard leftward to the lip above the adjacent boulder. Swing around with care to avoid scraping your back, and top out. A pain avoiding the lower rock, but otherwise fun.

2 **The Fang** v4 ★ ☐
From the jug at the back left, climb directly out the roof past the good jug rail to gain the hanging fang at the far end. Swing onto the fang and pull through to the summit.

3 **Toothless** v3 ☐
From the jug at the back left, climb out the roof to the good jug rail, then gain more good holds out right and cross the back wall of the cave to an easy exit.

SAD PARROT MAIN AREA

Up-canyon from the Pow Pow cave and just down-canyon from the Strength In Numbers Boulder, head uphill to the Sad Parrot Area, up on the east rim (right as you look up canyon). This spot is just up and left from the Bird Cage.

PARROT FASHION BOULDER

4 **Parrot Fashion** v0 ☐
Climb the wall, beginning by moving diagonally rightward across the crack.

5 **Arse La Vista** v4 ☐
A traverse from left to right passing through the archway formed between two blocks. You can walk the first part of the way as there is no clear distinction between the boulder and the ground!

6 **Syd Barrett** v4 ☐
Start sitting to the right of the arch and climb left through the arch, then immediately up the wall.

BERTIE BLUNT

Up behind the Parrot Fashion Boulder, on the left is:

7 **Bertie Blunt** v0 ☐
Sit start and move right and up over the prow.

NORWEGIAN BLUE BOULDER

The honeycombed wall to the right has several generic v0 boulder problems and ...

8 **Blue** v2 ★★ ☐
A slightly contrived but fun problem. Start sitting at the leftmost pockets of the honeycombed wall, next to a block in the ground. Pull up into higher pockets, then launch left to slopers. Match, then lock off for the top.

9 **Norwegian** v4 ★ ☐
A challenging traverse, staying low from right to left, choosing the pockets carefully, and finishing with *Blue*.

SAD PARROT BOULDER

10 **Flake** vB ☐
The offset to flake.

11 **Spike** v4 ☐
Stand start with a shallow slot for the right and a crozzly crimp for the left. Pull up and gain the summit by use of a tiny excrescence.

12 **Sad Parrot** v3 ★ ☐
Sit start at some pockets and climb the wall with a very long reach to start, either with the left hand or the right.

13 **Mad Parrot** v0 ☐
Sit start.

14 **Bad Parrot** v0 ★ ☐
Sit start on big flat pockets at the nose of the buttress. Pull hard, then high-step.

15 **Rad Parrot** v7 ★★ ☐
Sit start as for Bad Parrot (above). Traverse the lip right to the right-most crimps on the lip. Make hard moves up right to another line of crimps higher on the slap. Pull over and up.

16 **Bob Parrot** v3 ☐
The slab left of center.

17 **Bob Parrot Sit** v6 ☐
Sit start at crimps on the lip of the undercut slab. Pull up left and rock onto the slab using very small sharp holds. Cold conditions might be useful.

18 **Bob Parrot (Of Maine)** v2 ★★★ ☐
Start standing using the rightmost set of crimps on the slab.

On the boulder abutting the right side of the Sad Parrot slab is:

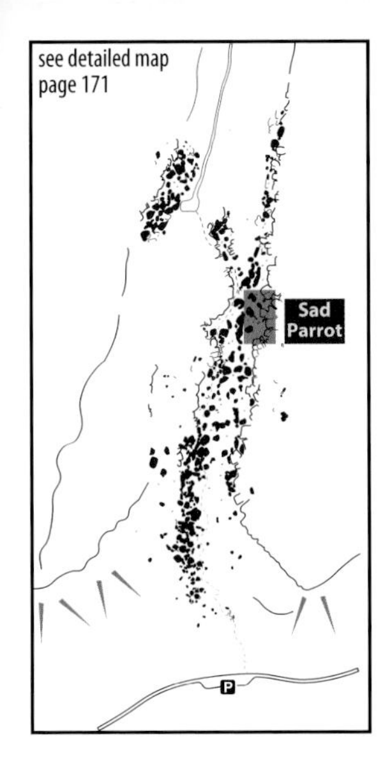

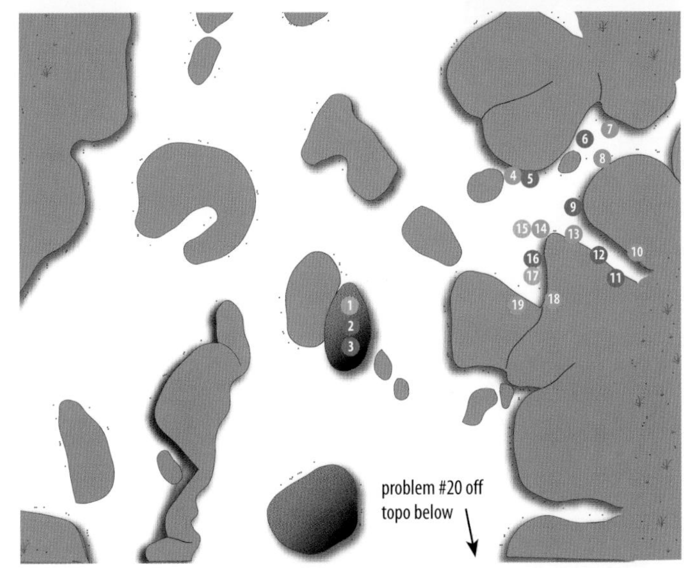

⑲ **Tight Arete** v1 ☐

Sit start the short overhanging arete and try to avoid bumping your back on the rear boulder as you finish.

Fifty yards along the rim toward the canyon mouth is a large squarish block with a blank wall facing north:

⑳ **Unnamed** v0 ★ ☐

The left arete of the square-cut face on good pockets.

STRENGTH IN NUMBERS

Facing up the canyon is the overhanging face of the outstanding Strength in Numbers Boulder with its eponymous three-star problem. It is located just down-canyon from the Ice Caves area, and 100 yards or so up-canyon from the Pow Pow Area. The central feature of this area is the world-class highball *Strength in Numbers* (v5, and no gimme), which is on everyone's tick list for its straight-forward aggressive climbing and gripping finale. The rock on this boulder is generally pretty good and most of the other problems are also worthwhile.

1 Community Spirit v1 ☐
More bold than difficult. Traverse out on good holds, then up.

2 Unnamed v6 ☐
Use a totally unreliable flexi-flake and crank for a half-moon pocket, then join *Community Spirit.*

3 Strength in Numbers v5 ★★★ ☐
The original SIN: A superb problem that has a bit of everything from big hard pulls to technical moves and a nerve-wracking finish. Sit start on the undercuts. Lunge up to the giant mouth, then follow a line of flakes to a very challenging finish. Pad the base well and take a spotter to help avoid the rock below. The standing start at the large hueco is the same grade.

4 SIN Variation v6 ★★★ ☐
Sit start around to the right at pockets. Move up, then traverse left to join *Strength in Numbers* at the large hueco. A fun start that makes the finish even tastier.

5 Come Together v7 ★ ☐
Sit start at underclings as for *Strength in Numbers.* Gain the flakes above the hueco then pull right, using the left hand in a shallow pocket. Throw your foot over to a good hold and grope onto the right wall using crozzly holds and blind faith.

6 Let The Happiness In v4 ★ ☐
Sit start on pockets. Go up, then left along a rail of crimps to the edge of this face. Climb up from here using a pinch to gain a shallow hueco, then up to the large sloping huecos, finishing left to a jug. A little contrived, but good climbing.

7 Chemical Romance v2 ★ ☐
Sit start on pockets as for *Let the Happiness In.* Climb directly up the wall, passing a chossy hole to more delicate and tenuous climbing above.

On an alcove in the west rim, just up canyon from Strength in Numbers is:

8 Unnamed v2 ☐
A short wall with a couple big pulls. A sit start is possible at about v4 with a hard pull off the ground using a pinch-undercling, but it's kinda stupid.

STRENGTH IN NUMBERS

Dan Brayack climbing the ultra-classic *Strength in Numbers* (v5) at the Sads, one of the Tableands' finest problems, first done by Mick Ryan around 1997. Photo: Dan Brayack.

THE ICE CAVES, OUTER AREA

This little area is formed by a collection of generally small boulders with a variety of options with good holds on gentle overhangs, mostly short, sometimes extraordinarily short, and often warm-up style, but with some good rock. *Hot Pants* (v5) is probably the stand-out. An utterly unimpressive wall with some surprisingly good climbing that has become a classic despite itself. Opposite, is the formidable *Chef's Arete*: enough said. However, my favorite piece of rock here is the Hauck a Loogie Boulder with enough variations to keep just about everyone in Sad happiness for an hour or more.

1 The Crack Problem v4 ☐
Sit start at a painful sidepull very low. Climb the crack. Weird undercling moves to a thuggish finish. Better than it looks, other than that first hold.

EMMA'S BOULDER

This forms the side wall on the west (left as you look up-canyon). See topo opposite for location.

2 Emma v2 ★ ☐
For full value, begin this problem at the large hueco around to the left. Move right, then up by a hard lock to a flake.

3 Unnamed v1 ☐
Start as for the above problem and climb up left.

SHORT ARETE BOULDERS

4 The Short Arete v3 ★ ☐
Sit start in a horizontal. Pull around the bulge and up.

5 The Overhanging Nose v0+ ☐
Start low on horizontals and climb the nose on huecos.

There is also a fun v2 squeezed in the cave behind *Short Arete,* from a shelf up and right into daylight.

HAUCK A LOOGIE BOULDER

6 Low-Angle Arete vB ☐
The low-angle arete.

7 Gotta Be Kidding Me! v5 ☐
Only if you're really desperate ... Sit start at the right side of the small wall and climb it via some tiny and painful holds.

8 Sir Isaac Hayes v1 ☐
Sit start and climb the left side of the face. The standing start is v0.

9 Hauck a Loogie v2 ★ ☐
Start standing below and just left of the flake. The left hand is in a narrow horizontal slot, and the right in a choice of small pockets. Reach up with the left,

10 Hauck a Loogie v3 ★ ☐
Same problem, different problem. Start standing immediately beneath the flake with the right hand in a distinct smooth pocket and the left in a choice of many pockets. Climb to the flake directly.

11 Hauck a Loogie Sit start v5 ★★ ☐
A sit start to the second variation. Begin at the pockets. Make a big pull up right. Use body tension to reach the flake.

12 Hauck a Loogie Eliminate v7 ★★ ☐
A right-trending eliminate: Climb the sit start from the pockets to more spraggled pockets and dreadful crimps. Don't touch the flake (or holds left of it), but reach out right to a good pocket and finally edges up high.

13 Slice and Dice ☐
The wall immediately right of Hauck A Loogie. Reportedly something was climbed here, and supposedly a sit-start. But it looks near impossible. Perhaps something broke, or this was some kind of strange joke.

On the rock at right of the Hauck A Loogie Wall is:

14 Unnamed v1 ☐
Sit start on the flat edge and climb up using any combination of holds that suits your fancy.

On the boulder on the other side of the path to Hauck A Loogie is:

15 Funkadelia Bdelia v0 ★ ☐
Short warm-up.

16 Parliament v0 ★ ☐
Another short warm-up. Climb the tiny arete from a sitting start. Good variation: traverse left, then up!

THE HOT PANTS BOULDER

17 Hot Pants v5 ★★ ☐
Somehow this is attaining classic status! Sit start at the horizontal ledge/crack. A painful finger-jam may be helpful to get started. Grab a buttery sloper and use strength, dynamics, or trickery to gain better holds to the right, then up. Or consider trying this on a cooler day.

18 Up For The Down Stroke v4 ☐
Start standing with a bad pinch for the right hand at about six feet; the left on a sidepull down left. Make one hard move to gain better holds, match, then pull big to the top.

19 Unnamed v1 ☐
Climb the very short wall on decent holds.
On the way up to the East Rim and the Prozac Nation from the Hot Pants Boulder, at left is:

20 Flush vB ☐
Stem the scoop. No cheating.

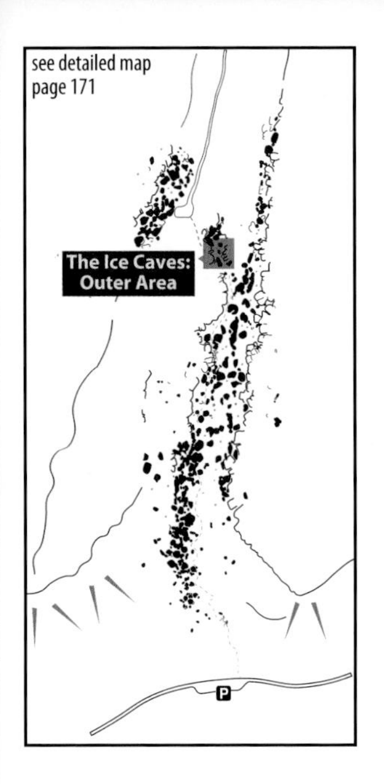

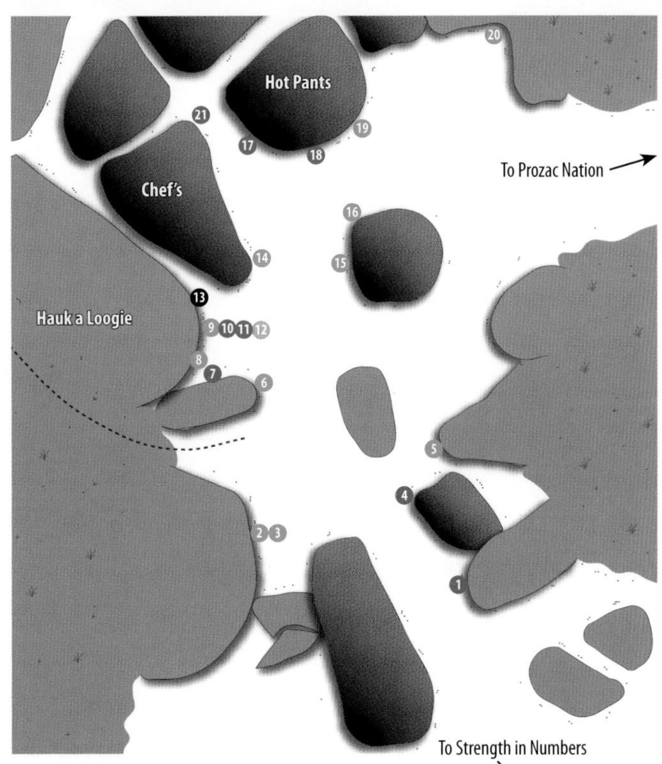

SHORT ARETE BOULDERS

HAUCK A LOOGIE BOULDER

Facing Hot Pants and forming the entrance to the Ice Caves is:

21 Chef's Arete v5 ★ ☐

Originally considered v8 and once a scene of much thrashing and screaming from climbers bent upon ticking a massive new line. This is not nearly the problem it was intended to be. Sit start with the left hand on the lowest sidepull, or on the upper one if you want to make it easier. Sneaky beta will reduce this to a two-move v3. But you can still take the v8 tick if you think you deserve it.

ENTRANCE AND HOT PANTS

THE ICE CAVES, THE CAVES

To me, this is the quintessential Sads. Good rock, cool temps from the narrow caves and passageways, and hard, powerful climbing. After a few visits you find yourself adjusting to this area, steadily gaining an appreciation, a yearning even, for those dim recesses that revive your human desire for the security of rock surroundings. You wrestle with a set of obstinate crimps, slopers and pinches on good hard stone. You smell the dirt in the earth-cooled air, and rub the chalk on your hands as you sit on a pad, squeezed in a gap between boulders. Next thing you know, you just can't get enough of it. You want to climb here all the time. You want to spend the rest of your life here. You are sad, sad, sad ... especially when you've done everything, and are forced to move on! Could it happen to you? It could, it most definitely could.

EROTIC TERRORIST/RORSCHACH TEST

MACKEY CAVE

This cave is formed by the northwest wall of the canyon and the back of the Chef's/Mackey Boulder. To enter, step over the three-feet high boulder blocking the Ice Cave entrance and turn left. Or, walk over the slab to the right of *Hauck a Loogie*.

1 Cream Horn v3 ★ ☐
The wide crack splitting the back of the overhanging wall is fun. Laybacking is a good option and getting past the lip of the neighboring boulder without touching it is the crux.

2 Layback Crack v0 ★ ☐
In the corner is a fine fingertip layback crack.

3 Mecha-Streisand v8 ★ ☐
On the northwest arete of the Chef's/Mackey Boulder. Start with the left hand on a tiny seam/crimp, and the right on the lip one foot right of the arete. Make a powerful pull then an awkward mantel.

4 Mr. Mackey v7 ★★ ☐
Incorrectly called *The Ninth Wave* in the previous guide. Start below the lip with both hands in an undercling/sidepull. Make a hard stab to grab the lip (can be very hard for the short!). Move left a little along the lip and top out, or pull straight over. Moving further left makes this harder.

5 The Ninth Wave v8 ★★ ☐
Sit start with both hands in a smooth flattish hold in an obvious depression at the edge of the boulder; move left along the lip and top out as for the next line—you can top out at almost any point, so take whatever grade you feel you deserve… !

6 Project ☐
Continue *The Ninth Wave* further left to *Mecha-Streisand.*

ICE CAVE ENTRANCE

Approaching from down-canyon, walk into the steadilly constricting slot that is blocked by a three-feet high boulder. This channel and the opening just beyond the boulder is the Ice Cave entrance.

7 Loaded v1 ★★ ☐
The scoopish line at the entrance on the right wall next to the embedded rock. A fine climb.

8 Shaft v5 ★ ☐
Just to the right of the block, sit start with right hand on a funky scoop pinch/undercling and the left matched or in a poor undercling at left. Make hard moves to gain a deep pocket then a long reach to the finishing slab. Beware the rock below!

9 Erotic Terrorist v6 ★★ ☐
Start at the back of the roof and, using all kinds of trickery, climb the roof out and right, staying clear of the wall on the left. Take care on the exit.

10 Rorschach Test v11 ★★★ ☐
Sit start with the right hand on a crimp beneath an overlap and left on the crimp just above. Begin with a big move right. Continue traversing right powerfully to a tricky move to gain the right edge of the boulder. Pull around onto the slab. Crimpy!

11 Project ☐
Start as for *Rorschach Test*, but climb up and left through the scoop.

12 Shizaam v5 ★★ ☐
Stand start the blunt arete with right hand on the knob at about seven feet. A couple of difficult moves are followed by a relatively easy exit (that needs care up high).

13 Shizaam Sit v11 ★★★ ☐
The full sit-start: Begin with the left hand low on a crimp about three feet off the dirt, and the right in a sidepull with a tiny pinkie pocket around to the right. A left heel-hook next to the left hand may prove useful to get started. Either vicious moves via

poor intermediates, or (perhaps easier) a wild dyno, will gain the holds of the standing start on which this finishes. Intermediate versions have been rated, each a move higher, at v9 and v7.

⑭ Undercling Problem v3 ★ ☐
Stand start on an undercling and climb up and left into the top of *Shizaam*.

⑮ Fueled by Hate v5 ★★ ☐
Start standing with left hand on a sidepull on the arete and right hand on a tiny crimp. Make a hard long deadpoint (or use other means necessary) to gain large pockets up and right, pull over onto the slab groping blindly for the good finishing holds.

⑯ It's All About Love v8 ★★★ ☐
A sit start to *Fueled By Hate*, with the right hand on the offset seam and the left on a tiny crimp. Begin with a big move up to a crimp/pinch using some annoyingly bad footholds.

⑰ Frostbite v8 ★ ☐
Sit start as for *It's All About Love* (or slightly left, if you prefer). Move up and gain the arching crack, moving left along this to where the arch stops and there is a good edge. Go straight up with a delicate move past a couple of small crimps. Watch your head and back at the exit! A more direct finish has also been done at about the same grade.

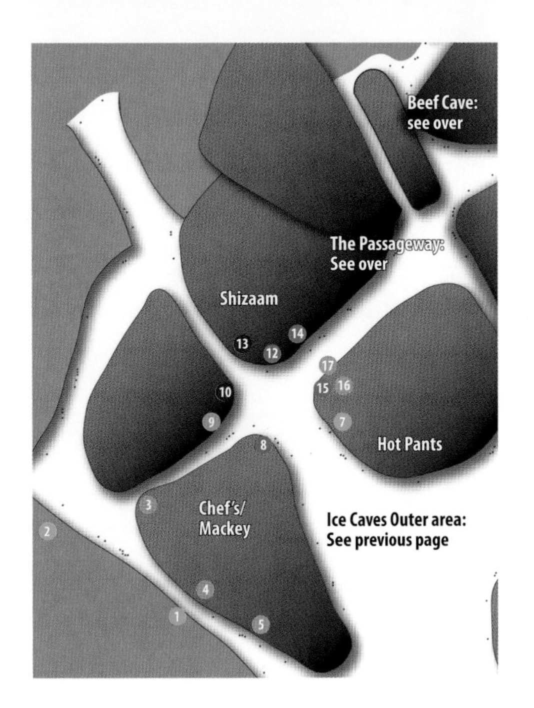

SHIZAAM

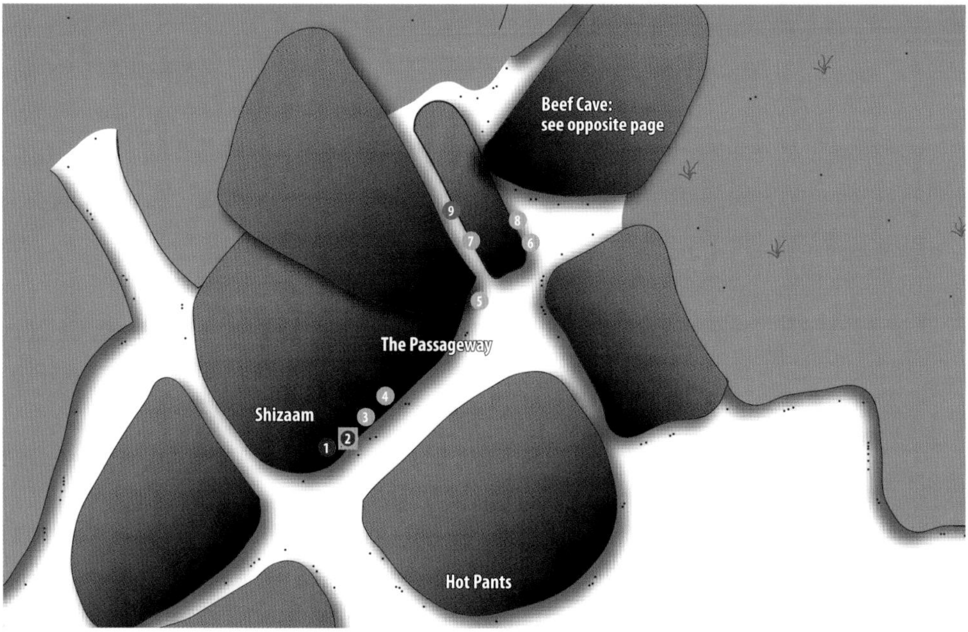

Beef Cave:
see opposite page
The Passageway
Shizaam
Hot Pants

THE PASSAGEWAY

Turn right on entering the Ice Caves to enter this passageway leading to the back of the caves. On the left wall of this passageway are:

1 Bubba Escapes the Ward v10 ★★ ☐

Sit start with left hand on very low sidepull; right hand on small but positive slanted crimp. Move left hand to pocket, set a left heel, and then bust a big move up into the undercling to join the *Undercling Problem*. The same line missing the first move is about v9.

2 Water Hazard v10 ★★ ☐

Sit start as for *Bubba Escapes the Ward* (starts with left on low sidepull): Move up and right using some trickery and a long move to gain a good crimp at the lip of a small overlap. Match and reach up again to a good jug in the break. Top out.

3 Water Hazard Right Start v9 ★ ☐

Sit start with the left hand on the right hand of *Water Hazard's* original start. Climb straight up.

4 Byrolian Traverse v6 ☐

A way to use some rock that would otherwise not be climbed! Begin at obvious crimps high on the left side of the corridor. Traverse left, staying below the big break above. Climb down using a small undercling to gain the big undercling of the *Undercling Problem*; finish as for this.

5 Darkness at Noon v8 ☐

Start sitting with the left hand on a micro crimp *below the sidepull/undercling*, and right on a crimp sidepull. Begin with a slap to a bad sloper with the right, then move the left hand into the good sidepull. Continue up and over. Spoiled by lack of space.

At Darkness at Noon, *the passageway makes a jog left, and then right, and there is a boulder suspended over the passageway. This provides:*

6 The Mothership Has Left v7 ★ ☐

Start standing at the left side of the face. Make a scary and powerful move up and left to a pocket. Pull through to the top. There is a rock at your back that you may need to pad.

7 Mothership Has Left Sit Start v8 ★ ☐

Start sitting below the big flake of the *Mothership Connection* start (flake is off), begin with a hard move up left, and then pull around the roof to join the standing start.

8 The Mothership Connected v6 ★ ☐

Begin at holds about four feet right of the left edge of the suspended boulder. Pull on and climb right by a couple of hard moves to join the top of the *Mothership Connection.*

9 The Mothership Connection v4 ★★ ☐

Start at a huge hold on a block at head height. Climb via a horizontal crack to gain and climb the front face of the hanging boulder.

THE ICE CAVE/BEEF CAVE

Further into the depths of the Ice Caves, enter a chamber with a roof formed by a huge block. The following four problems provide various solutions to climbing this ceiling.

1 Beefcake v10 ★★★ ☐

Start on the undercling, feet on the back wall and follow the pair of rails straight out the overhang and left using left foot toe-hook trickery. Continue left along the rail and, using a pocket in the upper wall if necessary, pull around left into the daylight, finishing up the pocketed wall.

2 Beautiful Gecko v12 ★★ ☐

Start on the undercling with feet on the back wall just right of Beefcake. Start by pulling around to grab an independent line of crimps above *Beefcake*. Follow these left to finish as for *Beefcake*. After holds broke (repeatedly), this may just be worth v12.

3 Beefy Gecko v11 ★★ ☐

Start as for *Beefcake*; climb the start to gain the slot crimps and then move right across the roof (avoiding touching the neighboring boulder) to finish at the jug on the far right, as for *Windchill*.

4 Windchill v9 ★ ☐

Start as for *Beautiful Gecko* but instead of moving left along the rail, pull directly up the overhang, then right. Finish with both hands on the jug at the right corner. Drop off.

5 Feel Like A Barnacle v7 ☐

Start by pulling on as for *Beautiful Gecko*, from underclings, using the rock at the back of the cave for feet. Move right, continuing to use that same rock for feet until you can gain the jug at the lip of the prow. Done.

6 Wheel of Beef v11 ★ ☐

Climb Feel Like a Barnacle, then head left across the roof (avoiding touching the neighboring boulder) and top out as for *Beefcake*!

7 Aquatic Hitchhiker v10 ★ ☐

Begin with the left hand on a good crimp on the left side of the hanging prow and the right hand on a funky pinch on the right side. Pull on and set feet (you do not use the back wall on this line!); make a couple moves out the prow to gain the jug at the lip. Drop off, or …

8 The Aquarium v12 ★★ ☐

As for *Aquatic Hitchhiker*, but from the jug finish, shake out and head left, as for *Wheel of Beef* (above), through the cave to finish on Beefcake, or …

9 Light at the End of the Tunnel v8 ☐

From the hanging jug at the end of *Windchill* and *Aquatic Hitchhiker*, climb up the face, close to the boulder at right, to a sketchy lunge at the top. A lot of pads are needed to protect a terrible landing.

10 Project

Link *Aquatic Hitchhiker* into *Light at the End of the Tunnel.*

11 Project

Low start to *Aquatic Hitchhiker* or *The Aquarium.*

Jake List crosses the roof on *Beefy Gecko* (v11).
The Beef Cave, site of many a late night sausage party and stuffed with double-digit problems, is the place to be for some powerfull pulling. It is equally suited as an escape from summer heat or winter snow.
See page 205. Photo: Dan Brayack.

PROZAC NATION BLUFFS

The bluff at the Sad Boulders' north-eastern limits provides plenty of enjoyable bouldering in a spectacular open setting. Never mind the caves, the cramped passageways, the grovelling speleological oddities that will make you Sad mad. This area is the antidote to all that darkness and doom: Prozac provides the glowing eternal sunshine for the cordless mind. You will have wide vistas and warm rays here. There are some tall airy lines up to about v5, sometimes requiring a bit of care and good padding. There are a couple of harder testpieces too, and some short powerful moderates to work out on. The Crystal Boulder tops my list here with four lines, from v2-v4, all worth doing.

CRYSTAL BOULDER

The furthest left boulder covered by this guide is a tall, clean piece of rock with some great problems.

1 Diamond v2 ★★ ☐
Start at the left edge of the buttress. Climb up and right to a large flake, then up the wall on pockets. Alternatively, start below and right of the flake.

2 Crystal v3 ★ ☐
Sit start at the big sidepull. Climb straight up the wall on good holds. Excellent.

3 Unsung Gem v4 ★ ☐
Sit start on the jug and climb over the small roof to a hard pull to pass the headwall. Tough up high. Fortunately the landing is flat, and hopefully padded.

4 Local Boy Does Good v4 ★ ☐
Sit start as for *Unsung Gem* but go diagonally right and make a huge move to pass a blank section. With serious determination, make some frightening pulls to gain the top.

JERRY FALWELL BOULDER

5 The Hysterical Bear Incident vB ☐
The slab around on the left.

6 Porn Again Christian v2 ★ ☐
The series of huecos to a tricky finish.

7 Jerry Falwell, Porn Star v1 ☐
The lichenous wall.

PROZAC NATION BOULDERS

8 Flawless v7 ★ ☐
Around on the left side of the boulder in an alcove is an overhanging groove-to-arete. Sit start at the jug at the base of the groove. Make some hard moves to gain the deep pocket high on the arete, then, climb more easily up and right to the top.

9 Prozac Nation v2 ★★ ☐
Start by climbing a short wall to gain a large flake at the lip of a roof. From the flake make a big move up left to the vertical handle-bar hold, then up right to flakes and the top. Can be climbed from the back of the roof at about a grade harder.

10 Pencil Dick v5 ★ ☐
Sit start at the left side of the short wall. Climb via a hard pull to an easier finish leftward to the flake. The stand-start is about v3.

11 Unnamed v4 ☐
Sit start to the right of *Pencil Dick*, with the left hand on the first good right foothold of that problem. Climb up using sharp pockets to a long move to the top.

12 Pocket Pussy v1 ☐
The right blunt arete of the wall.

SNAPPER BOULDERS

This line of cliff/boulders has a prominent high buttress at its left.

13 Garden Pest v0+ ★★ ☐
The smooth slab is punctuated by small slots.

14 The Crack v0 ★ ☐
Sit start at the base of the crack and make a hard pull into it. Top out more easily.

15 The Snapper v5 ★★ ☐
The tall wall. Low down the rock is friable, but it improves above. Start with a good right pocket. Pull into the sidepulls and move up right into underclings. Gain a spike up right, then pull through to a hidden hold and the top.

16 Fire Pit v2 ★★★ ☐
The right arete of the buttress is climbed by some committing moves to good holds.

17 Crack and Wall v0 ☐
The crack and wall.

18 Laughing Cow v1 ★ ☐
Around to the right of the Snapper Boulder in a little bay is a cylindrical feature. Sit start on edges and climb up the tube (or start standing).

19 What Mick Missed v0 ☐
Climb the striking fin of rock a few yards right of *Laughing Cow.*

CRYSTAL BOULDER

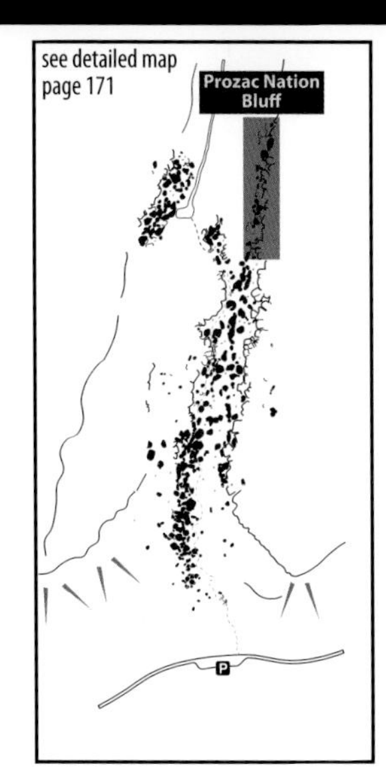

JERRY FALWELL BOULDER

OVERVIEW PROZAC NATION

SNAPPER BOULDERS

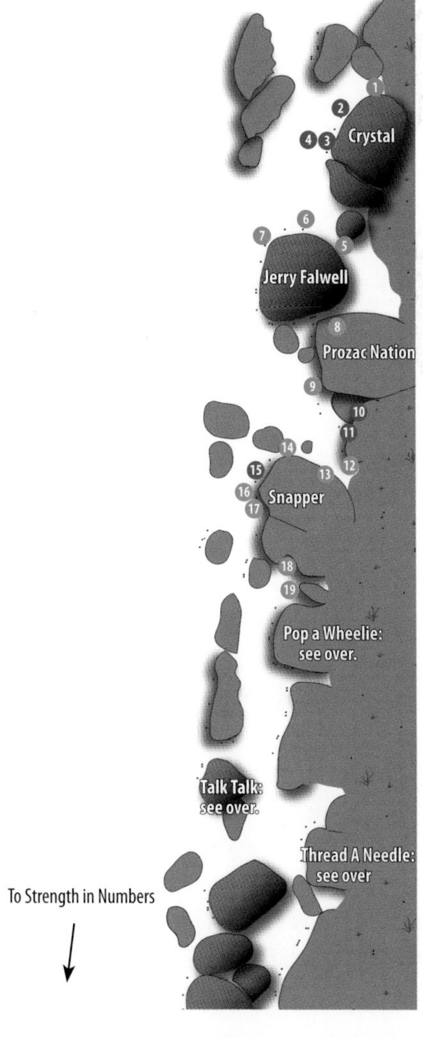

TALK TALK , VALIUM, AND BOMBER BOULDER

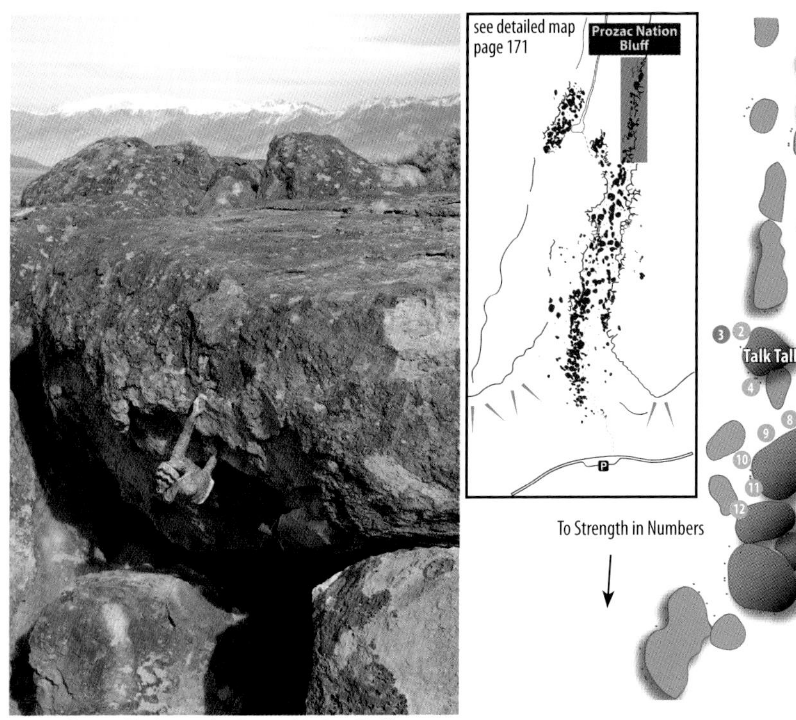

Jen on *Prozac Nation* at the Prozac Nation Bluffs.
Photo: Wills Young

POP -A-WHEELIE BOULDER

POP-A-WHEELIE BOULDER

This boulder is along the rim immediately to the right of the Snapper Boulder

1 Pop-A-Wheelie v4 ★ ☐

Contrived. Start at the left edge of the roof at a big hueco. Climb rightward to the arete, then make a hard move up and left to the good finishing holds.

TALK TALK BOULDER

This boulder is down below the rim and is near the right end of the boulders listed here.

2 No Talk v1 ☐

Sit start at the good flake and pocket. Make a couple of hard pulls directly up the left side of the boulder.

Kevin Daniels pushing past the fear on the Tim Steele classic *Professional Widow* (v4, highball). See page 212. Photo: Wills Young

3 **Talk Talk** v4 ☐
Sit start at a good flake and pocket at the left side of the boulder and climb right via a hard undercling move, then up the rounded arete at right.

4 **Shit-Talk** v2 ☐
The right arete from a sitting start, the right hand with a sidepull, the left a pocket.

VALIUM BOULDER

This boulder forms part of the rim above the Talk Talk Boulder.

5 **Unnamed** v1 ☐
The left edge of the face.

6 **Valium** v2 ★★ ☐
Climb the wall using a left-facing flake. Avoid the large sidepulls at left.

7 **Thread the Needle** v2 ★★ ☐
The right side of the wall.

BOMBER BOULDERS

Boulders below and right of the Valium Boulder and right of Talk Talk.

8 **Bishop Bomber/Pound Sign** v0 ☐
The left side of the face provides several options, all the same difficulty.

9 **Caveat Emptor** v0 ☐
Nearer the center, climb the wall passing pockets to a big undercling near the top, or move left avoiding the undercling.

10 **Shop Till You Drop** v1 ☐
The right side of the face, staying off the loose-looking flakes at right.

11 **Teen Angst** v0 ☐
For the record: the chossy wall right of the arete.

12 **Lonely Teenage Bedroom** v0 ☐
Up the wall right of the crack to an undercut hueco and the slab above.

KINDERGARTEN AREA

This is the group of boulders above and west of the turn-around at the end of the dirt road that arrives at the Sad Boulders from the north. There are a lot of big blocks here, as well as cliff-line stretching both north and south. Potentially a huge area, not everything known to have been done is recorded here. There are some great little climbs to reward the curious, including the intriguing *Slunk* (sit start, v9), which is a broken version of a previously far easier line. The trio of hard low-ballish problems on the *Mr Frosty* rock (v6-v8) are all good, and *Whiskey, Beer, and Spliff Hits For Breakfast* is a classic.

PARKING BOULDER

This stand-alone boulder is to the right of a pull out at the end of the dirt road. It has two problems up a short wall:

❶ **Unnamed** v1 ☐
The short wall at the left side.

❷ **Unnamed** v1 ☐
The short wall ...

There is a giant slab facing the pullout that blocks access to the boulderfield above. Up and left of this great slab of rock is another one, very similar though slightly more bulging on the downhill side. Behind this second large rock is a small alcove with a block sitting over it at left. Here you will find:

❸ **Mr Frosty** v8 ★★ ☐
Sit start at pockets at the base of the blunt arete. Climb via a big move left under the block above, then continue left and up the scoop. Cool moves.

❹ **Unnamed** v7 ★ ☐
Sit start down and right on pockets. Make a big move over the bulge with your right hand to a big flat pocket. Climb up the rib from here with difficulty.

❺ **Unnamed Variation** v6 ★ ☐
Sit start as above on pockets. Make a big move, but this time with the left hand. Then press across into the groove and up. Weird.

The boulder just south of the Mr Frosty Cave has:

❻ **Unnamed** v3 ☐
The painfully well-featured wall that faces downhill.

The boulder left of this has some v0 climbs also facing downhill.

SLUNK BOULDER

This unique boulder is just below the top of the bluff, up and slightly left from the Mr Frosty Cave. You can't fail to recognize the smooth curl of rock when you see it.

❼ **Slunk** v9 ★★ ☐
Sit start and climb the arete with difficulty and without escaping onto the slab at left. Very awkward since a crucial hold broke off the original line.

❽ **White Men Can't Jump** v-ouch! ☐
Leap from the low cliff line across from the Slunk boulder to grab the top of the Slunk Boulder.

❾ **Unnamed** v1 ☐
Climb the south-facing wall of the boulder.

BEANO BOULDER

❿ **Unnamed** v2 ☐
The wall on the uphill side of the boulder.

⓫ **Beyond Beano** v1 ☐
The right arete of the uphill side of the boulder.

⓬ **Unnamed** v0 ☐
The downhill face of the boulder.

PSYCHO BILLY BOULDER

This is just below the cliff line and directly up and right of the parking spot (and 30 yards right of the Mr Frosty cave, as you look uphill).

⓭ **Psycho Billy Cadillac** v2 ☐
Sit start and climb the southern end of the boulder.

RIM JOB BOULDER

Found just in from the rim, further right again, about 50 yards or so north along the cliff from the Slunk Boulder, or 30 yards along from the parking spot.

⓮ **Whiskey, Beer, and Splif Hits For Breakfast** v4 ★★★ ☐
Start low and climb the wall with a hard move to start, keeping a cool head at the top, and avoiding the left arete. Nice positive edges and biggish moves on a neat piece of rock. Climbing the left arete is a grade easier.

⓯ **Give Me a Rim Job** v6 ★★ ☐
Start low again, and climb up and right with a hard move to catch the top of the right arete. Expect a bit of a heart-flutter on this one.

Lastly ... and not to be missed is:

TIM'S HIGHBALL BOULDER

One-hundred yards along the cliff line to the south of the main Kindergarten Area (left as you face the cliff). Follow the faint (closed) jeep track south until you see it.

⓰ **Professional Widow** v4 ★★★ ☐
Climb the super-high, but solid and good-quality face to a big jug at two-thirds height. Then back off, or go for broke.

15
14
2
1
13
10
11
4
5
3
7
8
12
9
6
please park on Chalk Bluff Road
Strictly NO CAMPING/FIRES
16 to Professional Widow (see photo 211)

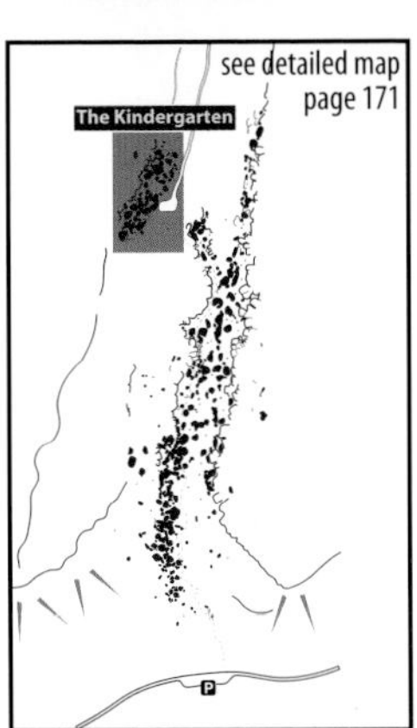
see detailed map page 171
The Kindergarten
P

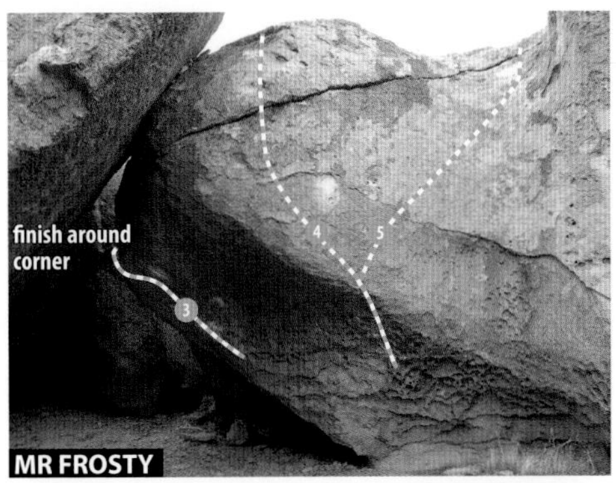
finish around corner
3
4
5
MR FROSTY

14
15
RIM JOB BOULDER

7
SLUNK BOULDER

16
TIM'S HIGHBALL BOULDER

Buttermilk Country

CHAPTER 3

Buttermilk Country: cool air, blue sky, and boulders. Photo: Wills Young.

BUTTERMILK COUNTRY

A view over Buttermilk Country at dawn. Photo: Wills Young.

The Buttermilk Country is a region about ten miles west of Bishop comprising rocky knolls, rocky ridges and a few large craggy peaks rising to about 8000 feet. Effectively this region is a range of foothills to the massive eastern scarp of the Sierra Nevada (see Geology page 20). The hills are interspersed with gravely flats and meadows watered by snowmelt, direct precipitation (including frequent summer thundershowers), and the occasional stream. The higher elevations of the Buttermilk Country provide suitable conditions for Jeffrey pines (primarily near McGee Creek), and wide swaths of sagebrush. Up behind Grouse Mountain are grasslands where, in summer months, cattle graze and where once the buttermilk of Buttermilk Country fame originated. At lower elevations, the sages disperse and occasional pinion pines are more thinly scattered or disappear altogether and the predominance is for gravel slopes with sparse vegetation leading between the quartz monzonite boulders and cliffs that are the attraction of hikers, climbers and all those who love a good scramble on the rocks.

The bouldering around the Buttermilk Country involves technical and precise footwork plus a lot of crimping on sometimes very aggressive edges of golden monzonite or a little bit of smooth incut patina. You may grab a few rough slopers to top out and grapple with a few more on some of the lower angled testpieces. Typically the faces run from slabs through to gentle overhangs, with some extra-steep exceptions. Of course, with nearly 1000 problems you'll find a little of everything. It's worth conditioning your fingertips to the Buttermilk areas in general by pacing yourself at first and ideally building some calluses.

In this guidebook, the Buttermilk Country is divided up into sections, beginning with the Buttermilks Main area, also known as The Peabodies area, and moving on to all the outlying areas beginning on page 301.

patagonia®
patagonia.com
1%
FOR THE PLANET
© 2009 Patagonia, Inc.
Bean Bowers. JOSH WHARTON

Buttermilk Country

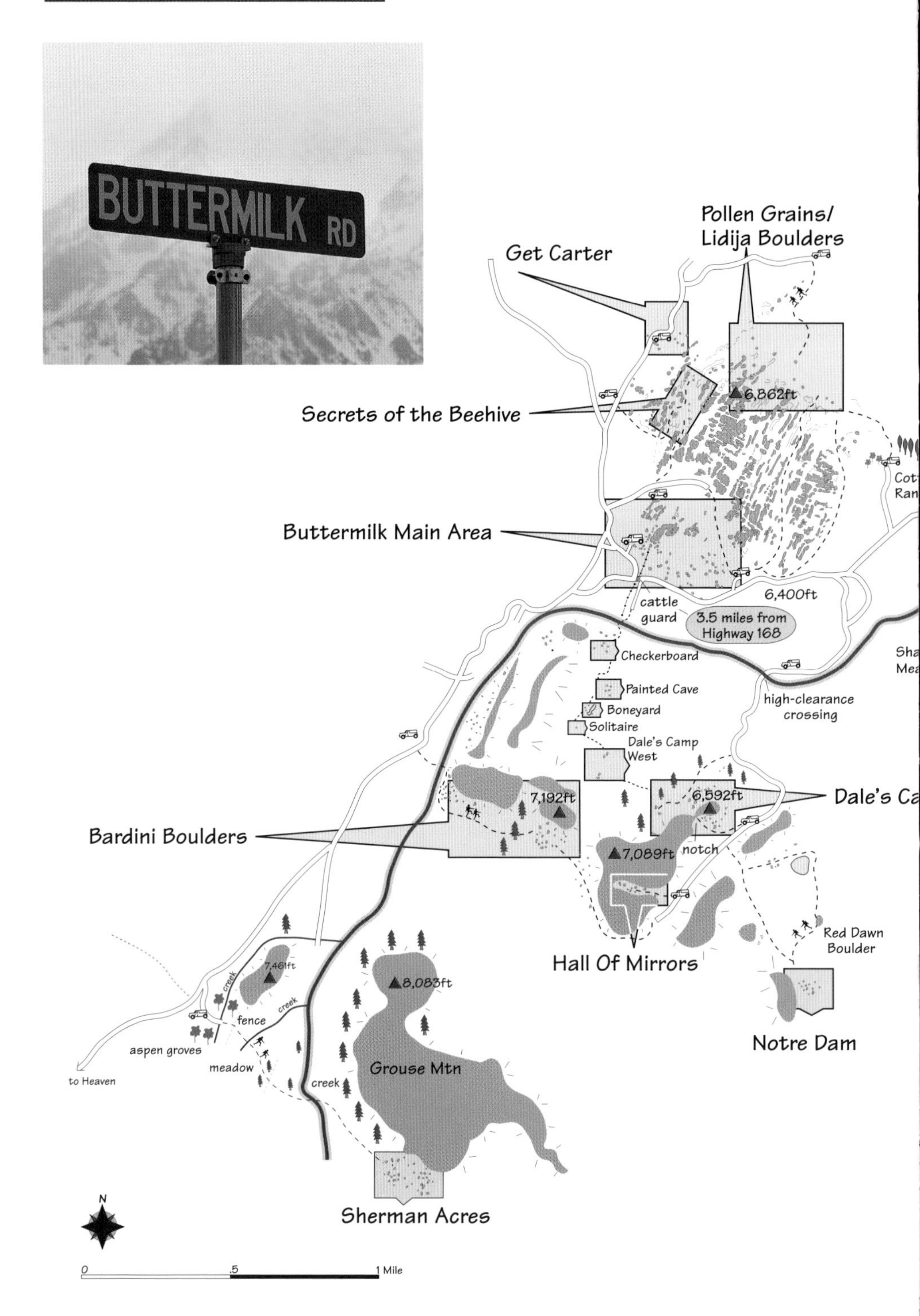

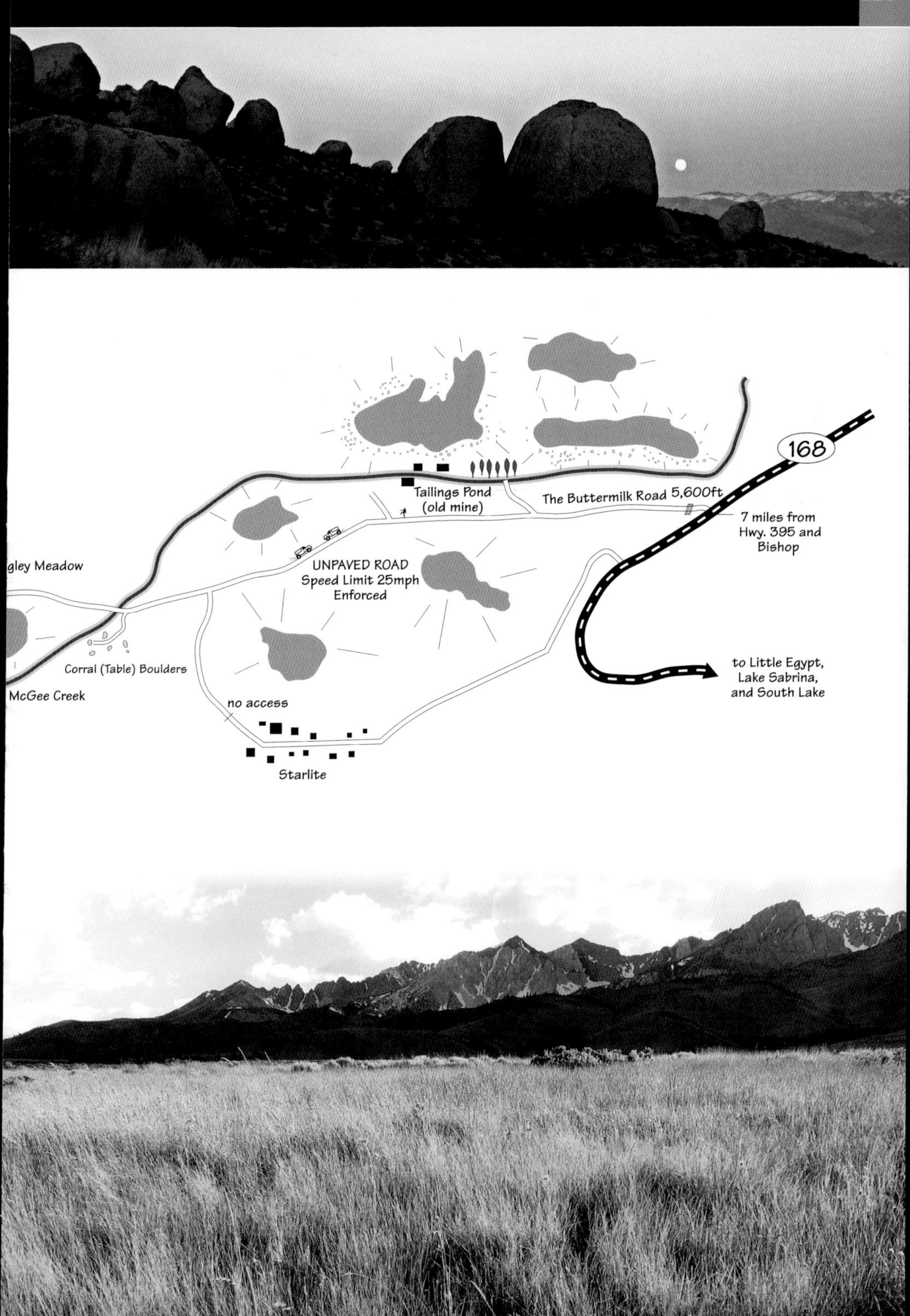

These meadows that lie beyond the Main Buttermilk Bouldering Areas provide the summer grazing for cows that once produced the Buttermilk for which the area is believed to have been named. Photo: Wills Young.

Buttermilks Main / Peabody Boulders

The evening sunshine warms the boulders after a stormy day at the Buttermilks Main area. Photo: Wills Young.

The Buttermilk Boulders Main area is also sometimes referred to as the Peabody Boulders. These are the sixty-plus boulders lying on a predominantly south-facing slope of Buttermilk Mountain, beside Buttermilk Road at about 6400 feet (1950m) altitude. From the giant Grandma and Grandpa Peabody Boulders at the east, to the Birthday Boulders on the slope's west side, these boulders make up by far the greatest concentration of large boulders in the entire Buttermilk Region. Of course, the few giants above the Birthday Boulders, and around the corner, are included in this dense group, with all the boulders within a few minutes' walk of each other. Most people habitually call this group 'The Buttermilks.' However, the entire Buttermilk Country is also referred to as 'The Buttermilks,' and so to clarify we use the term Buttermilks Main Area, or The Peabodies for this group in the guide.

The Bouldering

The Peabodies bask in sunshine virtually from sun up to sun down. This creates a perfect bouldering environment during winter, but if you're looking for cooler temps in spring, summer, or early fall, show up late in the evenings to enjoy the pleasing hour or more of shade after the sun drops behind the Sierra crest. The boulders here are generally big, and many of the problems extend from tall to very tall, though the landings are often gravely and fairly level, so a pair of crashpads will typically suffice. If your fingertips tire before you do, you can always enjoy the views, the environment, and the atmosphere. Without a doubt, this is one of the most spectacular bouldering areas in the world. Don't miss it!

For ease of navigation, use your guide's left cover flap to mark this map. Find the boulders you want by the page references here.

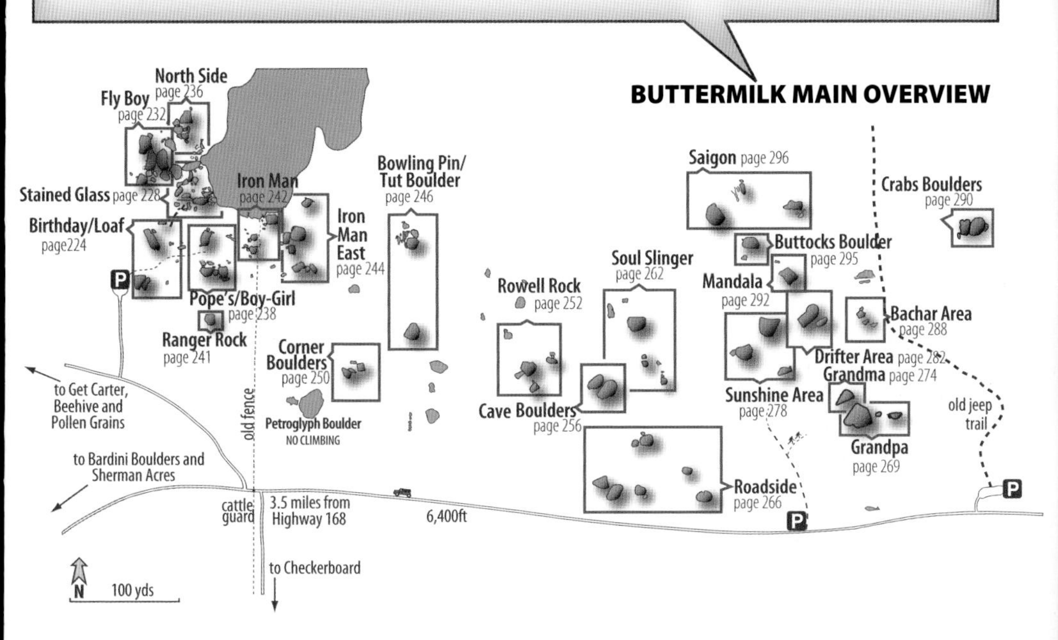

Directions:

From the junction of Hwy395 and Hwy68, in downtown Bishop (the crossroads of Main Street and West Line Street), head west toward the Sierra Nevada Mountains. If coming from the south, you'll know the junction as it is the first stop light. Coming from the north, this junction is about 0.5 miles after Schat's Bakery, just after Wilson's Eastside Sports (which, naturally, is on the east side of the road).

Those coming from The Pit campground, and all points north, will take a short cut, by making a right turn—due south—at Ed Powers Road, 1.4 miles east of Pleasant Valley Dam Road, and a couple miles outside of Bishop city limits. Head 2.4 miles along this road, straight across at the stop sign, to join Hwy 68 west of Bishop. This avoids Main Street, and reduces driving by several miles.

From the 395/168 junction in the center of Bishop, drive 7.2 miles west on Hwy168 (initially West Line Street), and turn right onto Buttermilk Road. If arriving at the Ed Powers Road junction with Hwy168, this will be about 2.5 miles. Head west along Buttermilk Road for a little less than 3.5 miles to find the giant Peabody Boulders up on a hillside at right as you round a curve (see map on previous page).

Note: Do *not* speed along this dirt road. The speed limit is 25 mph, and the road is patrolled. One way to upset all the locals around here is to drive too fast and throw up a massive plume of dust along the Buttermilk Road.

Parking

You can park below the Grandma and Grandpa Peabody Boulders at the side of the road, where a marked path leads up the hillside into the boulderfield. Alternatively, you can continue up the gentle hill, cross an abandoned cattle guard and turn right to reach the upper parking area beside the Birthday Boulders. Consult the overview map to know where you want to climb and park accordingly. It is, of course, easy to walk from one end of the boulderfield to the other, so choice of parking is not critical. On busy days, park anywhere along Buttermilk road, staying well to the side. Be aware that when facing up the gravelly hill, rear wheel drive light trucks can have difficulty pulling out of a parking spot in forward gear, so consider turning around and facing down the hill, rather than parking too tight in front of another car. **Please do not under any circumstances pull off the road, anywhere,** or you will turn this fragile area into a dust bowl.

BIRTHDAY BOULDERS

This area was named for James Wilson's birthday party held here in June 22 1975. One of the cleanest and smoothest pieces of rock at the Buttermilks is the "Birthday Face" on the first boulder by the parking lot, with a trio of excellent north-facing lines—*Birthday Direct* (v3), *Birthday Left* (v0), and *Birthday Skyline* (v3). The former is a fine introduction to hard bouldering, demanding good technique and crimp strength in equal measure. Flat landings are the norm for lines in this area. Nevertheless, some of the Loaf problems will feel serious; and they are, sometimes requiring a lot of confidence high off the ground. *Nan Bread* (v3), *Yeast* (v3), *Sheepherder* (v2), and *Dough Boy* (v3) are ideal for those who are looking to hone some footwork and to steady their head.

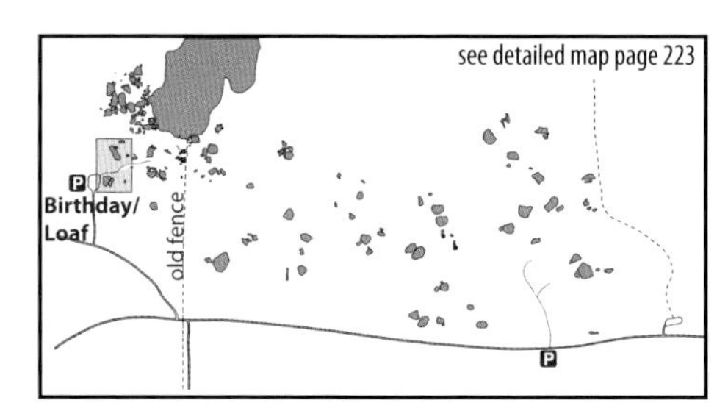

BIRTHDAY BOULDERS

These boulders lean against each other, just a few yards from the upper parking area.

1 Unnamed v0 ☐
Climb the left side of the west face. Use the crimpy rail for your feet, before moving directly up the slab.

2 Birthday Mantel v0 ★★ ☐
Right of the left arete is an obvious two-hand sized flattish hold: Mantel this, then proceed up the slab.

3 Unnamed v0 ☐
Right of *Birthday Mantel* is a shallow scoop with a low rib feature on its right. Start by climbing the rib and finish on the slab.

4 Unnamed v6 ☐
The bulge is climbed by squeezing some rough slopey holds.

5 Unnamed Scoop v6 ☐
Begin below the right side of the scoop. Pull off the ground with difficulty by squeezing a vague rounded rib to gain a footing in the scoop, then continue more easily.

6 The Way Down v0 ★ ☐
This obvious line of holds is also the easiest downclimb.

7 The Eh Train v9 ☐
Sit start at the arete and climb directly up using some slopey sidepulls and finish direct or make a move rightward to the top of *Alcove Problem*.

8 Alcove Problem v7 ★ ☐
Sit start with a slanting rail on the left. At the lip make a big move up and right, then over, or go direct on worse holds. The stand start is v6.

9 Unnamed v2 ☐
To the right of where the boulders meet, climb up a wide, shallow scoop with awkwardness at first to gain better holds that lead easily on to the top.

10 Unnamed v3 ★★ ☐
Begin at a huge hueco/pocket, and somehow stand up into it. Doing this in a single dynamic movement, beginning with the left foot placed beside the hands, is a fun trick. Continuing up the slab requires a cool head, and ideally, cool holds.

11 Bard Route v6 ★ ☐
Start standing with an assortment of unsatisfactory holds. Make a very tricky move off the ground, then climb the wall which requires concentration to the end.

12 Bard Route, Sit Start v8 ★ ☐
Sit start *Bard Route* from low to the right at a large knob for the right hand and small sharp crimp for the left.

13 The Prow v2 ★ ☐
Sit start at underclings or a little higher, and climb the prow. The standing start is v1.

14 Enough T v4 ☐
Just right of where the boulders meet, start hanging sloping crimps with both hands about 5 feet up. Move up to sloping holds, then over the bulge using a heel or toe out left. A long-armed "sit start" from some friable and extremely painful crimps is possible if you are very light and impervious to pain.

15 Parking Problem v9 ☐
Sit start with the right hand in an obvious sidepull and the left on a slanting crimp. Make one or two very hard moves up and right to gain a good crimp at the base of a hanging arete. Continue up slightly on the right side.

16 Birthday Left v0 ★★★ ☐
Climb the left side of the smooth wall with good incuts. A sit start, though it looks desperate, is only a grade harder when you figure out the move. You can also start sitting here and climb up and right to join the next problem at about v2.

17 Birthday Direct v3 ★★★ ☐
Climb the center of the smooth wall using deft footwork, a gaston (or two), a long move and a lot of tenacity. One of the finest little testpieces in the area; not too high, and with a flat landing.

To Stained Glass, Flyboy & North Side Areas
The Loaf
To parking
Birthday Boulders
BIRTHDAY BOULDERS
BIRTHDAY BOULDERS
BIRTHDAY BOULDERS

BIRTHDAY BOULDERS

18 Birthday Skyline v3 ★★★ ☐

A forced, but excellent line: Climb the arching rail of crimps that forms the rightmost edge of the patina. You begin by making a slight rock over to the right, but quickly swing the feet back around left to stand on small glassy dishes, moving up left with feet on the vertical wall. A tricky reach left up high brings you to the top of *Birthday Direct.* Exits out right make good easier alternatives.

THE LOAF

Beginning at the upper left side:

19 Unnamed v0 ☐

Climb the face on solid holds.

20 Unnamed v1 ★ ☐

Left of the arete, climb the wall using the good patina and an awkward move.

21 The Rising v4 ★★ ☐

Begin at opposing sidepulls and make a hard move to a crimp. Pull through with this to gain sidepulls and the top. A left start, using a large, but flexing hold down on the left is a little harder.

22 Nan Bread v4 ★ ☐

Climb the wall precariously using some patina past hard moves to gain good flakes up high.

23 Yeast v3 ★★ ☐

Climb the wall just left of a prominent black-streaked groove, beginning with nice bulbous holds, but ending with small crimps that lead extremely tenuously around a slight bulge on poor footholds. Frightening.

24 Sheepherder v2 ★★★ ☐

Begin at a prominent black streak and move up and right into a tall, shallow groove. Exit this with caution and good footwork. A 'rite of passage.'

25 Dough Boy v3 ★ ☐

Begin where the base of the boulder forms a corner and climb up the very blunt rib with hard moves on sidepulls to an uneventful topout.

26 Tall Guy's Revenge v5 ★ ☐

Make a huge reach to gain a sloper and pull onto the slab. Stack pads: you may need several! Rating uncertain for this Puhvel special.

One of the most delightful problems in the Buttermilk Country is *Birthday Direct* (v3, page 224) at the Birthday Boulders (Buttermilks Main Area). This glassy face of perfect rock is an entry-level footwork testpiece that can frustrate even the strongest climbers. Photo: Wills Young

STAINED GLASS AREA

The Stained Glass area is on the hillside, above the Birthday and Loaf Boulders (page 224) and the Pope's Hat Boulder (page 238). The Stained Glass Boulder is fairly innocuous from below, but when you walk around the back of it, you see an amazing sight: *Stained Glass* (v10) itself, an exquisite open groove of flawless rock. So smooth are the footholds, in fact, that the name is not only apt, but accurate—the quartz monzonite really is polished to glass here. Sadly, one crimper on the line feels more like the edge of a broken bottle. Still, it will be hard to find a more attractive line than this anywhere: It is simply a beauty. Also here is the Five and Dime Boulder, with another immaculate wall of solid patina at a much more amenable level of difficulty (v0 to v3).

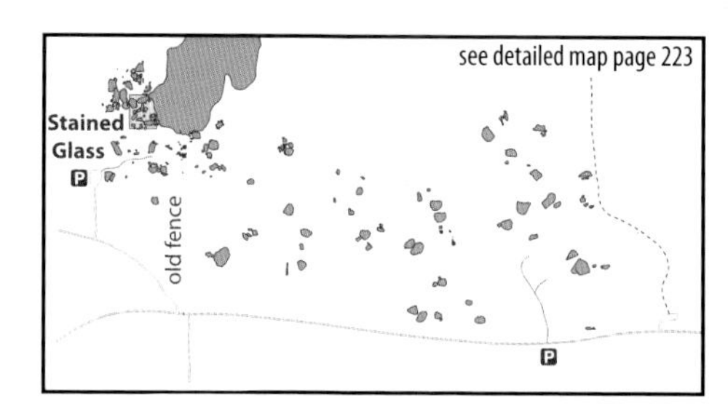

From the Loaf Boulder, walk up the hill toward the large Stained Glass Boulder to find, directly below the Stained Glass Boulder's south face, a boulder with an obvious white rail feature on its east side:

1 Unnamed v0 ☐
Sit start on the right side. Follow the rail up left and climb over on rounded holds.

STAINED GLASS BOULDER

The problems are described from the north east side moving rightwards around the boulder.

2 Blood Spud v10 ★ ☐
Sit start at the obvious good crimp and climb the northeast arete using tiny holds and squeezing with the feet. A good spot and pads are needed due to an uneven landing over a boulder.

3 Stained Glass v10 ★★★ ☐
Climb the smooth, clean, gently overhanging groove on crimps and slick footholds to reach a tiny left hand crimp in the headwall. Make a massive move to the lip. A world class line requiring a combination of strength and technique.

4 Stained Glass Sit v10 ★★★ ☐
A slightly more sustained version of the above from a sit start, for those who must take it one step further!

5 Stained Glass Right, Sit v11 ★★ ☐
A hard, sharp, but good problem. Sit start at the large hold, move up into the groove, then make a hard move horizontally right by way of a razor crimp, tiny footholds, and more tiny crimps to top out at right.

6 Unnamed v3 ★ ☐
Start off small boulders. Pull on and climb up, then directly over the top on grainy slopers. This feels quite bold unless, perhaps, it is very clean.

7 Broken Glass v5 ★ ☐
Start standing with both hands at the lip of the small overhang. Make a hard pull up with the right to a flatty, then climb left to join the previous line.

8 Project ☐
A sit start to the previous line looks like it would be a grade or two harder, and worth doing.

9 Project ☐
The center of the south face looks like it is climbable, possibly!

10 Project ☐
A series of crusty flakes lead up the east wall toward the arete of *Blood Spud.*

Above and leaning against the Stained Glass Boulder, is another largish boulder:

11 Affirmative Action v7 ★ ☐
Opposite *Stained Glass*, on the boulder leaning against the Stained Glass Boulder: Jump start and climb up and left by a big move. Avoid touching the Stained Glass Boulder as you top out.

12 Unnamed v4 ☐
Directly opposite *Blood Spud* (#2), begin hanging holds at the lip low at right (just left of a boulder). Make a couple of hard pulls to gain and climb the slab.

13 Snake Pit v5 ☐
Sit start low left in a cave and climb up patina to a scary move around the lip with an angled rock slab below. You'll need a few pads for this, and the rock quality is not that great in the roof. Maybe it will clean up.

A clump of boulders lie on the hillside to the left of the Stained Glass Boulder (seen from below).

14 Unnamed v0 ☐
Traverse from right to left on the west-facing side of a long, flattish boulder. See topo opposite for location. Start with your feet on flakes halfway along for a comfortable warm up on big holds. Starting lower to the right bumps the rating a grade or so.

STAINED GLASS BOULDER

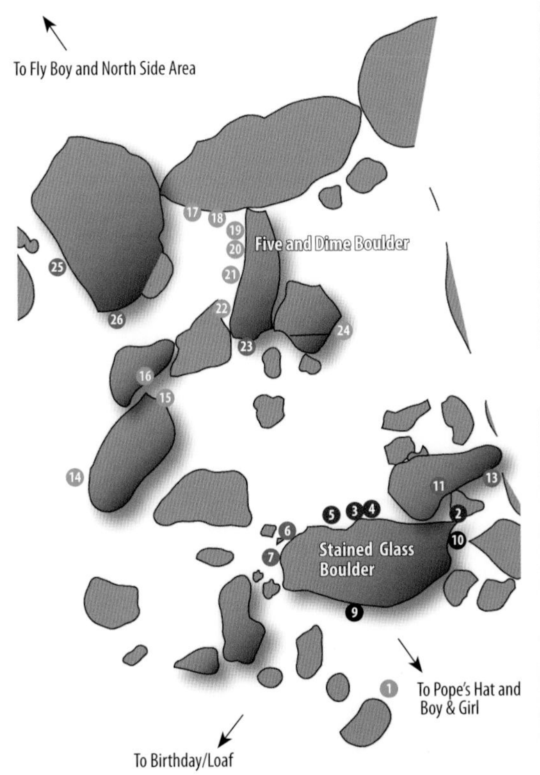

STAINED GLASS BOULDER

HILLSIDE LEFT OF STAINED GLASS BOULDER

FIVE AND DIME BOULDERS

⑮ **Unnamed** v1 ☐
On the left side of the alcove/shallow cave, start on a crusty flake at low right and climb up and left to a good hueco and over.

⑯ **Unnamed** v1 ☐
The slab on the right side of the alcove is climbed directly up the center on good holds, with a hard move off the ground.

FIVE AND DIME BOULDERS

The Five and Dime Boulder's patina wall, along with the surrounding boulders, forms a kind of room. On the north side of this is a low boulder with two mantel problems:

⑰ **Unnamed** v0 ☐
The left mantel.

⑱ **Unnamed** v0 ☐
The right mantel.

The Five and Dime Boulder itself has a beautiful patina wall facing the mountains with:

⑲ **Five and Dime Left** v0 ☐
Make a couple of moves up the short far left side. It helps to be tall to pull off the ground, or let's say it's a little more interesting if you're short.

⑳ **Five and Dime** v1 ★★ ☐
Climb the flawless wall of patina starting with a shallow flat pocket for the left hand and a good blocky crimp for the right.

㉑ **Five and Dime Right** v0 ★ ☐
Climb the pristine wall starting with both hands at a spike hold.

㉒ **Unnamed** v0 ☐
The short route up the right side of the wall, starting off the boulder below is a little scary due to the landing.

㉓ **Five and Dime Prow** v3 ★ ☐
The prow that faces *Stained Glass*: Start hanging from holds at the lip on the right and make a big move up left. Pull over onto the slab.

To the right is another slab on a different boulder, which is vB, or maybe v0 on its right edge. On this boulder but around right is:

㉔ **Unnamed** v0 ☐
One hard move over a bulge on big holds.

A low boulder to the west of the Five and Dime Boulder, which stretches toward the Fly Boy Boulder has a short, crusty west face above a sandy landing, with:

㉕ **Unnamed** v4 ☐
Sit start at flakes below the highpoint, if they are still there. Crusty.

㉖ **Unnamed** v4 ☐
Begin sitting at crusty sidepulls on the right side of the south-facing nose. Pull up and over on dreadful grainy holds.

The giant boulder to the left of this crusty boulder is the Fly Boy Boulder (page 233).

Tilly Parkins, of Australia working the moves of *Stained Glass* prior to her first female ascent of this amazing crimping and dynamic testpiece (November 2008). Photo: Mark Withers.

FLY BOY AREA

The Fly Boy Area includes three big boulders in a row, one above the other on the slope up and left of the Stained Glass Area (page 228). The lowest boulder (Bun Boulder), has a few fun slab lines at the bottom end of the v-scale, facing the mountains. The center, Big Wall Boulder has a couple of tall lines that feel more like short solos, plus a short, but scary mantel line. The outstanding Fly Boy Boulder, the upper of the three, is a huge block with something at every grade. One of these is the eponymous *Fly Boy* (v6 or v8 sit), which is a brilliant steep (45-degrees) problem, especially from the sit, requiring a positive attitude and a few pads. I've seen one person stick the lip, swing out violently, swing back in to kick the rock, and then back-slap from 10-12 feet. Proof, if you needed any more, that a boy, flying, is about as graceful as a tossed sack of potatoes. On the front side of the boulder are a few other notables, including one of the Buttermilks' most mind-blowing lines: *The Fall Guy* (v9), also known from the low start as *Haroun and the Sea of Stories* (v11/12). This has got to be up there with *Evilution, The Mandala, The Checkerboard, Saigon, etc.*, as a contender for best problem in the area. Just take a close look at the incredible golden patina on this huge 45-degree overhanging line! That is one hell of a boulder problem ... Long, sustained, and—other than the landing—perfect.

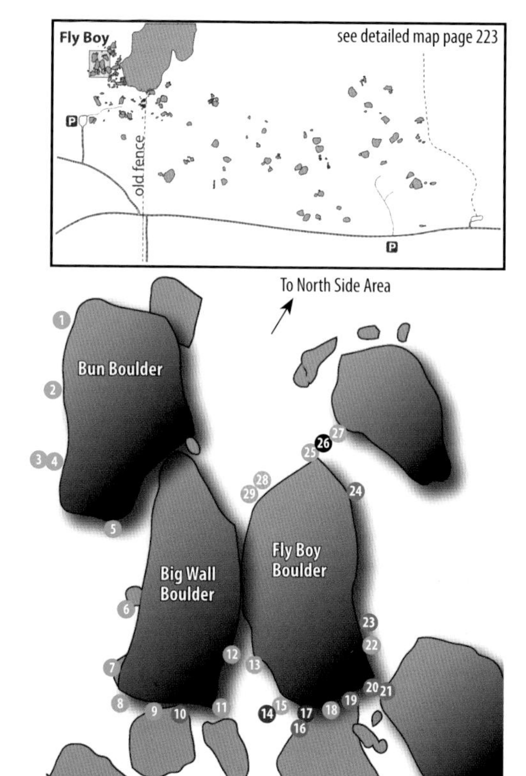

BUN BOULDER

The low angle face of this boulder, facing the mountains, can be climbed pretty much anywhere. Some ideas are:

1 Unnamed v0 ☐
The groove: Begin at the left side and follow a rightward slanting groove up and right to a good knob high up on the slab.

2 Unnamed v0 ☐
The direct: Climb directly up over a slight bulge.

3 Unnamed v0 ☐
Right to left: Start where there is a basketball-sized impression near the ground. Climb up and left via the line of least resistance.

4 Unnamed, Exit Right v0 ☐
Start where there is a basketball-sized impression near the ground and climb up and right.

5 Unnamed v0- ☐
The very crusty large flakes at the south end of the boulder are hardly worth climbing.

BIG WALL BOULDER

6 Big Wall v1 ★ ☐
Climb the big west-facing wall near its right side, past some sketchy flakes, moving right or left to finish.

7 Action Potential v2 ★★ ☐
Begin on the block on the left side of the arete and climb the arete until you can move up rightward. A scary highball requiring a steady head.

8 Potential Action v7 ★ ☐
Begin several feet right of the arete with both hands on a good crimp in a small corner. Climb up and left past some cool crimps and sidepulls to join the previous line.

9 Unnamed v2 ★ ☐
Fine climbing up the patina on the tall south face leads to an exciting move at the top.

10 Big Mantel v4 ★ ☐
Climb flakes to a hard and bold mantel above the rock slab. Pads needed.

11 Unnamed v1 ★ ☐
Begin hanging at a large jug on the arete, pull around right onto the right foot, then up the wall.

12 Unnamed v0 ☐
Climb the wall starting off a large rock.

FLY BOY BOULDER

13 The Fall Guy v9 ★★★ ☐
An astonishing line, originally climbed starting with the right hand in a shallow hueco, left hand on a bad pinch up high. Pull on, then make a hard move to gain the good hueco above. Make another hard move out left, then go up and finally left again on good crimps to a pumpy topout. A magnificent, powerful and sustained line. A mass of pads and/or spotters are needed.

14 Haroun and the Sea of Stories v11 ★★★ ☐
A low start to the above problem, beginning with both hands in the underclings down and right. Hard moves using a high heel hook gain the holds where the standing start begins.

15 Bulging Grain v7 ★★ ☐
Start with both hands in the lowest underclings at the back of the overhang. Move up and right by some hard moves to gain a jug, then make a powerful snatch for the lip. Pull a long move to a sloping dish and mantel onto the nose above the rock slab. Either climb on using tenuous holds above the sketchy landing, or give up and jump down.

16 The Nose v3 ★ ☐
As above without the roof start. A big move to a sloping dish and a tricky mantel is followed by a bold and tenuous low-angle face or, for those less ambitious, a leap down.

17 Fakir School v10 ☐
Start as for *Bulging Grain* to gain the lip. Heel hook and move right across the lip using a small flake in the overhang, to gain a tiny inset crimp. Finish by good holds on a faint rib as for the next problem.

18 Unnamed v2 ☐
Climb the blunt rib from a pair of poor crimps with a couple of moves to a shallow hueco.

19 Unnamed v4 ★ ☐
The wall to the right of the rib is climbed, avoiding the large hueco up and right. Start hanging with the left hand on a slopey hold and the right in a good deep edge.

20 Unnamed v5 ★ ☐
A sit start to the previous problem, beginning low and right where the end of a flake seam meets the lip of a low roof. Instead of climbing directly up, move left with difficulty to join the standing start. A slightly contrived but good problem.

21 Unnamed v3 ☐
Sit start where a flake seam meets the lip of a low roof. Make a hard pull through to a big hueco directly above, then easily up.

22 Unnamed v0- ★ ☐
Make a couple of moves past the crack on the left side of the east face.

BUN BOULDER

BIG WALL BOULDER

BIG WALL BOULDER

FLY BOY BOULDER

Lisa Rands, *Fly Boy* (v6 or v8). Photo: Wills Young.

23 Unnamed v3 ★ ☐
Climb the wall to the right of the crack without the crack, beginning at a left-facing sidepull.

24 Almost v4 ☐
Sit start on the sloping rock, at a right-facing sidepull and a good crimp. Pull up and right to more crimps, and finish more easily. Almost a good problem.

25 Fly Boy Arete v5 ★★ ☐
Sit start right of the arete at the obvious large jug and/or sidepull. Climb across left and pull around and up the arete using a confusing array of holds, none of which seem to help much.

26 Unknown ☐
An eliminate line staying just right of the arete and not using the arete has been climbed. Brilliant (not).

27 Fly Boy Sit-start v8 ★★★ ☐
Sit start at the obvious large jug and/or sidepull and make a series of hard moves up and right on good crimps to the exciting crux move to the lip.

28 Fly Boy v6 ★★ ☐
The overhanging face is climbed to an exhilarating finish. Start off the rock at right with sidepulls.

29 Flight Attendant v8 ★ ☐
Gain the same starting point as for Fly Boy, but with the left hand on what you would normally use for the right hand of Fly Boy. Bust a hard move up and right to a positive but distant hold, with the rock slab distracting below. Pull through to the lip. The sit start goes at around v9. A good spot required.

LISA RANDS * THE MANDALA V12 * PHOTO: WILLS YOUNG
HIGHBALL
Crash Pads
The Royale: 48 x 36 x 4"
Highball 4000: 48 x 41 x 4"
Highball 5000: 60 x 48 x 5"
VooDoo
Climbing Holds
Bouldering Gear
ORDER ONLINE: voodooclimbing.com
OR CALL: 928-527-0406

North Side

see detailed map page 223

old fence

NORTH SIDE BOULDERS

This small area lies north of the Fly Boy Area (page 236). There are a couple of outstanding highballs here, *East Side Story* and *Larger Than Life*, which climb a tall and pretty solid face on the North Boulder that looks toward the Fly Boy Area. There is also a very picturesque patina slab around the back of the same boulder with some easier lines. The Scoop Boulder is kinda crusty, but might clean up.

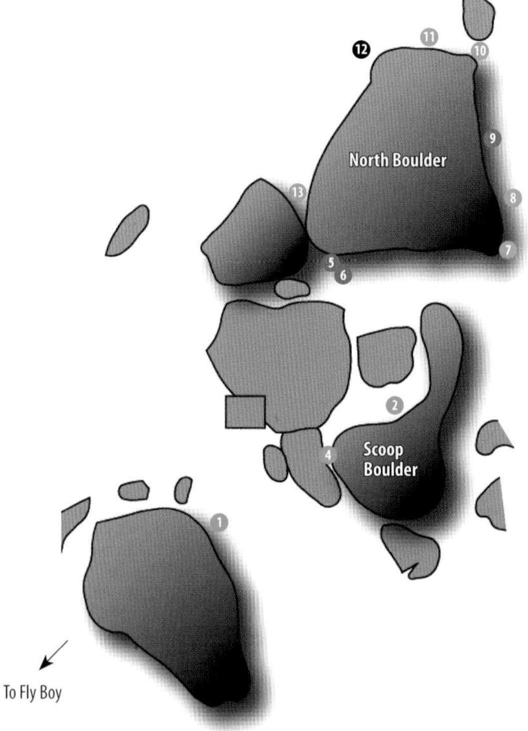

Neighboring the Fly Boy Boulder, just to the north, is another boulder, and on the north (far) side is:

1 Unnamed v0- ☐
Mantel, beginning from a hanging start on a good hold.

SCOOP BOULDER

2 Scoop v2 ★ ☐
Climb the scooped wall from the middle, moving left across the seam to the easiest exit: bad landing.

3 Project ☐
This face could be climbed direct, but the rock looks very grainy and unpleasant.

4 Erosion v1 ★ ☐
An excellent-looking line. Climb the heavily featured arete using large grainy sidepulls and big huecos, pulling around left at the top. The decomposing rock and terrible landing make this a must do for diehard adventurists out there!

NORTH BOULDER

5 East Side Story v3 ★★ ☐
The excellent tall south wall of the boulder is climbed beginning at the left by stepping off the rock, then moving up and right past good edges to finish with a huge move to a thin patina. The landing improves after the start, but this is very tall.

6 Larger Than Life v3 ★★ ☐
Begin as for the previous line, but after the first long move up and right to a good hold, climb up and slightly left, by a very scary move using a slanted right-hand crimp/pinch to reach up with the left hand to an obvious edge. Finish on good edges with great care.

7 Unnamed v0 ☐
The southeast arete is climbed from the base of the nose with a hard move off the ground.

8 Unnamed vB ☐
This low-angle bowl also serves as a downclimb.

9 Unnamed v5 ☐
Super-crusty fragilistic climbing on crystalline crimps to flakes and a groping finish over the crumbly lip. Yikes.

SCOOP AND NORTH BOULDERS

East Side Story, an excellent and long-overlooked highball up beyond the Fly Boy Boulder. Photo: Wills Young.

⑩ Unnamed v0 ★ ☐
Make a couple of nice moves on the solid patina of the pretty northeast arete.

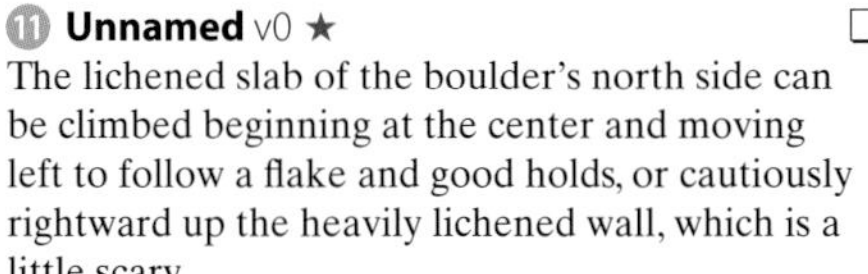

⑪ Unnamed v0 ★ ☐
The lichened slab of the boulder's north side can be climbed beginning at the center and moving left to follow a flake and good holds, or cautiously rightward up the heavily lichened wall, which is a little scary.

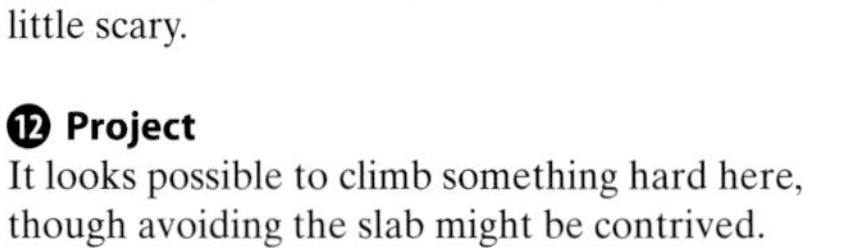

⑫ Project ☐
It looks possible to climb something hard here, though avoiding the slab might be contrived.

⑬ Mount Tom View v0 ★ ☐
Lean in off the tall rock at right to reach good patina and climb up and left to top out with great care on the lichened rock.

⑭ Project/Unknown ☐
On a boulder that forms part of the cliff band east of the Scoop Boulder is an arete with a rib that looks pretty good.

POPE'S HAT AREA

The Pope's Hat Area is named for the very tall boulder that looks every bit like the Pope's hat. The Boulder was labeled Pope's Prow on some early topos, leading to some confusion with another *Pope's Prow* on the Mandala Boulder. Here are a couple of extremely tall solos (left and right), the right one being the origin of the Pope's Prow confusion. It was climbed by Mike Pope and known as *Pope's Problem (aka No Girlfriend)*. The Boy and Girl Rocks have some powerful little sit-starts on the uphill side of the west-most boulder (v0 to v4), while *Verdad* (v5), on the east one, is worth a look. *Scenic Crank* (originally v6, now v8 or v10) is perhaps the best line in the area, an old Dale Bard problem that used to have a giant "cheat stone" under it, but fell into neglect after the block disappeared leaving an intense jump start, or a very fierce low start.

POPE'S HAT BOULDER

Beginning with the undercut north (uphill) side of the boulder and moving rightward around it, find:

1 Unnamed v2 ☐
Hang start between two low rocks. Make a couple of hard moves.

2 Unnamed v2 ☐
Junky: Sit start with crusty moves to join easy climbing above.

3 Unnamed v0 ☐
Climb the west face, just left of the right arete.

4 Unnamed v3 ★ ☐
For the adventurous only: Climb the face above the overhang from a standing start. The difficulty quickly eases, but great care is needed.

5 Pope's Roof v7 ★ ☐
Sit start at the large hold in the back of the roof. Use heel-toe locks to gain the lip, and turn this with difficulty to join the previous line, which adds an absurdly tall and scary finish to a really short and powerful problem!

6 Pope's Hat v10 ☐
Sit start at the large ledge at the back of the roof. Climb right on some incredibly painful crimps; make a big move out right, then up to finish as for *Pope's Problem* below. Hellish.

7 Pope's Problem, a.k.a. No Girlfriend v4 ★ ☐
Begin at high crimps to the left of the boulder's southeast arete, pull up and left to a good ear, then climb the face/blunt arete to the top. Another adventurous solo.

8 Unnamed v1 ☐
Sit start at a flake on the right side of the west wall.

BOY AND GIRL ROCKS

At the right side of the south face of the west boulder find:

9 Scenic Crank v8 ★★ ☐
Facing midday sun, this pretty south face sees few ascents, but is well worth doing on a cold or cloudy day. Begin with a jump off the ground from a left hand undercling to a small crimp. The difficulty of the first move depends on your height and whether you stack pads. Share at the crimp and make a couple of hard pulls (a good pinch out right is useful). The top steadily eases. The cheat start with both hands on the crimp is about v6.

10 Scenic Crank Low Start v11 ★ ☐
Begin hanging (no jump) with hands on crimps about four feet off the ground. Make an extremely hard pull to gain the higher crimp. where the high-start begins Make another hard pull to bring your feet up and reach right to the pinch. Carry on with pumped forearms.

The east boulder at right has:

11 Unnamed v1 ☐
Gain the deep hueco and climb the crunchy face if you feel brave or careless.

12 Unnamed v0 ☐
Sit start at a flake on the small boulder and climb up and over. There is also an easy problem at right.

13 Unnamed v1 ☐
The northeast arete moving up and right to top out. Use a heel hook and add a grade if you can't reach that high flake to start.

14 Verdad v5 ★ ☐
From the right side, begin with the left hand on a flake and the right on a shallow crimp. Pull up to a good hold high, then left to a crimp flake. Continue left along the lip of the boulder to top out at its apex.

Now back on the west boulder:

15 Unnamed v4 ★ ☐
Sit start from crimps on the left side of the cave, go up directly. A little sharp, unfortunately.

16 Unnamed v1 ★ ☐
Sit start with a solid incut patina for the left hand and an undercling for the right. Pull up to a good hold, and on.

17 Patina v0 ★ ☐
From the right side of the cave, at a big jug, climb up left. Or use a left hand gaston to pull rightward at about v1.

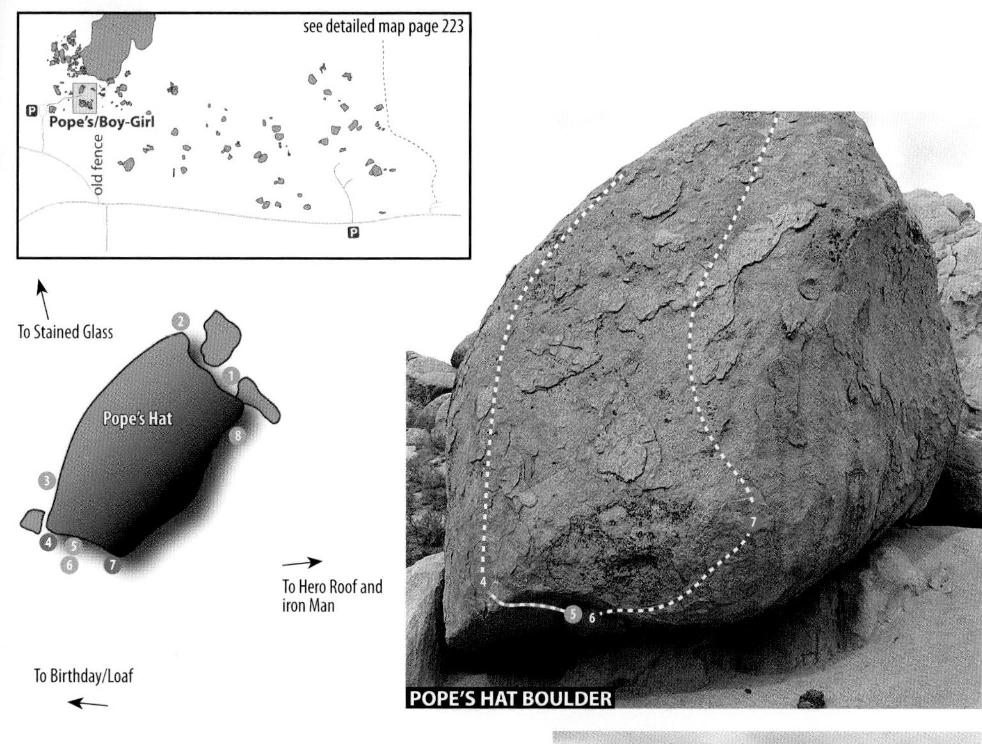

POPE'S HAT BOULDER

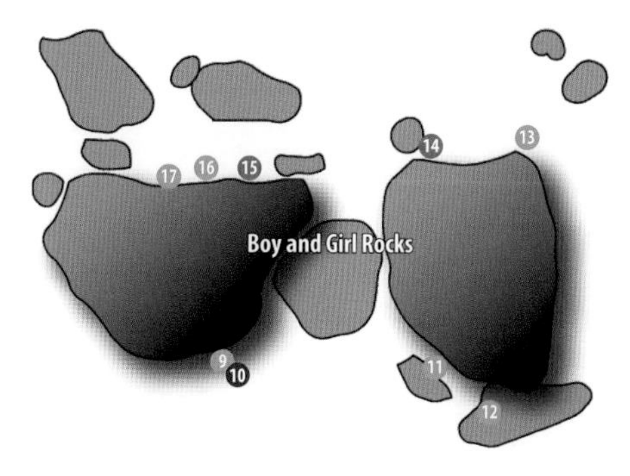

BOY AND GIRL ROCKS

BOY AND GIRL ROCKS, EAST BOULDER

BOY AND GIRL ROCKS, WEST BOULDER

Letting rip on the amazing *Iron Fly* (v9) page 243. Photo: Wills Young.

RANGER ROCK

Ranger Rock is downhill from Boy and Girl Rocks, it is low on the slope east of the Birthday Boulders. It has a little bit of everything up to about v6, all on good rock. It has great level landings and relatively short climbs for the area, making it one of several great places to begin a session, and a great place to improve skills needed for the bigger badder lines of the Buttermilks.

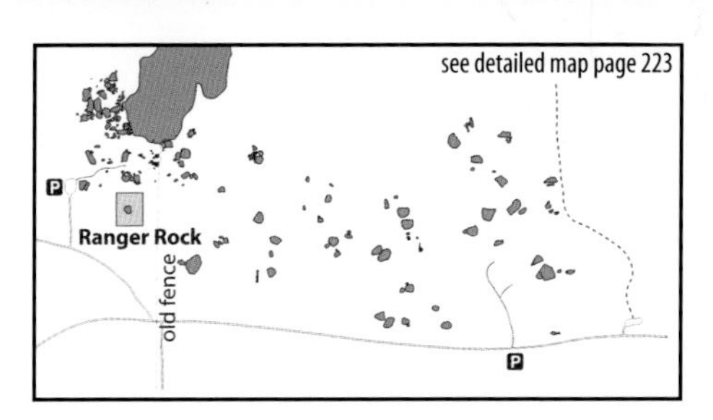

RANGER ROCK

RANGER ROCK

RANGER ROCK

1 Unnamed v3 ★ ☐
Sit start at the large hueco. Climb out of it rightward and then move back left to ascend the blunt nose.

2 Unnamed v5 ★ ☐
Sit start at the large hueco. Climb up and right to meet the top of the *Rail Problem* (below).

3 Rail Problem v5 ★★ ☐
Sit start at the good patina flake and follow the rail to the end. Make a hard pull up to crimps and step onto the rail.

4 Rail Problem Right Exit v4 ★ ☐
Sit start at the good patina flake and follow the rail to the deep incut. Move right to knobby crimps and climb up directly above these.

5 Unnamed v2 ★ ☐
Climb the slab just above the small boulder. Use the boulder to reach in to a good left crimp and a small right knob. Starting on similarly positioned holds lower to the left is a grade or so harder.

6 Unnamed v2 ★★ ☐
Climb the delicate slab. One of the best of its genre and not too high.

7 Unnamed v0 ★ ☐
Climb the slab to the right, on good holds.

8 Unnamed v6 ☐
Sit/hang start with hands on sloping holds at the lip of a small overhang: Make a couple of hard moves, then climb easily up

9 Unnamed v2 ☐
Climb the sloping rib, just barely to the right of the last problem, beginning with the right hand on a fairly obvious sidepull.

10 Unnamed v1 ☐
Find a way up this face where there are many options.

11 Unnamed v0 ☐
Climb the left crack.

12 Unnamed v0 ☐
Climb the right crack

13 Unnamed v2 ☐
Climb the face with knobs from low holds, starting with the right hand on a crimp.

IRON MAN AREA

I've broken the Iron Man Area into the main Iron Man Area (this section), and the Iron Man East Area (page 244). This spot is characterised by two boulders that are relatively low for the Buttermilks. The main attraction is undoubtedly the *Iron Man Traverse* (v4), a justly hallowed problem that is a must for every climber. I would not call it a gimme at this grade, but the ease with which every move can be practiced makes it amenable to everyone. *The Hero Roof* (v0) is another must do, on great holds, but requiring some punch at the lip. There are a handful of other excellent two-star lines. Those pulling hard will enjoy the superb *Iron Fly* (v9). More tricky than big, this is a special find for dyno lovers.

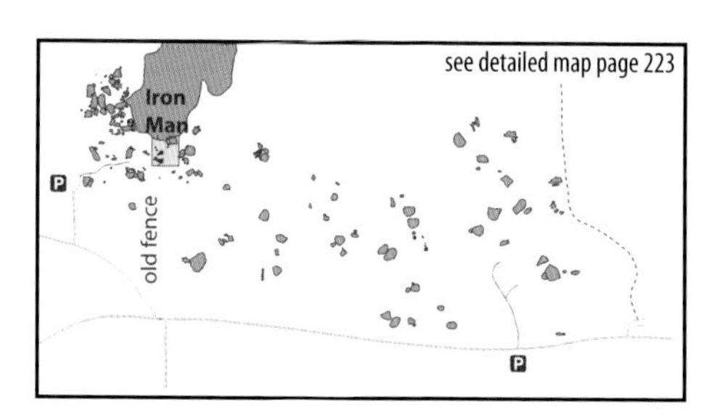

THE HERO ROOF BOULDER

1 Groovy Grit v1 ☐
Climb the groove from a standing start.

2 Just Grit v7 ★ ☐
From the sloping hold at the lip of the boulder, and with feet on a big ledge at the base, make an awkward dyno up to the sloper at the start of the previous problem. This assumes that the starting hold still has some crystals you can pull on. Continue direct, or right per *Just Dishy* (see below).

3 Dishy Grit v6 ★★ ☐
Begin under the groove and climb up and right via shallow dishes with a hard mantel-style move and a very grainy finish up to the right. Will clean up to be a fine sloper problem.

4 Just Dishy v8 ★ ☐
Make the starting dyno of *Just Grit* and join *Dishy Grit.*

5 Easy Grit v5 ★★ ☐
Begin with a right hand pinch and the left on the arete, and climb up right.

6 Hard Grit v8 ★ ☐
A low start to *Easy Grit* where the left hand is on the lower hold (not on the upper arete), and the right hand is in the poor sloping sidepull a few feet below the pinch.

7 Rib Direct v5 ☐
Start at the big jug/hueco and dyno through to the big jugs directly above (eliminating holds right).

8 Rib Direct Sit Start v7 ★ ☐
Sit start at two hand-sized blobs and join the previous problem: A toe hook could prove useful to make the first move.

9 Rib, No Rib v1 ★ ☐
Start with both hands in the deep incut dish/pocket. Pull right, then up.

10 Rib, No Rib, Sit v6 ☐
Sit start at the two hand-sized blobs and join the previous problem.

11 Hero Roof v0 ★★★ ☐
Sit start at the right side of the overhanging wall and climb up and left, following the edge of the wall on great holds, pulling the lip to more big holds: Heroic.

12 Unnamed Slab v0- ★ ☐
The slab, starting at the left side is pretty nice.

13 Unnamed Crack v0- ☐
On the southwest side of the boulder, climb the crack.

Just uphill from the Hero Roof Boulder, facing the overhang is another boulder. The southeast corner of this has:

14 Unnamed Jump Start v1 ★ ☐
Jump to the good jug and try to style your way up. Fun.

IRON MAN BOULDER

15 Unnamed v2 ☐
Sit start the crack at the left side of the boulder.

16 Iron Man v4 ★★★ ☐
This ultra-classic traverse is a world class favorite and relatively friendly on the skin. Begin with big flat holds and follow a steadily shrinking rail until it disappears, forcing a snatch for the full-hand-friction of the boulder's lip; then mantel over to glory. Begin with both hands at the very far left.

17 Iron Man, Footless v6 ★★ ☐
Surprisingly, the traverse (previous problem) is not that much harder without using your feet, if you move fast! The feet go back on after sticking the lip at right.

18 Iron Cross/Iron Circle v6 ★ ☐
Do *Iron Man* (above), then, without topping out, traverse the lip of the boulder back to the crack.

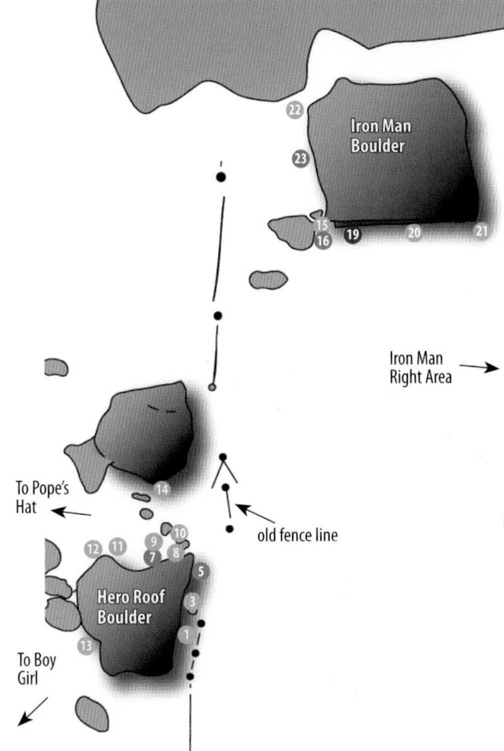

19 Iron Slap v10 ★ ☐

Start hanging the sloping rail. Grab a micro-crimp and use a heel to gain more crimps and then the lip. Pull over with some difficulty to finish. The fin/crack at left is not used.

20 Iron Fly v9 ★★★ ☐

An amazing dyno: start with hands on the rail and throw a very tricky move to a hidden flat edge beyond the lip; mantel over. The line also goes static by a heel hook and a lock-off, followed by difficult groping across left, then over—this feels like an entirely different problem.

21 Magnetic Attraction v6 ☐

Follow the blunt arete up and left, from a sit start at right: cold, cloudy weather a must.

Around the back of the Iron Man Boulder, on its west side, are two more excellent problems:

22 Iron Monkey v7 ★★ ☐

Sit start on the left, with the right hand just right of a vertical sidepull: traverse the lip rightward and pull over just before reaching the boulders at right.

23 Unnamed v4 ★★ ☐

Sit start with hands in the crack; make one move to the lip, and then pull a hard mantel.

IRON MAN EAST AREA

East of the Iron Man traverse are some boulders, large and small, both up-slope and down. I wouldn't' say there is a stand out classic in this collection, though there are plenty of good climbs. There's a nice v0 in *Hager Arete*, some good vBs and some good-looking, very tall projects on the Golden Wall Boulder, as well as the uphill-side slab of the same boulder which has perfect rock and a tall problem/short solo, *Glass Slab* (v0). *The Grovel Roof* (v3) almost makes it to classic status too. The run-and-jump is a good laugh, while the topout requires a complete change of gears.

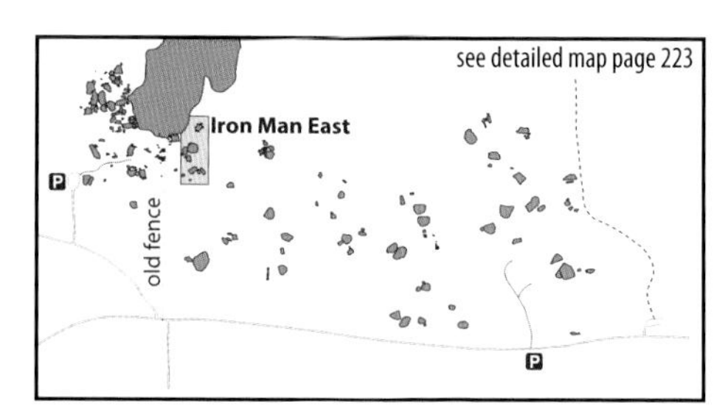

THE HAGER BOULDER

This is up and right from the Iron Man Boulder

1 Unnamed v0 ☐
At this grade, the face is climbed from its left side.

2 Hager Arete v0 ★★ ☐
The excellent northwest arete is fun and exciting.

3 Hager Face v4 ☐
Climb the face, following the crimps up and right.

4 Unnamed Arete v0 ☐
The south arete is climbed straight on from its base.

5 Unnamed vB ★★ ☐
Right of the arete is a fine slab with a nice rail of rising crimps.

GOLDEN BOULDER

The giant boulder down and right from the Iron Man traverse, named for its huge golden south face (with a stellar big project). On the northwest side of the boulder, facing the *Iron Man* traverse are:

6 Glass Slab v0 ★★ ☐
The left side of the slab above the horizontal crack requires a cool head and/or a very long reach. Gain the dishes, and move up left to the arete.

7 Unnamed v1 ★ ☐
Sit start the crack at right with a hard move, climb the crack and traverse left along it, and up the arete.

8 Constellation v10 ★★ ☐
Sit start in the crack and climb to the boulder's lip. Follow the lip angling up rightward all the way to the apex of the boulder. Top out. There is a tough move over the adjacent block where pads and spotters are needed, plus more trickery to bring you to a redpoint crux manteling over at the end of the traverse.

9 Project ☐
The Golden Boulder's south face provides a big challenge, beginning toward the right side of the smooth wall with some small crimps/laybacks. Dishes directly above lead to big patina up and left.

10 Project ☐
Another possible line is to move out right up the blunt arete and around rightward higher up. Begin as for the previous line, or possibly further right.

Next to the Golden Boulder, just left of its giant south face, is a smaller boulder with a few problems on its south and east sides:

11 Unnamed v3 ★ ☐
Climb the left side of the undercut prow that faces downhill. There is a small right hand pinch about six feet up to start.

12 Unnamed v2 ★ ☐
Climb the right side of the undercut prow that faces downhill. The first holds are high, so if you're short you may need to jump from the ground.

13 Unnamed v0 ☐
On the left side of the east wall, start off of big jugs high above the ground. Make a much harder start if you are too short to reach these.

14 Unknown ☐
Reportedly, climbing the crack between the boulders (I don't know which direction), was once considered a fun challenge, to Steve Schneider anyway.

THE GROVEL ROOF

This is just below the Golden Boulder. It is a narrow wall capped by a small jutting overhang.

15 Grovel Roof v3 ★ ☐
Run and jump to get started, (or climb the face with great difficulty) then grovel over the overhang! Fun and a little bit frightening up there.

THE TWINS

Downhill from the Grovel Roof are The Twins. There are some vB problems here and a couple of v0 climbs:

16 Unnamed vB ★★ ☐
On the left side of the south face is an excellent vB problem.

17 Unnamed v0 ★ ☐
At the right side of the downhill face, begin just left of a scooped section. Climb straight up toward a prominent shield of patina at the top.

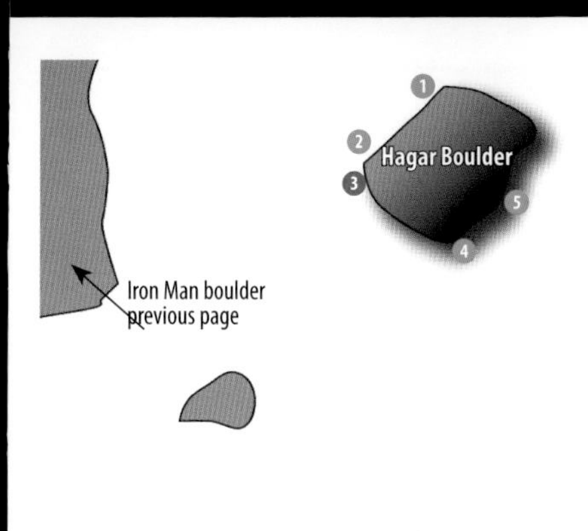

HAGER BOULDER

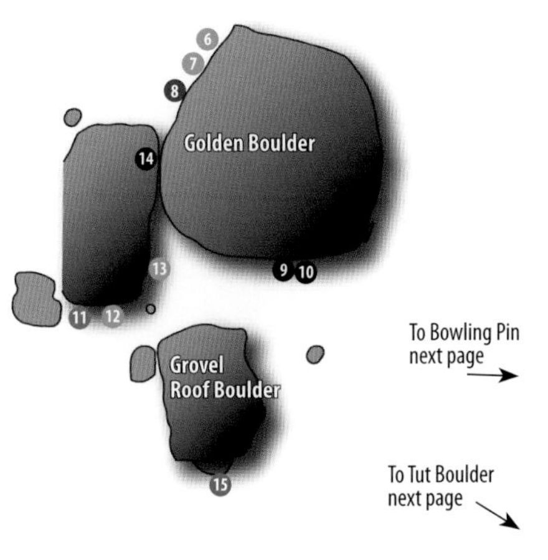

GOLDEN BOULDER

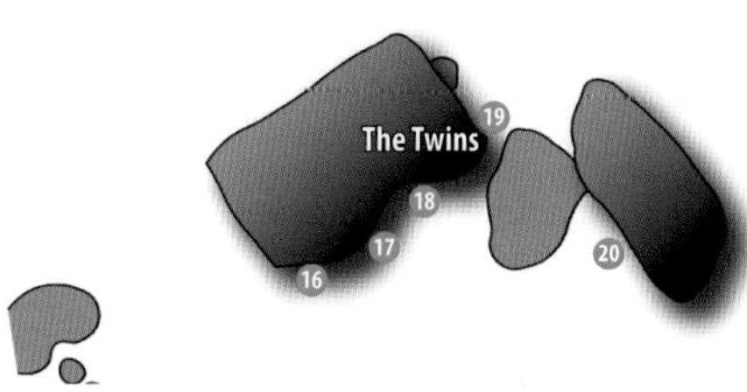

GROVEL ROOF

18 Unnamed v1 ☐

Sit start at the right side of the scooped section, with the left hand high in a deep hueco. Pull up, change the left to an undercling and move up and left.

19 Unnamed v0 ☐

Begin by reaching in from a rock to a high right-hand knob. A low start hanging on the overhanging nose looks possible, though the rock is a bit grainy.

The right twin (as you look uphill) has:

20 Unnamed v0 ☐

The left side of the south arete of the right twin has crusty incut holds.

THE TWINS

BOWLING PIN / TUT AREA

Two great boulders sit in the central section of the Buttermilks, stranded in the no man's land between the popular Iron Man areas to the west and the Rowell Rocks and Cave areas to the east. Both boulders offer a selection of top class lines *Bowling Pin* (v4) is an awesome problem, combining some hard pulling, some balance, and some confidence up high. Most other lines here are also good, including the Original Line, an oft neglected gem, which is pretty high, but with an okay landing. The Tut Boulder is definitely a popular one, with many relatively safe, relatively short lines, sometimes with steep starts, above good flat landings and a stack of options from v0 classics to v8 sit-starts. The perennial favorite duo of *King Tut* and *Funky Tut* are a pair of low-angle face problems on the south side of this boulder—ultra-classic Buttermilk climbing on protruding features and poor footholds.

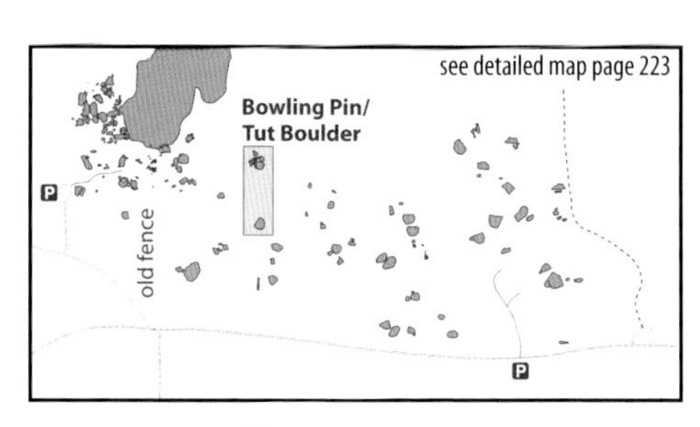

THE BOWLING PIN

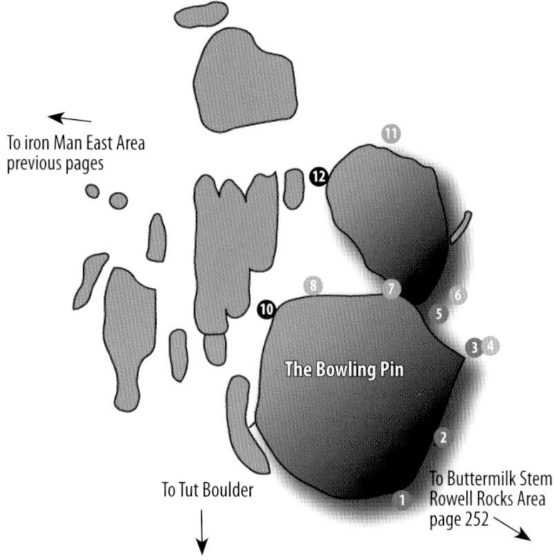

THE BOWLING PIN

This is a giant boulder, across the hillside right of the Golden Boulder, and uphill from the Tut Boulder.

1 Gutter Ball v5 ★ ☐
Begin with a left-facing sidepull at the very left edge of the east face and climb direct on bad crimps to gain the left edge of an obvious horizontal/crescent hold high on the right wall. Force the exit up and slightly left to the gutter/scoops.

2 Original Line v3 ★★ ☐
Climb the vertical east face by the easiest means to gain the big crescent-shaped hold (hard move). Sidepull this with the left hand and continue direct.

3 Bowling Pin Arete v4 ★ ☐
Start standing at the right arete of the east face and make a couple of sharp pulls to better holds. Pull up to a standing position on a big flake, and then finish up the grainy slab with trepidation.

4 Bowling Pin Arete Sit Start v6 ★ ☐
Sit start at sharp crimps and join the previous line.

5 Bowling Pin v4 ★★★ ☐
Pretty hard for the grade, since breaks: Climb up the undulating wall on an assortment of interesting crimps and sidepulls. Make a sweet move left to a standing position on a flake, and finish boldly.

6 Bowling Pin Sit Start v6 ★★★ ☐
As above, but sit start at opposing crimps, which adds a couple of hard moves.

7 Ten Pin Trial v8 ★★ ☐
Sit start at a deep undercling eight feet right of the previous problem. Traverse left to join *Bowling Pin,* beginning with very hard moves on small crimps.

8 Bowling Pin Traverse (High version) v6 ☐
Begin six feet right of the previous problem at a double-dished hueco. Climb left and then up, and then left through a squeeze between the boulders on some painful and questionable flakes to join The Bowling Pin.

9 Unknown/Project ☐
Start as for the previous problem and move up then slightly right with a questionable undercling and then good holds that lead to a high, grainy nightmare over a bad landing.

⑩ Unknown ☐

Right of the previous problem is an incredibly thin, but perhaps solid flake (well, kinda solid?). Climb from this, up and over on good features.

On the uphill side of the Bowling Pin, is a smaller boulder, with:

⑪ Unnamed v2 ☐

On the uphill side of the smaller boulder, sit start at a ring hold and climb up and left.

⑫ Project ☐

The west-facing wall above a low block has some rough texture, but seems solid.

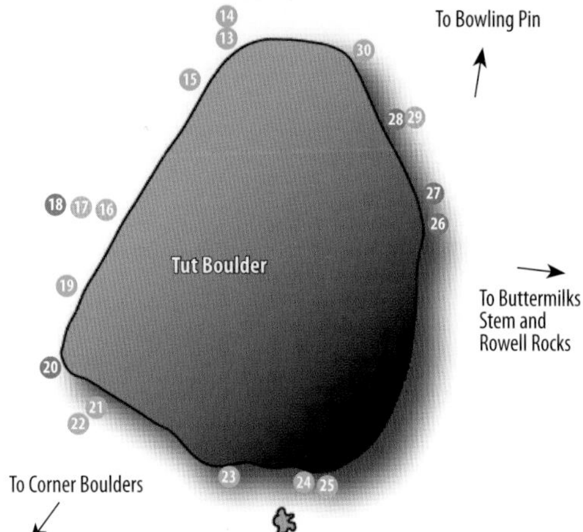

TUT BOULDER

A boulder with a plethora of excellent problems, *King Tut* and *Funky Tut* being the most sought-after classics. Starting at the northwest corner and working counter-clockwise, find:

⑬ Unnamed v1 ★★ ☐

Sit start at polished plate with crimps on the left: climb up and left with interesting moves and a variety of holds.

⑭ Unnamed v0 ★★ ☐

Sit start at the polished plate with crimps: climb up and right, then make a tricky press onto the rail.

⑮ Unnamed v0 ★★ ☐

Climb the crack and deep huecos. Sit start: v4.

⑯ Milk the Milks v6 ★★ ☐

Sit start with the lowest two crimps. Pull hard to gain good incuts at the lip, and then traverse six feet left along the lip of the boulder, before launching up the upper wall on sloping edges.

⑰ Tut Traverse v8 ★ ☐

Begin as for the previous line, but keep traversing, turning the corner to the north face, where some hard moves lead left until your feet are on the starting holds of *Lululator* (see over). Top out.

TUT BOULDER

TUT BOULDER

⓲ **Egypt (No Crack)** v3 ★ ☐
Sit start with the left in the upper crimp. Make one hard move up right, and then climb directly up by using a couple of protruding xenoliths, but without the crack.

⓳ **Egypt (Crack)** v0 ★ ☐
Climb the crack.

⓴ **Wimberries** v4 ★ ☐
Sit start at good holds and climb the arete.

㉑ **King Tut** v3 ★★★ ☐
Climb the face directly on weird slopey protrusions.

㉒ **Funky Tut** v3 ★★★ ☐
Begin as for *King Tut* but move right a few feet until it is possible to move up right to a deep hueco. A footwork-intensive testpiece with a rewarding finish.

㉓ **Ay** v1 ★★ ☐
Climb the pretty runnel past a grey pinch.

㉔ **Howard Carter** v0 ★ ☐
Near the right side of the south face, climb up past big patina plates.

㉕ **Howard Carter Sit Start** v6 ★ ☐
Sit start at good orange patina incuts. Climb up and left to join the previous line.

㉖ **Tut Crack Left** v5 ★ ☐
Sit start with the right hand in the crack, left hand to the left, and move up then left onto the slab, using both the crack and holds left.

㉗ **Tut Crack** v3 ★ ☐
Climb the crack from a standing start. The sit, sticking to the crack only, is at least v6.

㉘ **Lululator** v4 ★★ ☐
The scooped wall. The rating assumes a start from the high crimps.

㉙ **Lululator Low Start** v8 ★ ☐
Sit start with the left hand on a poor diagonal crimp and the right hand on a tiny crimp, the third (rightmost, and lowest) of a row of three in a diagonal line. Climb up and left. oo

㉚ **Unnamed** v2 ★ ☐
To the right of the scoop are a lot of good platey crimps which can be climbed by a few different variations at around the same grade.

Jeff Sillcox rolls out of hibernation to burn up some winter fat on the Tut Boulder (*King Tut*, v3 ,opposite).
Photo: Wills Young

CORNER BOULDERS

This is a tight cluster of three large boulders off on its own, low on the slope below and right of the Iron Man Area, and below and left of the Tut Boulder (page 247). There are many good problems here, often fairly tall and vertical, such as the superclassic *Leary/Bard Arete* (v5), a sustained climb up a prominent feature.

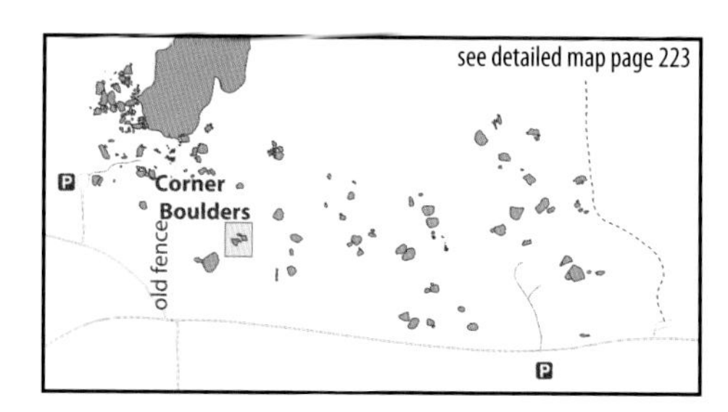

The west-most boulders lean against each other and are described first.

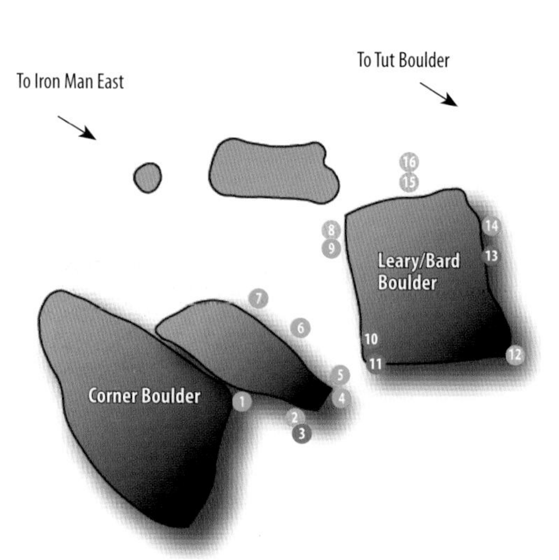

1 Corner Crack v1 ★ ☐
Layback, stem and struggle up the overhanging corner.

2 The Little Arete v8 ★★ ☐
Sit/hang start at two side-by-side holds on the right facet. Climb the left-leaning arete diagonally leftward, using small sidepulls for the right hand, plus a high step, and/or a big span up left.

3 Little Arete Right Exit v5 ★ ☐
Start as for the previous line. Use a sloping dish for the left hand to pull across right and out to the arete at right, and then the brown knob up high near the right arete.

4 Unnamed v0- ★ ☐
Climb the arete on the left side.

5 Unnamed v0 ★ ☐
The arete on the right side is also good.

6 Unnamed v1 ★ ☐
The wall about three or four feet right of the arete has some tough crimpy moves to start.

7 Unnamed v0 ☐
The wall past a slash or short crack with a big move to a sloper up high.

LEARY/BARD BOULDER

8 Curbed v6 ★ ☐
Sit start at a low hueco and climb up via some hard initial moves on sloping pinches. Top out on improving incuts.

9 Hobbs' Problem v2 ★★ ☐
Climb the clean vertical wall, using the large inclusion, or not, as you prefer.

10 Leary/Bard Arete Left v5 ★★ ☐
Climb the arete on its left side to a slightly grainy and scary topout. A seldom-climbed alternative to the standard testpiece (#11).

11 Leary/Bard Arete v5 ★★★ ☐
The classic: Climb the arete on its right side, beginning with some awkward thin face moves. Required climbing for every upwardly mobile Buttermilker!

12 The Eighth Degree v6 ★ ☐
A very hard pull off the ground (depending how high you stack pads, perhaps) using all the flexibility you can manage. Start using either a sidepull with the right, or with a low crimp far right and the left hand on the arete. The pull onto the slab up high is awkward on sloping holds.

13 Unnamed v3 ☐
The scoop and slab is climbed from a left-facing sidepull, moving up and right.

14 Unnamed v1 ☐
Vertical pulls to a slab.

15 Unnamed v6 ★ ☐
Sit start at sloper/crimps and make a very hard pull up into a good undercling hueco (crux). Move up and left to the rib/arete and follow this to the large patina plate (or pull left early with more difficulty).

16 Grit Dreams v9 ★ ☐
Begin as for the previous problem, but instead of moving up and left, move up and right to a deep hueco. Continue right by grabbing the undercut arete, and pull up onto this with a scary high step onto the protruding nose. Top out up the slab. Other variations have been done on this undercut nose, such as starting low right, climbing left, and then back right, also at about v9.

Lisa Rands climbs the ultra-classic *Leary/Bard Arete* (v5, opposite), which can give some climbers the shakes at the topout. Photo: Wills Young.

ROWELL ROCKS

This area is just a stone's throw east of the Tut Boulder and a hop, skip and jump across the slope west of the Cave Boulder. It provides mostly footwork-intensive climbing on thin faces and frictiony walls. *The Buttermilk Stem* (v1) is a mega classic . Every climber, no matter what their level, does battle with this and the sit-start is a humbling v4 that is rarely flashed. Downslope is the Rowell Boulder with the wickedly thin and astonishingly popular *Junior's Achievement* (v7), which used to be one of those v8 gimmes that just cried out to be down-rated. Does anyone want to climb this nasty sharp wall of crimps any more, for a mere v7 tick? Damn right they do, it's a great little crimping testpiece. Big, burly climbers will find it hard going, but for the small and spritely it's an excellent project! As for more powerful stuff, there's the surprisingly good *Sidewinder* (v10) and the slopey and shouldery *Brian's Project* (v9).

Stem Left (v5, opposite), is a fun variation on the Buttermilk Stem Boulder. Photo: Wills Young.

BUTTERMILK STEM BOULDER 📷

The Buttermilk Stem Boulder is just uphill from the Rowell Rocks, a group of boulders that are west of the Cave Area.

1 Unknown ☐
Sit or make a low start in the back of the cave on the west side, on a pinch and flake, and climb out the roof and over. Unfortunately the flake is about to break, though another method could be used to complete the line. The rock at left is obtrusive and could prove painful.

2 Unnamed v4 ★★ ☐
Stand start at the high left pinch/undercling and slopers at the edge of the roof, and climb over the bulge on nice slopers.

3 Brian's Project v8 ★★ ☐
Sit start with the left hand under the bulge on a crimp and the right on bad slopey crimp. Climb up and left to join the previous line.

4 Unnamed v0 ★ ☐
Climb the low-angle blunt rib.

5 Stem Left v5 ★★ ☐
Jump to a deep hole, left of *Buttermilk Stem*, then force a line up and left past a knob and some sloping handholds. The bigger hueco/scoop up and right is not used: Forced but good.

6 Stem Left, Sit v6 ★★ ☐
A sit start to the previous problem from the right.

7 Unnamed v2 ★★ ☐
Jump to the hole and climb up rightish using the rib, to the big hueco.

8 Buttermilk Stem v1 ★★★ ☐
This is the classic stem problem with a hard move off the ground, which is actually pretty easy when you know how. Photo overleaf.

9 Buttermilk Stem Sit Start v4 ★★★ ☐
Do the weirdest sit start around. Rarely onsighted.

10 Cheezy Brit v2 ★ ☐
Climb the arete on its right side, beginning with the right hand on a good hold out right, and the left on the arete. Though a little grainy, this is fun and will clean up.

11 Cheezy Brit Sit Start v7 ★ ☐
Sit start and move up the arete, moving to the right side (using a very high left foot on the arete) to join the previous line.

12 Matt's Project v6 ★ ☐
Start at the arete and traverse right across diagonal slopers to gain patina and a slab.

13 Matt's Project Sit v9 ★ ☐
Another good sloper special: Sit start as for *Buttermilk Stem* and contort and wriggle your way into the arete at right as for *Cheezy Brit Sit Start*. From here join *Matt's Project*.

ROWELL BOULDER

BUTTERMILK STEM BOULDER

ROWELL BOULDER

This is a giant boulder that is downhill from the Buttermilk Stem Boulder and just across the hillside west of the Cave Boulder.

14 Sidewinder v10 ★★ ☐
Sit start in the small roof with a good crimp and an undercling. Make a brutal move or two out the overhang to gain a big flat hold above the roof. From here, move up, left slightly and mantel into the scoop. A great combination of power and technique with a high finish.

15 Buttermilk Gem v1 ★ ☐
Make a mantel (little hop off the ground—crux) then tackle the giant slab straightish.

16 Junior's Arete v1 ★★ ☐
Climb the arete, staying to the right side.

17 Junior's Achievement v8 ★★ ☐
Climb the face, aiming for a pointed right-facing patina that is high to the right side of this smooth east-facing facet. Begin at left with a right sidepull, or to the right at a pair of small crimps. Aim for a good right sidepull, then that large patina up high: both ways are thin and sharp.

18 Unnamed v1 ★ ☐
Climb up passing to the right of a slanting crack by using a spike undercling.

19 Unnamed v3 ★ ☐
As above, but eliminate the spike undercling and follow the crack line up and left.

20 Unnamed v1 ★ ☐
Climb the scoopish wall past a hanging flake.

21 Unnamed v0 ☐
This arete also serves as a downclimb.

22 Mooned v9 ★★ ☐
A great line for tall, flexible freaks. Begin at a good blocky crimp just right of the left arete, and another tiny bad crimp higher (use a pad or two, if needed). Make ridiculously hard high steps and balance moves up the face on dreadful holds.

23 Project ☐
Climb the wall with a pair of right-facing sidepulls low down.

24 Absent Friends v6 ☐
Reportedly this is a line on the blunt arete, presumably staying to the left side to avoid the next line.

25 Rowell Face v1 ★★ ☐
A fairly sustained and serious highball up the face right of the arete.

26 Rowell Face, "Fright" v4 ☐
This is the sketchy line stepping directly off the top of the big boulder. Glassy footholds, bad handholds including a thin crimp that feels like it will break, all over a bad landing, make this a bit of a frightener.

POTHOLE BOULDER

Just up and right from the Rowell Boulder is a low boulder with a line of pothole huecos:

27 Project ☐
A ridiculous sit start up the very short bulging wall on the west end.

28 Pothole Traverse v1 ☐
Sit start at right and climb up then across to the left.

29 Pothole Direct v0 ☐
At the right side, go straight up.

About ten yards downhill from the Rowell Boulder is a relatively small boulder. On the northwest side of which is:

30 Unnamed Mantel v0 ☐
A mantel problem.

This boulder also has potential not recorded here.

Mike Brady pressing some flesh on the ultra-classic *Buttermilk Stem* (v1, page 252). Photo: Wills Young.

CAVE AREA

Two giant boulders form a large cave left of the Soul Slinger area, with the lower, larger rock providing several steep boulder problems on its cave side, plus several more vertical lines on the outside. The cave interior is regularly a big "scene" with many people hanging out, staying cool on warmer days, or trying to avoid snow during stormy weather. People climb here when icicles hang like chandeliers from the gap in the cave roof—those pushing the higher grades hoping the cold rock will give grippy conditions on the smooth slopey lip of the notorious *Buttermilker* (v13). People also climb here when the sun is so intense they daren't leave. *The Cave Route* (v6) is always being sessioned; half caving, half climbing, the butt-dragging thuggy moves will usually lead to a few back slapping encounters at the crux, just five feet off the ground!

With much of the attention of climbers being focused on the interior of the cave and its wealth of steep, powerful climbs, the contrasting vertical problems on the outside have been relatively overlooked in the past, and on the downhill side of the boulder, people continue to make "first ascents" of lines likely done years before. The best of these is the superb *Roc Trippin'* named after the Petzl "Roc Trip" event during which it was (again?) claimed as a first, but the *Mystery Bard Route* to the right is also a lost gem. All in all, there's much to be done here.

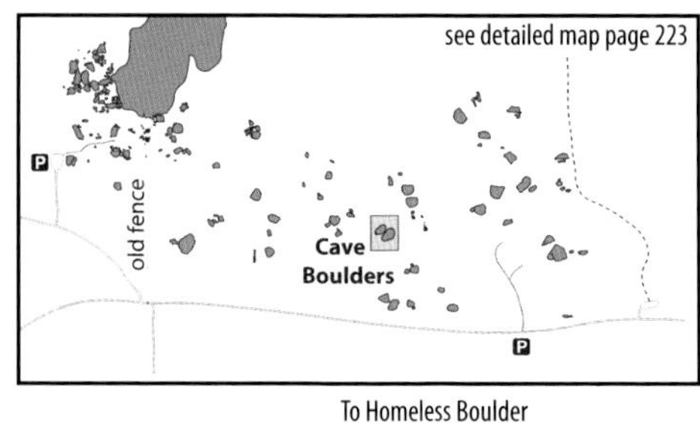

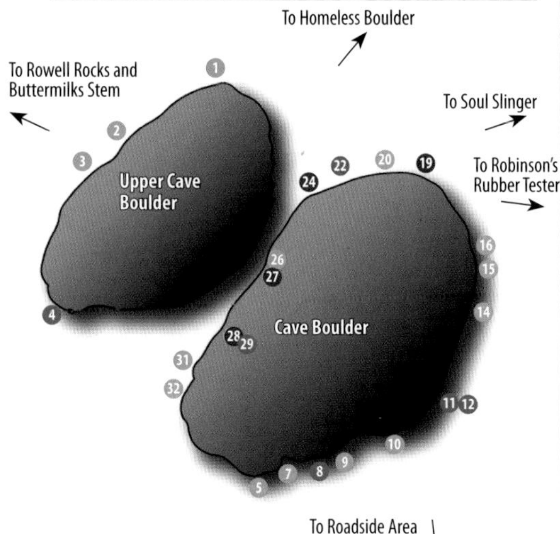

UPPER CAVE BOULDER

This is the big boulder that forms the north wall of the cave uphill from, and touching the Cave Boulder. On the uphill, outside face, moving left to right, find:

1 Unnamed v2 ☐
Start off a low rock and climb up with a hard couple of moves on sharp crimps: crusty.

2 Unnamed v0- ☐
The slab is climbed using good edges, but is uninteresting and the downclimb (at right) is awkward.

3 Unnamed v0 ☐
The slab further right has a couple of interesting moves (the downclimb further right, though, is a little awkward).

4 Unnamed v3 ☐
Sit start and climb the nose of the boulder. Begin with crossed hands.

CAVE BOULDER

This is the huge boulder that forms the southeast side of the big cave.

5 Roc Trippin' v7 ★★ ☐
Pull off the ground with difficulty to gain a good incut crimp. Continue over the bulge with hidden dishes both left and right.

6 Project ☐
An excellent sit start to the previous line will add a grade, or two.

7 Mystery Face v6 ★★ ☐
Climb the face, which is reasonably easy (and good) after the first heinous moves.

8 Bush Pilot v5 ☐
Start at a good incut and climb the vertical wall.

9 Unnnamed v6 ☐
Six feet right of the previous line, use a pinch sidepull for the right hand to make a ridiculous high-step. Reach to a hard-to-see edge high up for the left hand, and walk it out to the top.

1
2
3
tricky descent and jump
4
On nose
UPPER CAVE BOULDER

5
7
8
9
10
11
12
CAVE BOULDER

CAVE BOULDER, EAST FACE

⑩ Grain Pain v0 ☐
Start at the big flake jug and climb up by good holds.

⑪ Unnamed v4 ★ ☐
Begin at a deep incut hold, that is reasonably high up. Climb up and then left with a big move. Start low off small sharp crimps to add one move and bump the grade to v5.

⑫ Unnamed v5 ☐
Begin as for the previous problem, but climb right to a deep hueco. Start low and bump the grade to v6.

⑬ Project ☐
Climb the wall past some slanting features.

⑭ Unnamed v7 ☐
Begin with the right hand at two small knobs forming an awkward crimp, and climb the wall. There is also a wide crimp/pinch for the left at about 7 ft up.

⑮ Pain Grain v5 ★★ ☐
Painful, but good: Start at an undercling for the left hand and climb the wall. A small hidden crimp up high in the rib might be useful to pass the slopey section.

⑯ Pain Grain Sit Start v7 ★★ ☐
Sit start the previous problem down and right, beginning with a big move.

⑰ Project ☐
Directly above the sit start to *Pain Grain* is a small crimp. Higher right are more crimps and features.

⑱ Project/Unknown ☐
A hanging slab has some holds that can be gained from a crusty sidepull and other crusty holds just under the lip. Even a sit start might be doable, though not on the best rock.

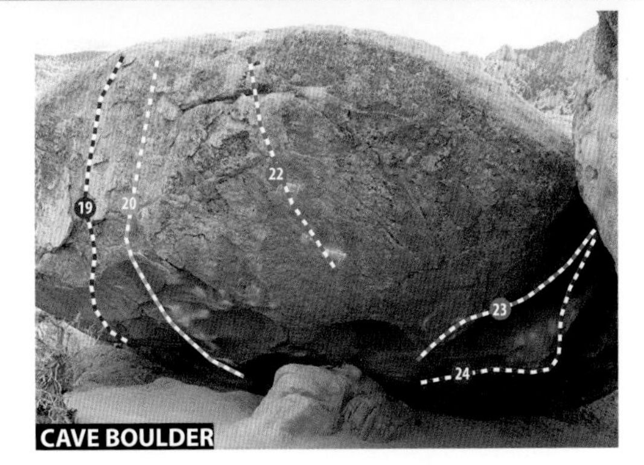

CAVE BOULDER

19 One Mule Wonder v10 ☐
Long ago a pleasant v5 sit, this is now one of the harder lines on the boulder: Start low with a very sharp sidepull crimp. Heinous.

20 Cave Route v6 ★★ ☐
Start virtually lying down and follow the line of flakes out the very steep roof. Pull around onto the slab and call it good.

21 Homeostasis v6 ☐
Reportedly a line moving right out of *Cave Route* into the next line. At this grade, a standing start?

22 Dyno Problem v3 ★ ☐
From the low boulder, reach in to a finger jug in the brown patina. Match hands, then move up with a couple of big moves and/or a dyno.

23 Lactose Intolerant v5 ★ ☐
From a standing start by the embedded rock, just left of The *Buttermilker's* start, pull on and follow a line of flakes up and right to join the top of *The Buttermilker*.

24 The Buttermilker v13 ★★ ☐
Sit start down and left on a large sidepull. Climb across right to underclings, then out to slick holds and a challenging move to grab a decent horn. Top out. The standing start from the underclings (v12), though not the original is a good problem in itself. Photo overleaf.

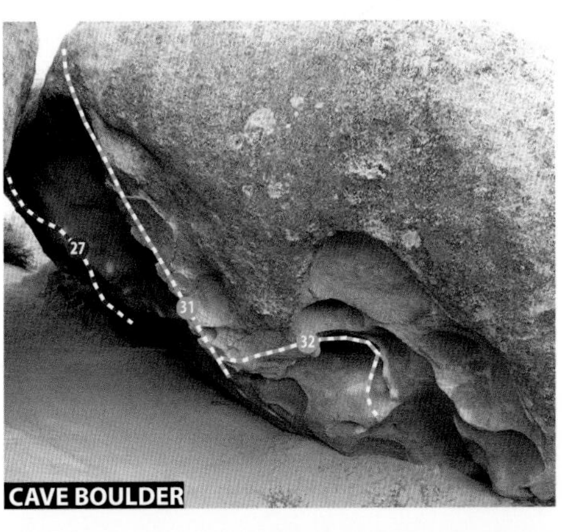

CAVE BOULDER

25 The Buttermelter v11 ★ ☐
In the giant scoop right of The *Buttermilker's* start and just to the left of the V-shaped feature at the start of *Moonraker*, begin at underclings with the right hand on a "ball." Throw in a knee-bar (pad very useful) and move your right hand over to the glass dish of *The Buttermilker*. Use a crimp and some crafty footwork to join *The Buttermilker*.

26 Moonraker v8 ★ ☐
Start on good underclings. Traverse right and make a tenuous pull into a standing position in the giant scoop. Pull out of the scoop to the right to join *Inner Sanctum* to the highest patina. Topping out is optional.

27 Little Forgotten v10 ★★ ☐
Begin with both hands on underclings as for *Moonraker.* Make a couple moves up to gain the deep hueco directly above, and a hold to the right of this. Move up past a knee-bar to a big span left into the large scoop and the finish of *The Buttermilker*. Some breaks since the last guidebook, have made the moves left a bit harder, so the rating, as always, is in debate. Fun varied climbing.

28 Already Forgotten (a.k.a. Buttermilker Traverse) v11 ★ ☐
Sit start at flakes below the left side of the giant scoop/alcove at right. Climb directly up the left side of the scoop to the rightmost crimps of the Moonraker traverse. Reverse this traverse to gain the big hueco and then continue up and left to join the ending moves of *The Buttermilker's* topout. Crumbly.

29 Shelter from the Storm v5 ★ ☐
Sit start at two low flakes. Make a move to slopers and then a big move right to another sloper. Finish on Inner Sanctum to the upper patina.

30 Wheel of Cheese v10 ☐
Now you're really desperate. Start as for *Shelter from the Storm* and climb up the rib of *Inner Sanctum* until you can reach left to some enticing looking pinch/underclings. Move left across these and join the last section of *Little Forgotten*. Total cheese.

31 Inner Sanctum v2 ☐
The tall and inviting rib of patina unfortunately leads to a dead end where some very long legs might come in useful. Begin on the left with both hands on a sloper and climb to the highest patina. Broken holds have rendered the exit desperate. Facing right, then turning and stemming looks like the best option.

The Cave Boulder has some excellent mid-grade to hard lines on steep rock. Here Daniel Woods hangs from *The Buttermilker* (v13, page 259), a testpiece established by Chris Sharma in 1999. Photo: Tim Kemple.

32 Gleaming the Cube v8 ★ ☐
Start with hands on the edge of the giant sloping scoop on crimps or pinches. Pull to the better slopers higher, then up right, and back left to finish on *Inner Sanctum*. A high start from the better slopers is an excellent v6.

33 Project/Unknown ☐
Right of *Gleaming The Cube* are some more slick, bumpy crimps and pinches.

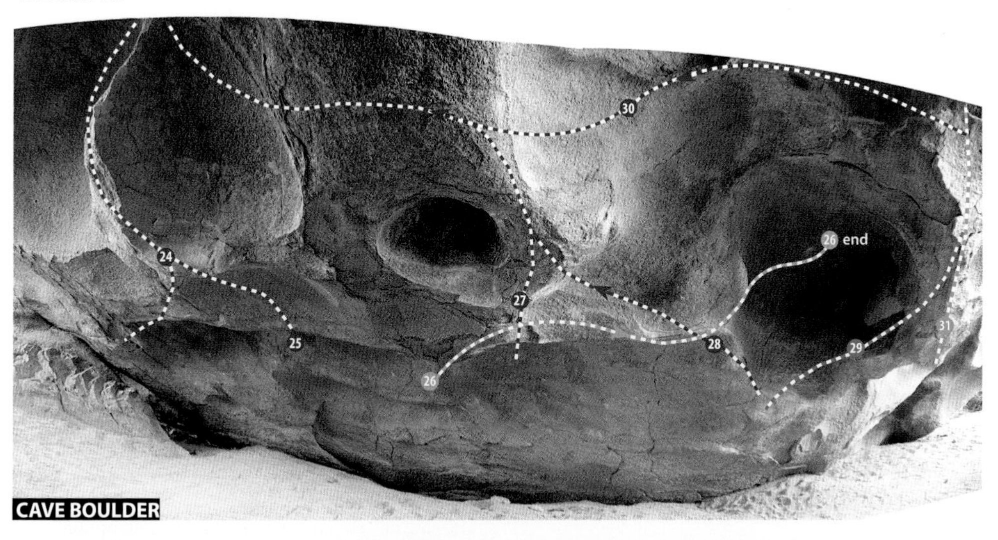

SOUL SLINGER AREA

Named after the fantastic *Soul Slinger* (v9), I've also included the Fit Homeless Boulder in this area. The Fit Homeless Boulder has two superb vertical faces on its east side. Both of them, *Yayoi* (v8), and *Yayoi Right* (v7), are extreme crimp and foot-intensive testpieces with high, hard finishes. Many good solid face climbs at relatively easy grades (v0 to v2) over good landings are on the uphill side of the Fit Homeless Boulder, left of the steep patina testpiece *America's Fit Homeless* (v9), a low-ball classic.

The Soul Slinger Boulder is home to *Soul Slinger* (v9) itself, one of the best lines in Bishop and understandably popular. It has technical and intriguing moves up a prominent, beautiful feature. The positive first holds give a false impression to many who think this might be a pushover. But compensating for lack of balance by trying to muscle up the line simply doesn't work. Lower down the slope, the excellent *Robinson's Rubber Tester Slab* provides great amusement at the entry level of v0 to v1.

Handsome and unsung bouldering maestro Michael Gennaro tests the friction on the old-school butt-kicker, *Pope's Prow* (v6, page 293). Photo: Wills Young.

FIT HOMELESS BOULDER

A big boulder uphill and slightly right from the Cave Boulder, with a tall, blank-looking vertical east face. Starting at this east face and rotating around the boulder, counter-clockwise, find:

1 **Yayoi** v8 ★★ ☐
Climb the smooth vertical face with gastons, opposing sidepulls and poor footholds to a gruelling finish at the slot. Seems very hard if you're short.

2 **Yayoi Right** v7 ★★ ☐
Using precise footwork, follow sidepulls to a rail at the lip and a long last reach to top out: very sustained. Start from the left, or direct.

3 **Unknown** ☐
The wall at the far right, just left of the black streak appears to have a couple of hard moves off the ground to gain good holds higher.

4 **Unnamed** v0- ★★ ☐
Climb the left side of the north wall with the scoop, or make a nice sit start at v1.

5 **Unnamed** v0 ★★ ☐
Just left of a small patch of yellow lichen, climb the wall with good patina sidepulls, staying straight.

6 **Unnamed** v0- ★★ ☐
Climb the good patina.

7 **Unnamed** v0 ★★ ☐
Climb the wall above the blocky ledge. Stay to the right, which is tricky to the end.

8 **Unnamed** v2 ★★ ☐
Sit start the previous line with one very hard pull.

9 **America's Fit Homeless** v9 ★ ☐
Sit start with a sidepull and one of two crimps below this, or with both low crimps. Crimp up and left.

10 **Tenterhooks** v8 ★ ☐
Squat start at the right side of the boulder, matched on side-pull crimps. Move the left hand up to a bad sloper, move your feet up and huck to another bad sloper. Continue on more slopers over the top: a slopey and insecure experience.

On a smaller boulder just west of the Fit Homeless, and directly up slope from the Cave Boulders are:

11 **Unnamed** v1 ★ ☐
The southeast arete has some good patina and shallow parallel cracks. Begin with hands in the lowest part of the left crack. Climb up, rightish, but then step left as soon as possible to top out. Alternatively, continue up slightly right and top out by stepping onto the top of the right crack (v3).

12 **Unnamed** v3 ☐
Sit start in the hueco and climb up and then left to a good incut. Continue slightly left to top out. Or, if you're feeling brave and have a long arm, make a harder finish direct to a good edge way back over the top.

13 **Unnamed** v3 ☐
At the far right of the east face, sit start and climb up the grainy wall above a big hueco. Make a huge move to a deep jug at the top. The standing start is v1.

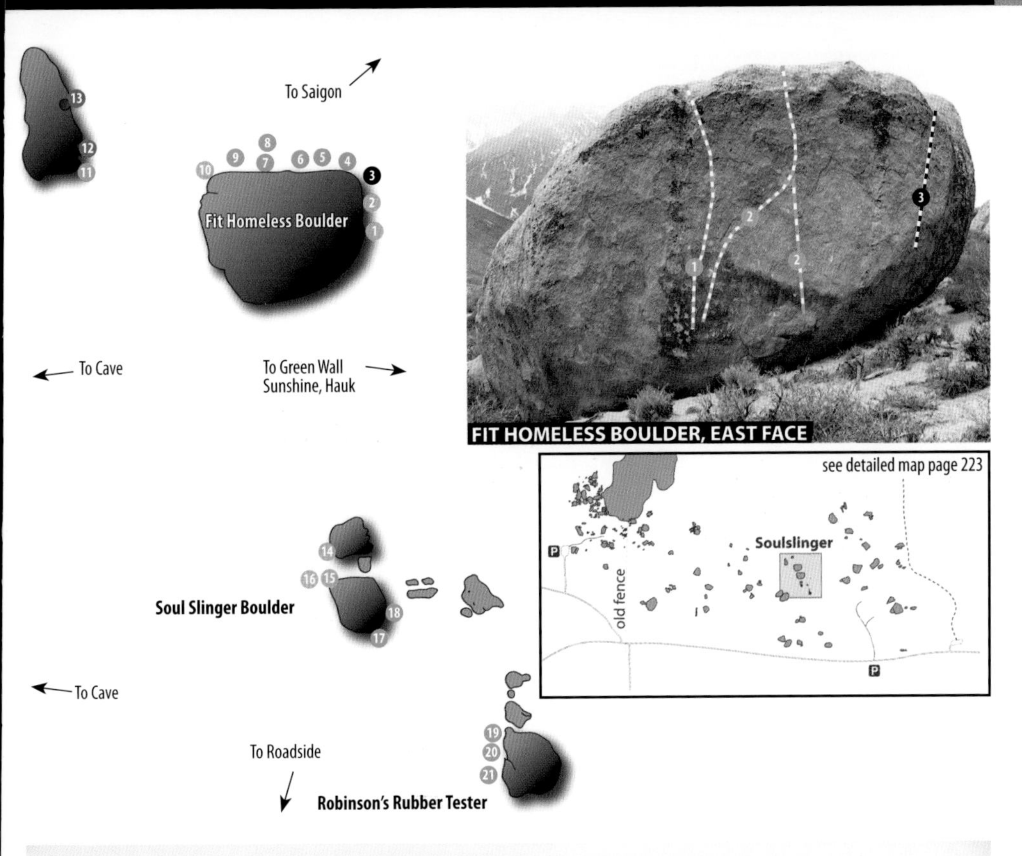

FIT HOMELESS BOULDER, UPHILL FACE

SOUL SLINGER BOULDERS

ROBINSON'S RUBBER TESTER BOULDER

SOUL SLINGER BOULDERS

These sit almost touching, on the slope east of and slightly uphill from the Cave Boulder, and just down from the Fit Homeless Boulder.
The upper of the two boulders has:

14 Akila v7 ★ ☐
Begin with a sloping crimp on the left side of the wall facing Soul Slinger (below), and climb the wall direct. A pinch high right and some high steps may prove useful.

On the lower boulder, find:

15 Soul Slinger v9 ★★★ ☐
The pretty arete is climbed using positive patina and a poor pinch to a tenuous and balancy sequence leading to a long stretch to the "grab me" bucket at the lip. How cool is that? Utterly brilliant! It can't be v9 though, can it? Make up your own mind, I guess.

16 Soul Slinger Right v8 ★★ ☐
Cold, cloudy day? Begin as for *Soul Slinger* and make a big pull from the two good incuts to a rounded hold on the right wall. Bring the left hand around and pull across to the deep hueco in the right wall. A direct finish up the arete on more rough slopers is possible if the friction is especially good.

17 Unnamed v0 ☐
Climb the southeast side of the boulder up past a large left-facing sidepull with one awkward move at the start.

18 Unnamed v0 ☐
To the right of the previous line, climb the wall on good holds.

ROBINSON'S RUBBER-TESTER SLAB

This is downhill from the Soul Slinger Boulders, facing west toward the Cave Boulder and mountains.

19 Unnamed v1 ☐
From the left arete pull around right and climb the right side of the arete.

20 Robinson's Rubber Tester v0 ★★ ☐
Climb the slab up the center.

21 Unnamed v0 ☐
The south arete.

Sasha Turentine on the Bard classic, *Green Wall Center* (v6), page 280. Photo: Wills Young.

ROADSIDE AREA

This area, which is down the slope from the Cave Area has many high quality climbs over flat landings, making it especially good for the v0 to v4 climber, with a variety of lines that are sometimes short and easy to spot. *The Rail Problem* (v3) is one such problem. There are also some higher lines, including the excellent *Roadside Highball* (v3), a technical face to a delightful and committing lock off way up high.

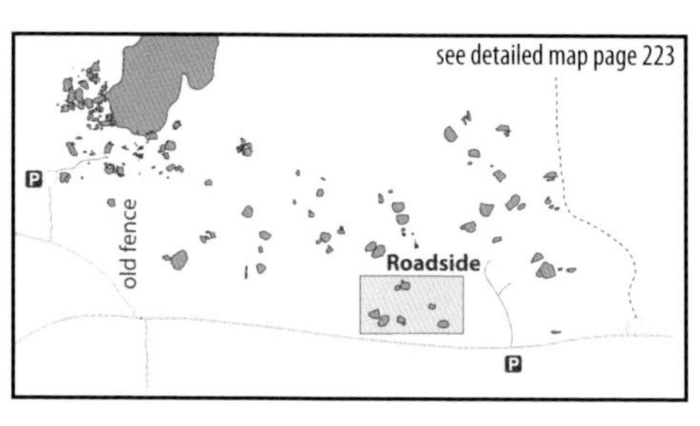

ROADSIDE BOULDER

ROADSIDE BOULDER

XENOLITH BOULDER

See the topo, opposite to locate this boulder that is very close to the road (no photo):

1 Heavy Grit v7 ★ ☐
From the big slot/xenolith, pull right and up the arete.

ROADSIDE BOULDER

Beginning at the left side of the south face, find:

2 Unnamed v0- ☐
Climb the blunt end of the boulder with some deft footwork.

3 Unnamed v0 ☐
Climb the smooth patina.

4 Roadside Highball v3 ★★★ ☐
Begin at the left side of the scoop and move delicately up past tiny crimps to a tricky reach right to the deep slot at the top. A delightful footwork test with a rewarding finish.

5 Project ☐
A little grainy still, and perhaps contrived: Move across the scoop from left to right to summit on the blunt nose, just right of the deep hueco (avoiding this to stay right of the previous line).

6 Unnamed v2 ★ ☐
Just right of the arete, reach high to start and climb up using a good right sidepull, staying left at the top. A low start is also possible but is hard, and grainy.

7 Unnamed v2 ★ ☐
From a high start, climb directly up the faint rib, just right of the previous line.

8 Unnamed v4 ★ ☐
Sit/hang start low on the slanting rail. Climb almost directly over the bulge. Pull slightly left to stand above the lip and then continue direct quite easily.

9 The Roadside Rail/Rail Problem v3 ★★ ☐
Sit/hang start low on the slanting rail. Move up and right along the rail. When this ends, use a crimp above to move up and right to good jugs.

10 Unnamed Arete v0 ★ ☐
Climb the arete with good flakes.

11 Unnamed Sit start v6 ☐
Sit start at a flake (which hopefully is still there). Move to a tiny right crimp, then pull through with the left to a better crimp and up.

12 Unnamed v3 ★★ ☐
Sit start at the far right side with the right hand on a sidepull flake. Climb left, then up following the line of sharp incuts along the lip before pulling up on good holds.

13 Unnamed v1 ★ ☐
Sit start as above, but pull directly up and over on good holds.

14 Unnamed v4 ☐
Sit start at flake just right of the small boulder. Climb up directly on sloping crimps.

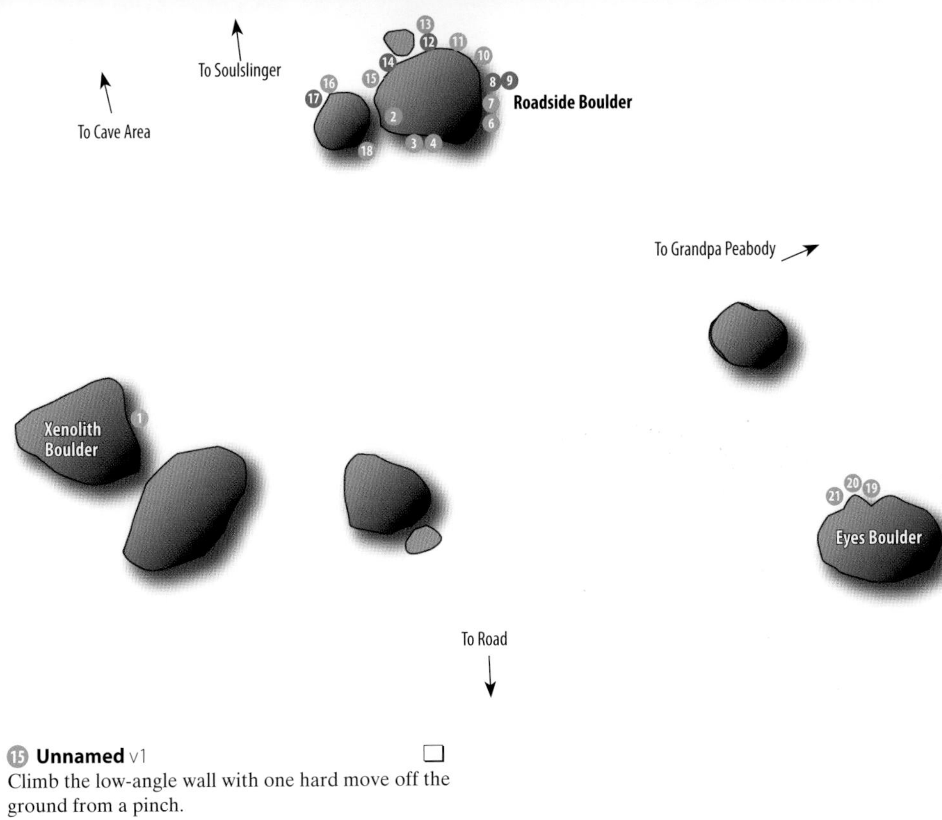

15 Unnamed v1 ☐
Climb the low-angle wall with one hard move off the ground from a pinch.

On the small Scoop Boulder next to the Roadside Boulder are:

16 Unnamed v1 ☐
Begin on patina just left of the west-facing scoop. Move up and right using poor holds but with good feet and top out above the scoop.

17 Marsha's Scoop v4 ☐
Climb the scoop, beginning with a right hand crimp/ undercling. Tricky.

18 Slots v3 ☐
On the roadside face at right: Climb from one slot to the other and over, with a big move.

EYES BOULDER

The boulder nearest the road to the east has a pair of eye-like huecos on its northwest side.

19 Unnamed v0- ☐
Climb the scoop with a big flake.

20 Unnamed v0- ☐
Start at the flake and move up right around the rib.

21 Unnamed v1 ☐
Start at the pair of huecos and climb up and left (reaching left to the rib make this much easier than pulling through on thin patina directly above).

ROADSIDE BOULDER

ROADSIDE BOULDER & SCOOP BOULDER

Kevin Jorgeson, *Southwest Arete* of Grandma Peabody. Photo: Jim Thornburg.

GRANDPA PEABODY

This is the big'un. It sits just 100 yards above the road, something of an obscure tourist attraction. Boulders sitting whole above ground simply don't come a lot bigger than this, let alone within 2 minutes of a road. There are some seriously high problems on this piece of rock. The south side of the boulder, facing the road, presents one of the most impressive and difficult bouldering challenges in the world. Here are the outrageous lines of *Evilution* (v12), and *Evilution Right* (v11). There is a tradition of highballing and "headpointing" (soloing after toprope practice or inspection) on this boulder dating back to the time when Dale Bard soloed his own former mid 5.12 toprope climb, *Transporter Room*, in 1983. For more about that, check out the history section of this guide..

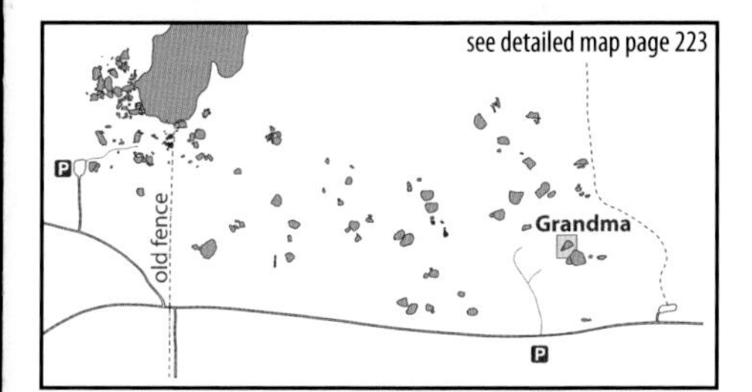

GRANDPA PEABODY

1 Footprints v9 ★★ ☐
Stand start at the lowest good holds and climb out, up, and left through the steep overhang on deep flakes. Make a hard move at the lip to gain the upper slab. The physical crux is over, but the mental test comes much higher up with an insecure sequence above a patina flake. Don't look down.

2 Project ☐
Climb the wall left of the cave problem, stepping right to the big slanted ramp to finish (descend from here or continue up). A sit start may be possible from the small boulder at right.

3 Cave Problem v4 ★★ ☐
Sit start far in the back of the cave on a good flake and climb out via slopers to a good rail, followed by a big move over a bulge to the upper crack. Match and drop off!

4 The Big Easy v7 ★ ☐
Stand start at the good holds of *Cave Problem* (above) and make a big move to the large ramp. Lean out around the bulge to find some crimps that lead up, past a crux pull, into the shallow, black-streaked groove. Some high steps and lock-offs on positive edges gain easy ground and the top.

GRANDPA PEABODY — FOOTPRINTS

Andrew Wilder, *Evilution*. Photo: Wills Young.

5 La Belette v11 ☐
Sit start below the next line using crimps, far to the right. With a couple of hard moves to start, traverse left around the corner to the big diagonal crack. Drop off.

6 Rastaman Vibration v12 ★ ☐
Begin at a very high left-hand pinch: make an outrageous move up with the right hand to a good but small crimp, and then climb up and left by long lock offs between good crimps into a tall scoop/groove. Head up the groove to an awkward step across rightward, high above the ground. Seriously highball.

7 Project ☐
Sit start the previous line. This natural, uncontrived start will add considerable difficulty.

8 Evilution v12 ★★★ ☐
Surely one of the best problems on earth: the front face of this, one of the world's biggest boulders, is climbed via immaculate 45-degree patina to a gruelling encounter with the lip and short headwall. Begin by using a cheat start to reach a pair of crimps. Make a series of hard moves up to a good left facing jug high on the face. Shuffle left and then push on up past poor crimps into the right side of a wide shallow groove that leads to the summit. Bring as many crash pads as you can muster, and a pair of crutches.

9 Evilution Direct v11 ★★★ ☐
A direct finish to the previous line, which is slightly more serious, though believed to be physically easier (time will tell regarding the grade). From the left-facing flake, continue up and right to the lip before pulling a crazy lock off to reach good crimps. Bring all the crash pads in Bishop, and a wheelchair.

10 Project ☐
A low start to *Evilution* looks plausible with a couple of extremely hard moves.

Anthony Lamiche making the FA of *Evilution Direct* (v11), straightening out Kehl's original masterpiece on Grandpa Peabody's south overhang. Photo: Stephan Denys.

11 Project ☐
The line of small holds leading out the right side of the overhang have been climbed to a decent flake/finger-jug at about v13 (Matt Birch). From there, the top out is perhaps just possible if the holds don't break, though the climbing will remain hard and very high.

8
9
6
3
5
11
?
GRANDPA PEABODY

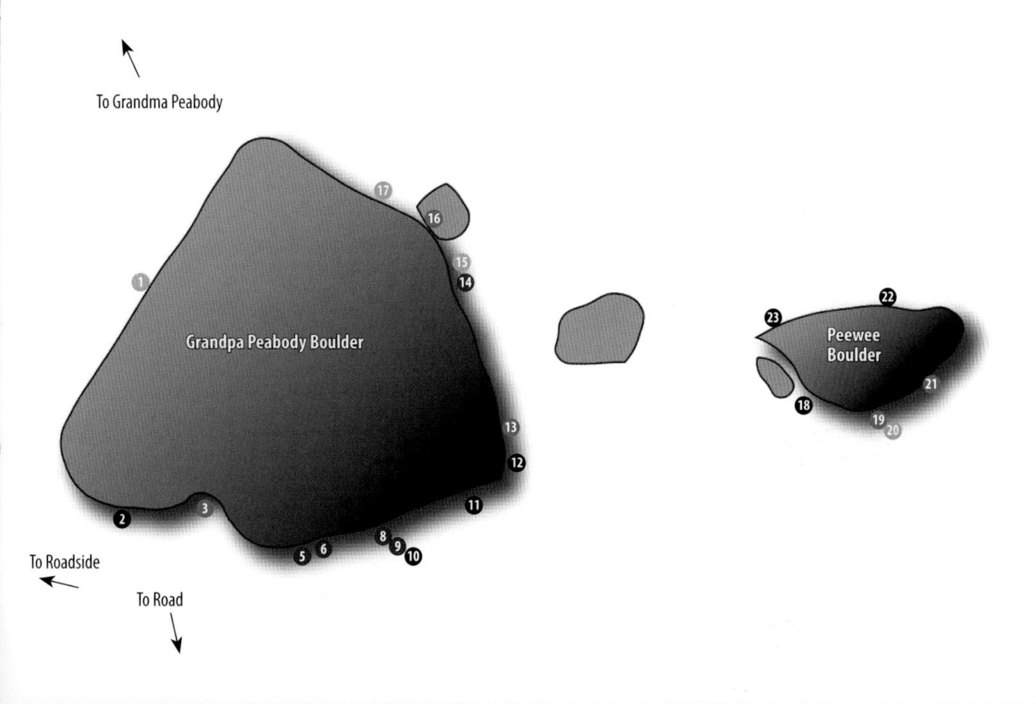
To Grandma Peabody
Grandpa Peabody Boulder
Peewee Boulder
1
2
3
5
6
8
9
10
11
12
13
14
15
16
17
18
19
20
21
22
23
To Roadside
To Road

⑫ Unknown ☐
Good holds lead to some crusty looking rock and an impasse at some deep runnels.

⑬ Transporter Room v5/5.12c ★ ☐
The original super-highball of the boulder, which was originally toproped, later bolted, then soloed and de-bolted! From a deep hueco near the ground climb a black streak to the rightmost of two very shallow huecos. Move to the left hueco (and good holds), and then onto lower angle ground to the summit.

⑭ Ambrosia v11 ★★★ ☐
They can't come much bigger than this! The latest super-highball of the boulder, which was once a toprope project, never bolted. Follow the gold streak just left of the black streak to the top of the boulder. Begin down and right with some very hard moves on small crimps that lead first left, then up to beneath a shallow hueco. Gain the hueco for a brief respite before heading into the no-fall zone past v7/8 pulls to a relatively easy but sustained finish.

⑮ Slicer v9 ☐
Begin to the right side of the east face, about ten feet left of the arete, at a left-facing sidepull. Move up past a pinch and then right (very sharp holds) to the arete. Climb down from the arete.

⑯ East Arete 5.10ish ☐
An extremely high arete.

⑰ Advanced Rockcraft Arete 5.8ish ☐
From a boulder, step onto the slab, traverse right and climb the north arete. This is the easiest way up the boulder. It's also the easiest way off.

PEEWEE

Just east of Grandpa Peabody, find another large boulder that appears very small by comparison:

⑱ Unknown/Project ☐
The face above the small boulder has a tricky move to a knob. Crumbly.

⑲ Unnamed v3 ☐
Grab a good flake and pull left to gain a hole in the middle of crazed patina.

⑳ Unnamed v2 ☐
From the same start, climb direct using the right side of the patina and some crimps at right.

㉑ Unnamed v3 ☐
From poor crimps, make a hard couple of moves up to the brown patina sidepull.

㉒ Unknown ☐
On the uphill face, right of the downclimb, sit start at thin patina and climb left and up. See topo page 271.

㉓ Unknown ☐
To the right of the uphill face, climb rough rock up the blunt right arete. See topo page 271.

Kevin Jorgeson climbs *Ambrosia* (v11).
Photo: Tim Kemple.

GRANDMA PEABODY

This monster block sits just uphill from the even bigger Grandpa Peabody. It is also seriously huge, with a couple of soaring aretes to solo, and some fairly extreme highballs on the huecoed northeast face. This northeast side's wide swath of steep patina—a striking golden-brown color, streaked with yellow lichen—is also home to one of the highest concentrations of relatively safe, short problems, most of them excellent and all with fine, flat landings. There are some of the hardest lines in Bishop here including the superb sit start to *Thunderbird*, also known as *Direction* (v13), *The Mystery* (v11/12), and Baburre (v11 or v12). There is also one of the most popular v5s, *Go Granny Go*, and the perennial favorite, *Center Direct* (v10).

GRANDMA PEABODY

GRANDMA PEABODY

Beginning with the Boulder's east side and moving rightward, find:

1 East Arete 5.10 ☐
The extremely tall arete.

2 Unnamed v0- ☐
Climb the scoop, moving low right and then up.

3 Unnamed v2 ☐
From the small hole, mantel up.

4 Unnamed v2 ☐
Climb the wall to the right of the hole.

5 Unnamed v5 ★ ☐
A deceptively tricky move gains the deep hueco.

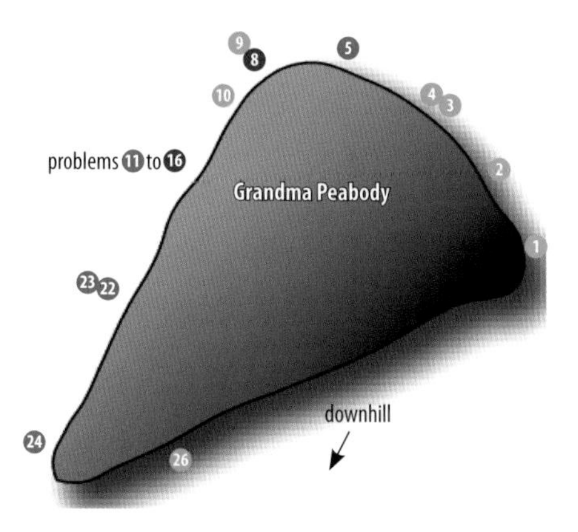

Buttermilk Country. Photo: Wills Young.

Korni Obleitner works the moves of Direction. Photo: Zlu Haller.

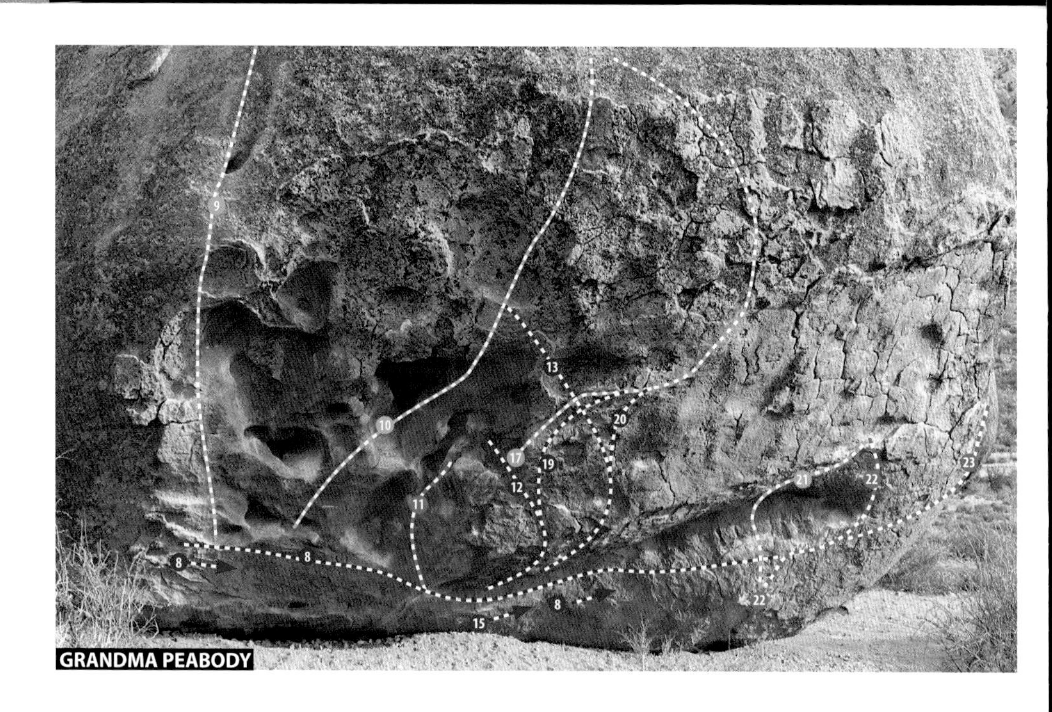

6 The Oracle v13 ★ ☐
A natural link-up of *Babeurre's* start into *The Mystery* adds some pump, though a knee-bar half-rest will help a little.

7 True North v13 ☐
A very hard link-up of *Babeurre's* start into Direction with a knee-bar breather. Top of the grade.

8 Babeurre v12 ★★ ☐
This low-level traverse of the boulder's steep face, begins at a good jug on the far left. From the good holds near the center, drop down with difficulty, move right on underclings and make extremely difficult moves on shiny patina and glassy rock very close to the ground, to gain good flakes to the right. Finish by climbing up the right arete to the rail of big jugs at about twelve feet up. Not really a boulder problem, the rating reflects the pump factor!

9 Essential Peabody v0 ★★★ ☐
A mini-route up the left edge of the patina face to a hole, then up and onward to the summit! Note: this is pretty much the easiest way down, though you can also backtrack the slab slightly to the left to a low point before jumping!

10 North Face Direct v2 ★★ ☐
Climb huecos, trending right, with a hard pull to the big pointed jug 20 feet up. Above the angle eases.

11 Slipstream v4 ★ ☐
Sit start with underclings: Climb left to huecos a right sidepull and then a jug. Drop off.

12 Center Direct v10 ★★ ☐
Sit start at the underclings. Climb directly up the overhang using some nice patina, a left sidepull/undercling and some glassy crimps to gain the good jug up and left.

13 Direction v13 ★★ ☐
You'll need some direction for this squeezed line, that nevertheless climbs beautifully. Sit start at the underclings and climb the overhang slightly right of *Center Direct*. Use a good left crimp to make a huge move with the right hand to an undercling sidepull. Bring the left up to a good sidepull and move the right to a micro crimp. From here, a long fierce move gains the small crimps in the shallow depression high left. Match with some difficulty, and move up left to big huecos high on the boulder. Finish on the *North Face Direct* (or downclimb from the good jugs).

14 Thunderbird v11 ★ ☐
The standing start to the previous line was the original, now superseded by the sit start.

15 Babeurre Short v11 ★★ ☐
Start at the underclings as for *Center Direct* and climb right, staying low across bullet hard patina on micro crimps and dreadful shiny footholds to finish up the right arete.

16 The Mystery v12 ★★ ☐
A very pretty rising traverse with some immaculate patina. Begin as for *Center Direct*, at the underclings. Climb diagonally up and right to gain crimps just at the lip of the small bulge, finishing with a big move

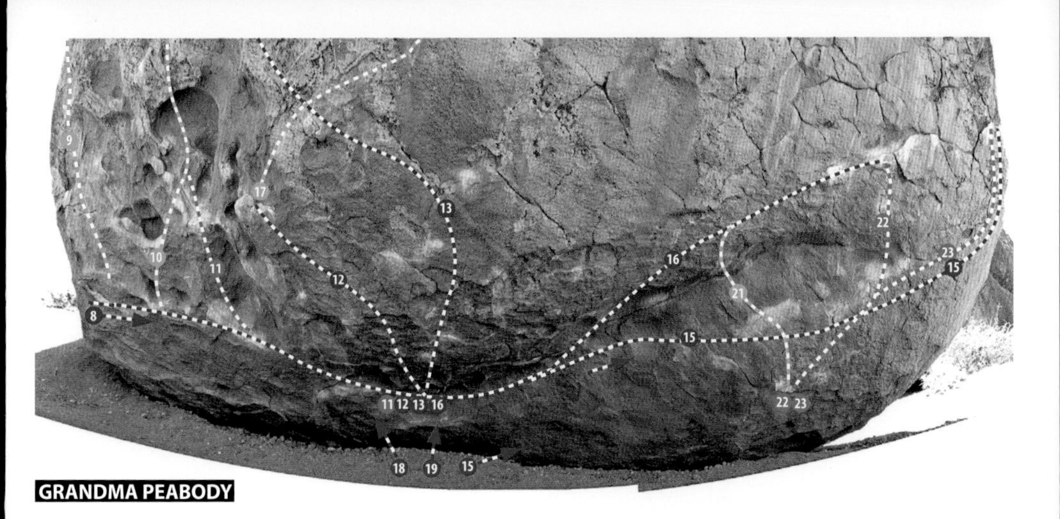

to join the top of *Go Granny Go*. The lower wall is used for the feet, not the hands, which stay in the underclings or on the bulge above. Often considered v11.

17 Magnetic North v8 ★★★ ☐
Begin at the jug "finish" of *Center Direct* (see photo above) and climb up and right on perfect patina. A hold out right in a small shallow depression is the key to this line. Gain it with the right hand then pull a hard move up from here (high heel useful) to good patina above. Move left to top out as for *North Face Direct*.

18 North of Center v11 ★★ ☐
A sit start linking *Center Direct* into *Magnetic North* (both described above).

19 Direct North v14 ★★ ☐
A sit start that links *Direction* into *Magnetic North* (both described above). Incredible rock; very sustained.

20 Project ☐
Secret project.

21 Go Granny Ho v7 ★ ☐
Start sitting at the left-facing flake. Pull up past a long incut crimp and cross into one of two small holds in the crease where the angle changes. Pull into the undercling and reach up left to a crimp. Make a long move right to join the top of *Go Granny Go*.

22 Go Granny Go v5 ★★ ☐
Sit start at a good flake and climb up and right to good holds. From these, pull directly up to good incuts above a scoop by any number of options. Drop off. A teaser.

23 Go Granny Go; Right Finish v5 ★★ ☐
A brilliant problem with fantastic moves and great rock: Sit start at a good flake and climb up and right to good holds, and then further right to the arete. Continue up to the good incuts at about 10 feet. Climb down or drop off.

24 West Corner v4 ★ ☐
Climb the edge of the patina on the arete to the good jug rail at 10 feet. Climb down, or drop off.

25 Granny High v7 [highball icons] ★
Begin as for the *West Corner*, the short climb up the patina rib to the jug. From the jug move up and right past a crimp and a couple of hard and bold moves to join the classic *Southwest Arete*.

26 The Southwest Arete 5.9ish [highball icons] ☐
Climb the smoothly split slab, then left to the souring arete and up this for a classic Peabody photo-op.

SUNSHINE/GREEN WALL/HUNK

These three excellent boulders are uphill from the Grandma and Grandpa Peabody boulders and slightly to the left. The aptly named Sunshine Boulder's south face is a popular warm-up spot, even though the lines on it are very tall. It basks in the sun and so is an obvious choice on cold days. The testpiece *Good Morning Sunshine* (v1) is one of those enticing lines that sucks you in with some interesting moves and then forces you into a gripping finale. Highly recommended! The Green Wall Boulder is named for the memorable smooth patina on its north side, streaked black and green by pretty lichens. This wall is relatively short but demands acute concentration on the slick footholds, plus deadpoint accuracy with the fingers. This is hard old-school climbing on perfect rock that everyone should get to grips with. Don't miss it. The Hunk is a giant block that has at least one amazing line: *The Hunk* (v2) itself. This huge highball slab is not only pretty, but the climbing is great; positive edges are linked by a few long reaches and confident footwork up high gains the final jugs.

SUNSHINE BOULDER

SUNSHINE BOULDER

SUNSHINE BOULDER

Uphill from the Peabodies, and over to the left, this pretty boulder soaks up the early rays of the sun, summer and winter. The tall slab has several classic problems that are not to be missed:

1 **Unnamed** v0- ★★ ☐
The rounded arete, beginning with thuggery from the left, or with finesse from the right.

2 **Unnamed** v0- ★★ ☐
The face, about six feet right of the arete, past a couple of high steps.

3 **Unnamed** v0 ★★ ☐
Slightly right of the previous line, moving right slightly to an upper sidepull, either by standing on an obvious know, or by moving right a little higher up.

4 **Good Morning Sunshine** v1 ★★★ ☐
Climb a line way over to the right side, with a tricky series of crimpy moves up high. Engaging climbing in a fine position.

Around the back of the same boulder are:

5 **Unnamed** v1 ★ ☐
Sit start at a flake in the overhang and climb over.

6 **Unnamed** v1 ★ ☐
Climb up to a large undercling and pass this to good holds up left.

7 **Unnamed** v1 ☐
Climb the wall above the rock slab and exit right with great caution.

8 **Unnamed** v1 ☐
Climb up the wall above the rock slab and exit left precariously.

9 **Unnamed** v2 ☐
Just right of the rock slab, climb the face moving slightly left, and top out with care.

GREEN WALL BOULDER

Beginning at the west face, and rotating around the boulder rightward, find:

10 **Unnamed** v5 ☐
Low on the left side of the west face, near the cave, sit start by the boulder (squeeze). Climb up and left to the big jugs and call it good. It also looks possible but much harder to continue through the cave if you have long arms and the sharp crusty patina doesn't break.

11 **Project** ☐
Pulling the bulge above the start of the previous line might be possible.

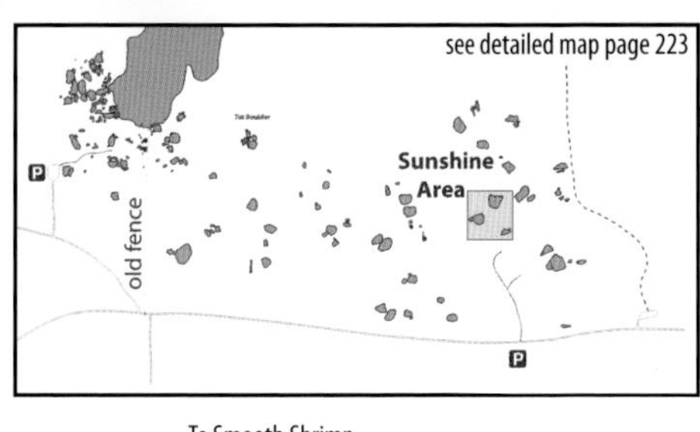

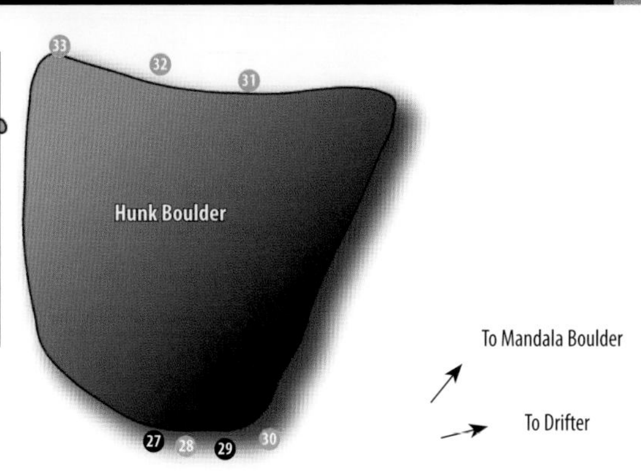

To Smooth Shrimp Buttocks and Saigon

To Soulslinger and Fit Homeless Boulder

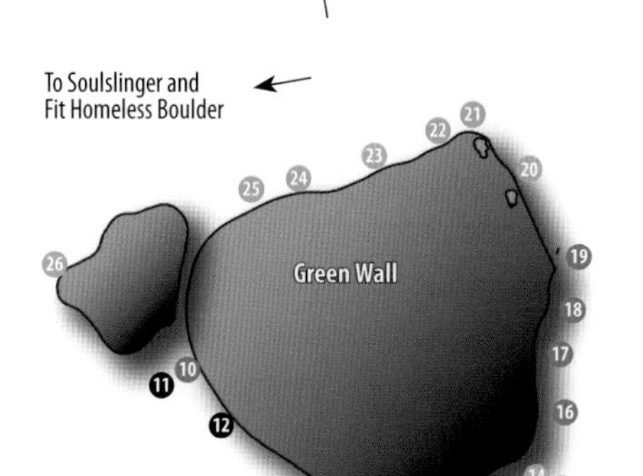

To Grandma and Grandpa Peabody Boulders

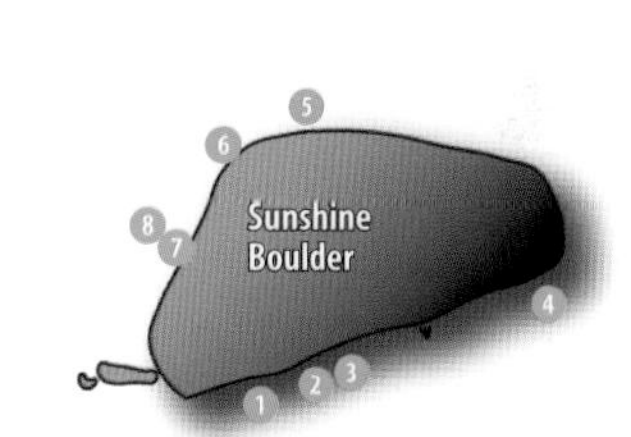

12 Project ☐
Up to the prominent scoop. Hmm ... no holds on this one! I swear I saw some once.

13 South Face v5 ★ ☐
A hard move off the ground from a left-hand sidepull/pinch is followed by relatively easy but airy highballing on rounded edges. A low start looks possible to the right.

14 South Arete v6 ★★ ☐
Climb the beautiful south arete from the left side, beginning with awkward moves on sidepulls. Move up and right to big holds on the arete's right side to top out.

15 South Arete Sit Start v7 ★★ ☐
Sit start at the large hueco and climb up and right to join the previous problem.

16 South Face of the Green Wall v5 ★★ ☐
Begin about eight feet right of the brown-streaked south arete, with the left hand on a spike crimp. Climb up and left to the big hold on the arete. Alternatively climb direct and move left higher up.

17 The Groove v4 ★ ☐
Begin with the left hand on a high pinch and pull up into the groove. Stay direct by some hard stemming to the extremely insecure top. It is possible to escape left at several points.

GREEN WALL BOULDER

18 East Rib v3 ★★★ ☐
Climb the rib, just right of the groove, beginning with a slanting sidepull. Great confidence is needed up high.

19 Unnamed v4 ★★ ☐
Gain the rib of the previous problem from the right.

20 Meticulous Ridiculous v8 ☐
About 8 feet from the right side of the east face, begin at left-facing sidepulls and climb the wall up rightward with difficulty passing more sidepulls. With deft footwork make a long move to gain a sloper near the arete. Another hard move up from here brings you to a deep hidden slot and the summit.

21 Green Wall Arete v1 ★★ ☐
Climb the arete on good holds.

22 Green Wall Essential v2 ★★★ ☐
A super-technical line on perfect rock: The aim is to get your hands on the first horizontal fracture in the patina about ten feet up, and then make a couple of moves to the summit. Begin either at the left-facing sidepulls, or better, from the thin crack at right.

23 Green Wall Center v6 ★★★ ☐
A crimping and footwork testpiece: Begin just right of a yellow and black streak where there are opposing sidepulls. A tricky high step with the right foot may help.

24 Unnamed v0 ★ ☐
Climb the crack with a pod which quickly eases after the start.

25 Unnamed v0- ☐
The face at the right side above the low overhang. The sit start is possible (about v4 now?), but junky.

On the neighboring small boulder just west of the Green Wall Boulder, find:

26 Unnamed v2 ☐
Sit start and climb flakes.

THE HUNK

Just uphill to the right of the Green Wall Boulder is the giant block of The Hunk. Beginning at the south side of the boulder and moving rightward, find:

27 Unknown ☐
Jump off that low xenolith to the seam and climb up the groove/crack.

28 Unnamed v6 ☐
The shallow groove with decomposing rock is extremely thin and crumbly, but climbable for all that, so long as no more holds are tweaked off.

29 Project/Unknown ☐
On the uphill face (see image opposite, top), right of the groove, the small facet or square-cut prow was climbed before holds broke.

30 Unnamed vB ☐
Climb just right of the blunt arete. Downclimb the same.

31 Unnamed v2 ☐
Start at the grey patch right of patina and make a couple of unpleasant moves on small crimps right to join the following line.

32 The Hunk v2 ★★★ ☐
The imposing wall of orange rock is climbed, beginning at the right side, and angling steadily left and then up. The hardest moves are down low, but the top requires some cool.

33 Rhubarb Crumble v8 ☐
The very blunt prow of grainy rock is climbed from a standing start if it is cold enough to hold the crystals. The sit start is about v9.

Emma Young gets an alpine start for *Good Morning Sunshine* (v1), previous page.
Photo: Wills Young.

DRIFTER BOULDER

The giant Drifter Boulder (also known as the Smoking Boulder) is one of the finest boulders at the Buttermilks. It sits upslope from the Peabody Boulders and also has a small companion, the Lower Smoking Boulder, listed in the next section. There are several outstanding problems here, including High Plains Drifter (v7), a world class line, and a former highball testpiece of the area that was first climbed by Dale Bard in the late 1970s. Many a climber makes it through the initial powerful crimping moves only to fail at the tricky "drift" move right off of a sloper. It's almost as though there's a fear of sticking the move because doing so means pressing on, even higher off the deck, with gripping lock offs between thank-God edges. In addition to this you will find a fat stack of excellent lines to either side, including the excellent *Change of Heart* (v6), and more.

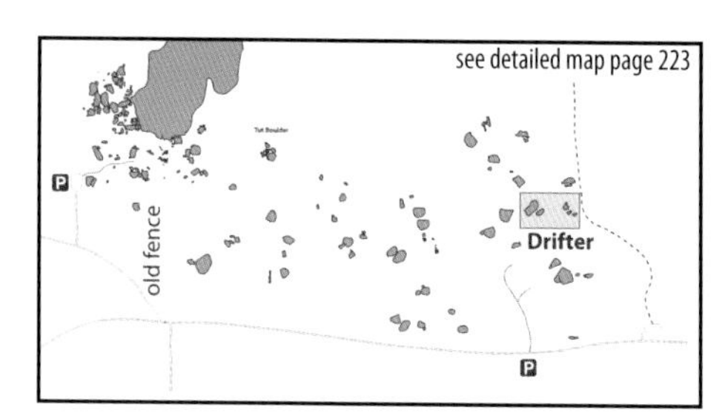

DRIFTER BOULDER, EAST SIDE

DRIFTER BOULDER, NORTHEAST SIDE

DRIFTER (A.K.A. SMOKING) BOULDER

Beginning at the downhill side of the boulder (facing the Grandma Peabody):

1 Unnamed "B2" v4 ☐

There is an old line toward the left side of this big wall that is rarely climbed, but listed in an early guide as "B2." Make a hard move to gain a patina plate, then continue boldly on more patina, moving left to the easier angle as soon as possible.

2 Mordecai v11 ★★ ☐

In the tall corridor between the Drifter and the Cosmonot/Lower Smoking boulders, about three feet left of an obvious narrow orange streak: Begin with a very low right hand only a foot or so from the ground and a hueco-esque left hand pinch. Make a hard first move to a right hand crimp Long moves between small crimps lead to an exit on slopers. Rating unconfirmed.

3 Bard's Scoop Left v6 ☐

Dale Bard did the intimidating left exit to the next line, with a big pull to a jug, back in the 1970s. Scary with some questionable-looking rock!

4 Bard's Scoop Right v6 ☐

The tall face has a very shallow scoop with two exits. This is the right exit. See the line on the photo.

5 Unnamed v5 ★ ☐

Sit start just right of the large, shallow hueco on opposing diagonal sidepulls. Climb direct.

6 East Face Sit Start v4 ★ ☐

Sit start as the previous line and climb right two moves to a good jug, then up onto the slab before downclimbing and dropping off. Good rock.

7 Les Trois Maunets v11 ★★ ☐

The left-to-right traverse that ends on *High Plains Drifter*. Begin as for the previous two lines. Traverse right and turn the corner by some very difficult moves. Cross the face to an okay rest before dropping down into the deep incuts at the start of *High Plains Drifter,* and finish up this line. Yikes!

8 The Dripper v4 ★ ☐

Climb the blunt northeast arete by the polished flakes, to the upper slab.

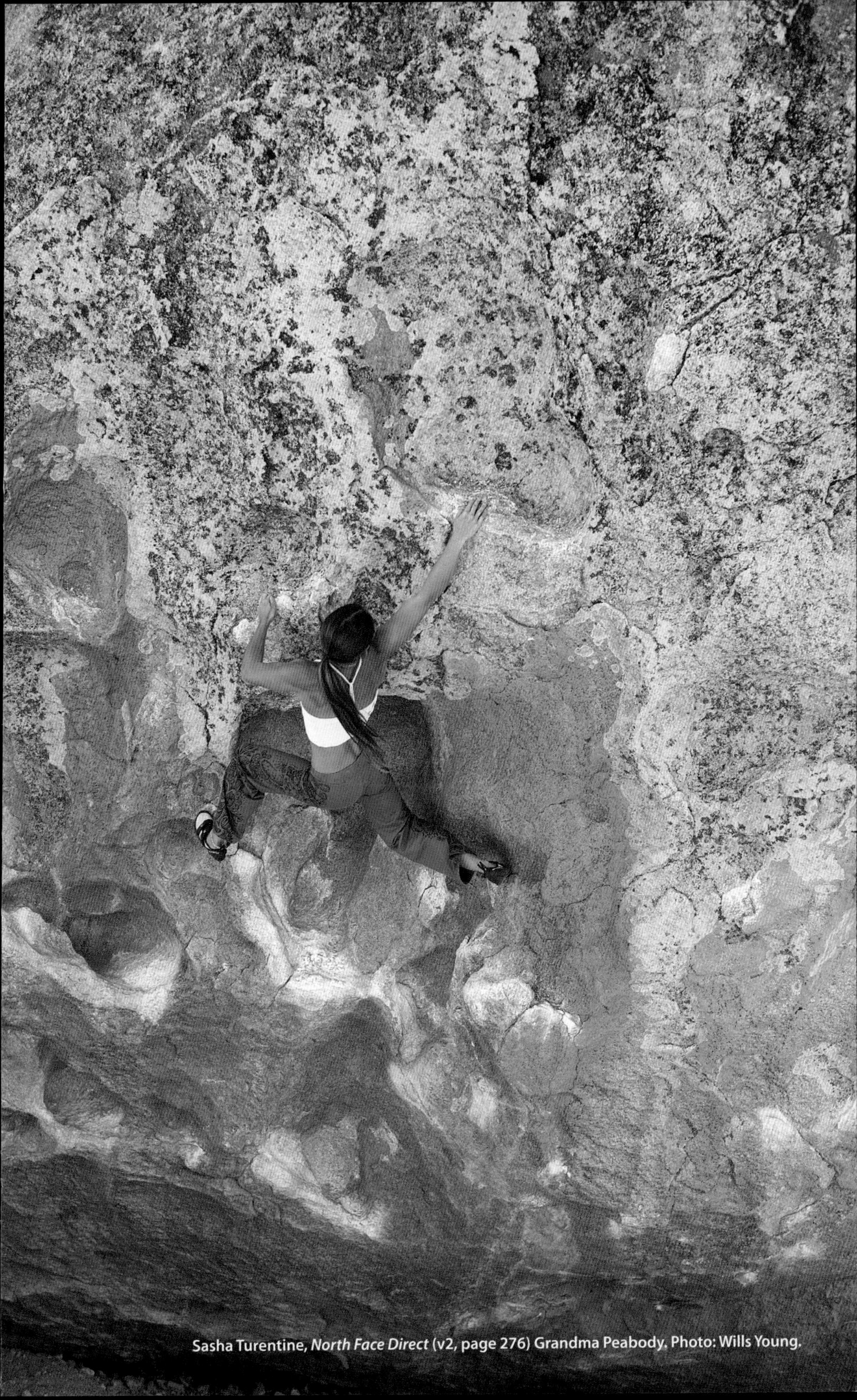

Sasha Turentine, *North Face Direct* (v2, page 276) Grandma Peabody. Photo: Wills Young.

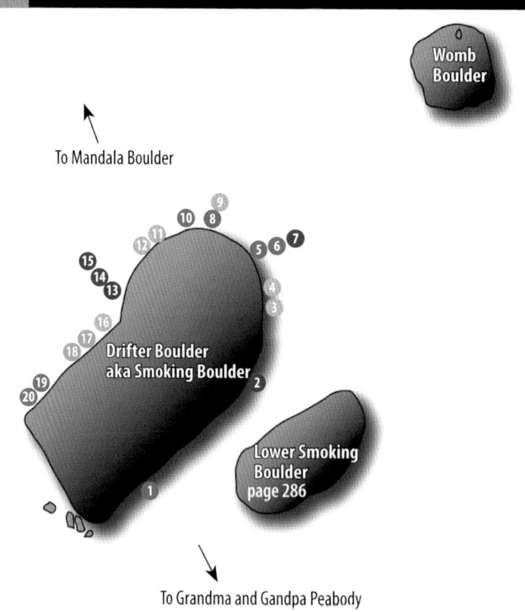

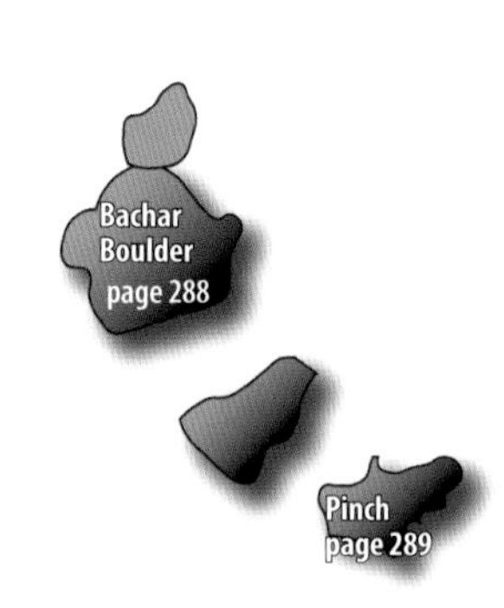

Mule deer are frequently seen in the Buttermilk Country.

9 The Dripper Low Start v6 ☐
Start the previous line at a right-facing sidepull (both hands), and make a couple of very painful moves to join the standing start.

10 The Knobs v5 ★★ ☐
Right of the arete, use pinches/crimps to gain a foot-wide boss. Then make a huge rock-over on the right foot and a very long reach to gain holds up and right.

11 Change of Heart v6 ★★★ ☐
Begin with hands matched at the deep incut crimps six feet off the ground. Climb direct with a long move to gain a big sloper that is quickly followed by good patina.

12 High Plains Drifter v7 ★★★ ☐
The ultra-classic Buttermilks testpiece: If you can climb this grade but haven't done this line, you better step up! Start with hands matched at the deep incut crimps about six feet off the ground. Move right and powerfully up to a good inch-deep crimp for the right hand. Pull to a sloper, and then execute the drifter move up right to another sloping crimp. Keep a cool head and pull past good patina plates to the upper slab. A magical testpiece!

13 Plain High Drifter v12 ★★★ ☐
Another great problem: Start at the obvious smooth pinch/sidepull. Pull on and make hard moves to a smooth, but tiny crimp far up and right. Options for this are either: 1. Use a micro crimp for the left hand (a small, but important thumb-catch broke in 2002) and make an excruciatingly hard press across to the right; or 2. If tall enough, invert the left hand on the patina sidepull, grab an intermediate for the right and make an unlikely-looking deadpoint to the high right crimp from good footholds. From there, launch up and left to the inch-deep "jug" of *High Plains Drifter* and finish on that line.

14 Plain High Dyno v10 ★★ ☐
A fun trick: From the starting patina ear of *Plain High Drifter,* leap up and left immediately to a good crimp. Pull through to join *High Plains Drifter.* The idea is that you don't use the ground as a launch pad. Of course if you do, you're only cheating yourself, right?

HIGH PLAINS DRIFTER: The ultra-classic Buttermilks testpiece: If you can climb this grade but haven't done this line, you better step up!

⓯ Plain High Drifter, Right Exit v12 ★ ❑
Start as for *Plain High Drifter,* but from the small right crimp, figure a way to continue right with another hard move to gain easy ground.

⓰ Drifting High v7 ❑
Start at the shallow groove as for the easiest way up (named Smoking). Climb up and left to a large right-facing flake. From this, make a massive span left to join the top of *High Pains Drifter*, and finish on this: long arms essential.

⓱ Smoking v0 ❑
This is the wall and crack system that leads to low-angle ground, and so to the top of the boulder. It also serves as a downclimb.

⓲ Unnamed v0 ❑
Climb the wall on good patina to the ledge.

Several traverses can be done starting at left and leading either to the previous line, or to an exit up the face to the right (around v7 for the latter). The face at right can be climbed pretty much anywhere, but two suggested independent lines are:

⓳ Unnamed v3 ❑
An obvious knob sits about 12 feet up the wall. Start below and two feet right of this. Pull on and make a hard high step with the left foot to start, climb to the knob and over to the ledge.

⓴ Unnamed v3 ❑
Climb the black/gold boundary with hands to either side, moving slightly left to a sloper to gain the ledge.

㉑ Project ❑
A sit start at glassy crimps looks possible, with one very hard move.

DRIFTER SATELITES

Two boulders neighboring the Drifter Boulder are the Lower Smoking (aka Cosmonot) Boulder, which is just downslope (overlooking the Grandma) and the Womb Boulder, which is just upslope just a few yards from the Drifter problems. Both boulders have some fun lines. Of particular note is the bizarre *A Birthing Experience (v1)* on the Womb Boulder. Don't miss it. There is also Sharma's strange, reachy, and rarely repeated testpiece, *Crankenator* (v13), first done in 2002 during the Petzl "Roc Trip."

LOWER SMOKING BOULDER

WOMB BOULDER

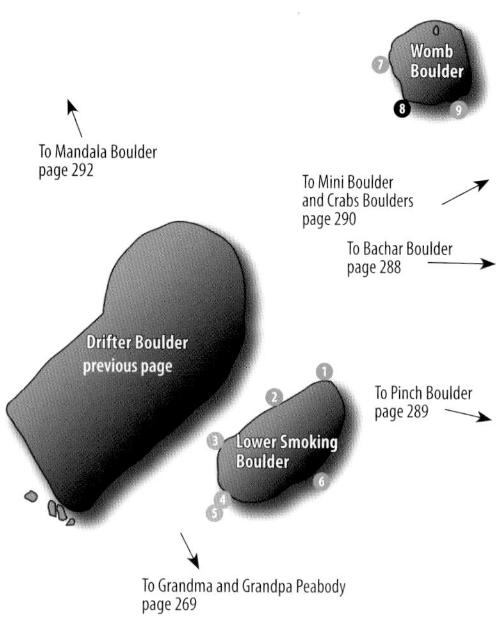

LOWER SMOKING BOULDER

Directly uphill from the Grandma Peabody, sitting adjacent to the Drifter Boulder is the smaller Lower Smoking Boulder, which has:

1 Unnamed v0- ☐
On the uphill side, jump to the jug in the bulge and climb over on more jugs. Then back-track and jump down, as this is the easiest way off.

2 Unnamed v1 ★★ ☐
Sit start at a hueco and climb up via flakes.

3 Unnamed v7 ★ ☐
Sit start at the big sloper and a left undercling down low. Climb up right to good holds right of the arete by a tricky sequence. Finish at the jug before the angle change, or continue to the summit via a long traverse up leftward on sketchy thin patina.

4 The Cosmonaut v6 ★ ☐
On the west side of the boulder, sit start at a right-facing flake and traverse very low leftward to gain good holds that lead up the blunt arete. Stop at the upper jug, or continue up leftward across sketchy thin patina.

5 Croft Problem v8 ★ ☐
Sit start as for the previous problem, but move up almost immediately past a shallow dish/pocket with a hard move, to gain the upper jug from the right side. Finish as for the previous problem.

6 Unnamed v2 ☐
The southeast face.

WOMB BOULDER

This little boulder is just uphill to the east of the Drifter Boulder.

7 A Birthing Experience v1 ★ ☐
Crouch into the very small, low cave. Squirm out leftward and up the short wall.

8 The Crankenator v13 ☐
Long arms and a cold, cloudy day are a must for this hard, strange problem. Begin sitting at the right side of the shallow cave and slap out right, and then up via some invisible holds.

9 Yo! Basecamp v0+ ★★ ☐
A great companion line to the famed Robinson's Rubber Tester (page 264).

Some say the left is harder, some the right. Both have tricky moves on glassy feet. Classic Buttermils. Lisa Rands climbing *Bachar Problem Left*. Photo: Wills Young.

BACHAR AREA

The Bachar Area, with the excellent Bachar Boulder and a couple of other small blocks, should not be overlooked. The1970s testpieces established by John Bachar on the Bachar Boulder's south face are still testing today, while the *Sharma Scoop*, though unimposing, is nevertheless worthy for its wonderful movement, and something of an obscure gem. The Pinch Boulder and Mini Boulder both offer some lowball fun with short intriguing climbs.

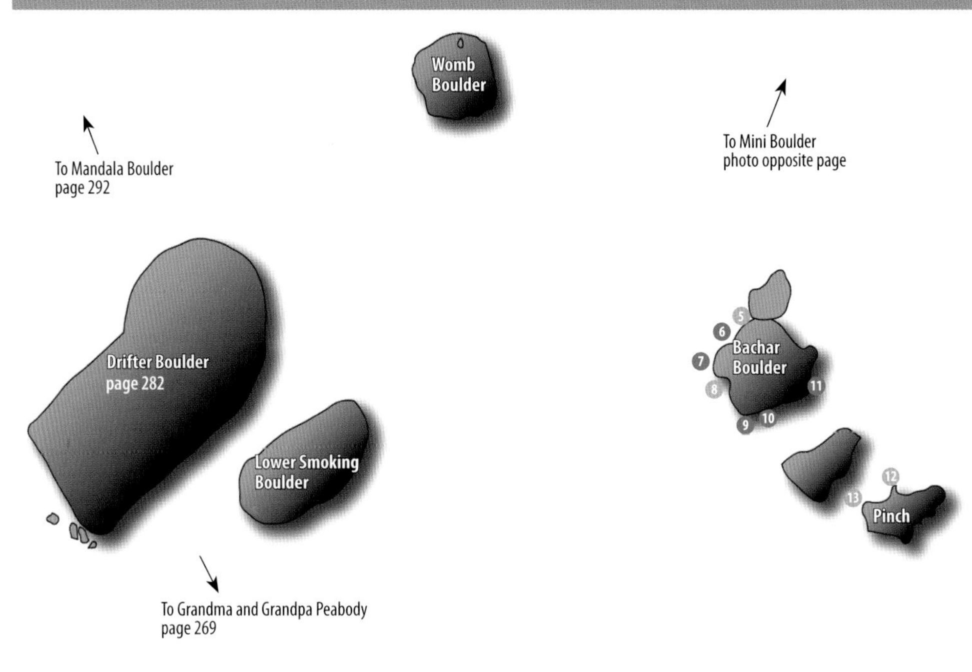

MINI BOULDER

The Mini Boulder is found just up the slope from the Bachar Boulder.

1 Unnamed v4 ☐
Sit start below the large patina jug on deep patina crimps. Pull to the jug, then up and left with a hard move to a slopey crimp in the black rock. The top's a jug.

2 Project ☐
About two-and-a-half feet down and left from an obvious deep slot/jug is a right-facing crimp. Sit start; gain the crimp, and then the top.

3 Unnamed v6 ★ ☐
Start at sloping but crystalline crimps about four feet up. Begin with a press right to a foot-long crescent shaped hold; match this, and climb over the top on poor crimps.

4 Unnamed v3 ★ ☐
Begin sitting with the left hand on a sidepull/pinch about three feet up (choose the best of several options here) and the right hand also on a crimp/pinch on the face to the right. Make a hard move to gain the arete, then climb up this on sloping holds.

BACHAR BOULDER

This boulder is to the east of the Drifter/Smoking Boulders. It is relatively small, but has a few very good lines.

5 Some Crust v6 ☐
Start super-low at a big incut hueco. Pull up to good jugs and then out right, past some tenuous crystalline holds, to top out just above the start of the next line.

6 Unnamed v4 ★ ☐
Sit start with an incut sidepull for the right, and an undercling for the left hand. Climb up and right with a hard move around the bulge.

7 Unnamed v4 ★ ☐
Sit start at a big flake and throw a sweet dyno off a big jutting foothold to the deep huecos.

8 Sharma Scoop v8 ★★ ☐
This tricky scoop is usually done by a jump start from the ground, but can also be done without, which is now harder. Getting established in the scoop and groping out of it requires some trickery and/or a day with cold and overcast conditions. Whether you exit left, right, or even straight up, it's the same good fun. Should be on everyone's list.

MINI BOULDER

8a Charlie's New Squeeze/Letting Go v10 ★ ☐
Charlie's New Squeeze begins at two tiny, sharp, opposing sidepulls up high: Step on and throw left hand to the rounded knob in the right side of the *Sharma Scoop*. Climb the blunt rib above. The original, *Letting Go*, is the jump start from a couple of pads.

9 Bachar Problem Left v5 ★★★ ☐
The perfect glass-smooth patina is climbed by a couple of hard moves with all the holds facing the wrong way. Photo previous page.

10 Bachar Problem Right/Golden Boy v5 ★★ ☐
The right of the two Bachar problems has more slick footholds and underclings.

11 Unnamed v5 ☐
The scooped wall right of *Golden Boy* has a very hard press off the ground from low left and an awkward finish. Alternatively, shift upslope, reach high up right to start, and drop the grade a notch or two!

BACHAR BOULDER

PINCH BOULDER

Just downhill from the Bachar Boulder are a couple of small boulders, the lower one has some very short, but good problems on its overhanging north side.

12 Working Class v8 ★ ☐
Sit start (highish) at double pinches. Slap a move up the pinch with the right hand. Continue up right to gain a crimp below the lip, then over. The left exit is considerably harder.

13 Pinch Arete v7 ★★ ☐
Sit start at the right arete with a pinch for the right hand. Pull over the left foot to start, and then seek slopers over the lip that lead to a hard mantel. A traverse left through the scoop into the previous line, requiring long legs and great flexibility, is reported.

PINCH BOULDER

CRABS BOULDERS

By walking east from the Mini Boulder or the Bachar Boulder, you will find the remains of what was once a four-wheel-drive track. Walk uphill along this track a short distance to find, at right, and just east of the track, a cluster of boulders.
See map on page 223 for location. (The Crabs Boulders are at the right edge of the map.)

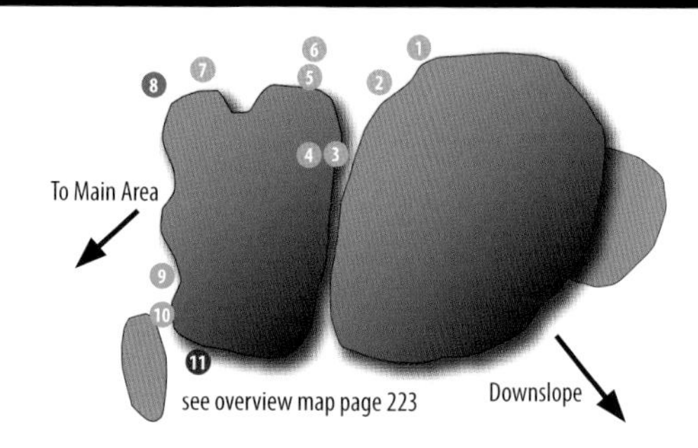

1 Brazuca v7 ☐
Gain the giant hueco from a sit down and left. From a sidepull/pinch in a rib, make a big move to the giant sloper and up to join *Rasta Slab*.

2 Rasta Slab v7 ★ ☐
Sit start low at a deep hueco. Pull up to an undercling/sidepull and then reach over to crystalline crimps in the slab. Make a hard move to gain a pinch at the side of a huge hueco. Work up into an undercling and tiptoe up the slab. Interesting climbing, but very rough rock.

3 Crabs on my Nipples v7 ★ ☐
You need some tough skin to handle this! Sit start at a deep hole three feet up. Climb up right past painful patina to a large dish. Move up further right into a sharp sidepull and swing around the arete to gain a big jug on the overhanging face. Move up and right past an even bigger jug and on further right to a good diagonal hold on the left side of a body-sized scoop. Press into the scoop and over.

4 Finders Keepers v9 ★ ☐
Follow *Crabs on My Nipples,* but finish straight up from the good right sidepull (patina plate) with a long move directly to the top.

5 Keep Searching v8 ☐
Begin with a low sloper with the left hand and a good sidepull with the right. Make a very hard move with the left to a good incut crimp, and then climb past good holds (one crusty/breakable) to the huge jug. Finish direct from the right sidepull (patina plate), with a long move with the left hand to gain the lip.

6 Brazilian Monkeys v8 ☐
The right finish to the previous line is a touch easier but worth the points for the first move.

7 Breakaway v6 ☐
Break a way through the choss to the top of the boulder and try to leave something behind for others to climb on.

Kevin Daniels, *Action Potential* (v2), page 232. Photo: Wills Young.

8 Unknown v5 ☐
Start lying down at a big hueco. With a knee bar or two useful, pass the second deep hueco and reach to the good incuts a wide jug. Above this jug is a deep slot, but don't go there. Move diagonally up and left with a couple hard pulls to gain very dubious incuts at the lip (care!), then over slightly right. Going straight to the slot above the jug makes this about v3.

9 Unnamed Mantel v1 ★ ☐
Jump or reach up to sloping ledge and press it out.

10 Unnamed Slot v0 ☐
Jump or reach the slot and climb up (the right side is easier, but watch out for the rock at your back).

11 Capoeira v10 ★ ☐
Start at an obvious crimp for the left hand and pull up and right with a hard press off a high and distant foot hold.

*Another notable problem not shown on the maps or images is **downhill and east of the Crabs Boulders** on an egg-shaped boulder nestled in a ravine:*

12 Catcher in the Rye v6 ★ ☐
The obvious west-facing line (facing the Crabs Boulders). Variations are possible at the start and you can either pull out right to a good edge or, better, go directly over past a sloper. A bit crusty but fun.

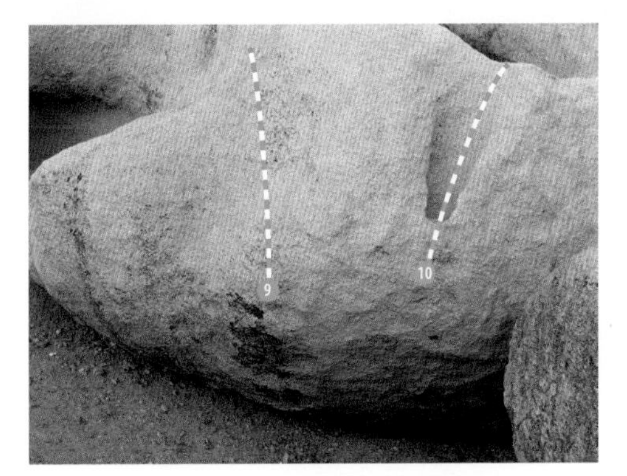

MANDALA BOULDER

Once appropriately named The Prow Boulder, this block with its two prows at either end of an invincible wall of glassy rock, holds some exceptional problems. At right, on the downhill end, is *Pope's Prow* (v6), a superb line, an old-school spoiler that will vex many an accomplished power merchant. At left, on the uphill end, the "Wow Prow," known since its first ascent in March 2000, as *The Mandala* (v12 or v14 sit), a modern benchmark, and one of the world's most famous boulder problems.

Beginning just left of that uphill prow (The Mandala) and moving rightward around the boulder, find:

❶ Butterfinger v12 ★★ ☐
Climb the wall left of *The Mandala* on some dreadful slopey crimps. Doesn't seem to get climbed a lot since some breaks made this harder… or impossible?

❷ Project ☐
A sit start to the previous line from the right looks possible.

❸ The Mandala v12 ★★★ ☐
Begin with the crimp above the undercling with the right hand, and left hand on the low crimp. The correct start involves stacking only the pads needed to reach the high crimp, no more. Pull on and climb either by a long move up right-handed after moving the left to the undercling, or by a long move left handed after transferring the right into the undercling. Aim for the big ear-like flake up right. Then left to a good incut. Set the feet, grab the lip, and roll over. *Yowza!*

❹ The Mandala Sit Start v14 ★★★ ☐
Sit start down and left on low opposing sidepulls and maneuver to a tiny two-finger crimp with the left hand. Jump to the good incut with the right hand and join the standing start: an amazing crimping testpiece with powerful flowing movement from start to finish. Alternately, from the sit, climb directly up to a high and very sharp left hand sidepull, then, telescope your right arm rightward to wrap the big glassy undercling of *The Mandala*. Hold the swing as you come in with your left to the good crimp and away you go ... The latter sequence is nigh impos-

Dave Graham sticks the new opening move while making the second ascent of *The Mandala* (v12, this page; also see next page) in early October 2000. Photo: Wills Young.

sible for those without the height to make the span or control the swing, but some have said it is a fair bit easier than the original.

5 The Mandala Direct v12 ★★ ☐
Follow *The Mandala* to the good "ear" hold--the rightmost hold in the middle of the line. From here, make a cross through to a good but small crimp with the right hand. Bring the left to another good crimp out left at about the same level. Now, instead of moving left as for the normal finish, go straight up by a hard punchy move with the left hand to a high and distant crimp. Roll through with the right to another crimp just over the bulge, and top out. Not quite a two-for-one special as the direct version is a good bit harder than the original and a touch reachy up high.

6 The Mandala Direct Assis v14 ★★ ☐
If you're not convinced the regular sit is worth all 14 points, this one's for you: Take the regular sit start to *The Mandala* (described above) and throw in the direct finish for good measure

7 Pope's Prow v6 ★★★ ☐
Climb the prow on its left side. This amazing problem is both baffling and compelling at the same time. It feels simple and yet impossible. An intriguing sit start goes at about v8, beginning sitting at right.

8 Pope's Prow, Right v5 ★★ ☐
For some reason, climbing the right side of the prow is easier, but doesn't have quite the same allure. It is, however, a good lesson in balance and finesse.

9 Whipped v5 ★ ☐
Layback a dark xenolith with the left hand and make a big stretch to a hidden crimp. Pull leftward and exit relatively easily, but frighteningly, via a shallow scoop.

10 Devoted v8 ★★ ☐
Sit start left of the southeast arete, at a good flake. Climb direct using a slanting feature, some very poor hand holds, and good balance.

11 Devoted Traverse v6 ★ ☐
Sit start as for Devoted and traverse up rightward to gain good holds near the right arete. Pull onto the slab: Weirdly awkward.

12 Unnamed v5 ☐
On the right side of the rounded southeast arete, sit start and climb via flakes. Holds have broken here.

13 Unnamed v1 ☐
Several generic short pulls are possible on the northeast side of the boulder.

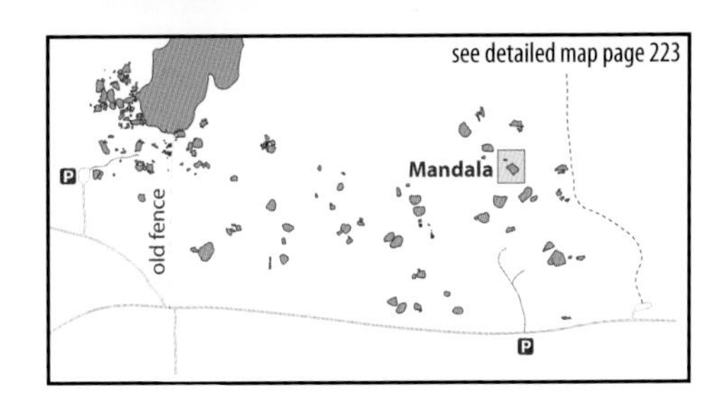

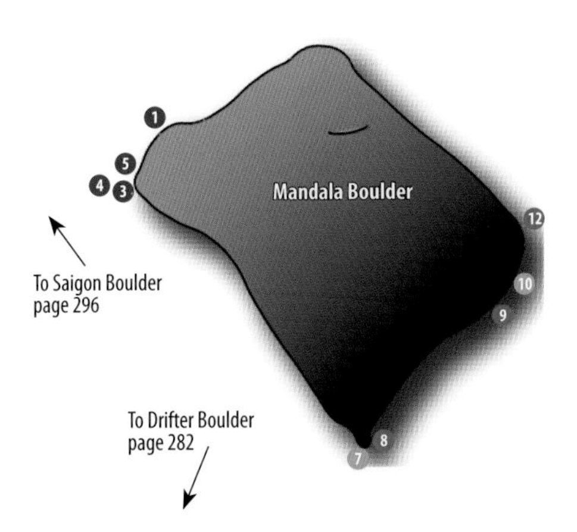

MANDALA BOULDER

MANDALA BOULDER

The Mandala

Icon of a New Era

By Wills Young

Lisa Rands making the first female ascent of *The Mandala*. Photo: Wills Young.

When Chris Sharma pulled off the first ascent of *The Mandala* in early 2000, word spread that he had solved one of the finest unclimbed lines in the Western States. Peter Croft, a Bishop local and longtime Sierra pioneer, described it as the best unclimbed line on the East Side, bar none.

In a famous video, Chris Sharma is shown completing the first ascent and then making the cheekily provocative joke (mistaken for a serious comment by most) that, "if I were to rate it, I'd call it v16—*but I'm not going to rate it.*"

How hard was it? Fueled by Sharma's deliberate obfuscation, rumors were rife. Sharma insisted that for him, this was his hardest ascent. In this, he was likely sincere. It was an extremely hard problem for him, the initial moves being giant deadpoints and burly snatches to tiny, though positive edges that faced in awkward directions. Even for others it might have been v13 the way Sharma climbed it.

However, the second day that Dave Graham checked out the problem five months after Sharma's ascent, a photographer took a small step ladder up to the boulder to gain a better perspective for shooting. Graham was working the first two moves and beginning to get a feel for them. He asked to use the ladder to clean the holds, and while standing on it Graham noticed a tiny edge out right. This micro-crimp, unchalked, was almost impossible to see from below. Using it, though, just minutes later, Graham whipped off the second ascent, and then climbed the line again and again for sheer fun.

Within months, the jaw-dropping nature of the line, Sharma and Graham's positions as the new Crown Princes of Bouldering, plus Josh Lowell's *Dosage* video showing Sharma's ascent all contributed to making *The Mandala* one of the best known problems in the world.

The parallels with Yosemite's *Midnight Lightning* are clear. Back in 1978, first Ron Kauk and later John Bachar, equally revered as the gods of rock climbing, climbed the quintessential American boulder problem in the crucible of American climbing, Yosemite Valley. Twenty-two years later, the new generation, Sharma and Graham, pulled the *new* icon of American bouldering in this new crucible for cutting edge ascents: both lines striking, both lines awe-inspiring, and both lines representing the benchmark upon which every up-and-coming boulderer had an obligation to be measured.

It is interesting to note also, that both Bachar and Kauk had eyed *The Mandala* back in the late 1970s, when they had gazed at it in wonder. Bachar says that the two of them joked that perhaps, long into the future, John Gill's great grandson might one day climb the line. What Bachar had not reckoned with was the exponential increase of interest in bouldering that would begin just ten to 15 years later. *The Mandala* was flashed by Anthony Lamiche in November 2002. in January 2008 Lisa Rands was the first woman to climb the line.

SMOOTH SHRIMP / BUTTOCKS BOULDER

This boulder is just uphill from The Mandala Boulder. It has some fun patina pulling on fairly short steep and powerful problems (though they lead to the summit of a very tall rock). Climbers pushing higher v-grades will find this a suitable place to warm up, with *The Flake* (v0), steep and juggy, an excellent problem to get the big muscles working. The harder lines, the best being *Perfectly Chicken* and *Bubba Gump*, are excellent projects for those preferring to do their hard pulling close to the ground.

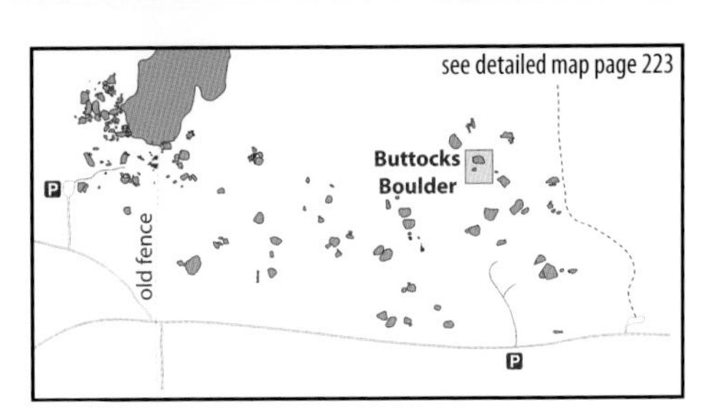

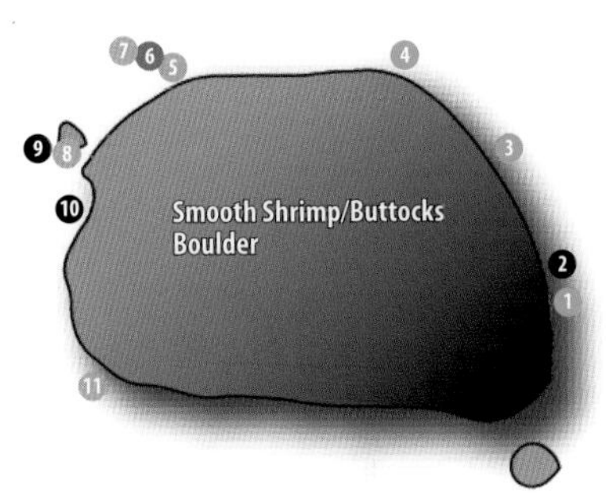

SMOOTH SHRIMP BOULDER

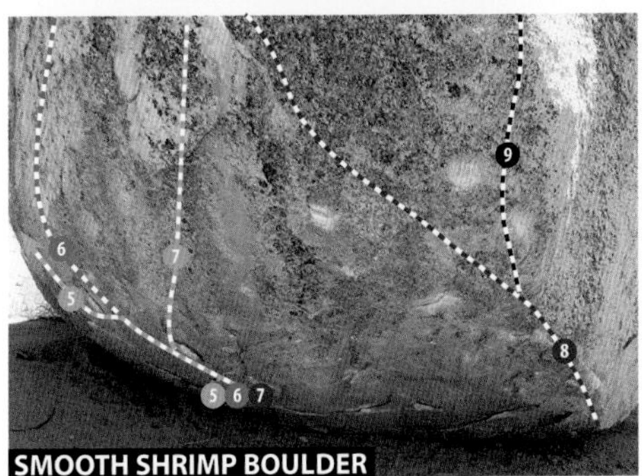

SMOOTH SHRIMP BOULDER

Beginning at the overhanging northeast face with its obvious crack, and moving rightward, find:

1 The Buttocks v2 ☐
Climb the crack.

2 Unknown/Project ☐
Sit start just right of the crack, and climb the wall on sharp holds moving diagonally right. Hard.

3 The Flake v1 ★★ ☐
Sit start and climb the flake crack on excellent rock, pulling onto the slab, from which you might find it easiest to descend by the same route you just ascended.

4 Unnamed v1 ☐
Sit start at a horizontal hold.

5 Smooth Shrimp v6 ★ ☐
Begin at the low left-facing flake per the photo. Climb left across the lip of the boulder, and top out at the easiest exit far left. Those who enjoy full-on butt-dragging can extend this line further right to start as for #8.

6 Perfectly Chicken v5 ★★ ☐
Begin at the low left-facing flake, and climb almost directly up slightly left with a hard move to get established on the vertical wall. Again, those who enjoy full-on butt-dragging can extend this line further right to start at the same point as *Bubba Gump*.

7 Cocktail Sauce v10 ☐
From the start of *Perfectly Chicken*, climb the overhanging wall just right of the arete, using a shallow two-finger pocket.

8 Bubba Gump v10 ★★ ☐
Sit start low right on a thin sidepull flake and climb up left along the rail. Use a flexi-flake with the left hand and slopey crimp above the overhang for the right. Gain the good incut and finish on good patina.

9 Project ☐
Climb the prow, starting as for the previous line.

10 Project ☐
The groove immediately to the right of the prow (previous line) almost seems possible.

Now, moving far over to the right of the previous lines, at the southwest arete find:

11 The Bomb v9 ☐
On the downhill side of the boulder, at the far left: Sit start and climb up the left side of an arete with tiny crimps, before pulling around and stepping right onto the slab. No topout.

SAIGON AREA

At the top of the slope, way up above the Grandma and Grandpa Peabody, above the Mandala Boulder and the Smooth Shrimp Boulder, are a few more boulders, one of them a giant, the others smaller. The big one, the Saigon Boulder is named for the eye-catching arete, *Saigon*. It is believed that this prominent line somehow evaded ascent until Tommy Klinefelter strolled up and connected the plates of patina from the left side of the arete to the right, using his long reach and powerful fingers to get past a blank-looking section. Now it is on everyone's tick list, and rightly so. Meanwhile the same boulder also provides some harder and some easier three star lines, the *Monkey Dihedral* (v2) being an engaging easier classic, demanding grace and invention. Across to the right of the Saigon Boulder is the small Porcelain Boulder which also has some great climbing, and further right still is the Sharma Traverse Boulder with its popular, pumpy, powerful, and puzzling traverse of the same name.

SAIGON BOULDER

This is the huge boulder with a massive southeast arete, sitting high on the hillside above the Buttocks Boulder, which in turn is up from the Pope's Prow/ Mandala Boulder. Beginning at the boulder's southwest side and moving rightward, find:

1 Fight Club v11 ★★ ☐
Jump to sloping holds at the lip of the boulder, grab some more poor holds and press out a mantel. Then, move up and left along a ramp to a tenuous topout.

2 Fight Club Direct v11 ★★★ ☐
A direct finish to *Fight Club* goes by a very treacherous series of slopers.

3 Project ☐
Aim for a pointed right-facing ear and sidepull 3 feet right of the arete.

4 Project ☐
An amazing project! Climb the wall left of the arete, heading up to an obvious protruding hold and a very highball topout.

5 Saigon v6 ★★★ ☐
A beautiful and engaging line. Follow good patina up the left side of the face, and then pull around right by way of a small crimp and perhaps by groping a sidepull sloper low right with the right hand. Snatch for that teasing jug, stick the move, and make a couple of hard pulls to gain the summit. Wow! Several pads are useful, though the landing is pretty flat.

6 Saigon Direct v9 ★★ ☐
Climb *Saigon* and stay with the flakes on the left side of the arete until you can make a big pull to gain an obvious wide pinch high on the arete. Match this, then pull around to the right with a wide span to a good sidepull, by stepping on the hold typically used for the left hand on the regular *Saigon*. Sustained and little scary for sure!

7 Saigon Superdirect v10 ★★★ ☐
A very proud line: As for *Saigon Direct* but when you gain the obvious wide pinch high on the arete, keep it with the right hand and make a punch for slopers over the top with the left. Pull over and start celebrating, or take the huge plummet back to planet earth! A flat, but a very high crux!

8 Unnamed v0 ★★ ☐
Climb the wall about 10 feet right of the arete on excellent patina.

9 Unnamed v3 ☐
Climb through a small bulge with awkward footwork and a long move to poor holds. Pull up and then right to join the next line.

10 Unnamed v0 ☐
Climb the wall above the shelf, trending right or left on excellent patina.

11 Unnamed v2 ★ ☐
Begin as for the *Monkey Dihedral* (below), by pressing into the groove. Gain a good crimp high and left, with the right hand and continue direct (slightly left at first), staying right of the previous line.

12 Monkey Dihedral v2 ★★★ ☐
Intriguing: Pull up into the groove, and use balance and finesse to move up to a good crimp. Pull right, with dexterity, past the top of the crack and onto the slab to finish.

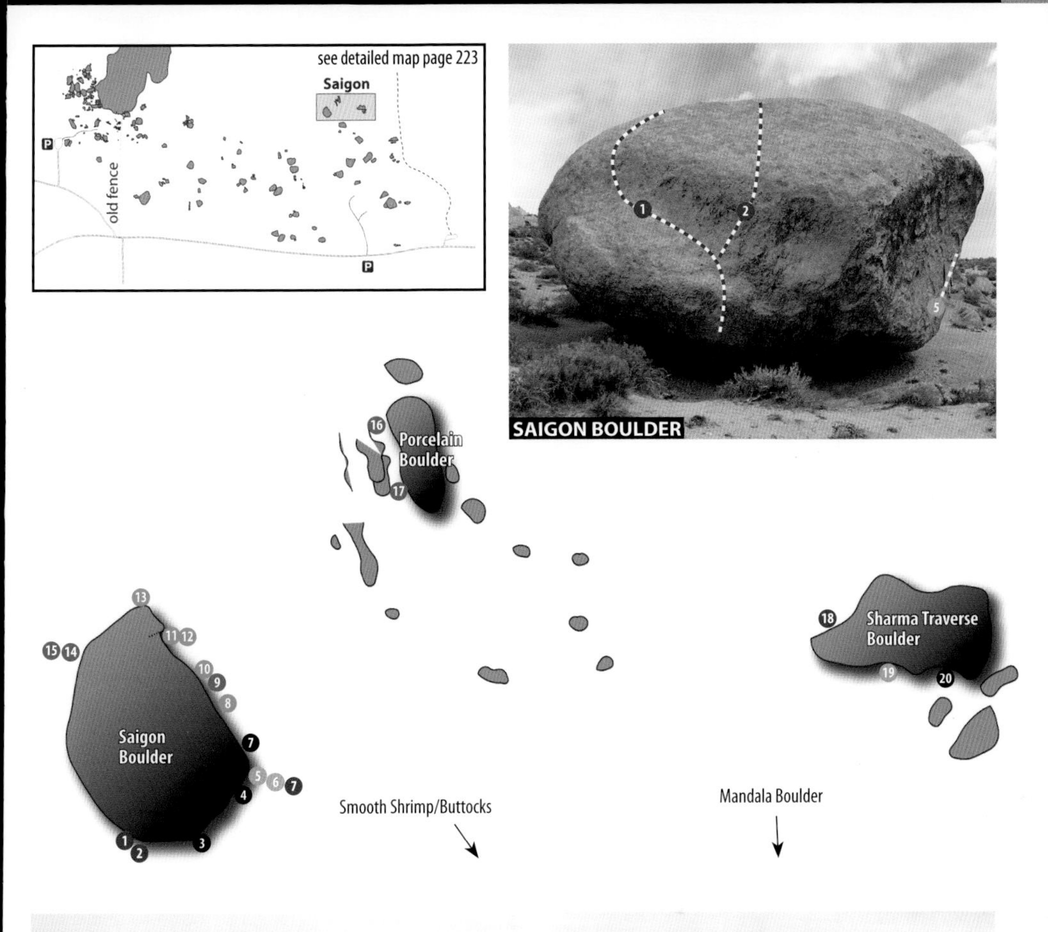
see detailed map page 223
Saigon
P
old fence
P
SAIGON BOULDER
Porcelain Boulder
Sharma Traverse Boulder
Saigon Boulder
Smooth Shrimp/Buttocks
Mandala Boulder

SAIGON BOULDER

SAIGON BOULDER

PORCELAIN BOULDER

SHARMA TRAVERSE BOULDER

⑬ Unnamed v2 ★ ☐
On the north (uphill) side of the boulder, just right of the arete, pull on and over, using a good crimp and large patina sidepull, if you can reach!

⑭ Unnamed v3 ★ ☐
Further right there is a small slightly crusty crimp beneath the lip of the boulder (let's hope it stays there!). Place the right hand on the crimp and jump up left (from the ground) to gain good patina, which quickly leads to more good holds and then easier ground.

⑮ Topside v5 ★★ ☐
From the same starting crimp, beneath the lip, jump (from the ground) up right to slopers, and make a couple of moves right on more slopers. Pull hard to grab a huge lone jug. Exit left with a very long move to a pinch and then good patina. Brilliant problem!

PORCELAIN BOULDER

Up and right from the Saigon Boulder is a narrow boulder with a couple of superb problems on its west side:

⑯ Raggedy Ann v3 ★ ☐
Begin low left. Traverse right, then up to a giant jug that calls your name! A long move from a crimpy sidepull gains the jug (much harder if you're short). Definitely scary due to the ravine and rock below. Spotters and pads are extra-useful here.

⑰ Doll Face v4 ★★ ☐
From a right facing sidepull, move right to another right facing sidepull, then up. A hard move right gains the arete. Excellent. A careful spot would be wise.

UPSIDE BOULDER

SHARMA TRAVERSE BOULDER

Across to the right from the Saigon Boulder is a low boulder with a big overhang on its north side, facing slightly west. This is home to:

18 The Sharma Traverse v10 ★★ ☐
Start low at right. Traverse the lip left to a huge move between patina holds at the edge of the roof. Finish up and over the blunt nose with great difficulty.

19 Backside Mantel v6 ★ ☐
Reach into sidepulls from the low boulder. Reach over the lip to poor slopers and pull a desperate mantel.

20 Unknown ☐
At right is an alcove with splintery patina holds. The left side of the alcove has a rib with some crimps. Above is another horizontal crimp. Up and right is a deep hueco. Connect these somehow.

UPSIDE BOULDER

A two-or-three-minute walk directly up the hill from the Saigon Boulder/Sharma Traverse Boulder will bring you to this large and little-known boulder host to one amazing line and a couple of other worthwhile problems.

1 Unnamed v8 ☐
On the northwest side is a slightly crusty bulging wall. Start high, at a crack and climb up and right with the small boulder at your back (a little scary). There's a hard move turning the bulge on grainy rock, but it will probably clean up. Beware the rock below the topout.

2 Project ☐

3 Upside v8 ★★★ ☐
Sit start and climb the beautiful tall, smooth wall via nice crimps and long moves. Super high quality face climbing. A short walk for an easy tick?

4 Early Exit v5 ★ ☐
Stand start and climb the wall with technical moves on good rock. **Sit start** at about a grade harder.

4 Big Dave's Big Find v5 ★ ☐
Climb the wall from a standing start.

You will need steel fingers for this crimping testpiece. Tim Steele shocks his tendons with a run on the immaculate glassy incuts of *The Checkerboard* (v7/8, page 258). Photo: Wills Young.

Checkerboard Area

A view of the Checkerboard area, looking south from the end of the spur road.

The Checkerboard (v7/8, page 306), is one of the world's most amazing boulder problems. Rock simply does not come better than this! Even though the Checkerboard Boulder sits across from the Buttermilks with its impressive sheer west face in full view, the blank-looking appearance of the wall put off all-comers until February 2000. It was then that Chris Sharma, having hiked over and eyed the line briefly, envisioned a potential area testpiece on the giant rock. Imagining a massive dyno would be necessary to link the lower holds with the easier upper section, Sharma went over with a couple of extra pads. It turned out, after a brief inspection (while climbing), that holds were hidden by a streak of black lichen, and a key crimp was situated far out to the right. It only took a couple of tries to put up what has to be a contender for best line on the entire east side, with Sharma making the first ascent in his inimitable style, from the low start.

If that problem is not reason enough to make the visit, there are plenty of good relatively moderate problems dotted across this small area. The Edge of Reason Boulder is particularly noteworthy with numerous good problems at a broad range of grades. Another five minutes' walk around the hillside to the east will bring you to the Painted Cave Area (see page 307).

Directions

Drive: The Checkerboard boulders are situated opposite the Buttermilks Main Area, across the creek, which runs west to east. First follow directions to the Buttermilks Main Area (page 220). The final approach to the Checkerboard is by a small side road which follows a decaying fence line crossed by the main Buttermilk Road (between the lower roadside parking area, and the upper Birthday Boulders parking area). The boulders are visible from the Buttermilk Road, and it is easy to leave your car parked either there, or at the Birthday Boulders parking area, and walk the 100 yards southward to the end of this bumpy side road. See the map, page 307.

Hike: 5-10 minutes. From the turnaround at the end of the short side road mentioned above, walk down a steep slope, cross a stream and head up the other side. Off to the left, as you arrive at the top of the slope is the gold and black streaked north face of the High and Mighty Boulder with a cluster of boulders nearby. The Edge of Reason Boulder is directly up the hill above these, while the Checkerboard Boulder itself is up the slope and slightly right. Photo above; topo next page.

THE PAWN

HIGH AND MIGHTY BOULDER

THE KNIGHT BOULDER

THE PAWN

This is 25 yards up and left of the High and Mighty Boulder.

1 Unnamed v2 ★★ ☐
The northwest arete: From a good jug, press out a tricky move.

2 Pawn v0 ★ ☐
From a low flake, gain a palm-sized chicken-head and pull around left and up.

3 Unnamed v3 ★ ☐
On the uphill side, stretch to reach a pair of slopers. Reach over to knobs, and way back to a good knob, while making a hard mantel over the lip.

HIGH AND MIGHTY BOULDER

Even though this boulder is impressive and tempting, I can't really recommend any of the climbs, unless you're seeking a very adventurous experience. It is little-climbed, grainy, and some of the holds on the north side are undoubtedly friable. These lines would be great if they cleaned up though.

4 Unnamed v1 ☐
Climb the right of two cracks to a deep hueco. Use the undercling in the hueco to reach up and over. Very grainy.

5 Unknown ☐
The blunt left arete of the impressive north wall with grainy holds and patina. Great care needed.

6 The Welsh Route v4 ☐
Climbed by some visiting Welsh climbers, who don't know better. From the left arete moving right, or perhaps originally, by a lower start further right, climb the towering north wall, on positive edges, some of which may not be entirely solid.

7 Unnamed v0 ☐
Climb mossy, juggy patina and follow it leftward before topping out. Downclimb the small arete to the right. A direct start up right of the gold streak is possible at about v2 on very lichenous rock.

GREEN SLAB BOULDER

Right of the High and Mighty Boulder is a small group of boulders on a ridge, with:

8 Queenie v3 ☐
The green slab in a corridor facing west has been climbed, though there doesn't seem to be any particular line standing out. It is green: very, very green.

THE KNIGHT BOULDER

On the ridge behind (above and right) of the High and Mighty Boulder are:

9 Knight v5 ★★ ☐
Start just right of a slanting arete at some good crimps. Avoid the arete by a big move up right to a knob, pull through to a left-facing sidepull to top out. Backtrack and drop, or climb off the southwest side via knobs and drop to a small boulder.

10 Project ☐
A low start to the previous line looks good.

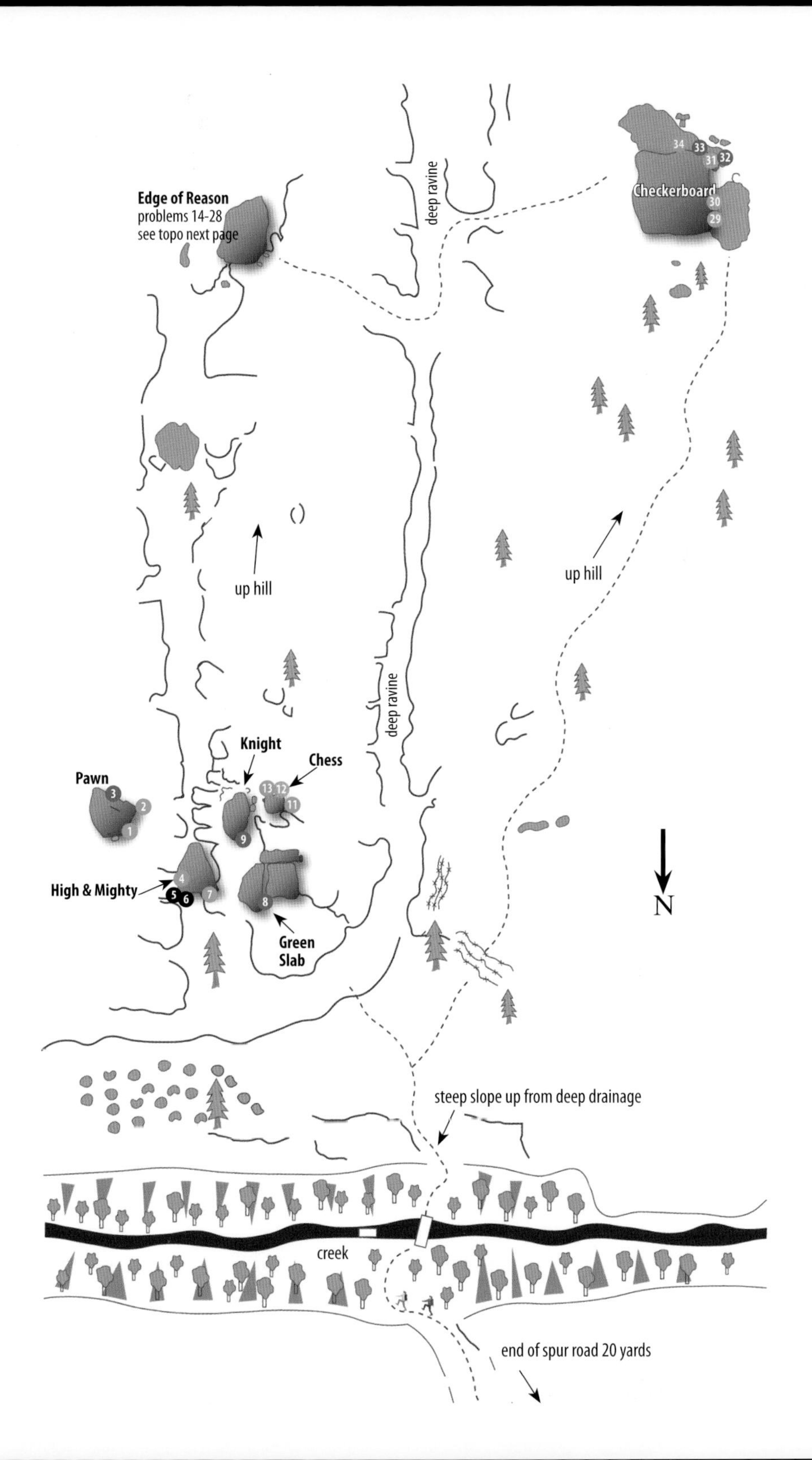

Edge of Reason
problems 14-28
see topo next page
deep ravine
Checkerboard
34
33
31
32
30
29
up hill
up hill
deep ravine
Knight
Chess
Pawn
3
2
1
13
12
11
9
High & Mighty
4
5
6
7
8
Green
Slab
N
steep slope up from deep drainage
creek
end of spur road 20 yards

CHESS BOULDER

EDGE OF REASON BOULDER

CHESS BOULDER

The relatively small boulder at the upper right of this small grouping has:

11 Chess v2 ★ ☐
The rounded arete and west face presents a fun challenge with a tricky press onto the left foot at mid height.

12 Kings and Castles v6 ★ ☐
From the right side of the arete climb the face and arete, by a very hard press onto a pointed knob with the right foot. Use the right arete too, as needed, but pull up and around left to finish. Very grainy but will clean up and perhaps become easier.

13 Draughts v0 ★ ☐
Climb huecos on the arete.

EDGE OF REASON BOULDER

14 Unnamed v2 ★ ☐
Hang the jug, pull to the sloper, and then mantel using some incuts.

15 Colin Goes Mental v7 ★★ ☐
A traverse from left to right, beginning at the previous line's start and finishing on the patina face and arete at the far right. Great rock.

16 Unnamed v2 ★ ☐
Start at patina jugs and execute another slopey entrance onto the slab. Low start also goes.

17 Zero Mantel v5 ★ ☐
Hang the big rounded boss and grope awkwardly until able to step up onto the slab, avoiding jugs far to the left. Listed as "v0" in Mr. Ryan's previous guide: Mick, were you having a laugh, or what?

18 Kick the Boss v6 ★ ☐
Pull up to gain a decent right-hand edge at the lip, and press out a mantel stepping onto the holds out left.

19 Freeze Short v8 ★★ ☐
Sit start at a small flat edge for the right hand and a sidepull for the left which is just 2 feet right of a grey patch. Climb up left to gain an edge at the lip with the right hand. Finish as for the previous line. (Note: a direct finish, using the left hand on the edge at the lip is easier and tends to force you onto the giant patina holds at right.)

20 Freeze All Cylinders v8 ★★ ☐
Sit start, as above, but keep moving left to finish on Zero Mantel. Excellent rock and movement to a heartbreaking finish.

21 No Sense, No Reason v4 ★★ ☐
Begin as for Freeze Short and climb the beautiful overhanging patina up and right.

22 Edge of Reason v3 ★★ ☐
Sit start at the arete and climb it. The standing start is about v0. But you will also want to downclimb it (or the wall left, then drop).

23 Warming v1 ☐
The flakey wall right of the arete and left of a black streak is slightly crusty, and reachy.

24 Rose v5 ★ ☐
The thin flakey wall right of the second black streak. Jump, as necessary to gain the flexi flake. Follow it up to an intense lunge to grab the deep incut slot.

25 Project ☐
Gain crusty friable-looking flakes, and climb up into the shallow scoop.

26 Stand to Reason v7 ★ ☐
Jump start, or reach in to crimps above a xenolith. Climb up using a good flake, a sloping knob and a series of high steps. Nice climbing to a very grainy finish. Will be better and perhaps easier if clean.

27 The Left Lindner v9 ★ ☐
From the big black xenolith toward the right side of the face, follow flakes leftward by big moves on sidepulls, crossing the previous line and finishing with a dyno for the deep slot at the top of Rose. This could also be linked into the previous line.

28 Crack and Ramp vB ☐
The grainy crack and ramp can also be used as a descent, though I prefer to descend next to the southwest arete, on the opposite side.

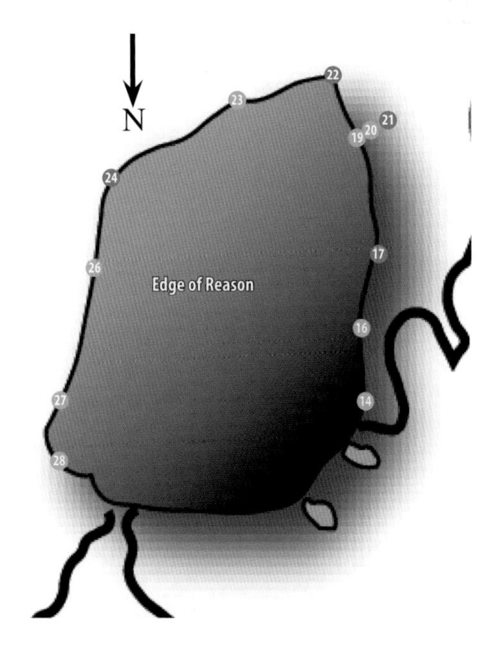

THE CHECKERBOARD

29 The Checkerboard v8 ★★★ ☐
One of the finest in Bishop! Start at a prominent flake jug above the grainy slab, and follow the amazing patina up and across to the far right before a long hard pull gains holds leading into the good upper flakes. Take care: The rock at left has broken more than one leg! Beginning higher, off the top of the low rock makes the problem a little easier (v7).

30 The Checkerboard Direct ★ v8 ☐
Reach from the high point of the rock mound to start. Climb straight up with a scary move to poor crimps, and reach right past another bad crimp to gain good holds and the exit. Perhaps more a question of confidence than difficulty.

31 The Checkerboard Right v9 ★★ ☐
Broken since originally climbed. Begin at right from the rock slab and climb up leftward to a big move left to gain a crimp sidepull on the clean patina face. Make a hard move up to gain the good right-hand incut of the regular Checkerboard, from which the big "last" move is made to join the good flakes leading to the summit.

32 Checkerboard Crack v5 ★ ☐
Start as for The Checkerboard right, but climb the shallow scoop to gain a good sidepull and then jugs.

33 Arete v3 ★ ☐
The blunt southwest arete is climbed by a deep slot.

34 King Me v10 ☐
Underwhelming alongside *The Checkerboard* is this sit start to the previous problem: Begin with right hand on a pinch, and left on a sloping edge. Pull into a knee scum, and make long compression moves up and rightward.

35 Knob and Slab v2 ★ ☐
The black water streak right of the southwest arete is followed starting at the smooth black cobble. This is also a descent (jump the last few feet).

Painted Cave Area

This is an enjoyable area, with fantasic views across to the Peabodies and into nearby canyons. There are a handful of good problems on half a dozen boulders. The area offers a bit of a retreat from the main Buttermilks, as the approach hike of 10-15 minutes stops most from even contemplating climbing here! The gem here is the problem itself (v6), which has some fun juggy moves on big huecos leading to a series of slopers on a short headwall: a great change of pace from the typical Buttermilk crimping fare. (v5) is a good, tall problem too that could clean up to be a classic. At a much more amenable level, (v2) is a fun, technical little groove that is worth seeking out.

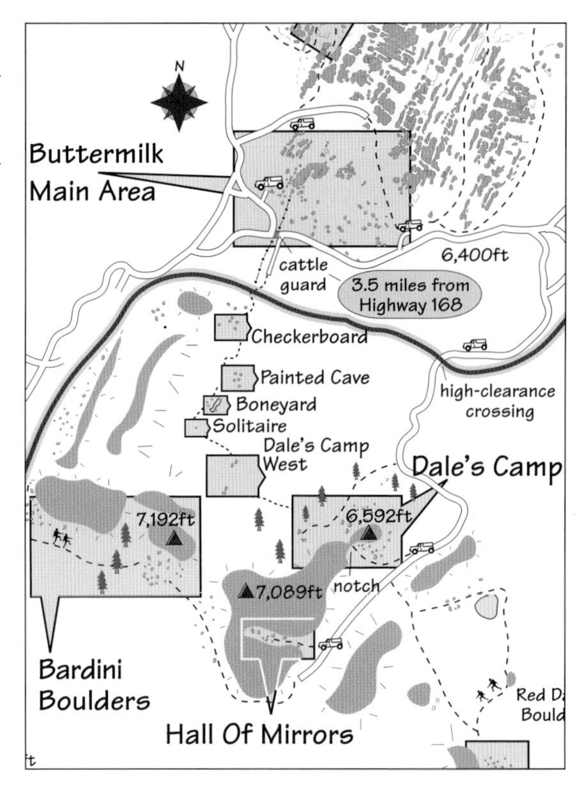

Directions

Drive: As for the Checkerboard Area, page 301.

Walk: 10-15 minutes. Follow directions to the Checkerboard Area (page 301). But, after crossing the stream, and arriving at the top of the ravine, walk ahead and then left to follow a small wash downhill. Where that wash takes a sharp turn to the left (dropping toward the steam), head up rightward out of the ravine. From here, head west, and slightly south away from the Checkerboard Area, contouring the hillside.

PAINTED CAVE BOULDER

PAINTED CAVE BOULDER

CHARLIE BROWN BOULDERS

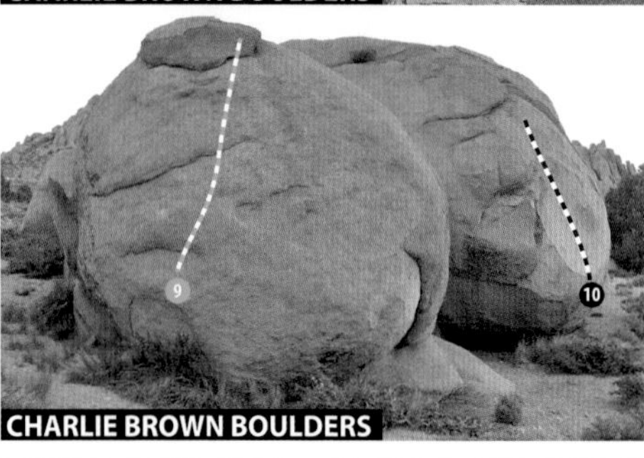
CHARLIE BROWN BOULDERS

PAINTED CAVE BOULDER

This boulder is clearly seen on the approach due to the distinctive slashes on its north side.

1 Undercling Problem v7 ★ ☐
Pull into underclings on the left side of the north face and make an urgent slap to gain a large grainy pocket in the slab above. Continue up, with right underclings and step onto the slab to finish.

2 Slashface of the Buttermilks v6 ★ ☐
From a awkward start at the left side, follow seams and good edges up right, pulling over the top with a pumpy finish using a lone crimp and a knob. A large chunk came off the start since the last guide, making it harder.

2a Slashface Sit Start v8 ☐
A tricky sit start to the previous line.

3 Slashface Right Start v7 ☐
Start to the right, at the large blob and make a long hard move via a crimp to join the previous line.

4 Painted Cave Standing Start v4 ★ ☐
Climb the headwall from the big hueco on shallow sloping dishes.

5 Painted Cave v6 ★★ ☐
This is the gem of the area. There is some graininess at the top, but the moves are great. Sit start at right on the giant hold in the cave and traverse left into the big hueco to join the standing start.

CHARLIE BROWN BOULDERS

These boulders are just west of the Painted Cave and clearly visible on the approach.

6 Charlie Brown v3 ★ ☐
From a slanting foothold, climb up and over on hard-to-find edges on the slab. Sit-start at about a grade harder.

7 Harder, Browner v4 ★ ☐
To the right of Charlie Brown is a similar line that is perhaps a tad harder.

8 Pig Pen v5 ★ ☐
Begin with both hands in underclings and make a couple of hard moves onto the slab. (The flake at right is not used.)

9 Unnamed v1 ★ ☐
On the smaller boulder's southeast side, start with good holds and make a high step and tricky rock-over move.

10 Unknown ☐
A sweet looking mantel into the obvious scoop at the end of the larger boulder. Hard!

11 Georgia O'Keefe v0- ★ ☐
Climb the groove. The left side and the right side can also be climbed independently.

12 Evening Snow v7 ★ ☐
From slopey edges, make a reachy move up to more small edges.

13 Unnamed v2 ☐
From the right side, force a line left across the crimps to the top of Evening Snow (above).

14 Unnamed v1 ☐
Climb up to an undercling and then up the slab.

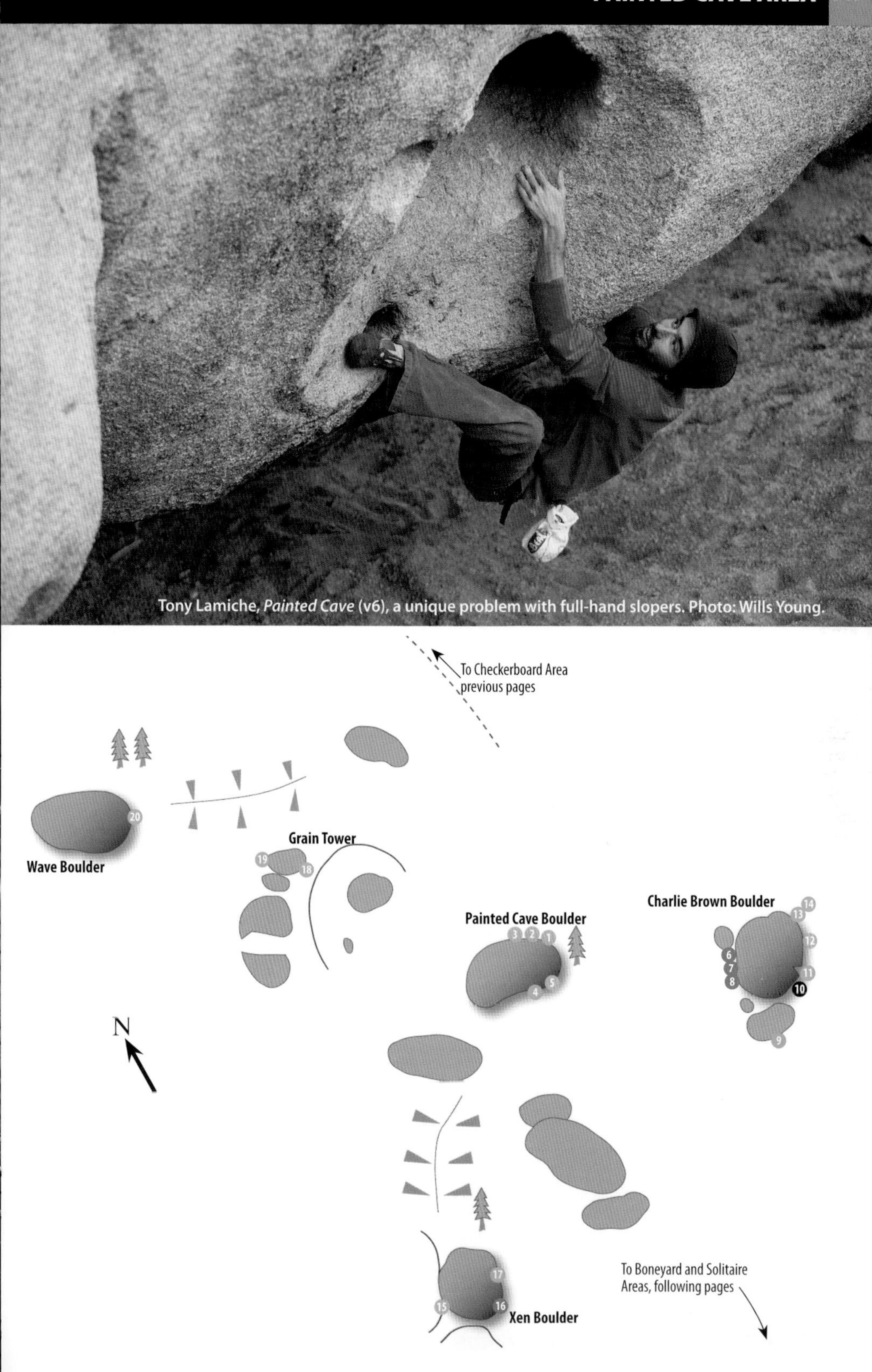

Tony Lamiche, *Painted Cave* (v6), a unique problem with full-hand slopers. Photo: Wills Young.

CHARLIE BROWN BOULDERS

XEN BOULDER

XEN BOULDER

XEN BOULDER

Find this boulder by looking out from the Painted Cave problem and slightly to the right. There is a drainage blocked by some low boulders. Up the drainage is the Xen Boulder, named after its xenoliths.

15 Unnamed v6 ★ ☐

Cheat if necessary to gain a good crimp/dish at the lip of the boulder with the left hand. Make a strenuous pull to gain a good xenolith knob, and then climb up into the groove.

16 Split Arete v3 ★ ☐

Climb the arete with some tricky laybacking.

17 Xen v2 ★★ ☐

Sweet, technical climbing up the groove with xenoliths, leads to a deep hueco up and right.

GRAIN TOWER

To find this boulder, face out from the Slashface problems on the Painted Cave Boulder; map previous page. Look diagonally to the left to see a drainage/ravine. Head into the ravine where a tower-like boulder is on the left with:

18 More Grainy Than Hard v1 ☐

The left arete on the east side is a world of grain.

19 Hangar 18 v1 ☐

On the west side, a strange lichen patch looks a little like an alien image. Climb the blunt arete/face.

BIG WAVE BOULDER

Further up the same ravine that contains Grain Tower (above) is the Big Wave Boulder. It is at the head of the small ravine, northwest of the Painted Cave Boulder.

20 Big Wave Surfing v0+ ★ ☐

On the downslope side of the boulder climb the crack leading to a low-angle slab.

The Boneyard

With a handful of good problems, this area is worth a quick stop to enjoy the wild concept of being a full 15 minutes from your vehicle. Enjoy the crazy rock-strewn landscape that extends for miles and remains little-explored. Climb some problems not listed, give them names, and put them in your next guidebook. Climbing here could also be a nice warm-up for those going on to the Solitaire Boulder (next page).

Directions

Drive: As for the Checkerboard Area (page 301).

Walk: As for the Painted Cave Area, and then, from the Painted Cave Boulder, face out from the Painted Cave problem and start walking contouring the hillside, aiming toward the distant Grouse Mountain, which is visible rising in the background beyond a v-notch in the relatively nearby hills. After a hundred yards or so, notice a tall rocky knoll with a small valley to its right. The highpoint of the knoll is formed by two large boulders (split east-west by a sheer-sided offwidth) and a small capstone. Head up the valley just right of the rocky knoll. On the southwest side of the knoll find the Bone Boulder, with a small dead tree by its side. Map and photo page 307.

BONE BOULDER

BONE BOULDER

Named for the low natural rock arch in the shape of a leg bone, in the corridor behind the boulder.

1 Bone Bulge v3 ★ ☐
Begin with a good left-hand sidepull in a shallow hueco and move up right to slopers. Make a big move up right to grab a sidepull sloper and step up and over the bulge with subtle body positioning.

2 Sierra Phantom v2 ★ ☐
Start at the left end of the big rail and climb directly up and over the bulge on slopers.

3 Rail Problem (Boneyard) v1 ★ ☐
Start at the left end of the big rail, and climb right and then up.

4 Dyno Problem v4 ☐
From a good knobby hold, make a long, powerful move up left to the right end of the rail, and finish as for the previous problem.

5 Shortie v1 ☐
Pull onto the wall above the Dyno Problem's start, by stepping in from the rock slab using a sidepull and crimp. Make one long move up and over. A low start looks possible. This is also a good descent.

6 Unnamed v1 ☐
In the corridor, from the center of the wall, make an interesting traverse left, and up, finishing on some suspect patina.

7 Macabre Proposition v4 ★ ☐
In the corridor, begin at the center of the wall and climb up to a large shallow hueco. Make a big stretch out of this, up to the right to a good incut, and reach through to the top. A left finish is friable, but around the same grade.

BONE BOULDER

OTHER BOULDERS

There are also many other possibilities in the area, including:

8 Trigger Hippy v4 ★ ☐
On top of the knoll, on the northeast arete of the summit block is a tall arete, which has a bolt at the top. Climb it on crimps over a very bad landing.

DALE'S WEST

The lower (Zen Flute) boulder at Dale's West (page 372), is visible a couple of hundred yards away by looking southeast from near the Boneyard across the small wash/valley. From the Zen Flute Boulder, you can hike up to the Green Hornet Boulder, and over the ridge to the main Dales Camp, arriving at the Hueco Wall Area (page 360).

Solitaire Boulder

This boulder has two extraordinary problems. *Solitaire* (v8) is a magnificent link-up of two long dynos on immaculate rock (this is an extremely hard problem for shorter climbers). The arete to the left is another beauty, requiring a very different style of climbing to top out on its slopers after a powerful start.

Directions

Drive: As for The Checkerboard Area.

Walk: 15-20 minutes. Follow directions to the Boneyard from the Painted Cave Area (page 307). From here, the Solitaire Boulder is visible, further along in the same direction. Map and photo page 307.

VIEW OF SOLITAIRE BOULDER FROM BONEYARD

1 **Judge Not** v9 ☐

On the steeply overhanging north face (visible on approach view, left) of the Solitaire Boulder, is this gymnastic climb on sadly crusty rock. Stand start, grab a small but positive edge and throw a big drive-by to gain a huge hold. From here either climb straight up via a thin right-hand sidepull of very doubtful sturdiness, or move up rightward via small crusty crimps and a couple of big pulls (probably harder). Hard to know if this will clean up to become a classic or just fall apart ...

2 **Eric's Dyno** ☐

Start low and throw a big move. Not the best rock.

3 **Evil Empire** v6 ☐

Start from a rail at four feet. Make two moves to good holds then a long dyno for the big edge. Pull up on some cool slopers and edges and make a big high step rock over. Aim for a big diorite knob to top out.

4 **One More** v8 ★★ ☐

Begin at a good sidepull and an undercling for the left hand. Move up left to a good incut, and then over on slopers.

5 **Project** ☐

It might be possible to climb from the arete at left across to join the top of Solitaire.

6 **Solitaire** v8 ★★★ ☐

Start matched at the good incut crimp and make a huge pull to gain a similar, and slightly bigger crimp up and left. Make another big pull to the hard-to-see hold over the lip. Then top out more easily. An amazing find. Hard for the short ... **Sit start** at v10 or harder (?) on friable rock.

7 **Unnamed** v7 ☐

Traverse right from the start of *Solitaire* to top out on the Groove (below).

8 **The Groove** v6 ☐

The groove is a bit junky, but it could clean up.

Nic Oklobzija slaps the big move on the incredile *Solitaire* (v8), opposite. Photo: Wills Young.

Get Carter Boulder

Long-time boulderer Bob Murray's age-old maxim states that you can hike all over creation seeking new stone, but all the best boulders turn out to be right next to the road. This is one amazing boulder. You can park next to it, it's a perfect height for bouldering, and it has some of the best problems you are ever likely to find. Not only that, but local guru James Wilson (of Wilson's Eastside Sports) used to call this place the Sunbathe Naked Boulder because Bishop's finest could typically be found airing their skin in a perfect wind-sheltered love-seat up on top. Scary thought, actually.

Here are two of the Buttermilk's hardest lines side-by-side— *A Scanner Darkly* (v12), and *Michael Caine Sit* (v12)—twin cracks leading up to both left, and right exits; plus two superb and very finger-friendly testpieces, *Grommit* (v4) and *Seven Spanish Angels* (v6) also side-by-side. The namesake *Get Carter* (v7) is also, and rightly, a perennial "fave" with hard moves close to the ground followed by a tricky exit.

Directions

Drive: Follow directions to the main Buttermilk Boulders' parking area below the Peabodies, (page 223). Continue as if going to the main Buttermilks' upper parking, by driving further up Buttermilk Road, making a right turn after the fence, and following the bumpy road briefly uphill then around a left curve. At this point, instead of driving up into the upper Birthday Boudlers parking circle (a right turn), continue straight on along the road, which soon curves right and heads downhill. The road shortly crosses another fence line. Just after going through the gap in the fence (sometimes a gate), stay and over some bumps, continuing downhill. After 0.2 miles from the fence, the road forks; take the right fork on road 7S04. Drive this fork for 0.4 miles to where boulders are strewn across the slope, and the Get Carter Boulder is adjacent the road on the right. Park just after the boulder.

Walk: Five yards to the boulder.

1 Goosepimple Exposure v0 ☐
Follow the left edge of the patina to reach the hollow at the top. Kinda the same problem as the next one, but starting left.

2 Sunshine Naked v0 ★ ☐
Climb the patina beginning as you like, to reach a deep hueco above. High-stepping over at the top is nervy, with no real hand-holds. Photo overleaf.

3 Roadside Crack v1 ★ ☐
Follow the patina crack up and right, beginning at the alcove. Some questionable patina on this one too.

4 Wallace v4 ★ ☐
Begin at the undercling and make a couple of hard moves to gain good holds on the left of the very shallow groove. The upper flake is very hollow. Press it out to the top with great care.

5 The Wrong Trousers v8 ★ ☐
Step onto the wall from the ground using a slick xenolith, and climb with an enormous press at first, and another hard pull using strange glassy pockets in the blank face, then a long move left to gain sidepulls and eventually exit holds: A little scary up high.

6 A Grand Day Out v10 ★ ☐
Begin at the blunt arete on the lowest holds of *Grommit*. Pull on and make a move left to a small sidepull. Pull onto the left foot and head up the face on small gastons and the occasional right hand crimp to an obvious (and slightly suspect) edge up high (care!). Finish with a long move to the top.

7 Grommit v4 ★★★ ☐
The rightward rising line of sidepulls is intriguing with a crux up high. It is a little scarier than it ought to be due to a rock slab behind the base. But it is well worth checking out with a spotter and a couple of pads.

8 Unnamed Link-up v7 ★★ ☐
A fun link from the previous problem to the next one.

9 Seven Spanish Angels v6 ★★★ ☐
Climb the amazing wall of knobs and blobs using body tension, awkward gastons and pinches, and perhaps a dyno. Confusing, yes, but you'll find something that works, and, if nothing else, it will be fun trying. Also known as *The Ruckus*. Photo overleaf.

⑩ Flecheros v8 ★ ☐
A surprising and amazing line up the blunt arete and face. Use a very poor left-hand crimp to start. Layback a blunt arete high up with the right hand and use a small sidepull for the left hand to gain a good slanted crimp. Make a big move to grab a good incut a few feet below the top and then up and over. The rock is slightly crusty, but so long as the starting hold doesn't disintegrate completely, this will potentially clean up to be very good.

⑪ To Kill Ya Corner v3 ★★ ☐
Reach the high good flake at a stretch and climb directly up the gold streak.

⑫ To Kill Ya Corner Sit Start v9 ★ ☐
Start below *Flecheros* on pinch/jugs and climb into *To Kill Ya Corner.*

⑬ Twin Cracks v9 ★★ ☐
Using both cracks, climb up left by some long moves with wide spans. Continue to the top of the boulder by some more long moves.

⑭ A Scanner Darkly v12 ★★ ☐
Sit start the previous problem. Begin with the right hand at the good sidepull in the right of the two parallel cracks (4.5 feet off the ground). Use the twin cracks to join the previous line.

⑮ Michael Caine v9 ★★ ☐
Start with both hands in the right of two parallel cracks. Pull up right by a powerful move to a sloper; cross under and move right to top out above *Get Carter.*

⑯ Michael Caine Sit Start v12 ★★ ☐
Sit start the previous problem. Begin with the right hand at the good sidepull in the right of the two parallel cracks (4.5 feet off the ground). Use both cracks to make all-out deadpoints to gain the better sidepulls of the right crack, where the standing start is joined.

⑰ Get Carter v7 ★★ ☐
Sit start with the right hand in a low sidepull, and climb the overhang with sustained hard moves and some clever technique. Follow the line up and left to a high rock-over (harder and better), or cut right early for the quick send.

Facing the road is a solid well-featured slab:

⑱ Holy Slab vB ★ ☐
The slab to the left of the flake crack is the downclimb.

⑲ Backside Crack vB ★★ ☐
The pretty crack is also a downclimb.

⑳ Burned and Bare v0 ☐
The arete to the right of the slab

㉑ Exposed Rearside v0 ☐
A short patina wall leads to a low-angle slab.

CARTER TWO

22 Mantel v0 ☐
Mantel and scoot off left.

23 Mantel and Slab v1 ★ ☐
Press out the mantel and head up right following a faint seam to the top. The airy finish is exciting.

24 Diedrin v10 ☐
Sit start at the base of the tiny dihedral. Right hand is *low* and left hand is higher on the small facet of the dihedral at a tiny crimp. Make a hard pull off the ground, cross right above left, and then make a big move up and left to the ramp. Top out — kinda highball — by climbing up and rightward. The top part is perhaps more fun than the hard start, though it needs some cleaning!

25 Unnamed v11 ★ ☐
From a high start (pads probably needed for a boost) with two sloping pinch underclings, make a tough highstep and balance awkwardly onto the slab, which eases higher. Rating unconfired. The low start is the sweet project in the works at time of press.

26 Project ☐
Something might be doable on the smooth, shiny south face of the boulder.

Julia Krueger catches some *Sunshine Naked* (v0, previous page). Photo: Dan Brayack.

Jerome Meyer sticks the crux move of *Seven Spanish Angels* aka *The Ruckus* (v6, overleaf), an extraordinary problem up blobs and dishes on the east face of the exceptional Get Carter Boulder. Photo: Stephan Denys.

Secrets of The Beehive Area

The Secrets area is a secluded spot on the west side of Buttermilk Mountain, with a mix of fine problems, including something at every level. It requires a bit of a hike — which is not entirely flat, so can be slow going after snows—but the area has its own aura, great views and some excellent rock. The super-highball *Secrets of the Beehive* (v6), first climbed by itinerant climbing legend Hidetaka Suzuki in the late 1990s, draws aspirants from far and wide, eager to sample the huge patina wall with its leg-shaking—hopefully not leg-breaking—finale. A stack of pads is a good idea for this big line. There are a couple of superb low-angle v0s in *Natural Melody* (left and direct), and excellent v9s, *Queen Sweet Nectar* and *Queen Sweet Nectar Left*, which are steep and powerful. There is just enough here that everyone will be well-rewarded by a visit.

Directions

Drive: Follow directions to the main Buttermilk Boulders' Peabodies parking area, (page 223). Continue as if going to the main Buttermilks' upper parking, by driving further up Buttermilk Road, making a right turn after the fence, and following the bumpy road briefly uphill then around a left curve. At this point, instead of driving up into the upper parking circle (a right turn), continue straight on along the road, which soon curves right and heads downhill. The road shortly crosses another fence line. Just after going through the gap in the fence (sometimes a gate), make a right turn. Drive down, and then uphill and park at a pull out on the right just before the hill steepens. Leave space in the parking area for others. (Map page 223)

Hike: In brief, for those who know the area, you head out past the Windy Wall and continue in a more-or-less straight line in the same direction until you are at the end of a valley that parallels the road below —the road to the Get Carter Boulder. The Secrets area is up above the Get Carter Area, but is most easily approached by this route.

After parking, walk up the steep road for about one hundred yards. A few yards before a bend to the right, head left toward the granite "domes" (see photos below). After crossing a ravine continue across a gravelly slope leftward to the entrance to a wide canyon. Walk through the canyon with the "Windy Wall" on your right. At the far side, walk around some boulders, and continue toward the next ravine. From here, you can see the Secrets area in the distance. Cross another ravine at its right side and continue to contour the hillside. You will soon pass through a group of large boulders. These are mostly not covered by this guidebook—except for one boulder high up on the right side—the Windy Wall Area (see 326). Keep walking, staying toward the slope's right side until you arrive at the Secrets area.

Legendary itinerant climber Hidetaka Suzuki settled in Bishop in the late 1990s, before moving on to a life of leisure in Hawaii. Here he re-enacts one of his first ascents in the region, *The Secrets of the Beehive* (v6, next page). Photo: Simon Carter.

NECTAR BOULDER

NECTAR BOULDER

1 Natural Melody v0- ★★★ ☐
Climb up into a scoop and over into another shallow scoop, then make a step up and left into the third scoop to top out. Intriguing low-angle climbing.

2 Natural Melody Direct v1 ★★★ ☐
Climb into the first scoop as for the previous line. And continue direct by laybacking the right side of the second scoop to gain a deep hueco by a very long move. Another excellent little climb.

3 No Words, No Talk v2 ★ ☐
Climb into the low scoop, and then move up and diagonally right to a good knob.

4 Royal Trux v2 ☐
Begin at a tiny left-facing crimp-sidepull. Climb the smooth wall.

5 Ballbuster v1 ☐
Sit start at the column feature. Climb up to good holds.

6 She Smells of the Sun v0 ☐
Step onto the left edge of the shallow scoop, and traverse delicately rightward and up.

7 Unnamed v1 ☐
Reach high/jump and make a couple of moves on the right side of the wall, just left of the "cave" entrance, using good huecos and patina.

8 Queen Sweet Nectar Left v9 ★★★ ☐
In the corridor, sit start at a pair of small right-facing sidepulls very low and begin with a hard move up with the left hand. Move up, and then left to the nice round hueco. Use this (undercling) to gain small shallow huecos up above and stretch left to good patina at the left edge of the wall. Top out on the slab at left.

9 Queen Sweet Nectar v9 ★★ ☐
Sit start at a pair of small right-facing sidepulls very low. Begin with a hard move up with the left hand and climb the wall up and slightly right using all the features.

10 The Buzz ★★ v2 ☐
Climb up huecos on the right side of the wall with a hard move up high.

SECRETS/TITAN BOULDER

11 The Secrets of the Beehive v6 ★★★ ☐
One of the best highballs in the Bishop area, this huge, gently overhanging wall is climbed on good flakes to a worrying finish where the patina runs out, high above a pea-gravel landing. A big line that even with the good drop-zone, deserves serious respect. A butt snag has been used by some at the upper crux! Now that really is putting your ass on the line! Photo preceding page.

12 No Place For Fear v5 ★ ☐
Sit start at a big hueco. Make a hard move up left to another big hueco, and then pull onto the wall. Climb this on slightly crusty patina to a hard finish. It might be worth scoping and cleaning this from above, unless it's seen a lot of traffic (unlikely!).

13 Flake Crack vB ★★ ☐
The crack is an excellent little climb.

14 Russ Walling, Bored Housewife v3 ★ ☐
The unlikely-looking problem is climbed on surprisingly decent holds to a long lock off to the patina at the top (or just left of it).

15 The Choadler Yodler v3 ★★ ☐
Climb the wall with some good moves on pretty rock, with care at the top.

16 Desert Stormer v1? ☐
Sorry, no precise info on the rating or line other than that it probably goes up past the rotten-looking circle of flakes. Reportedly about v1, but it looks harder.

17 Liar, Liar, Pants on Fire v1 ☐
Climb easily up right into a scoop, and then balance up rightward still and up to good, but fragile holds at the lip. Precarious and scary.

18 Pathological v6 ★ ☐
Start with two small crimps at the diagonal lip. Originally a hard eliminate that has easier options.

UNNAMED BOULDER

This boulder is opposite the The Swarm (next page).

19 Gossip v4 ★★ ☐
A proud and obvious line that is not the gimme it looks to be. Climb up into a hueco awkwardly, and gain slopey holds at the lip of the boulder. Teeter left to good holds and make a terrifying mantel up. A direct finish past the pinch will be a great cool weather version. There's a dreadful landing either way.

NECTAR & SECRETS BOULDER

UNNAMED BOULDER

SECRETS/TITAN BOULDER

THE STORY OF A BROWN WALL

Top boulderers who know how to pull hard and then harder on tiny crimps will arrive like bees to nectar at the astonishing smooth "Brown Wall," with its ultimate testpiece *The Swarm* (v14), first done by Matt Birch, of England after a season of uninspired attempts resulted in a visit by fellow Brit, Ben Moon. It was Moon's immediate progress on the line that provided the needed kick-in-the-pants for Birch to get the problem done (photo opposite). Dave Graham and Chris Sharma had been unlucky with their attempts a year or so prior — Sharma broke a hold after the crux on the line, and having badly split his finger could try no more on the razor edges during his then short visit in 2002, while Graham was only stopped after making quick work of the moves because a two-foot dump of snow prevented his return in December the same year. Birch then, finally took the prize, which has seen many attempts and few repeats since. Is it v13 or v14? Concensus so far puts it at v14. Dave Graham, one of four people to have climbed *The Swarm* (at time of press) agrees, and with a tick-list that is second to none we have to bow to his usually good opinion—at least until someone flashes it!

BROWN WALL BOULDER (A.K.A. TITAN)

20 Flight of the Bumblebee v8 ★★★ ☐
A beauty! Begin with a jump to gain a big jug. Follow the seam/crack up right past a couple of tricky moves to its end below a small overlap. Positive full-pad edges allow a breather here before the crux sequence. Make an insecure and teetery pull over the bulge, then reach right to the faint rib. With improving holds, carefully reach through to the summit. An extremely bold line over a blocky landing and certainly one of Bishop's toughest challenges!

21 The Swarm v14 ★★★ ☐
With bullet rock, a stunning line, and a dramatic location, this is surely one of the best crimping testpieces in America, if not the world. Start with both hands on a right-facing sidepull. Make some stupidly hard, but uncomplicated moves on tiny holds to gain and then follow the rail of small crimps to the right arete. Pull up and onto the slab.

22 Project ☐
A direct finish to The Swarm seems very plausible, though a fragile hold may break (hence the right version was initially preferred).

23 Unnamed v6 ★ ☐
Around the corner right of The Swarm, at the small overhanging northwest arete, sit start with the right hand high at a knobble pinch. A couple of hard moves leed to a fun mantel. Walk off or drop.

Matt Wilder bearing down on the small crimps of *The Swarm* (v13/14).

Luminance Block

The sheer number of gigantic free-standing boulders scattered across the Buttermilk country is astonishing. Even with the constant stream of visitors, and exploration by locals, some of these fabulous boulders remain untapped due to their sheer size, steepness, or paucity of holds. The Luminance Block is, or at least was, one of these. It is a truly magnificent piece of rock, resting in a gully between the Windy Wall and the Secrets (of the Beehive) Area. It had no significant climbs on it when the last guidebook went to print. Nevertheless, an "easy way up" had been established with a couple of bolts and some top climbers would visit and gaze at its many facets in awe and contemplation. Clearly it was on the radar.

Things began to happen here in January 2007 when Chris Sharma picked off the unnamed *Northwest Arete* during an exploratory visit. Later in November of the same year Kevin Jorgeson climbed *The Golden Rule*, a beautiful and sustained 40-foot route at the boulder's northeast edge. Jorgeson's line blends bouldering into traditionally protected leading to link a striking arete to an enticing crack. Shawn Diamond was next in the book with his solo ascent (after self-belay) of *Rise* another giant line but this time with a clear distinction between the steep and bouldery lower highball and the relatively easy slab solo. Shawn returned at the end of December 2008 to snatch up the most spectacular boulder problem on the block with his daring first ascent of *Luminance* — a problem-length climb, but with a heinous drop-zone. No doubt there will be more to come from this giant block — the project on the wall right of *The Golden Rule* was tried by Brit George Ullrich before his car broke down at the end of his visit! It will likely go at around mid-5.13 or perhaps an extremely highball v8/9?

Directions

Drive: Drive and park as for Secrets of the Beehive Area (page 318).

Walk: The approach to this block is the same as for the Secrets of the Beehive as described on page 318, except that you will need to look to your left about half way out toward the Secrets area (roughly below the Form Destroyer Roof) to see the upper part of this block. A couple of bolts on the uphill side of the boulder provide the way up if you're planning to check out a line by top rope — you can either climb, or simply drag your ass up using a quick draw or two to gain the summit.

Shawn Diamond on the opening move of his amazing contribution, *Luminance* (v10), which he climbed at the end of December 2008.

1 The Golden Rule v5/5.12 ★★★ ☐
Climb the overhanging northeast arete with a frightening move over a terrible landing to gain the lowest end of a curving crack. Kevin Jorgeson placed gear here on the first ascent. Follow the crack up and right a little and then climb direct to the summit. Photo: This page.

2 Project ☐
The attractive golden wall to the right of Golden Rule leads to a lichen-streaked finish. The thin face moves on this vertical line have been done.

3 Northwest Arete v7? ★ ☐
Climb the northwest hanging arete with a very big pull between good holds at the lip over a dicey landing. Rating unconfirmed.

4 Luminance v10 ★★★ ☐
Perfect rock and terrifying position make this mesmerizing line one of the boldest and most beautiful in all the 'Milks. Delightful crimps quickly lead you into the no-fall zone over a stepped blocky landing that drops away even faster than the face leads upward: a serious proposition. Begin at a good rail on the left side of the steeply overhanging wall. Climb right and then up. Photo: opposite.

5 Rise v5/5.12 ★★★ ☐
Another super-highball, this has some steep and powerful climbing leading to a scary, though relatively easy slab. Begin by pulling onto the left side of the hanging arete and climb up this over an okay-ish gravel landing to a move right onto the slab and the heady finish.

Kevin Jorgeson ties in for the first ascent of *The Golden Rule* (5.12, v5), December 2007. Photo: Andy Mann.

WINDY WALL BOULDERS

There are dozens of boulders in the southern end of the Secrets of the Beehive valley, spread across the slope from the end of the Windy Wall to the main Secrets area (page 318). Most of the problems here are not documented in this guide, and there is no topo of this area. However included here is the Form Destroyer Roof Boulder, which has several good lines on solid rock with a pleasant gravelly landing (v0-v4), plus the very short testpiece, *Form Destroyer* (v12). A photo shows the lines and a locator image will allow you to find the boulder.

Approach: Follow directions to the Secrets of the Beehive Area (page 318), but after leaving the Windy Wall area, walk across the right flank of the valley about 200 yards, as though heading to the Secrets of the Beehive Area, and locate the boulder on the right side, using the photo provided below. The boulder sits up on the hillside overlooking the valley and is 50 yards or so right of an area of ochre-colored rock.

FORM DESTROYER ROOF BOULDER

1 Unnamed v1 ☐
From a right facing undercling/sidepull in the roof, make a hard move left and climb over the bulge.

2 Unnamed v4 ☐
From a right-facing undercling/sidepull in the roof, climb right to a flake, over the bulge, and up.

3 Unnamed v1 ☐
Stand-start the previous line.

4 Unnamed Dyno v5 ★★ ☐
Fun, kinda height-dependent, and probably easier if you're tall, but most can do this with very high feet. Start with both hands on the embedded xenolith incuts. Walk your feet really high and deadpoint/dyno to the edge about six feet up! Top out.

5 Unnamed v4 ★ ☐
Sit start at a right-facing flake/jug, and climb left to join route 3.

6 Unnamed v3 ★ ☐
Sit start at a right-facing flake/jug and climb diagonally up right to good patina edges.

7 Unnamed v1 ★★ ☐
Awkward at the start the wall is climbed on good patina.

8 Form Destroyer v12 ★ ☐
A short sharp shock: Start at the undercling hueco, with your heel set in there from the get-go. Make a hard move to grab a micro-crimp in the roof. Walk your feet around and stab for the sharpness at the lip. Pull around and up the headwall.

FORM DESTROYER ROOF BOULDER

Suspended in Silence (V5, page 333) is a classic highball on the Lidija Boulder at the Pollen Grains (next section). Here, Yen gets a good spot at the scary upper section. Photo: Wills Young.

Eric Lang on the highballer's rite of passage *Jedi Mind Tricks* (v4, page 336)
— FA Tom Klinefelter 1997/8. Photo: Wills Young.

The Pollen Grains

Around the "back" of the Buttermilk Mountain from the Peabodies, on a delightful east-facing slope of gravel, at between 6300 and 6600 feet (about 2000m) live the Peabodies' nearest relatives, the Pollen Grains, a.k.a. the Lidija Boulders. In winter, this is generally a little cooler than the Buttermilks main area, due to its easterly aspect and the proximity of the shading bulk of Buttermilk Summit. There's a slightly longer drive and a 10-15 minute hike to reach this area, but the rewards are huge.

The Bouldering

The boulders at the Pollen Grains/Lidija Boulders come big, and bigger — no less than you've come to expect from the Bishop Buttermilk Country. You will find them sitting for the most part above good flat landings. *The Spectre* (v13), found here on the Spectre Boulder, is one of the hardest lines in America, seeing very few ascents, and is one of the Bishop area's toughest and proudest ticks (though undoubtedly something of a reachy issue for shorter climbers). Great highballing on easy terrain is another of the area's features. *Original Line* (v0) provides one of the best boulder ascents you can hope to find. Harder highballs are also available in quantity, with *Jedi Mind Tricks* (v4) being the big attraction for those seeking something less powerful and more thought provoking, while moving into the more punchy terrain you will find so much to go at that even the strongest climbers will be hard pushed to do them all — and we're talking world-class highballs here. One of these, *The Ninth* (v6), though requiring a bit of an uphill trek, is certainly one of the most striking lines on the East Side. Take pads; take your friends; and above all, *take care*.

Those looking for climbing that won't potentially leave them hobbling back to the car, or worse, will find some fun climbing here too, especially on the Honey Boulder, the north patina on the Lidija Boulder (a.k.a. Pollen Grain), over at the Beehive Ridge Area, and at the not-to-be-missed cave on the Beekeeper Boulder with the superb *Beekeeper's Apprentice* (v5).

Suspended in Silence (v5, page 333) — FA Mick Ryan late 1990s — could be the best v5 in the Buttermilks. Charlie Barrett climbing. Photo: Wills Young.

For ease of navigation, use your guide's left cover flap to mark this map. Find the boulders you want by the page references here.

POLLEN GRAINS OVERVIEW MAP

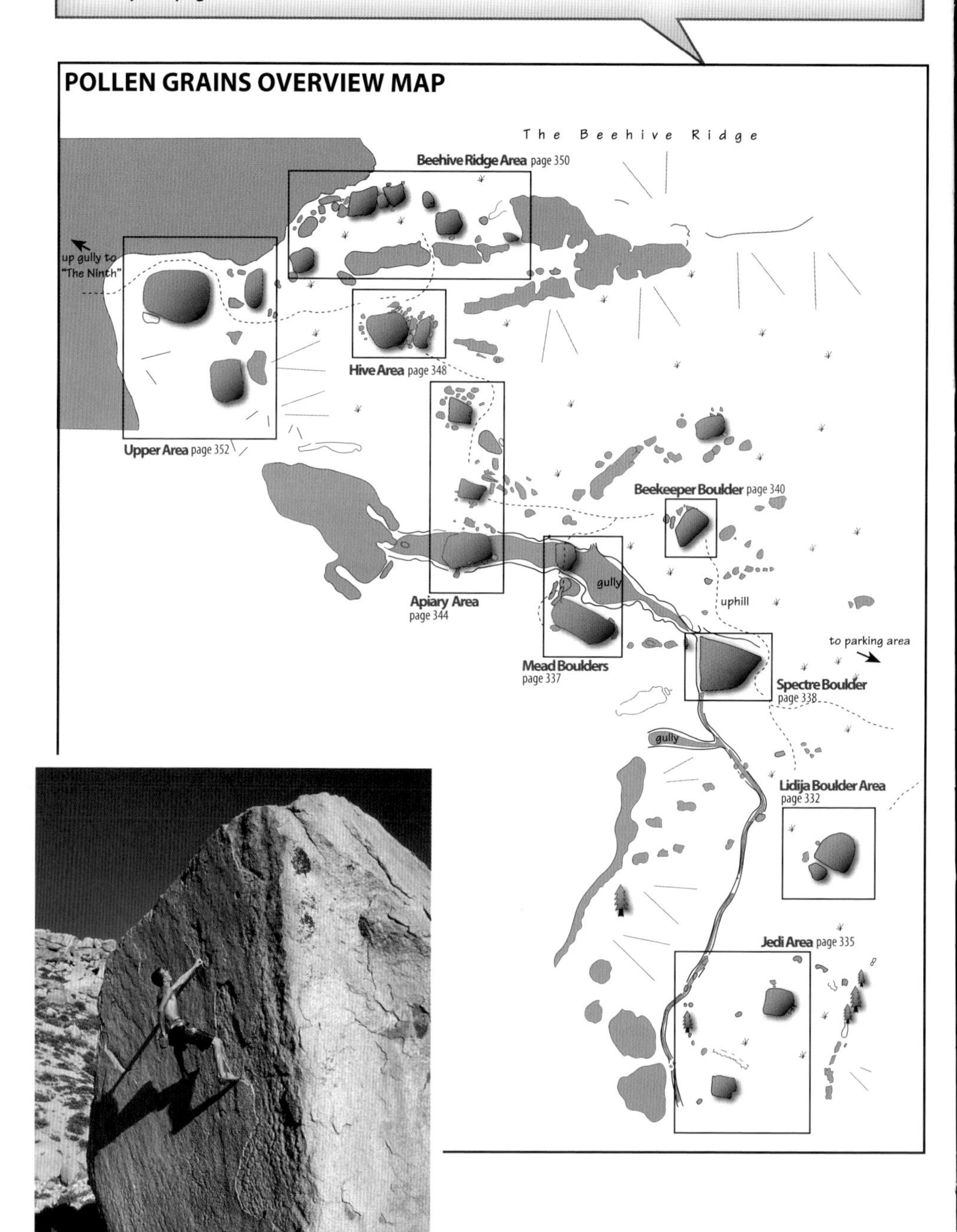

Victor Copeland hangs the creaky flake and eyes the summit of *Jedi Mind Tricks* (v4, page 336), a must-do for all aspiring highballers. A steady nerve and steady hand are needed in equal measure to make that next stretch. Photo: Mick Ryan.

Directions

Drive: Follow directions to the main Buttermilk Boulders' Peabodies parking area, (page 223). Continue as if going to the main Buttermilks' upper parking, by driving further up Buttermilk Road, making a right turn after the fence, and following the bumpy road briefly uphill then around a left curve. At this point, instead of driving up into the upper parking circle (a right turn), continue straight on along the road, which soon curves right and heads downhill. The road shortly crosses another fence line. Just after going through the gap in the fence (sometimes a gate), stay *left* and over some bumps, continuing downhill. After 0.2 miles from that last fence, the road forks, and you take the right fork on road 7S04. Drive this fork for 0.5 miles, passing the Get Carter Boulder (which is on the right). Make a right turn (first right after the Get Carter Boulder), and head uphill. This road leads to the turnaround at the Pollen Grains parking area. See the map on page 223.

Walk: Head south from the parking turnaround (see photos this page). At the top of the rise head 30 feet left of a pyramid-shaped boulder (viewed from this side anyway) and then contour the hillside, hugging the slope at right. After this, the boulders will shortly come into view and you drop down slightly to the first ones: the giant Lidija Boulder/Pollen Grain, the Honey Boulder and the Jedi Boulder are down to the left, while the Spectre Boulder is directly ahead (slightly right) and all the others are up-slope from there.

#1 View from the parking area

#2 Approaching the top of the rise

#3 From the top of the rise, contour the hillside roughly southward

LIDIJA BOULDER

There are two boulders side-by-side here, though the large one—a good 40 feet high—is the main attraction. This is the boulder that has the incredible contortionist's problem, *Lidija's Mouth* (v3, though very hard if you're short!), as well as two of the most interesting highball's around, *Drone Militia* (v6), which is brilliant and *Suspended in Silence* (v5)—big hard bouldering in a stunning position. Some good, but short patina problems are also found on the boulder's north side for those seeking a fun safe session.

LIDIJA BOULDER

LIDIJA BOULDER

LIDIJA BOULDER

1 Hunting Dog v2 ★ ☐
Sit start and make a hard move off the ground to gain good holds that lead to the giant patina. Drop off.

2 Gazelle v5 ★ ☐
A fun double dyno: Start with hands about the same level in opposing sidepull finger-jugs. Leap for the top patina!

3 Wanderlust v2 ★ ☐
Sit start with the right hand at a good sidepull and the left lower. Pull through to a good jug up left, and then climb diagonally up right finishing with a dynamic move to the good jugs. Drop off.

4 Snake Oil v6 ★ ☐
Sit start with the left hand at a good slanted incut. Climb direct or slightly right up the steep smooth patina. Aim for the sidepull for the left hand, and then the top, or go diagonally right at about the same grade.

5 Original Line v0 ☐
Climb patina till your feet are above the overhang. Move left to gain good holds, and then climb directly up on deep slots and good edges. Also the downclimb.

6 Unnamed v0 ☐
Scary! Climb the low-angle face, stepping up on thin patina to gain some grainy edges that lead to an impasse. Either step left and then make a hard move up to gain finishing patina knobs, or continue direct scarily to a step right. Either way, the climbing is bold and tenuous, though not hard.

7 Traverse v1 ★ ☐
Follow good patina left to join the The Original Line.

8 Left Aorta v2 ☐
Climb the left side of "the mouth," to gain large patina blobs, and up with a hard press from these.

9 Lidija's Mouth Direct v7 ★ ☐
Climb up into "the mouth" and use a pinch at the lip to gain crimps in the slash above. Match this, throw a foot out left and pull up and over on rounded grain. Somewhat contrived, but good.

10 Lidija's Mouth v3 ★★★ ☐
If this doesn't spit you out once or twice, you're a smooth mover! Great fun! Figure a way across the mouth from left to right and blindly grasp for that elusive hold around the lip. Holding on to it is not so easy, either. Finish at the patina up right, or continue to the top of the boulder. Laughingly hard if you are short.

⓫ Stamen Envy v10 ☐

Broken, but probably still climbable at the same grade. Sit start at right and climb up and left past a large pocket to the broken sidepull, then up the right side of the mouth to good patina.

⓬ Drone Militia v6 ★★★ ☐

A memorable highball that finishes by a move off a pair of "stuck-on" cobbles high off the deck. Begin to the left and make very tricky moves up right on shallow dishy sidepulls and such. From a large hold, move out right to a small edge, and then pull boldly up left past the cobbles. Entertaining and varied.

⓭ Drone Direct v10 ★★ ☐

Begin as for *Drone Militia* but after making the first hard moves to the good holds, go straight up to a hueco with your right hand. Pull up, to a bad sloper and throw to a patina jug a few feet left of the cobbles.

⓮ Droning Silence v8 ★★ ☐

Follow *Drone Militia* to the edge out right just before the move up left to the cobbles. Maneuver your left hand to this hold (crux) and then keep moving right to join *Suspended in Silence:* a pretty line with a lot of climbing.

⓯ Suspended in Silence v5 ★★★★ ☐

Another great highball with a flat landing tackles this tall face at its highest point, and is one of Bishop's most enjoyable lines! Begin at the left and use some clever moves to gain the large jug below the bulk of the line, or begin below that same big hold with a long dyno. A flake broke off the middle section of the line since the first edition of this guide, but that only made the problem cleaner and finer. Don't miss it. Photo page 329.

⓰ Project ☐

Hard, and a little grainy, the right side of the wall beckons.

LIDIJA'S BABY BOULDER

Around on the southeast side of the giant Lidija Boulder/Pollen Grain is a small wedge-shaped boulder, with a tall north and east side. There are several options here, with different finishes available for each start -- as suggested by the photo.

17 Black Light Blue Sit Start v3 ★ ☐
Sit start and make a hard shouldery move to join the flake up right. From this, directly move up left immediately to the big jug. Other finishes possible.

18 Moon Grey Blue v2 ☐
Start further right at rotten flakes. You'll be black and blue when you pull the holds off of this. Several exits, all junk.

19 Dangerous Brother v2 ☐
Hoh! You thought that last one was bad ...! Up the utterly worthless crusty flakes that are about to explode. Go on then ...!

20 Unknown Choss v6 ☐
Like choss ... ? You'll love this! Sit start at the undercling and pinch. Bust a big hard move up with the left hand to an angled crimp. Match right next to it on the crusty crimp. Step up on a crusty edge. Grab an open grainy sidepull with the left. Move right hand to crusty pinch sidepull. Set feet and launch to that totally loose flake up high. Rip it off the wall. Or perhaps hang it. Maybe both. Top out, or go home. Left exit anybody?

This intriguing rock formation is somewhere in the Pollen Grains. I will leave it up to the reader to find it.

Flowers bloom across the Pollen Grains, relishing the brief but frequent early summer thundershowers

JEDI AREA

Here are two excellent tall boulders with a couple of world class lines including the short but sweet *Cover Me With Flowers* (v2), on the Honey Boulder, and the main prize: the tall, sustained highball *Jedi Mind Tricks* (v4). There are a couple of excellent harder lines (of the non-highball variety) on the west side of the Honey Boulder too — *Cindy Swank* (v7) and *Finder's Fee* (v9), both with nice moves on solid patina.

HONEY BOULDER

1 Bouquet v3 ★ ☐
With a big stretch, get off the ground using a right-facing hollow flake. Grab a knob and make a precarious long move up left to a big hold hidden on the upper wall. Top out easily.

2 Charlotte Rampling v2 ☐
Sit start on flakes and make a big hard move to gain bigger flakes that lead to the top. Standing start: v0.

3 Heidi v0 ☐
Climb the right side of the wall with care on good, but thin, patina, moving left at the top to step over the summit.

4 Giselle v2 ☐
Sit start at a hollow blocky flake, and climb straight up.

5 Christine Keeler v5 ☐
Sit start with both hands at a large left-facing pinch/sidepull feature. Climb the arete by some hard moves to gain a grainy boss, and over.

6 Swanky Sit v9 ★★ ☐
Sit start with both hands at the large left-facing undercling/sidepull as for *Christine Keeler* (above). Move right by a hard move and a little trickery to join *Cindy Swank* (described next). An excellent and obvious addition that is well worth doing.

7 Cindy Swank v7 ★★ ☐
Start with hands at about 5 feet up. Make a couple of moves to gain the lip of the boulder and pull over with high steps. That ramp over left is not used!

8 Finders Swank v8 ☐
For killing time: Start as for Finders Fee with both hands on the good shallow hueco, and climb left and up to join *Cindy Swank*. Done after a good hold broke here in fall 2008. (*Finder's Fee* is not much changed by the break).

9 Finder's Fee v9 ★★★ ☐
Start at a good hold, five feet up. Move up left at first, then to the lip and over rightward to a good hold.

HONEY BOULDER

HONEY BOULDER

HONEY BOULDER

10 Lean Thinking v9 ★ ☐
Climb the very right edge of the wall, grabbing a small ear of patina with your right hand (careful!). Launch up and left and top out as for Finder's Fee, or slightly right.

11 Sara Eirich v2 ☐
Tall, thin, and beautiful ... but sadly a little flakey. Take care with this one!

12 Cover Me With Flowers v2 ★★★ ☐
Follow a beautiful diagonal seam/crack to a long move to distant finishing jug. Sit start to add a couple good extra moves at roughly the same grade.

13 Project ☐
Big move to jug on crusty face.

14 Unknown ☐
Munge.

15 Twiggy v0 ★★ ☐
Reach in off blocks to a left sidepull, or (v1?) begin matched at a good hold at the lip of the undercut base. Press across onto the slab and move up by interesting moves to good slots. This is probably the easiest way down — though you can also figure a way down the northwest slab onto the nose, and hang and drop from there.

HONEY BOULDER

JEDI BOULDER

16 Return Jedi v10 ★★ ☐
A technical thin-face testpiece on immaculate glassy rock with a high finish: Begin with both hands on right-facing sidepull crimps at the blunt arete. Pull to holds up and right on the smooth face with great difficulty. Move up and left to finish at the arete on hollow holds (care needed).

17 Jedi Mind Tricks v4 ★★★ ☐
The wall just left of the right arete is a gem that belongs on everyone's ticklist. A very tricky start with bad footholds, leads to sustained crimping on fairly solid, yet hollow flakes. A big move up right provides the mental crux. A left exit looks risky. Photo page 328.

18 Unknown ☐
The arete looks climbable by its right side.

19 Godman v1 ★ ☐
Climb the corner, following it to a finish high on the leftmost flake, or direct on the other flake. Both are scary up high.

20 Unnamed v0 ☐
Start at the right arete of the dihedral, but climb onto and up the slab on small hollow flakes.

21 Out of Focus v1 ☐
The arete starting on the broken flake with a slopey finish.

22 Out v0 ★ ☐
A short climb up the center of the wall on good holds. Also an option for a downclimb.

23 Out of Time v0 ☐
The arete left of the flake.

24 Flake Descent vB ☐
This grainy arete is also a descent option.

25 Loud Dark Eye v1 ★ ☐
Start low, grab the surprising cobble jug, and climb up left.

JEDI BOULDER

JEDI BOULDER

26 Massage From Below v8 ☐
Just left of where *Return Jedi* begins (see above), on the southwest facet, begin about five feet left of the blunt arete. From a good flake, bust a tough move up left to an edge and work your way up, joining the arete.

MEAD BOULDER

This beautiful boulder sits above a ravine, across from the Beekeeper Boulder, and up the hill from the Spectre Boulder. Seen from across the ravine (on the approach) it presents a huge wall of patina streaked with green and gold. Two bold lines tackle this wall. Around the back, the shorter steeper side of the boulder is featured and has good landings but the rock is a bit crumbly. The descent is by a very short crack at the northwest corner.

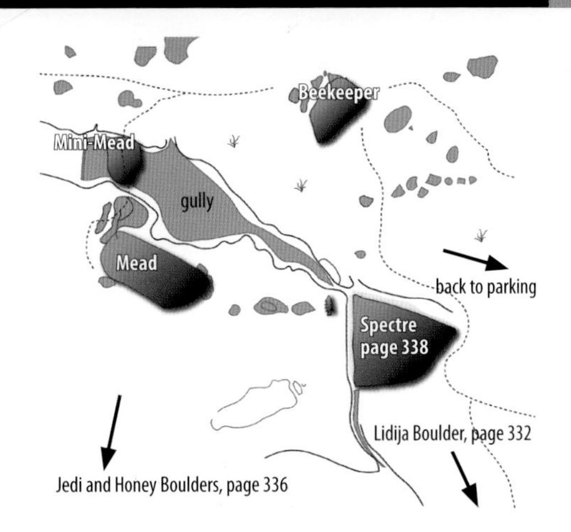

1 Vic's Demise v0 ★★ ☐
Climb the pretty face over an extremely bad landing on good patina. Begin by stepping off the top left point of a rock pedestal.

2 Slow and Steady v3 ★★ ☐
This bold solo begins just to the right of Vic's Demise, from the right side of the same rock pedestal. Pull around the roof with trepidation using some thin but incut patina. Make a traverse right (crux) before going up on perfect edges, and back left a little to the top.

MEAD BOULDER

Around the back, the uphill side of this boulder is also tall, though with decent flat landings. However, there is only one recorded line and a lot of potential highballing for those who fancy it:

3 Project ☐
On the steep overhang there are some positive glassy crimps. Potentially a decent line here, though extremely hard.

4 Mead v6 ☐
Around the back (southwest side) of the Mead Boulder is this decomposing line on the otherwise good-looking steep face. Start at a good but rotten edge and make long moves between crusty holds to reach and pass the lip.

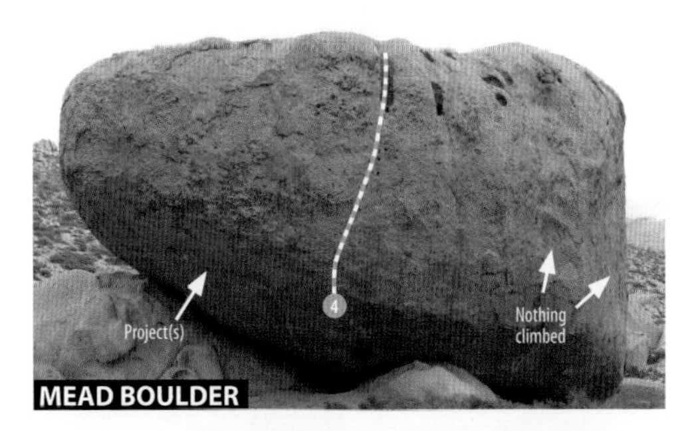

MEAD BOULDER

A long wall of vertical or near-vertical rock wraps the south and east sides of this large block. For those motivated to do some cleaning, there is plenty of scope here for super-highball first ascents.

MINI-MEAD

This small boulder is jammed in the ravine between the Beekeeper Boulder and the Mead Boulder. It has one excellent line.

5 Mini-Mead v0 ★ ☐
Begin at the good huecos and climb up onto a slopey ramp before moving up and high left to the huge patina jug. Reach back to an edge and step over. Airy! A good spot and some pads are needed due to the rock below at right.

MINI-MEAD BOULDER

SPECTRE BOULDER

Sitting alone in a shallow wash, and overhanging steeply and hugely on every side, this is simply an amazing looking boulder. The northeast corner has bullet-hard granite and one of the most outrageous lines this side of the Sierra: *Spectre* (v13). Sadly, few problems have been established, due to the boulder's overhanging blankness, although there definitely is some scope for more lines.

1 Valentino Traverse v7 ☐
Start at a big flake far to the left of *Spectre*. Make a huge move to the lip, and then traverse right for 15 feet. Mantel and stand up over the lip. Drop off.

2 Moonlighting v2 ☐
To the left of *Spectre*, pull onto the ledge by starting from a hand-jam at the lip. Drop off.

3 Spectre v13 ★★★ ☐
A stunning piece of steep granite, with just enough holds to be climbable: Begin at a large blocky jug with a long move to grab a crimp. Match this with difficulty and bust an even longer move out left (crux) to more crimps that lead to a tricky lip encounter. Either top out directly up the arete and left face (highball), or make some precarious moves across the wall to the right, and then up to join easy terrain (slightly less highball). Top out (very high-ball, but easy). Reverse and drop off.

4 Project ☐
From a high start, somehow climb up the arete right of Spectre.

Right: Charlie Barrett, *Spectre* (v13). This problem, on some of the finest glassy monzonite around, has a perfect jug start, climbs like a harder version of Yosemite's *The Dominator* and culminates with a high-ball slab finish. FA: Dave Graham, Jan 2001. Photo: Wills Young.

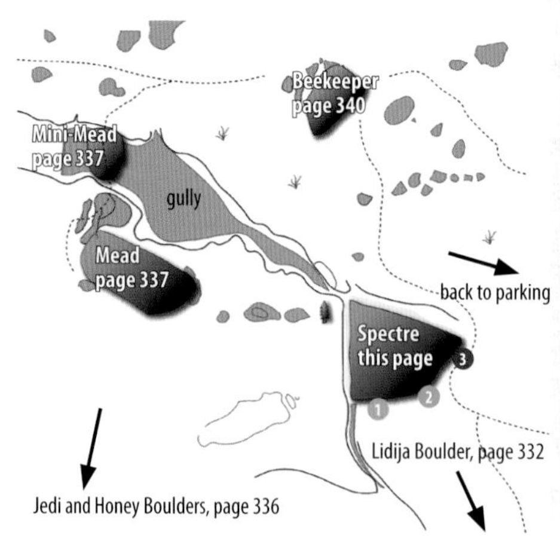

BEEKEEPER BOULDER

This is another wonderful block, with a combination of steep safe thuggery, and some tall (sometimes thin) highballing. The descent of the boulder, (by its northeast arete and north face) is quite thrilling, and potentially as hard as getting up! In fact, the first ascent of this boulder by longtime Bishop local, Dennis Jensen, resulted in the placement of a bolt to rappel off!

The ultimate line (*The Beekeeper*, v6), crosses a short roof at its steepest, moves right, busts a hard crux, and finishes up a super-highball face that is serious business. The Beekeeper's Apprentice (also v5), cops out after the low crux, though is good for all that. The two problems on the south side — *Golden Shower* (v10) and *Mesothelioma* (v7) are also striking highball lines with great movement.

Several "cave" problems begin at the same spot. These have numerous variations, and there are many combinations of sequences into different finishes possible, some of which are listed and named here. However, most people choose not to complete the lines, but rather drop from a jug as indicated on the image on the page opposite.

5 The Beekeeper v6 ★★★ ☐

The big one, all the way from low left to top right. Sit start — nay lie start — at the back left of the roof at a pair of huecos, separated by a pinch. Roll through to holds leading to a good basketball-sized hueco, and then further right to another, wider, flatter hueco. Move right from this to a hard crux to gain a jug at the base of features that lead up the face diagonally right. Up high, make a committing step right to gain a big patina jug, and then go directly up from this on flat edges, and a long reach right to a deep slot. More scary than hard ... But definitely scary.

6 The Beekeeper's Apprentice v5 ★★ ☐

As for the previous line through the crux to gain the jug at the start of the highball topout. Toe-hook trickery can help at the crux.

7 Beekeeping for Profit & Pleasure v4 ★ ☐

Start as for *The Beekeeper*, but pull immediately left around the lip to good, though painful, holds and climb up and right across the roof to the big jug. Drop from here (v3), or continue with a couple more hard pulls on sharp crimps to gain the large flake crack above (v4), which leads to a very highball topout — or not (caution: this is also the easiest way down).

8 Jensen Route v2 ★ ☐

Standing start to the previous line. The original easiest way up! Make sure you can climb down!

9 Follow the Pollen Path v4 ★ ☐

Begin as for The Beekeeper and follow The Beekeeper to the first large hueco. From here climb the flake above it leftward to the big jug. Finish as for the previous line with a few more hard moves to join the flake crack above, or drop off early.

Jeff Sillcox, *Mesothelioma* (v7), overleaf.
Photo: Tim Kemple.

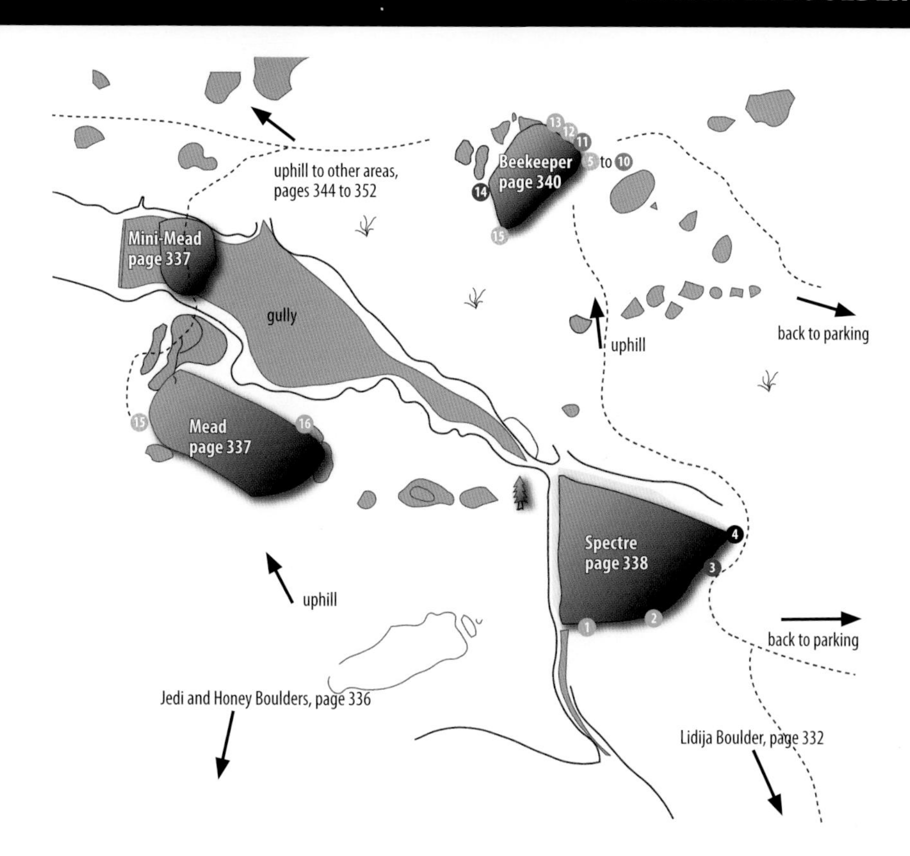

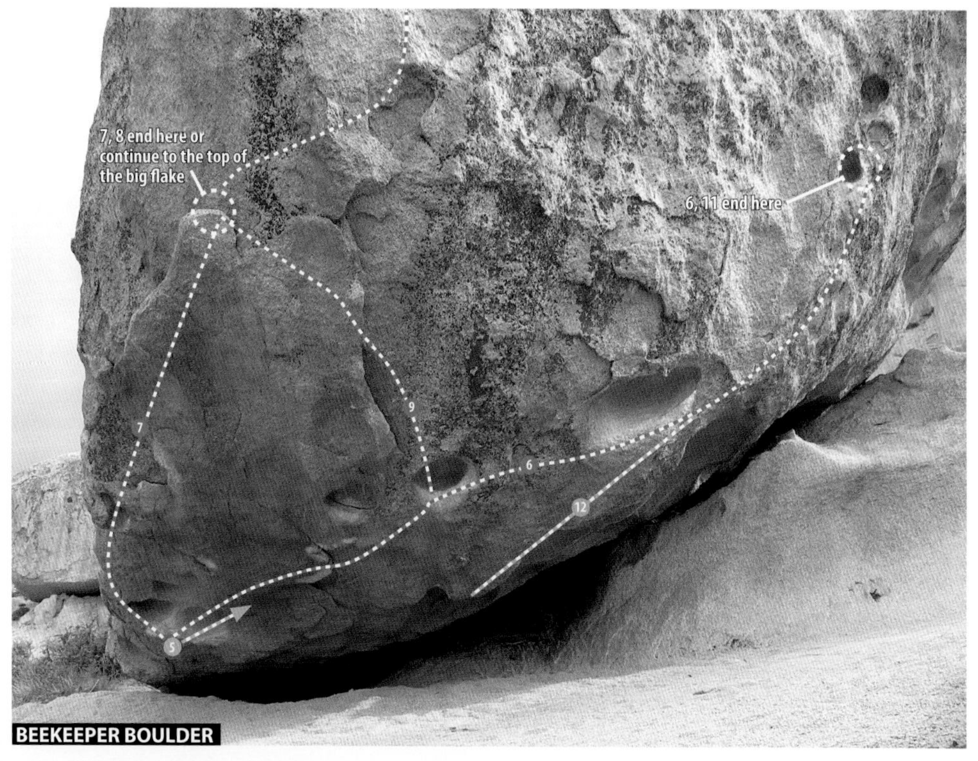

BEEKEEPER BOULDER

BEEKEEPER BOULDER

⑩ The Path v5 ★ ☐

As for the previous line, but from the big jug above the cave, move right and continue up the wall right of the arete for an alternate, but still very highball finish on good, spaced patina holds. The standing start is listed below.

⑪ Jensen Route v3 ★ ☐

Climb the wall from a standing start. Aim for the lone plate half way up followed by a big move to solid knobs above -- or cop out early before the patina plate by heading up left. Either way, you will likely step left before topping out. Take care on potentially breakable holds. The descent is slightly left, and is not easy.

⑫ Royal Jelly v6 ★ ☐

Shuffle under the boulder to grasp an amazing double-hand wrap at a strange keel-like hold. Bust a couple of hard moves up right to join the finish of *The Beekeeper's Apprentice*.

⑬ The Beekeeper Standing Start v2 ★★ ☐

An extremely thrilling climb, from which you must not fall. Follow the big sidepull slots and huecos diagonally up to a committing move right to gain a big patina jug. Then, very boldly step directly up and over the top on flat holds. Tall with a bad landing.

⑭ Golden Shower v10 ★★★ ☐

Start low, with both hands at a football-sized shallow hueco, down on the right side of the southwest arete. The tricky moves up the arete lead to powerful crimping and a massive lock-off to reach hard-to-see edges high in a shallow scoop. Not the greatest landing.

⑮ Mesothelioma v7 ★★★ ☐

Begin left of the southeast arete (step off pads as necessary) and climb the wall rightward with long moves on incut holds to a shallow dihedral. A committing layback or long reach gains the lip which is not exactly a jug. A few committing pulls will put you over the top. A sustained highball, with a slightly sketchy landing. Stunning! (Sit, at arete, v8). Photo previous page.

Josh Williams attempts *Golden Shower* (v10, opposite), which requires a good spot and many pads for most climbers. Photo: Wills Young

THE APIARY AREA

The Apiary Boulder has a few good low-angle climbs, and a nice v3, The Bee Sneeze. For me, the standout climb is the Scooped Face on the Honey Bear Bong Boulder, which is more like a solo, but with a low crux (a bit grainy) followed by super-cool moves between giant holds. *The Honey Bear Bong* (v7), a sit-start requiring a huge move at the start has smooth solid rock and a highball topout up a nice arete.

APIARY BOULDER

HONEY BEAR BONG BOULDER

APIARY BOULDER

1 Bee-have! v4 ☐
Climb just right of the northeast arete on left-facing sidepulls to gain very poor holds on the face at right! Pull up using the bad holds and move right to finish.

2 Project ☐
Optimistically use the slanted undercling to attempt the wall, which is sadly very grainy.

3 Unnamed v0 ★ ☐
Reach high to start at (or pop for) a cobble, and then continue up the wall.

4 Apiary Crack v0 ★ ☐
Begin just left of the crack and climb up to gain the crack, following it easily to the summit. Downclimb the north side by good patina.

5 The Bee Yard v6 ★ ☐
This might clean up to be easier: Start at the giant huecos, pull out of the upper one on extremely poor holds and step onto a small knob (right). Move up and left very precariously to a good hold and the crack. A direct finish looks possible in good conditions.

6 The Bee Sneeze v3 ★★★ ☐
Begin by using the right two huecos to make a big pop to a pinch. Roll through to a nice crimp and then surf rightward to good sidepulls at the blunt angle-change there. Pull up and over onto the slab rightward. The direct finish, is a little harder.

7 Unnamed v1 ☐
The wall right of the big huecos is climbed on positive, though perhaps hard-to-see edges.

8 Unnamed v0- ☐
The slab is climbed starting just left of the bush.

9 Unnamed v1 ☐
The rounded south arete is begun at right, but completed on the left side, with caution up high.

Lisa Rands enjoys some thuggish pulling on the steep underbelly of the Beekeeper Boulder (page 340). Photo: Wills Young

HONEY BEAR BONG BOULDER

⑩ Northwest Arete v3 ★★ ☐
Stand start and climb the very tall northwest arete, staying to the steep side all the way to the top.

⑪ Honey Bear Bong v7 ★★ ☐
Sit start at a short crack down and right of the northwest arete. Gain the arete at left by a hard move, joining the previous line.

⑫ Project ☐
The southwest arete.

⑬ Grandfather Hooler v2 ★ ☐
Grab the massive flake. Step up onto it. Move up and right to good holds that lead even further right to finish at the top of *Scooped Face* (below).

⑭ Scooped Face v3 ★★★ ☐
The beautiful scooped features are climbed with a hard start which is slightly grainy, followed by long moves between sinker buckets.

⑮ Project ☐
The steep, shallow seam and features just right of the southeast arete may need cleaning on rappel.

⑯ Project ☐
The extremely highball face looks vaguely possible.

⑰ Project ☐
The less high northeast arete also looks climbable.

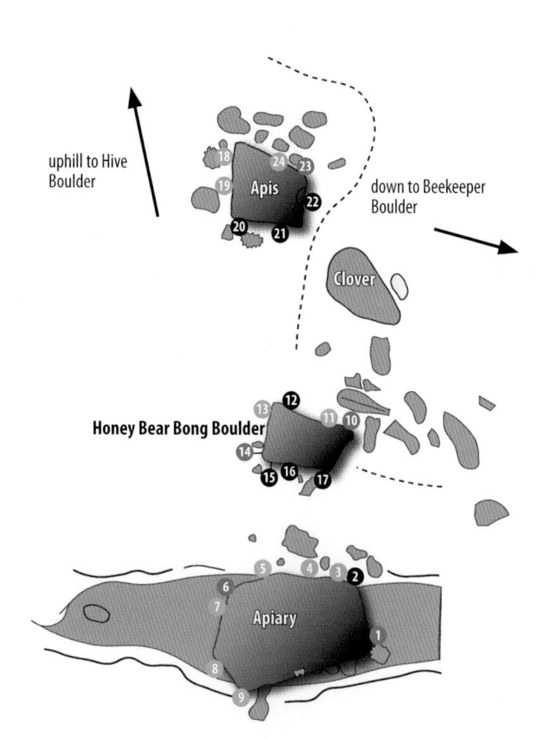

APIS

This is a larger boulder with a tall east face on the downhill side that has a couple of impressively blank, but maybe do-able projects.

18 Unnamed v0 ★ ❑

The short south-facing wall is climbed beginning with a good blocky hold and a hard move up and left to flat dishes.

19 Knobs v0 ★★ ❑

Climb the wall above the cave past a pair of knobs, starting hanging at a good jug at the lip. Finish right by a long move to a jug, or left with careful footwork.

20 Project ❑

The bulge looks to have a good hold to aim for.

21 Project ❑

Imaginary holds lead to a good xenolith.

22 Project ❑

The overhanging groove is grainy, but may be climbable if you can gain the hold up left by some trickery — jump? — and then move right. Kinda junky though.

23 More Than Nothing v3 ❑

The arete is climbed by stepping off the left side of the low boulder, with a good pair of sidepulls and a long move. Grainy rock on the underside of the overhang slightly spoils this one.

24 Unnamed v0 ❑

The patina wall right of the arete. Step off the low boulder's right side with tiny crimps and a hard move.

Right: Kevin Daniels climbing the excellent highball/solo, *Timothy Leary Presents ...* (v2, see over) on the Hive Boulder. This line has a scary start with a big pull to a good hold over a bad landing. You may be able reach in to avoid the crux start, but either way you'll have to keep your head at the top! Photo: Wills Young.

THE HIVE AREA

The Hive is a huge boulder just below a saddle in the ridge, with a series of scoops forming almost a giant ladder-like effect on its east face. This surrealistic rock formation provides the superb highball *Timothy Leary Presents ...* (v2). This beauty which was originally done as a precursor to *... Insanity* (v7) is one of the finest solos around with a very heady finish. Other highballs on this boulder have some pretty heinous-looking landing zones, with *On the Cusp* (v1), which like the first two mentioned was a Vic Copeland special, being particularly suicidal, while *... Insanity* (v7) has a hard move low down while the top is thankfully easy. The Honeycomb, next to The Hive has one nice highish v2, *The Horseshoe Problem*, which is a worthwhile find. Hopefully the excellent-looking *KD Presents* will clean up to be a classic addition too. Photos opposite; no topo.

THE HONEYCOMB

This boulder sits next to the much larger Hive Boulder. From the low east side, moving right, find:

1 Unnamed v0 ☐
Begin at a large jug and climb up.

2 Unnamed v0 ☐
Climb slots and huecos left of the nose.

3 Skin Grazer v2 ☐
Jump to a jug and pull up and over the very grainy undercut boulder.

4 Unnamed v2 ☐
Climb the arete which is hard (and grainy) at the start and top out with care.

5 The Horseshoe Problem v2 ★★ ☐
Gain the large cobble and climb up above it using small patina crimps and a big move to grab the horseshoe jug at the top: quite a stretch.

THE HIVE

Note: The way down from this boulder is a technical v0 slab with a bad landing: Take care!

6 KD Presents v5 ★★ ☐
Begin at gravelly pockets and climb up right to gain the large incut xenolith. Using a handhold up and right, step up onto the xenolith and press up to a standing position. Tip-toe onto the highest point (with a small fingertips edge out left useful). Grope, heart-in-mouth for the rounded finish. Really fun, if you can reach the top!

7 Turn On, Tune In, Cop Out v4 ★ ☐
This is the right exit to the previous line. Instead of stepping up onto the xenolith, make a roll-through and move out right to join *Timothy Leary Presents ...* .

8 Timothy Leary Presents ... v2 ★★★ ☐
Step in at right and climb the wall of giant horizontal scoops, beginning with a hard committing move. A second (easier) big lock off is needed at the top. You can add some more good climbing by doing a sit start down and left.

9 On the Cusp v1 ★ ☐
Step in high from boulders and climb good huecos to a terrifying finish above a death-defying landing. If that's not enough for you, add the low start.

10 The KD Factor v4 ★ ☐
Begin very low and right at a deep hole and begin with a long move to a large jug. From here, roll to an edge with the right hand, and squeeze through the gap between the boulders to gain better holds. Climb up and left to a rail below a large xenolith and then further up and left with a committing move on a sloping rail to join *Timothy Leary Presents ...* .

11 The KD Factor Left Start v2 ★ ☐
The left start makes a lot of sense: Skip the hard squeeze section and join the bold and airy fun.

12 Downclimb v0 ☐
Step right off a boulder (crux) and move diagonally right standing on large huecos, and then up on good patina. This is also a slightly awkward downclimb.

13 Project ☐
This looks to be a potentially fine problem, though with a bad landing.

14 ... Insanity v7 ☐
Step off the ground and with a couple of very hard moves gain a deep slot and buried xenolith jug. Reach left to find a big sidepull on the block there, and climb up easily, but boldly.

15 Project ☐
The wall right of the previous line, might be crossed from right to left to join the previous line.

16 Project ☐
Facing uphill is a giant wall that looks very hard and high, but might have just enough holds when clean.

descent
12
13
14
THE HIVE

4
5
THE HONEYCOMB

6
7
8
9
10
11
6
THE HIVE

BEEHIVE RIDGE

Just beyond the Hive Boulder and to the west (toward the Sierra Mountains) is the Beehive Ridge. From The Hive, you cannot see the problems in this area as they are hidden by a ridge of weathered rock. Walk through a gap or over the low ridge to find this little area with a half-dozen medium-sized boulders. Here are a few fun problems, with unusual holds and features, rarely high, and with good pea-gravel landings.

BOULDER 1

BOULDER 1

1 Unnamed v4 ★★ ☐
Adjacent to the north end of the ridge of rock, is a small but fine boulder. Sit start down and right on a big flat hold. Throw a heel on and pull to a good hueco, then up and left with hard moves.

2 Unknown ☐
Climb directly up the face to the upper holds beginning at a pair of crimps.

CRACKED COBBLE BOULDER

3 Unknown ☐
The tallest boulder here has a good-looking sidepull and hueco feature that leads to utter choss. Reportedly v2 (presumably leftward).

4 Supercracker v8 ★ ☐
Climb the wall with a big move to crimps and a good undercling. Move up and right from this undercling using terrible slopers and crystals and a hard step up. Then slink rightward into the top of *Cracker*.

5 Unnamed v0 ★ ☐
Start at patina flakes and climb up and right to join the next problem.

6 Cracker v1 ★★ ☐
Begin at the cracked cobble. Pull up to good patina and over rightward. With right on the cobble, reaching up left is easiest.

7 Scoop v5 ★★ ☐
Climb into the scoop from the right side and out the top. Awkward.

8 Cave v5 ★★ ☐
Sit start and pull into underclings in the cave. Move right to a good hold. Step on a patina edge across right to reach over the lip, but climb direct on small crimps and with a high step. (Moving directly rightward with a long reach is also possible at v4.)

BOULDER 3

9 Unnamed vB ☐
The green patina face.

10 Unnamed v4 ★ ☐
At the left side of the nose at the west end of the boulder, start at a high crimp and make a big move to a good finger-jug, then over.

SMALL COBBLE BOULDER

11 Blob vB ★ ☐
The green wall and cobble is compelling just for the look of it.

BIG COBBLE BOULDER

12 Project ☐
You would have to be about 8 feet tall to get off the ground on this arete, but if you are, it looks pretty nice.

13 The Cobble v2 ★★ ☐
Stepping on the big cobble, a little pop/jump from the ground gains some slopey crimps. Pull up to good patina. Short; fun; no gimme.

14 Unnamed ★★ ☐
Start low and climb the sidepull. An almighty good hold is hidden over the lip rightish.

A few other v0 or easier problems in this area are not listed here, though there is some fun exploring to do down the slope on some decent sized boulders

CRACKED COBBLE BOULDER

BIG COBBLE BOULDER

UPPER AREA

Uphill from The Hive are the last major boulders listed. While only a few lines are recorded with ratings, there are numerous huge highball projects to be done. The White Slab is one of the most beautiful pieces of rock in Bishop, and now home to some tall, excellent, and exciting climbs. Currently the proudest tick here is *The Ninth* (v7), a truly stunning line that climbs the square-cut arete tilting out over the ravine from virtually the top of the hillside. Having intriguing moves on pinches and sidepulls, leading to a gripping rock-over to the upper wall, *The Ninth* is spectacular in every way. Take at least four pads, and be careful on this one!

SMALL CAVE BOULDER

1 Small Cave Left v4 ☐
Grab a good incut with the right hand (high) and pull up and left to more good holds. A good one-mover.

2 Small Cave Direct v6 ★ ☐
A superb two-move wonder on great rock. From good incuts, make a hard pull up right to a funky pinch, edge. Hold it and reach to good holds. Done.

WHITE SLAB BOULDER

This boulder, seen from below presents a tall glassy slab that has a couple of the best solos around.

3 Unknown ☐
The tall northwest arete. Proud, but sadly junky.

4 Downclimb vB ☐
The face just left of the arete is basic. Positive holds and low angle make this the best way down.

5 Unknown ☐
Just right of the arete a low start on positive holds looks a bit crusty (not hard though).

6 Unnamed v4 ★★ ☐
From a low flake, climb up past good edges for the left hand to a long move up to grasp a good spot on the arete. Continue up the arete.

7 Project ☐
A low start to the previous line might be good.

8 The White Slab v3 ★★ ☐
Begin in an undercut scoop and make a hard couple of moves to get established on the slab. Then head straight up to the top on nice little edges.

9 J. Bachar Memorial Problem v1 ★★★ ☐
Climbed in memory of the late great John Bachar, soon after his memorial service. Start to the right of the previous line and pull on where easiest. Climb up rightward toward a blunt rib where a precarious move gains easier ground leading adventurously to the summit. A beauty!

10 Unnamed v3 ☐
Start at the right side of the small wall and climb up a little before gaining the slab up and right. Traverse left and up to join the previous line.

BIG ARETE BOULDER

The boulder is simply massive and many of the lines look very serious, requiring a load of pads, and/or top-rope inspection and cleaning.

11 Project ☐
No holds are visible toward the top of this north face, so it may be unclimbable.

12 Project ☐
The ridiculously high "Big Arete" on the northwest corner looks hard. A headpoint project, perhaps?

13 Project ☐
At the far right side of the west-facing wall is an undercling flake system leading to decent edges above a very bad fall zone.

14 Unknown ☐
One short pull will gain the lip right of the arete on the uphill side of the boulder.

15 Project ☐
A fine blunt rib looks to be one of the less serious lines, but is still very high.

16 Sierra Phantom v0+ ★ ☐
Up to and past a big xenolith to gain a shallow groove, with one tricky move requiring confidence.

17 Project ☐
Follow a slight rib up the black streak.

18 Project ☐
The slab right of the black streak leads to some big cobble jugs.

19 Project ☐
The curving slab and arete is very pretty.

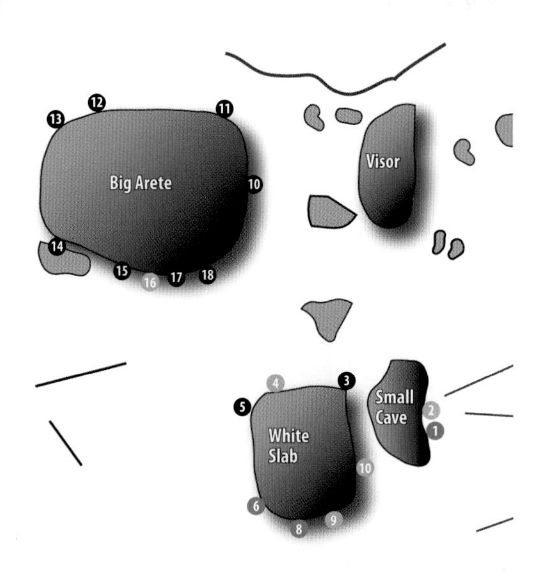

WHITE SLAB BOULDER

WHITE SLAB BOULDER

BIG ARETE BOULDER

WHITE SLAB BOULDER

BIG ARETE BOULDER

THE VISOR

⑳ **Visor Left** v2 ★ ☐
Start matched at underclings. Move sideways directly to the left lip. Throw a leg over and mantel up through the bite.

㉑ **Visor Direct** v4 ★ ☐
Start matched at underclings. Climb straight up to a shallow hueco. Toe-hook and move up left to the extraordinarily thin lip of the boulder. Continue all the way up the fin and top out.

㉒ **Unknown** ☐
Reportedly a v10 on this boulder, though I'm not sure where it goes, presumably rightward.

THE NINTH

㉓ **The Ninth** v6 ★★★ ☐
An utterly stunning line on the perfect square-cut arete that looms out like a cleaver from the top of the hillside. Begin with good sidepulls and pinches which lead to a big move up right to a hard-to-see incut. From there, make a precarious pull onto the left side of the arete. Continue to the top relatively easily but with careful footwork and longish moves on good crimps. A very serious, but extremely rewarding proposition. The top may require cleaning.

Mike Brady carefully negotiates the crux on the *John Bachar Memorial Problem* (v1 solo), on the pristine white slab of the White Slab Boulder. Photo: Wills Young.

Matt Wilder repeats his masterpiece *The Ninth* (v7 highball, opposite), first climbed in 2005, and one of the most beautiful pieces of rock on the East Side. Need an adrenaline rush? Photo: Wills Young.

Dale's Camp

Dale's Camp, named after Dale Bard, who once set up "home" here in the late 1970s, is an area of great beauty surrounding and including "Dale's Dome" (6592 feet, 2009 meters), a granitic knoll located half a mile south and slightly east of the Buttermilks Main area, south of Buttermilk Road. The dome and many of the boulders on the slope below are visible from the Peabody boulders, by looking south, across the valley. The setting is much the same as with the Buttermilks Main area, except that this spot is generally cooler, especially in the evenings when many of the boulders take more shade on the north side of the dome, or in the shadow of bigger peaks to the west. There are even some pinion pines and a few larger trees here. After snows, this area can be hard to approach, though no doubt the bouldering on the south side of Dale's Dome (for example, The Heart Prow area and Zeppelin area) will get plenty of sunshine.

Beavertail cactus at the Notch, Dale's Camp.

The Bouldering

With about 130 problems listed, this is a big area. It is typical of the Buttermilk Country (see Buttermilk Main area for more information), being predominantly a crimper's paradise. It is worth noting that visitors can easily climb at any combination of the small sectors of Dale's Camp in a single outing, as it takes but ten to 15 minutes to hike entirely around the dome. Some exceptional boulders not to be missed include the Led Zeppelin Boulder, a giant block on the south side of the dome, with some outstanding v2 to v4 problems, The Hueco Wall with its amazing, desperate and committing problem of the same name (v9), and the Zen Flute Boulder with some excellent lines including *Zen Flute* (v10), a Chris Sharma testpiece, which was named by others. For those looking for something mellower, The Notch provides one of the best circuits of short, moderate problems in a quiet and picturesque setting.

Directions:

From the turn off for the Buttermilks (the junction of Buttermilk Road and Highway 168), drive about 3 miles (the tops of the Grandpa Peabody Boulder will be just in sight above a ridge furher on). Make a left turn onto the second of two side roads. The road twists and turns for about 0.5 miles to where you can park off the road. Or, you can continue over very bumpy terrain, and eventually a creek crossing. If you do drive this section, you can continue along the track to pull in at a right spur in a shallow valley and walk up to the Heart Prow or the Hueco Wall areas, or follow the road as it curves back left and up around the hillside until it eventually heads back right and runs along below the Zeppelin area. See overleaf.

Hike: Most people will park up a hundred yards or two before the creek crossing. You can jump the creek just below the road crossing, or, if the water is too high here, head up-stream just 50 yards (the track takes you a little bit in the wrong direction at first but then back). You can hop the creek pretty easily even in fairly high water here, in a couple of places. Get onto the track and follow it out to the base of Dale's Dome -- a shallow valley at right leads to a turn around and camping site. Walk up the wash to the Hueco Wall area, which will be visible on the left after a couple of hundred yards, or go directly up the slope past the cracked boulder and on to the Heart Prow and Zeppelin areas.

The Led Zeppelin Boulder provides high quality rock and great moves in the v2 to v4 range. Shown here: *Dale's Right* (v2, page 368). Photo: Lisa Rands.

For ease of navigation, use your guide's left cover flap to mark this map. Find the boulders you want by the page references here.

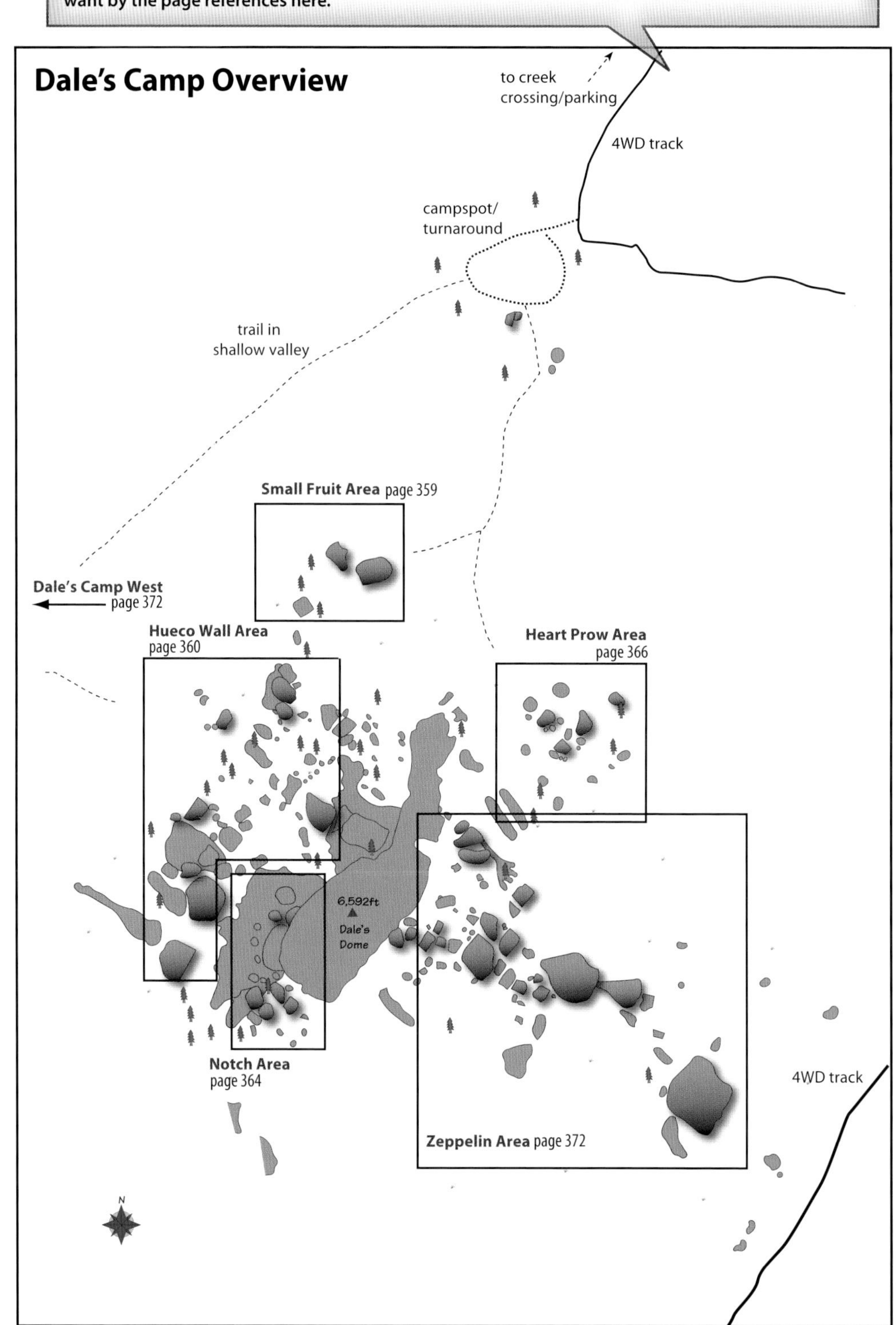

SMALL FRUIT AREA

These are the first boulders listed in the guide to Dale's Camp, though they are not the first ones reached on approaching from the jeep track. There are no individual photos for these boulders.

THE BLACK PLANET BOULDER

Beginning on the east end and moving rightward, find:

1 Unnamed vB ☐
Mantel into the grainy scoop.

2 Unnamed vB ☐
Climb the very short wall to the slab, beginning at a grainy sidepull.

3 Fear of a Black Planet vB ★★ ☐
Climb the slab, which is a fun easy problem.

4 Unnamed v2 ★ ☐
Just left of the arete, begin at a small seam and xenolith and climb the steep short wall.

5 Unnamed v2 ★ ☐
Sit start, and climb the short blunt arete.

SMALL FRUIT BOULDER

6 Tricky Grain v0 ☐
Oatmeal slab climbing on odd pockets.

7 Unnamed v3 ☐
The grainy prow can be climbed from the left by a high reach or jump up to a good jug to start.

8 Small Fruit v3 ★★ ☐
Climb the arete, using the good clean holds to gain a patina crack.

9 Scoopy-Doo v0 ☐
Mantel the xenolith and then traverse up and left along the lip to top out at the highest point.

10 Unnamed vB ★ ☐
Climb the right side of the left arete by scoops and good rock.

11 Unnamed vB ★ ☐
Climb the short solid face.

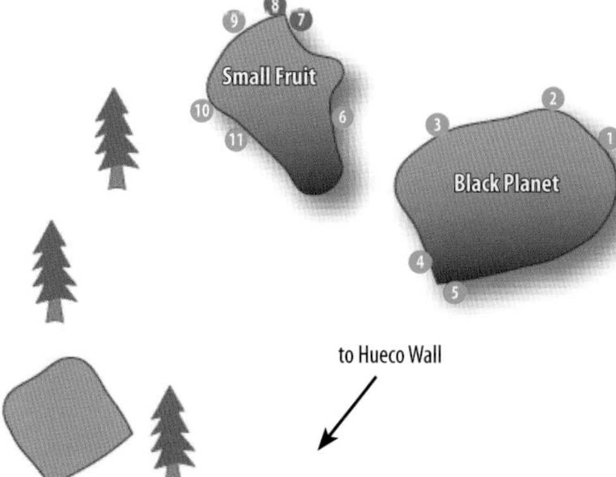

HUECO WALL AREA

The Hueco Wall area has one of the finest concentrations of hard bouldering in the Buttermilk Country, with several outstanding problems mostly in the v4 to v9 range including the amazing *Hueco Wall* (v9), one of Bishop's proudest lines. See map next page.

A-FRAME BOULDER

Across the hillside west of the Small Fruit area, and slightly uphill is the A-Frame boulder, which is a square block leaning up on another smaller block to create an A-frame cave.

1 A-Frame v4 ★★ ❑
Standing under the hanging prow, with thin patina at the lip, reach to a good incut just above it (or begin there if you can reach). Climb directly up with a long hard pull to start above a slopey, slab landing.

2 Unnamed v2 ★ ❑
Start at the left side of the slab with a tiny right crimp and poor left-hand holds. Step on and press up awkwardly to gain the good holds that lead to the top.

GIRLS OF WHISKEY CREEK

3 Wicked Pete v1 ★★ ❑
A right-hand start to the previous line involves stepping onto the slab and moving left to a good flat edge before climbing directly up.

4 Unnamed v0 ★ ❑
The right side of the slab is relatively easy.

B-FRAME BOULDER

This is the boulder just uphill from the A-Frame Boulder.

5 B-Frame v0+ ❑
Climb the short wall on edges with a couple of rounded holds at the lip.

6 Exoframe v3 ❑
Sit start the previous line using thin patina immediately below.

7 Out of Frame v4 ❑
Sit start at a large left-facing crack. Make a big move up left to a good wide crimp. Share this, and then move up and left again (crux) to thin patina and the topout.

GIRLS OF WHISKEY CREEK BOULDER

This boulder lies across the slope and slightly below the A-Frame Boulder. On the side facing downhill:

8 Girls of Whiskey Creek v6 ★★ ❑
Without jumping from the ground, make a gut-busting move up to a good flat hold at the base of the small crack. Move diagonally up left along the crack to a big move to gain the good slot, and then over.

9 Karaoke Night v6 ★★ ❑
As for the previous line to gain the small crack. Now move up right and over by long moves to good crimps above a low boulder.

A- & B-FRAME BOULDERS

Justin Alarcon using the magic on *Xavier's Roof* (v11). Photo: Wills Young.

HUECO WALL BOULDER

Up and right of the Girls of Whiskey Creek Boulder is the distinctive Hueco Wall—a smooth face with a single prominent shallow hueco nine feet up.

10 Project/Unknown ☐
Climb up into the scoop, and so to the top.

11 Project/Unknown ☐
Climb the rising left edge of the overhanging wall with some good patina, stretch right to good holds and over the lip on big jugs. Bad landing.

12 Hueco Wall v9 ★★★ ☐
A big line, one of the Buttermilk region's proudest: Start below and right of the prominent hueco. Gain the hueco and use an undercling in its upper edge to power through to big slopers at the lip of the boulder, where confidence is needed to top out.

13 Hueco Wall Sit v10 ★★ ☐
Sit start the previous line down and right.

14 Gastonia v8 ★★ ☐
Start at a good left sidepull in a shallow vertical hueco and climb directly up past a shallow vertical groove to a flat edge at the lip. Pull over without too much fuss on good xenoliths. **Sit start** at about v9.

15 Gastonia Sit v9 ★★ ☐
Sit start the previous line.

16 Xenolith Problem v9 ★ ☐
A sweet little problem, rediscovered: Start with both hands on the obvious thin xenolith/cobble, with a toe hook out right. Reach to the arete and over with a couple of hard pulls followed by a delicate finish.

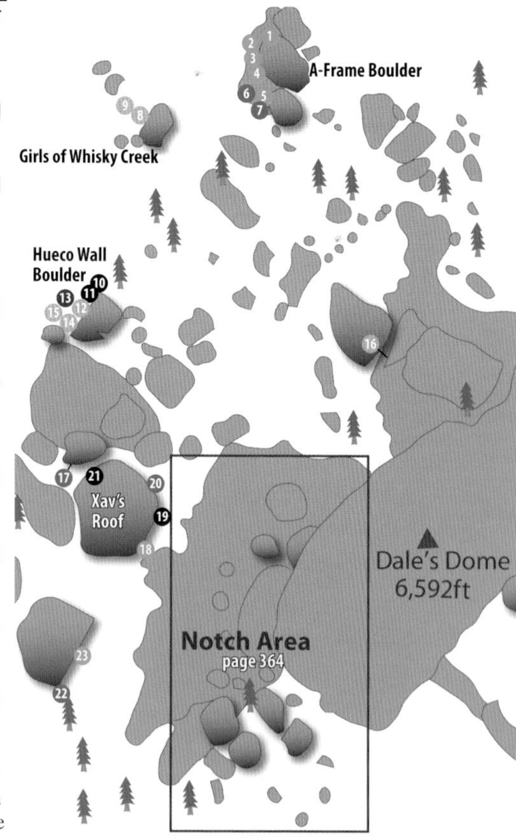

see overview map page 358

XAV'S ROOF BOULDER

HAIKU AND XAV'S ROOF BOULDERS

RANDY'S BOULDER

16 Randy's Problem v4 ★ ☐
Facing the Hueco Wall: Start matched at a horizontal and climb up on poor dishes and slopers.

SWISS ROOF BOULDER

About 20 yards up the slope behind and to the left of the Hueco Wall, is a large boulder aligned down the slope. A cave runs under it from its left side up to its top end. At the uphill end of the cave, find:

16 Swiss Legends v7 ★★ ☐
Named for the Tresch Brothers of Altdorf: Begin with both hands on the underside of the roof -- the right hand at a good inch-deep edge, and the left hand lower, at a decent sidepull. Step onto the rock and make a hard move to the gain the lip. Traverse bad slopers left to the arete, and up by means of this.

HAIKU BOULDER

On a small boulder on the slope beside the north side of the Xav's Roof Boulder is:

17 Haiku v4 ☐
Sit start and climb up the right side of the rounded arete by a big move to a good knob.

XAV'S ROOF BOULDER

The giant boulder up and right of the Hueco Wall. Beginning on the uphill side, find:

18 Downclimb v0+ ☐
Step off the rock to good holds which lead boldly to the summit. Also the descent.

19 Xavier's Roof v11 ★★★ ☐
Sit start and climb up the overhanging wall on sharp edges to a good flake that leads to the lip. Surmount the headwall using a right-hand sidepull, high feet and some kind of magic. Photo previous page.

20 Project ☐
A full sit start to *Xavier's Roof* starting below and slightly left.

21 Unnamed v3 ★ ☐
Sit start at the right side of the wall and climb up to a giant jug. Get stood on the jug using more good holds up and left, and then make an awkward move left across the lip of the boulder to gain a huge hueco/ledge.

22 Welshman's Leap v? ☐
Jump from the small rock behind to a jug on the big boulder, and climb up. FA by a Welshman of course.

23 Golden Age v8 ★★★ ☐
Does it get any better than this? Start on the right and climb the blunt arete until a big move up and left gains a good angled crimp on the face. Move left from here with a couple more hard moves to the incut patina that hangs over the void. Follow the good edges to the top, taking care, as it's not a total run-up. The friendly landing at the crux start makes this an accessible highball.

24 Project ☐
Between the previous line, and In the Bank is a blunt arete and wall that could offer a decent highball after some careful inspection.

25 In the Bank v5 ★★★ ☐
This outstanding highball takes on a beautiful scoop of immaculate rock. Climb up into the left side of the scoop. Move delicately up rightward to a small but positive sidepull from which a big committing move will bring either tears or positive crimps. Scoot right before stepping up onto the summit.

BIG SLAB BOULDER

26 Old Skool Arete v3 ★★ ☐
Sit start and climb up the leaning arete on its left side.

27 Biggie Smalls vB ☐
The slab is climbable almost anywhere.

THE NOTCH

On the slope above and to the right of Xav's Roof boulder is a collection of good-quality boulders, nestled against Dale's Dome, and on the saddle. Here find a great little circuit of vB to v3 lines. See the overview photo opposite.

COOKIE BOULDER

This boulder is at the back left of the Notch area, up against the steepening hillside. It is a curving, overhanging fin behind the Angle Boulder.

1 **Cookie Roll** v0 ☐
Thug some footless moves and roll out a mantel.

2 **Cookie Traverse** v1 ☐
Traverse the cookie from its right leftward to an obvious point where you can pull over into a scoop.

ANGLE BOULDER

In front of the Cookie is a small, pretty boulder with angular aretes, undercut on its downhill side, but with a flat landing to the uphill side.

3 **Unnamed** v0+ ★ ☐
On the downhill side, pull onto the left side of the hanging arete with a high right pinch on the arete and a left-hand press—a fun and committing move.

4 **Unnamed** v0 ★ ☐
On the downhill side, pull onto the right side of the hanging arete and up.

5 **Unnamed** v0+ ★ ☐
The left side of the uphill arete is precarious and frightening with no pad.

6 **Unnamed** v1 ★ ☐
The same arete climbed on its right side above the flat landing is an excellent little problem.

7 **Unnamed** vB ☐
The easy right arete on the uphill side, is climbed beginning with the high left hand hold.

THOUGHT SEEDS BOULDER

The north side of the boulder has several very short sit-start problems on good patina incuts, vB to v1, and on the front face are:

8 **Thought Seeds** v2 ★★ ☐
Climb the diagonal left arete up and right to a big move to gain a deep hueco at the lip, and more jugs further back.

9 **Free Your Ass** v1 ★ ☐
Avoid the intermediates and throw a big move to the deep jug on the right side of the face. .An excellent dyno that is easy if you commit!

BUSH WAR BOULDER

Adjacent to the Thought Seeds Boulder is another large boulder with:

10 **Bush War I** v1 ☐
On the south face, start in the deep hueco and undercling it to gain edges leading directly up.

11 **Unnamed** v3 ☐
On the north side, at left of a cave entrance, sit start wtih both hands in underclings. Make a very hard pull to good holds and up.

DON QUIXOTE BOULDER

This large boulder is behind the Thought Seeds Boulder on the left.

12 **Unnamed** v2 ★ ☐
Starting at a good flat edge about seven feet up, make a hard move to thin edges at the lip, and then reach back to the arete. Top out on the arete's left side.

13 **Don Quixote** v0 ★★ ☐
Start off the gravel and climb the arete's right side passing a good ledge. Avoid the ledge if you can!

14 **Brian's Slab Direct** v2 ★★ ☐
Begin at an orange streak (not left). Pull onto the slab and climb directly up using tiny crimps, a slanting seam, and careful footwork.

15 **Brian's Slab** v3 ★★ ☐
Begin as for the previous problem, but make a very tricky rising traverse right to a slanting seam/groove above a low boulder, and climb this. Pads needed.

CHARLATAN BOULDER

This boulder is adjacent the Don Quixote Boulder.

16 **Unknown** v? ☐
A line up the short overhang.

17 **Unknown** v? ☐
The hanging right arete is not as grainy as it looks... or is it?

18 **Charlatan** vB ☐
Mount the undercut slab using an obvious right-hand pinch, and make a long move to the lip and over.

19 **Unnamed** v2 ☐
Sit start with both hands in an undercling. Make one hard move to grab the left arete, and pull around and over the bulge.

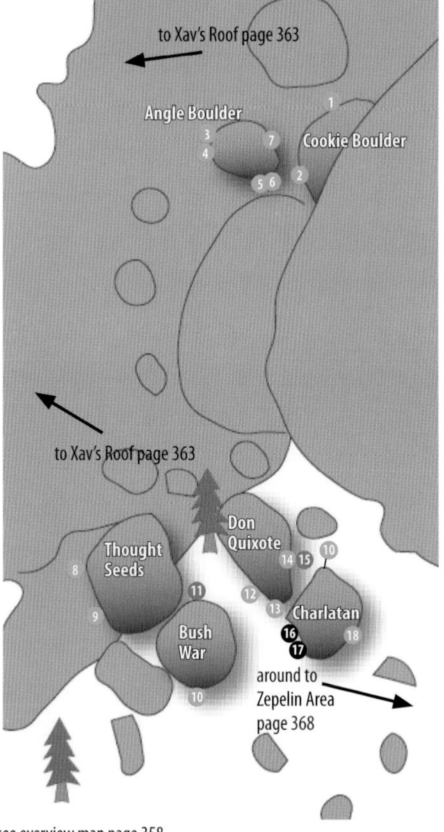

DON QUIXOTE AND CHARLATAN BOULDERS

DON QUIXOTE BOULDER

see overview map page 358

HEART PROW AREA

This area, at the north east side of Dale's Dome, consists of a collection of boulders scattered on a gentle slope. Good flat landings are the norm here, and the boulders are not too high. More problems are here than are listed in the guide. This guide covers the three main boulders and one boulder just below these.

HEART PROW AREA (looking down slope from the base of Dale's Camp)

SHARP BOULDER

1 Unnamed v1 ★ ☐
On the left side of the northwest face, sit start and climb left to the arete and over.

2 Unnamed v1 ★ ☐
Sit start below an orange patch at a good diagonal patina and climb over the bulge.

3 Cutlery v6 ★ ☐
Sit start as above, and traverse right on crimps to a slanted crimp, gain the slanted crimp with the left hand, and climb up and over.

4 Sharp Kitchen Utensils v4 ★ ☐
At the right side of the northwest face, sit/hang start with the left hand at a tiny xenolith and the right on a poor crimp slightly lower. Climb over the bulge.

5 What Dyno? v4 ★ ☐
On the southeast face, start at a lone slanted crimp. Dyno to the jug, or gain it statically by a crimp up left. Two or three pads are useful due to the block below.

CHICKEN HEAD BOULDER

6 Unnamed v1 ★ ☐
Climb the center of the short northwest face to a big hueco using careful balance.

7 No Chicken v1 ★ ☐
Start standing and climb the left side of the arete, reaching left at the top to the big hueco,

8 Choke the Chicken vB ★ ☐
Climb the right side of the arete to the big chicken-head xenolith. The sit-start is v3.

9 Simpatico v2 ★ ☐
Climb the right side of the southeast face using a poor xenolith, or edge, and a hueco low at right. Tricky.

HEART PROW BOULDER

10 Seam Traverse v0+ ★ ☐
Sit start and follow the good holds in the seam up and left (watch you don't scrape your back on the rock behind on exit).

11 Unnamed v0+ ☐
Sit start as for the previous line, and move right to a deep hueco and up.

12 Pet the Kitty v6 ★★ ☐
Sit start with the right hand at a pointy hold in a seam, and the left on a poor rough crimp. Climb up past good edges and positive xenoliths to a difficult move over the lip. Great moves; good rock.

⓭ The Crazy Dog Lady v5 ★ ☐
Start as for Pet the Kitty. Traverse right and top out on the left side of the prow as for Emotional Rescue.

⓮ Emotional Rescue v2 ★ ☐
Sit start with a left-hand sidepull and the right just above on a good edge. Climb up using the pinch and undercling feature, and positive patina on the left, and top out about four feet left of the arete. A hard last move if you're short.

⓯ The Heart Prow v1 ★ ☐
Sit start at the low ledge. Climb up the well-featured prow and exit just right of he heart-shaped hole (don't break it!). You can also exit left on Emotional Rescue at about v2.

⓰ The Shark v0+ ★★ ☐
Sit start on the right side of the prow at good patina. Follow the line of patina diagonally up left and reach right to a good hueco to top out.

⓱ Chorizo v4 ★ ☐
Sit start with the right hand on an excellent crimp, left on one not quite so good. Climb up and over the bulge rightward with a couple of nice moves.

AGENT ORANGE BOULDER

⓲ Agent Orange v3 ☐
Sit start at a hueco/slot. A hard move gains a good edge and so the top

⓳ Xenolith Slab vB ★★ ☐
This is a really nice easy little slab.

MORE: *There are a few more boulders and a few more worthwhile problems not described here.*

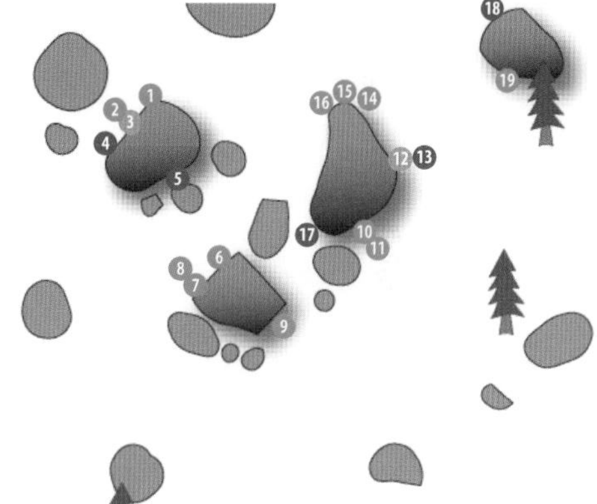

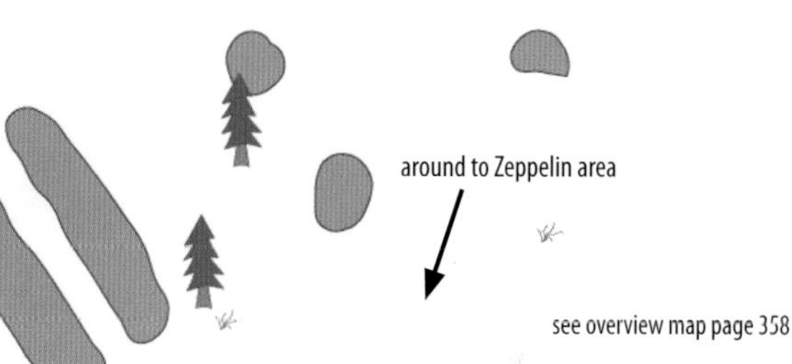

HEART PROW BOULDER

ZEPPELIN AREA

Just around the hillside about 100 yards from the Heart Prow Boulder is the Zeppelin area. There is a tight concentration of boulders, with small corridors and alcoves between them, arranged down the hillside from the edge of Dale's Dome. There are a few giants among these, including the enormous Cuban Roll Boulder, which stands alone, low on the slope. Aside from problems listed here, you will no doubt find more to do, and some pretty amazing projects too. See topo overleaf.

ZEPPELIN AREA and CUBAN ROLL BOULDER (on southeast side of Dale's Dome)

CUBAN ROLL BOULDER

1 Cuban Roll v4 ★★ ☐
Climb the big patinas to a roll over at the lip using a good hueco. See photo page 371.

LITTLE ZEPPELIN BOULDER

2 Unnamed v2 ★ ☐
Sit start at the far left side of the overhang. Make a move to the big incut at the lip on the left, and then up right and over immediately.

3 Unnamed v4 ★ ☐
Contrived but good: Sit start at the far left side of the overhang. Move to the lip, and follow it rightward to a good jug about two feet left of the right end. Share at the jug, then top out.

4 Led Zeppelin v8 ★ ☐
Start at good crimps just left of the low boulder on the west face. Make a long reach to a small crimp above, and then, with even more difficulty, toss for the lip.

5 Led Zeppelin, Sit Start v10 ★ ☐
Make a sit-start to the previous line from flexi crimps. You could also extend the sit lower to the right at about v11.

LED ZEPPELIN BOULDER

6 Model Dairy v2 ★ ☐
Sit start on the boulder around on the west side. Climb big patina incuts slightly right (one hard move) and then up on thin holds above a bad landing.

7 Unnamed v3 ★ ☐
As above, but move further right by a long reach, leading to good patina over the flatter landing zone.

8 South Face v6 ★★ ☐
Way harder than it looks and often sun baked, so wait for clouds to try this. Make a big move on good holds, and then step up onto these and levitate up using poor, slippery nothings! An extremely technical highball on excellent rock.

9 Project ☐
The arete right of the *South Face* looks feasible, just.

10 Dale's Left v3 ★★ ☐
Begin just right of the blunt lower arete. Move up to a crimp in a seam, then reach to small crimps above a bulge and so to the top.

11 Dale's Right v2 ★★ ☐
Begin just right of the previous line and climb up and slightly right on good solid edges by long moves.

⑫ Unnamed v2 ★ ☐
Jump to a good hold above the overhanging arete and mantel over.

On the slope left of the Led Zeppelin Boulder are a few small boulders. These boulders are listed here together. For locations, consult the topo next page.

⑬ Unnamed v1 ☐
Sit start and climb the short northwest arete.

⑭ Who's Your Daddy? v4 ☐
Traverse left to right across the lip of the downhill face, and then up.

⑮ Size Matters v1 ☐
Sit start, if your arms are long enough with the left hand on the left arete and the right hand on a pinch xenolith. Make a hard move and over. Without the xenolith, this is about v3.

⑯ Mick's Wonder v1 ☐
Start with the right hand in a thin seam/crack. Climb up and over on grainy huecos. Image below right.

⑰ Unnamed v1 ☐
Start at a big jug on the east face and make athletic moves up and over. Image below right.

LED ZEPPELIN BOULDER

LED ZEPPELIN BOULDER

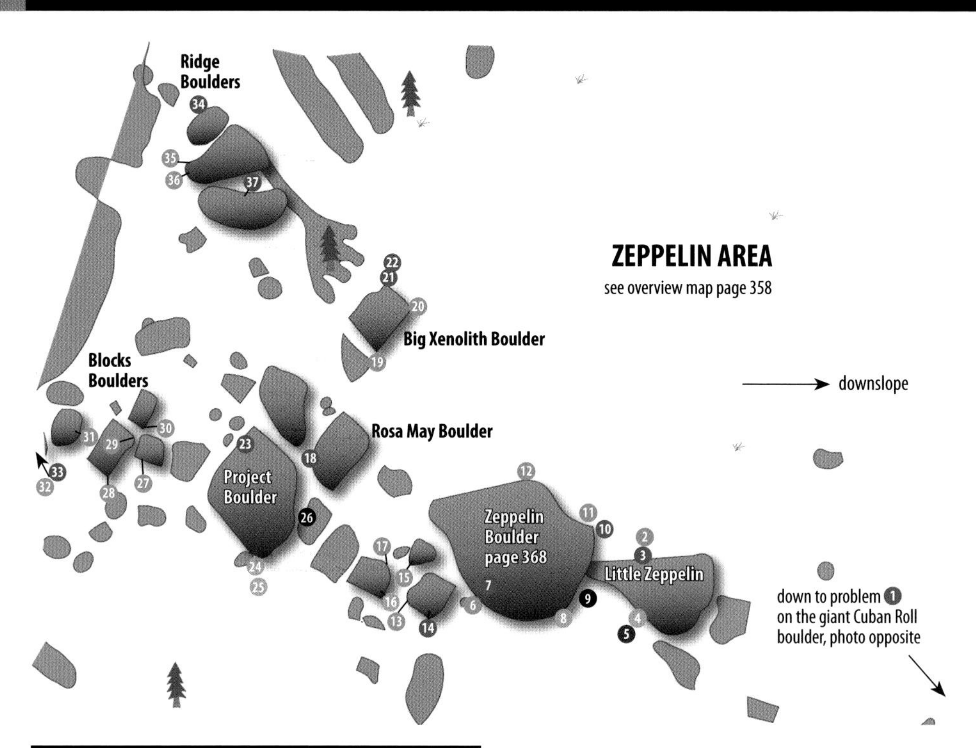

ROSA MAY BOULDER

18 The Legend of Rosa May v5 ★★ ☐
Beginning with a good, but sharp, right-facing sidepull, climb the porcelain-rock arete by a couple of hard moves.

19 Unnamed Arete v1 ★ ☐
The left arete of the downhill face is climbed on its right side, providing a fine little climb on good rock.

20 Unnamed v0+ ☐
The right arete of the downhill face is climbed on its right. Finishing direct with a long move is fun and a touch harder than matching at right.

21 Big Cobble Direct v3 ★ ☐
Sit start as for the previous line. Mantel the giant cobble with slopey holds above and finish directly up the arete.

22 Big Cobble Left v3 ★ ☐
As above, but with a left finish, by a long balancy press to a good hold.

PROJECT BOULDER

This is one of the big boulders of the group with a striking undercut prow facing downhil. The first problem listed is around on the uphill side. The others are on the front side. See the topo on this page.

23 The Jingle Dress Dancer v4 ★ ☐
Sit start off a low rock, and traverse the lip of the boulder left to the hanging arete, and then climb up the arete to the slab.

24 The Golden Pear v6 ★★ ☐
The blunt prow provides a proud line with a flat landing and one of the best climbs at the grade in the area. Start with crimps and make some pulls on positive holds. Grab the pear-shaped pinch in the seam with the left hand and move up and right to the slanted shelf and then the top.

25 The Golden Pear Left v7 ★★ ☐
The contrived left version of the previous line involves grabbing the pear with the right hand and moving up and left to a crimp before a slightly scary pull to the lip.

26 Project ☐
The pocketed wall on the southeast face has some cool holds leading to a scary topout.

BLOCKS BOULDERS

This is a collection of relatively small boulders, just upslope of the Project Boulder, including a couple of square-cut blocks.

27 Cow Lick v0 ☐
Traverse the lip up to a point, on the boulder below the two blocks.

28 Unnamed v0+ ★ ☐
The beautiful clean left arete on the larger block makes a fun climb.

29 Unnamed v0 ☐
The right arete of the larger block.

30 Unnamed v1 ☐
The arete on the slightly smaller block.

31 Unnamed v2 ☐
On the boulder just above the two blocks, traverse the lip from left to right.

LORAX BOULDER

This medium-large, tall boulder is at the upper left side of the Zeppelin boulderfield.

32 Unnamed v1 ☐
Climb the arete and slab on the upper left corner of the boulder.

33 The Lorax v4 ★★ ☐
Climb the crack rightward to the arete and up this without disturbing the flowering plant.

CABBAGE ROLL BOULDERS

Across the hillside to the right (as you look uphill) is a group of boulders that sit up above the Zeppelin area on a kind of ridge, the upper ones on a rock slab. The lower boulder has a cave beneath it.

34 Battleship Earth v3 ☐
On the uphill side of the upper boulder, sit start at crimps and climb slightly left and up.

35 Trundle v2 ☐
Sit start and climb the short dihedral.

36 Unnamed v0 ☐
The west end of the boulder looks kinda monstrous, but turns out to be okay.

37 Cabbage Roll v3 ★★ ☐
Jump to the lip of the lower boulder's uphill side, and pull a mantel.

MICK'S WONDER

Wills Young preparing for a *Cuban Roll* (v4, page 368). Photo: Lisa Rands.

DALE'S WEST

Dale's West consists of two boulders one about 50 yards above the other on a north-facing slope, just west of Dale's Dome, and just southeast of the Boneyard. The slope looks out across a shallow valley to the Peabody Boulders at the Buttermilks Main area, and also across the Painted Cave, Boneyard and Solitaire areas, which are just a few hundred yards away. There are several excellent problems on two boulders being pretty much as good as any around. The Zen Flute (v10) is an excellent area testpiece, originally climbed, but not named by Chris Sharma in winter of 2000, while The Green Hornet (v4) is a superb slab climbing exercise.

Directions: Dale's West is easily approached from the Hueco Wall area of Dale's Camp (see the locator photo below). It can also be approached from the other side entirely by way of the Checkerboard past the Painted Cave area and the Boneyard. See the Buttermilk Country overview map, page 220.

VIEW TOWARD DALE'S WEST FROM HUECO WALL AT DALE'S CAMP

GREEN HORNET BOULDER

1 Man Child v2 ☐
The arete at the left side of the east wall is climbed on small knobs.

2 Man Child Sit ☐
A sit start from low right is much harder.

3 Good Day Bruce v2 ☐
The grainy wall is climbed on small knobs.

4 Stain Grain v2 ☐
Climb the grainy ramp.

5 Project ☐
Dyno from decent holds to very bad holds at the lip.

6 Barn Door v6 ★ ☐
The arete and crack is climbed with much more effort than it looks like it would demand.

7 Balance v1 ☐
This is the left side of the north-facing slab.

8 The Green Hornet v4 ★★★ ☐
The mean green streak is climbed right of the slab's center. A technical, airy, and memorable line.

9 Hornet Right v5 ★ ☐
Follow the polished face right of The Green Hornet up and right to finish.

10 Cloud v1 ☐
Sit start under the right arete. Climb up on flakes.

ZEN FLUTE BOULDER

Directly down the hillside from the Green Hornet Boulder. Beginning at the west side of the boulder:

11 Unnamed v4 ★ ☐
Start from a funky spike/horn and pull up past a patina pinch. Not the best landing.

12 Unnamed Low Start v6 ★ ☐
As above, but begin down and right with the right hand on a tiny crimp. Jump from the ground or reach high to the good two-hand crimp. Beginning both hands low, without a jump start, also looks possible and considerably harder.

13 The Flake v7 ★★ ☐
Sit start at the base of the right-facing flake adjacent to the small boulder. Climb up the flake and reach left from its end to a slanted crimp (formerly there were better holds here). Use heel-toe contorsionism to match hands before reaching to the deep hueco.

14 Paralimpet v9 ★ ☐
Start low with both hands in the crack. Climb up past some sloping holds and a weird limpet-like knob.

15 Arete v3 ★★ ☐
Climb the arete on its left side.

16 Unknown/Project ☐
The arete can be climbed moving slightly to the right side to good sidepulls and what look to be decent holds beyond a tricky section. Probably not too hard.

GREEN HORNET BOULDER

GREEN HORNET BOULDER

GREEN HORNET BOULDER

ZEN FLUTE BOULDER

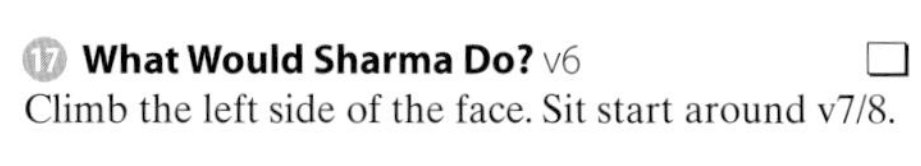

17 What Would Sharma Do? v6 ☐
Climb the left side of the face. Sit start around v7/8.

18 Sharma's Flake v9 ★ ☐
The flake runs out and a big span gains slopey, grainy holds at the lip.

19 Zen Flute v10 ★★★ ☐
The short solid wall is a puzzle to unlock. A left heel hook can prove useful. Figuring out which holds to use is not easy, as they all seem terrible at first. Also been done from a sit.

20 For Lovers of Grain v1 ☐
Climb the grainy ramp.

21 Northeast Arete v6 ★ ☐
Eliminate: Climb the arete WITHOUT the big patina jugs at right (these are not used for the feet or the hands). Difficult to start, this is quite scary up high, when moving up left to good holds from small but positive patina on the right wall.

22 North Face Patina v3 ☐
Climb the face from the good patina, left at first, and use some crafty technique to go back up and right.

23 North Face Low Start v3 ☐
Start low in the overhang. Make a hard move to the lip and then over and up the face.

ZEN FLUTE BOULDER

ZEN FLUTE BOULDER

Bardini Boulders

At an altitude of about 6950 feet (2100m), with a few large pinyon pines, this is a pretty area, similar though slightly higher in altitude than the Buttermilks Main area. The boulders are named after the very popular and colorful character, climbing guide Allan Bard (the late brother of Dale), known locally as The Great Bardini.

The Bouldering

Some stunning problems have been done here, including the very pretty *A Maze of Death* (v12), first climbed by Dave Graham in December 2002, and the awesome highball *This Side of Paradise* (v10), first bouldered by Matt Wilder in November 2005. Also on the giant Bardini Boulder is *The Beautiful and Damned* (v13), first done by Kevin Jorgeson in Jan 2007 and one of the hardest lines in Bishop. Besides these well-known desperate testpieces, the area has dozens of other lines that have been climbed — problems from v0 to v10 scattered across the boulderfield, many of them excellent. This area is well worth the visit for those looking for a break from the crowds, and a relatively guide-free experience — retro-style bouldering, just like the 1970s! The views are amazing, and the boulders can be spectacular. If you get there soon, you will enjoy many a first ascent experience — whether the climbs have been done before, or not.

Directions

Drive: Follow the main road up past the Peabody Boulders. Cross a cattle guard and fence line, and go straight. Continue along the road about 0.9 miles from the cattle guard, and look for a short left spur that angles sharply back. Park here, or near here.

Hike: This only takes about 15 minutes and is pretty mellow. Head east toward the ravine. On the far side of the ravine, note a large pine halfway up the slope. Cross the creek below this and head up the slope. At the top go rightward around the rock slab and then uphill with the slab at left. There is a large fallen tree pointing upslope. Head up the shallow ravine immediately above this fallen tree. This ravine splits after a couple hundred yards. Head up the ridge between the two ravines to reach the first boulders including the Maze of Death Boulder — it is a large boulder sitting on top of a steep rock slab. The rest of the Bardini Boulders are on the south-facing slope beyond this boulder.

Matt Wilder climbing *This Side of Paradise* (v10). The phenomenal arete, also known as the *Bardini Arete* is on the southeast corner of the spectacular, smoothly sculpted Bardini Boulder—the biggest in the area. Photo: Wills Young.

Jake List works *A Maze of Death* (v12) at the Bardini Boulders. Photo: Dan Brayack.

BARDINI BOULDER

1 The Beautiful and Damned v13 ★★★ ☐
Climb the gold streak and move right before slapping over the bulge to a sloper (crux). Move up left to gain a horn-like hold: Breather. Press on fearlessly, either up right at first by a fingertip reach to a slanted crimp (as used by the two ascensionists at time of press), or perhaps (?) by some slightly more physical pulls following the arete. Head into the no-fall zone with confident footwork to gain a small slopey black inclusion up high. Dicey, hard, and magnificent!

2 This Side of Paradise v10 ★★★ ☐
Climb the giant ship's prow with a hard move to gain a pinch up high. Grab a pair of crimps above this and make a long move to better holds and a relatively easy tiptoe finish up the slab. More phenomenal highballing! Photo previous page.

A MAZE OF DEATH BOULDER

1 A Maze of Death v12 ★★★ ☐
Sit start at a large right-facing sidepull. Climb the shallow overhanging groove with big moves on small, positive holds. Image: facing page.

2 Harry's Problem ☐
The wall right of *A Maze of Death* was climbed from a sit start. This line appears to have broken. Begin at or above a pair of shallow huecos, and climb the overhanging face on positive edges.

While many other excellent problems have been climbed at the Bardini Boulders, for now this area is being left for non-guided exploration, somewhere to go for a little peace and quiet, an escape from the crowds, a kind of step back in time. Please take care of the area, and enjoy it.

A MAZE OF DEATH BOULDER

Sherman Acres

VIEW OF THE SHERMAN ACRES APPROACH, AFTER HIKING A SHORT DISTANCE FROM THE CAR

At about 7600 feet (2300 m) with scattered tall Jeffrey Pines, this is another amazing area, similar to the Bardini Boulders in having a stack of great blocks, including many giants, with perhaps 50 to 100 unrecorded problems and plenty of potential. As with the Buttermilks Main area and the Bardini Boulders, the Sherman Acres are on a south-facing slope, but this time on the far side of Grouse Mountain, the highest peak of the Buttermilk Country. This area is named for the first person to seriously explore its bouldering potential, John Sherman, who spent a fair bit of time here in 1989 to 1990. He surely climbed all the classic lines he could find that had holds big enough to support his weight, and made the very proud ascent of *Sketch Pad* (v0-), a lichened north-facing highball slab. Visitors will also enjoy the excellent *Peewee Sherman* (v1) up the groove on the left side of the same slab, a problem which, though perhaps first climbed by Sherman, was respectfully named many years later in his honor. If you approach on foot (see below), you cannot miss this, as it is the first large boulder you'll come across, at the northwestern edge of the boulderfield. 'The Acres' has huge potential, and you are very welcome to claim a first ascent for pretty much anything above v1 — but do *not* tell Sherman about it.

Directions

Drive: Follow the main road up past the Peabody Boulders. Cross a cattle guard and fence line and go straight. Continue along the road about 2.3 miles from the cattle guard. At the first aspen trees at left beside the road, turn left onto a short spur that leads to a parking spot and a fence. Park here.

(Note: It is actually possible to drive all the way to the Sherman Acres, if you carry on along the Buttermilk Road. You follow the road a further two miles beyond the parking spot described above eventually reaching a creek. If you can cross this, you can then head back east along the bumpy road that leads to the Sherman Acres. This is not advised in anything but a reliable four-wheel drive vehicle with good clearance.)

Hike: The hike takes the better part of an hour, though undoubtedly you can cut this significantly with practice! It is only a little over a mile after all, but the path disappears into thigh-high scrub that makes hard going at times. You also have to cross the deep ravine cut by McGee Creek. From the parking lot head out along the obvious path, which soon disintegrates. You can soon see the spot where the boulders are located —though you won't easily spy the boulders themselves (photo above). Head more-or-less directly toward the destination. Drop into the ravine, cross this by means of bog aspens, and climb the other side to the boulders. An easy line could be found and maintained with a little effort.

Jeff Sillcox takes some air on *This Side of Paradise* (v10) at the Bardini Boulders, page 377. Photo: Wills Young.

CHAPTER 4

Druid Stones

The Druid Stones sit in a spectacular position overlooking Bishop and the Owens Valley Photo: Wills Young.

DRUID STONES

Two young girls, Felicity Ryan and Arianna Pope, who prove that hiking to the Drudes is a doddle. Photo Mick Ryan.

The Druid Stones are a collection of boulders reached by a long uphill path up a ridge that rises steeply into the Sierra foothills just a couple of miles from the southwest edge of Bishop. As the crow flies, this is one of the closest bouldering areas to town. Indeed, while climbing at the area, noise of motors or even music drifting up from the Bishop fairgrounds can give the place a slightly urban feel, a bizarre mismatch to the surreal beauty of the rock formations and tranquillity generally found here. Despite the close proximity, there is no road to the rocks and the 30-plus minute hike to the area keeps the crowds away. Its altitude of about 6150 feet (1875m) is 200-400 feet lower than the Buttermilks main area. Nevertheless, the views from the Druids across acres of rock-pinnacled terrain, down into the Owens valley, across the town of Bishop, and over to the White Mountains are unique and spectacular. Often a cooling breeze blows during warmer months. In winters you can climb here too: the distance from the Sierra crest means there is considerably less snowfall here than in the Buttermilk Country, and the afternoon sun warms the ridge for longer.

The Bouldering

This is undoubtedly one of Bishop's finest little areas. It can be tough the first time you boulder here, if you're not used to the hike, as you'll feel wasted even before you start. But after a couple of trips up the hill you begin to enjoy the exercise. There are several boulders here with immaculate patina providing some of the best "ticks" in the Bishop region. The Thunder Wall, the Skye Stone, the Sacrificial Boulder, and the Hall of the Mountain Queens stand out as the best individual blocks for quantity and quality. Not only are the problems good, but the landings are frequently good too. Besides the lines on these boulders, many outstanding problems are scattered across the boulderfield, all within a two to five minute hike of each other. There are loads of relatively easy (vB-v0) lines to climb, many unlisted, while for those looking to push themselves, anything with two stars or better will be well worth the hike.

Directions

Drive: From the junction of Highway 395 and Highway 168 (Main Street and West Line Street) in downtown Bishop, drive west on Highway 168 (West Line Street) for 1.5 miles to Barlow Lane (crossroads and stoplight). Turn left on Barlow Lane and drive 1.6 miles to a fork in the road. Take the right fork and drive about 1.3 miles to a dirt road on the left that runs parallel with a power line. Make a left on the dirt road and drive about 0.2 miles (past two power line pylons) to a narrow dirt road on the right. Turn right and follow this slightly bumpy and occasionally rocky road (good clearance will be very useful here) for 0.6 miles to its end at a turn around. If you don't wish to take your car down the bumpy road, stay on the paved road for a further 0.45 miles – that will make 1.75 miles from the right fork off of Barlow Lane (rather than the 1.3 described above). Park at a pull out next to another dirt road on the left. Hike this dirt road and make a right at its end to arrive at the parking spot (about 0.3 miles).

Hike: From the parking spot at 5000 feet altitude (1525m), hike out the end of the dirt road, heading southwest along a narrow path that rises gently with the hillside initially on your left. The path makes many switchbacks and eventually veers slightly westward, leading to the Druid Stones. Note: the zigzag path/old road you can see up to the left from near the parking lot goes nowhere: don't take this. This hike will take from 25 minutes to 40 minutes, according to your fitness level.

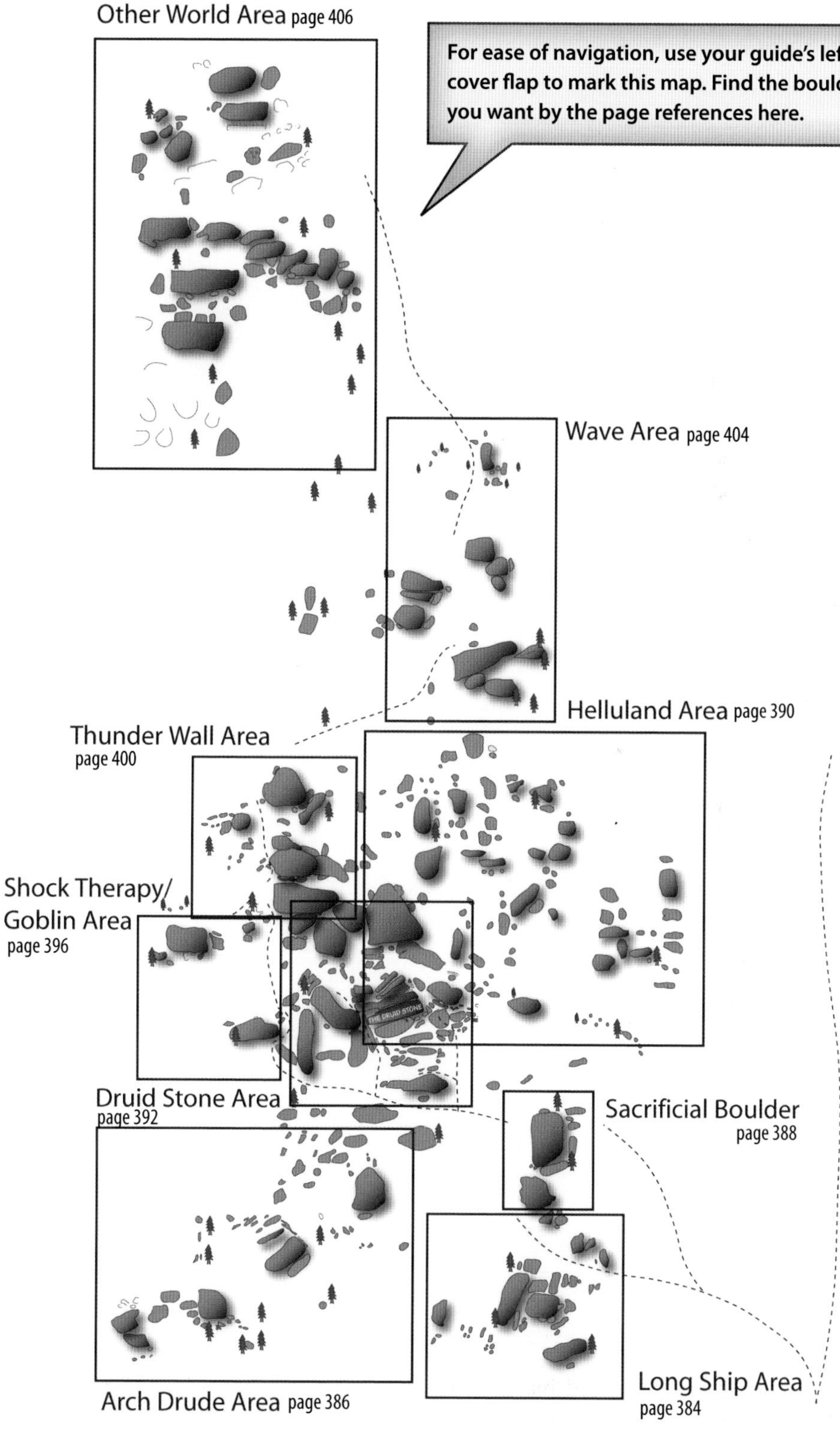

For ease of navigation, use your guide's left cover flap to mark this map. Find the boulders you want by the page references here.

Other World Area page 406

Wave Area page 404

Helluland Area page 390

Thunder Wall Area page 400

Shock Therapy/ Goblin Area page 396

THE DRUID STONE

Druid Stone Area page 392

Sacrificial Boulder page 388

Arch Drude Area page 386

Long Ship Area page 384

DRUID STONES VIEW FROM APPROACH PATH

LONG SHIP AREA

This is the first area you will come to if you follow the main path to the Druid Stones. Having arrived at the flat area at the top of the last uphill section, look to the left to see the Flying Viking Rock (which looks very much like a flying saucer) and the tall Long Ship. There is some good warming-up to be had here on the Norse Boulder, while the Erik The Bolder Boulder will give you some lessons in slabbage to set you up for some slightly crusty, but engaging highballing on the Long Ship itself.

NORSE BOULDER

This is a small boulder with some shady north-side warming-up possibilities.

1 Norse Crack vB ★ ☐
The left-facing flake is a nice little climb.

2 If It's Not Norse It's Scottish v2 ★ ☐
Sit down start in a hueco on the right side of the face. Make a couple of hard pulls to gain a rail and the top.

THE FLYING VIKING

This is the huge flat, wide boulder, tilted up like a flying saucer (as viewed from the west).

3 Unknown ☐
The right side of the overhanging south face looks climbable.

THE LONG SHIP

Somewhat crusty rock makes this nice-looking tall boulder less than perfect, but fun for those who like to get high off the ground.

4 Long Ship Crack vB ☐
The tall crack on the south side, climbed by stepping off a block below, is slightly crusty at the start, and about 5.6 or something like that.

5 Kicking Steps v1 ☐
This is on the same face as the crack, but way over to the right side. It begins from the ground in a small alcove, left of the southeast arete. Climb up and stand on a small crimp rail, then up with trepidation on grainy slopers.

6 Downclimb vB ☐
The east end of the rock is pretty much the easiest line of descent too, though you can also descend to the right of this line by grabbing the tree.

7 Gunhild v1 ☐
Climb the nondescript scooped slab near the tree. Descend by the tree or the west nose of the boulder, at left.

8 Erik Bloody Axe v0- ★ ☐
Climb the groove with patina to a crack.

9 Unnamed v0 ☐
The wall right of Erik Bloody Axe is climbable, but sketchy: highballish plodding on thin, flexing holds.

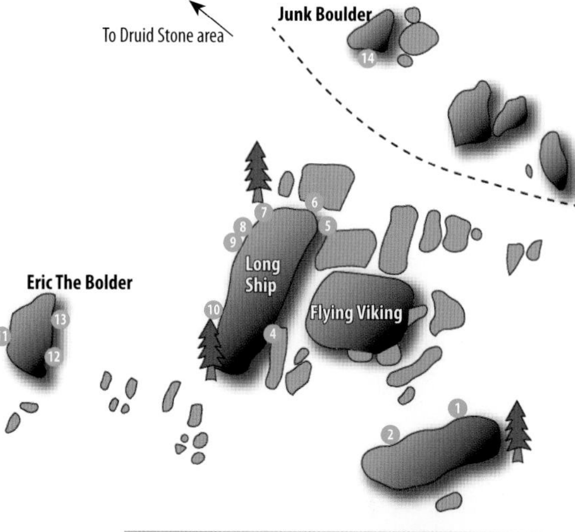

⑩ Mr. Gorgeous v0 ★ ☐
Begin at the right side of the face and climb diagonally up left to creaky thin flakes that provide a scary finish.

ERIK THE BOLDER

Here are a few good short problems.

⑪ Unnamed v0- ★ ☐
Around the back is a flake. Climb this with an undercling move to a good jug.

⑫ Celtic Soul Rebel v0 ★ ☐
Stand on a ledge to gain a high dish, and then climb the slab.

⑬ Erik The Bolder v0- ★ ☐
The slab is climbed at its right side.

JUNK BOULDER

⑭ Junk in Your Trunk v2 ★ ☐
Begin from the ground at a right-facing flake. Climb up and left. Move around left onto the slab where the rock deteriorates to munge. Top out by pulling ever-so softly and stepping up carefully.

ARCH DRUDE AREA

The *Arch Drude* itself (v5) is the gem of this little area that extends toward the slope overlooking both Bishop and the last quarter mile of the Druid Stones' approach path—don't miss this classic line.

ARCH DRUDE BOULDER

FINLANDIA AREA

GRANITIC ORDER BOULDER

ARCH DRUDE BOULDER

1 Flawed Genius v5 ★ ☐
Sit start at a right-facing sidepull. Climb up with some hard moves at first to gain a hueco up and left. A hidden flatty just above the hueco on the upper slab allows a move left to gain the top.

2 Arch Drude v5 ★★★ ☐
Sit start at right and make a hard move up past a hueco to gain good holds. Make a long move to a surprising finish.

3 Arch Drude (Left Start) v5 ★★★ ☐
Sit start at a right-facing sidepull as for *Flawed Genius*. Climb diagonally up right with hard moves to start, and then launch rightward to join the top of the regular Arch Drude (the previous line).

FINLANDIA AREA

Two boulders, two climbs:

4 Finland v1 ★ ☐
The very thin fin of rock is climbed up its always-grainy left edge. A grainy-but-good classic for munge hunters everywhere!

5 E3 5c v2 ☐
On the much larger rock, climb the rising right edge of the boulder, basically walking it out with nary a hand-hold, passing the rotten flake without using it, and making some frightening steps up to finish. There are some good vB climbs to the left.

GRANITIC ORDER BOULDER

6 Galar vB ★ ☐
Climb the southeast wall using a short crack. It looks great, but is over in a couple of moves. Traverse left (almost as hard) to descend.

The wall at right can be climbed almost anywhere, and there is also at least one decent vB on the west face.

PUBERTY BOULDERS

Two small boulders, two small climbs.

7 Teenybopper v5 ☐
Reported at v5, on the left boulder: Sit start on edges on the right in the trough. Climb up left.

8 Puberty v6 ☐
Reported at v6 on the right boulder: Sit start in the back of the blocky roof.

Above: Jeff Sillcox makes the big pull to the hole on *Arch Drude* (v5).
Photo: Wills Young.

see overview map page 383

SACRIFICIAL BOULDER

You'll find some great climbs on good rock here. The north wall is short with some fun little climbs (vB-v2) while the south-facing wall is tall and exciting, with some frightening topouts on sloping grain. If v2 or v3 is your speed, beware of the latter, as the landings are bad. The problems are excellent, but they are definitely not for the feint of heart, and could be disastrous if you fell from the slopey finish. This face also has one of the hardest offerings in the area, The Sloth (v9), with its superb topout on sloping dishes, which, this time fortunately, has a flat landing.

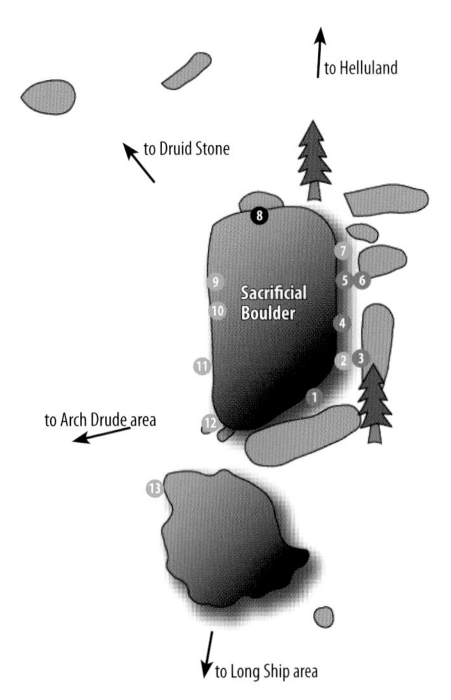

see overview map page 383

SACRIFICIAL BOULDER

1 Hung Up and Hanging Out To Dry v4 ☐
Start by reaching in high and making some footless moves over the bulge left of the sloth.

2 The Sloth v9 ★★★ ☐
Full value! Sit start on the rail in the roof. The left hand is at a good hold where the horizontal crack opens into a tennis-ball-sized pod (the rail continues further left, but is crusty). The right hand is just to the right at a good hold. Move right along the rail (the big hueco at right is on for feet, but not hands). After a couple of moves, go straight out the steepest part of the roof by long moves on small crimps to gain the huge block of patina up and left (rest). Use a right-hand sidepull to gain the lip and grope over to a nerve-racking finish on sloping dishes.

3 Sloth Stand Start v5 ★★ ☐
A standing start to the previous line is also a superb high problem over a flattish landing.

4 The Greatest Imperfection ... v6 ★ ☐
(... is Love, Love, Love. But I Can't Keep the Fire Away.) Yeah, yeah, whatever ... Sit start at the giant hueco at the right side of the roof. Climb up and then left to a huge smiley jug by contortions and long hard moves. Head up on good flakes to the top of the following line.

5 Fear of the Unknown Sit v5 ★★ ☐
Sit start at a right-facing sidepull and make a few hard pulls on small crimps to gain the huge patina jug. Continue as for the previous line. If the landing were flat, this would be a popular classic.

6 Fear of the Unknown (Stand) v3 ★★ ☐
Climb the face just right of the cave beginning with a move/jump to a huge left-hand jug. Top out by groping slopers and stepping onto patina. Beware of the landing.

7 Woodman, Woodman... v2 ★ ☐
(... Will You Spare That Tree?) Climb excellent patina, and finish on sloping grain, stepping up on the lip above a horrible landing and reaching back to a crimp. Good, but don't fall from this one!

8 See Whitey Fly ☐
Sorry, no rating for this. Supposedly you can leap to the upper patina from the low rock. Rightward looks most likely.

9 Unnamed vB ★ ☐
A good face climb.

10 Unnamed vB ★ ☐
Another decent face climb.

11 Through the Heart v2 ★★ ☐
Sit start at a low edge and climb the patina ...

12 Toxygene v1 ★ ☐
Start with two good high edges. Climb over the bulge to a sloping topout.

On a low boulder next to the Sacrificial Boulder, right of Toxygene, is:

13 Trollkind v2 ★ ☐
On the north side, sit start at a hueco and climb up and over. Short and awkward.

Above: Tiffany Campbell sticks the crux move of *The Greatest Imperfection...* (v6, next page) on the Sacrificial Boulder. Photo: Mick Ryan.

HELLULAND BOULDERS

Southeast of the Druid Stone itself is a boulderfield of scattered medium-sized boulders with a great many vB problems and several harder problems. Explorers will find plenty of options, and many good climbs that have been done before, but few of which are recorded here.

WILLIAM THE VOLLMAN

At the east side of the main Druid Stone grouping is a huge boulder, which is named William The Vollman Rock. Though not particlularly high, it is massive, and probably the second-largest boulder here (after the Druid Stone). **There is no easy way off this boulder, so don't climb it unless you're very sure of being able to get down OK.**

1 Unnamed v2 ☐
Climb the slightly scooped low-angle face directly off the highest of the low boulders below the face.

2 Unnamed v0 ☐
From the low boulder at right, climb up the low-angle face past good patina incuts. NOTE: As for the previous line, there is no easy way off this boulder.

3 Downclimb v0- ☐
From a low boulder climb the rich red-brown patina, and then back-track the same line ...?

HELLULAND

This is a large boulder just east of the giant William the Vollman Rock. It has a fine patina slab facing east with:

4 Goi vB ★ ☐
Climb the tall featured slab, starting at the left side.

5 Frilla vB ★ ☐
Follow the line to the right beginning where the base of the boulder changes angle.

6 Unnamed vB ☐
The right arete is climbed on its left.

7 Death Mantel v2 ★ ☐
Around on the south face on the right side is a scary mantel above a low boulder.

MISSACK

Heading further toward the east near a Further toward the east, near a huge tree, find:

8 Missack v3 ★★ ☐
An excellent little climb up the right-facing flake.

WIMMIN CAVE

Heading further toward the east On a boulder neighboring Missack in a cave facing northeast is:

9 Wimmin of Climbing v4 ★ ☐
Sit start at flakes and climb the cave overhang by huecos and crusty edges. There is another line to the left, but it's extremely crusty.

10 Scoop v0- ☐
The short but excellent scoop on the southeast side.

WIMMIN OF CLIMBING

HELLULAND BOULDER

MISSACK

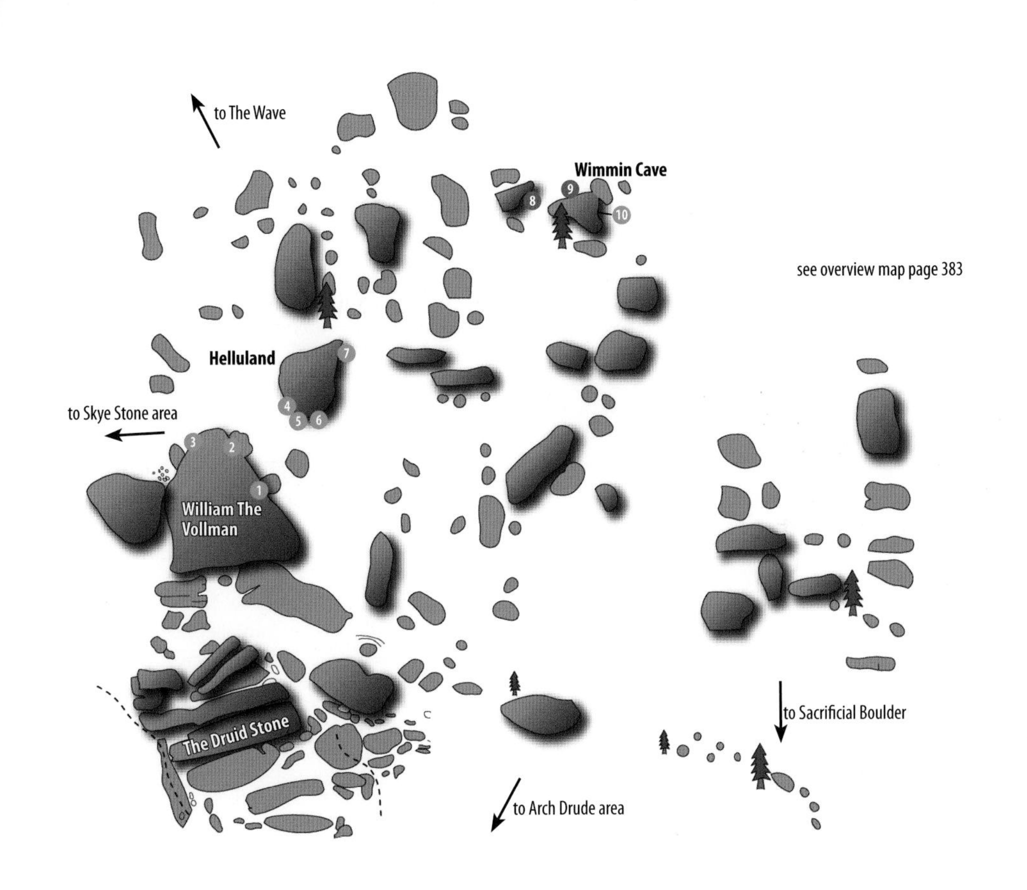
to The Wave
Wimmin Cave
8
9
10
see overview map page 383
Helluland
7
4
5
6
to Skye Stone area
3
2
1
William The Vollman
The Druid Stone
to Sacrificial Boulder
to Arch Drude area

DRUID STONE AREA

Adjacent to the Druid Stone are a few giant boulders creating small retreats and corridors. Here you'll find the Ice Flow, as smooth and nearly as cool as a glacial-cave wall, with some good, technical climbs. Also here are the Odin's Cave with a few steep athletic lines (though a bit sharp and crusty), and the excellent Blood Kin Stone with the superb Blood Kin (v1) a fun line on some interesting rock. Facing out from the Druid Stone Area is the Golden Child Wall, which is a very pretty wall with a couple of tall lines and the excellent testpiece Golden Child (v9).

One of the most significant climbing achievements at the Druid Stones came at the taped-up hands of two English climbers, Craig Smith and Stuart Littlefair, when they climbed the north crack and arete of the 60 foot tall Druid Stone and became the first humans to step on the summit of this rocky sentinel. They offered a rating of 5.12c R/X (UK E6 6b) and the name *The Key To The Whole Deal.*

ICE FLOW

ICE FLOW

This is a fine boulder with excellent face climbing. It looks small from a distance standing next to the Druid Stone, but upon approach you find it seriously big. The patina is solid, and the glassy rock provides a challenging start to the lines.

1 Sun Circle v0 ★★ ☐
Begin at the left side of the wall and make a rising traverse to finish on the right,

2 Winter Sun v2 ★★ ☐
The wall is climbed with a tricky start with a pair of good but high underclings.

3 Dreams of Winter v3 ★ ☐
At a very poor pair of underclings and some bad footholds pull on and up the wall, moving slightly right from a vertical crack.

4 The Ice Shirt v2 ★ ☐
At right, with the edge of a rock at your back, climb the wall with some longish moves on smallish crimps.

ODIN'S CAVE

GOLDEN CHILD WALL

Outside of the cave, on the The west face of the Odin's Cave Boulder forms the Golden Child Wall, which is home to:

5 Unknown v1 ☐
Beginning at good patina, follow a rising traverse up and left to a finish above the adjacent boulder.

6 Well of Weird v2 ☐
Starting as the previous problem, climb directly to a very thin and friable horizontal flake, and then over the top if it doesn't break.

7 Yggdrassil v2 ★ ☐
Begin with difficulty and climb up and then right onto the upper slab, or begin more easily further left.

8 Golden Child v9 ★★ ☐
Sit start at a right-facing undercling (both hands) with great difficulty (squeeze). Make an all-out snatch with the left to a high sloper and then climb the wall on good patina to a bit of a grovelling finish onto the slab up and left... Hard?

ODIN'S CAVE

Back at the cave's entrance, on a tall wall on a huge rock adjacent to the giant Druid Stone are:

9 Frey v1 ★ ☐
Climb the features of scoops, edges and sidepulls up the left edge of the porcelain wall without using the boulder at left.

10 Sheep Cat Lives On v4 ★★ ☐
Follow scoops, sloping ledges and a diagonal sidepull feature up the tall glassy wall above a nasty landing.

Moving into the cave, the overhanging brown west face, provides some sharp and slightly crusty lines:

11 Sleipnir v11 ☐
Begin left of the following line at a low shield and small crimps. Make a very hard move to gain the good flake at right. Continue low rightward across the wall and top out on Vinland (below). A shorter traverse, beginning as for the following line is reported at about v10.

see overview map page 383

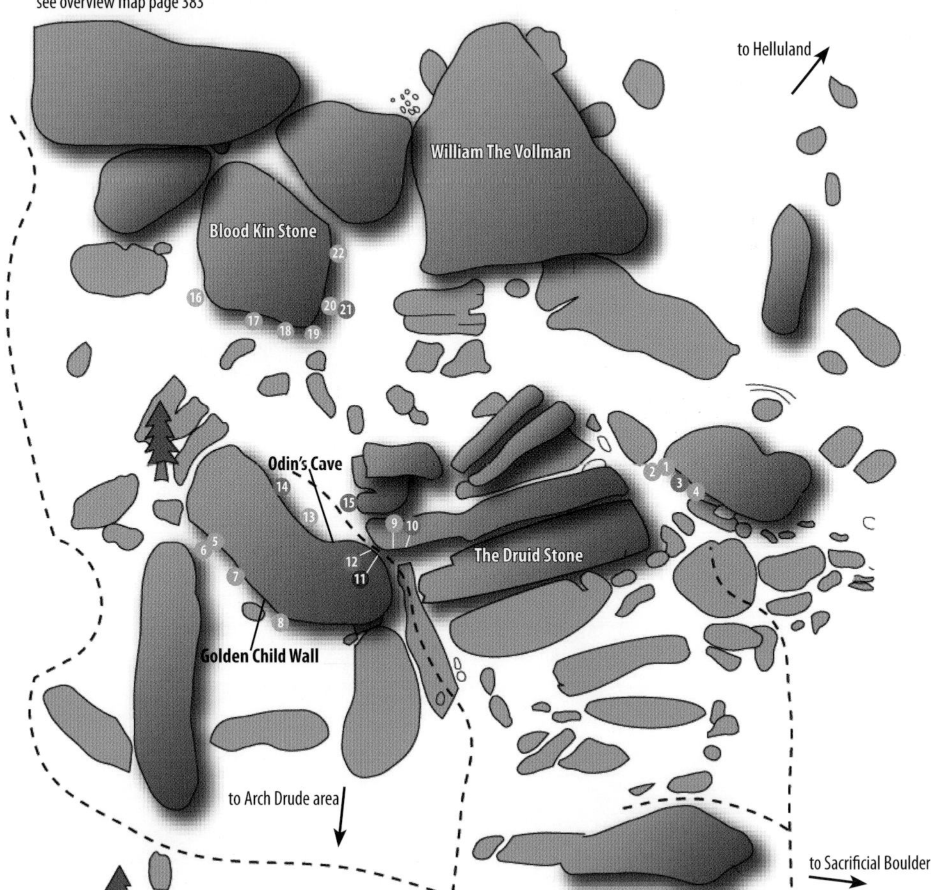

The Thunder Wall (page 400) provides one of the best pieces of rock in the Bishop Area making the Druid Stones a must for all climbers. Here, Lisa Rands climbs *Kredulf* (v4) in the middle of the wall. Photo: Wills Young.

BLOOD KIN STONE

BLOOD KIN STONE

12 Truth Crushed to Earth... v4 ★ ☐
(... Will Rise Again). Start with both hands on the low, left-facing flake. Climb up and right by a long move to a sharp jug, and then move up and slightly right to top out with care (a large rock looms at the back of the landing zone).

13 Pleiades v6 ★ ☐
Sit start near the center of the brown overhanging face, just left of annoying small block. Make one or two hard moves to gain a left-facing slanted crimp, and then up more easily into the scoop.

14 Vinland v4 ☐
Sit start at the right side of the overhanging face with a high right flake and a left-hand sidepull. Climb via a hard move to a jug and a long reach over the lip to a good hold.

15 Unnamed v4 ☐
Climb the fin-like boulder on the east side of the cave.

BLOOD KIN STONE

Up and over some low blocks To the east of the cave is this giant boulder which has some superb juggy patina on its south side, while around to the north-west is a cave. From here, moving to the right are:

16 Poltergeist v7 ★ ☐
Sit start in a cave and climb out the cave with patina edges to gain the slab.

17 Everlasting Soul v0- ★ ☐
The big committing slab toward the center or left, taking the line of least resistance.

18 Tribal Wisdom vB ★ ☐
Excellent patina just left of the southwest arete.

19 Jormungand v0+ ★★ ☐
Bold airy moves lead up the right side of the south-east arete.

20 Blood Kin v1 ★★★ ☐
Above a small cave, climb big patina sidepulls and jugs to a slab with a single hueco. Step up, and move slightly left to top out. A beauty.

21 Blood Kin Sit v4 ★★ ☐
Sit start in the giant hueco and make a hard reach out of it to join the previous line.

22 Downclimb vB ☐
The excellent patina of the main face leads easily either up or down.

GOBLIN ROCK / SHOCK THERAPY AREA

There are some boulders scattered down the hillside below the Thunder Wall, and also across the hillside to the right of it. The Goblin Rock is approached either from the inside of Odin's Cave by dropping downhill across some low rocks and gravel, or by walking downhill and then turning right (east) around some boulders from the Golden Child Wall. It is just twenty yards to the right of the Thunder Wall as you look at the Thunder Wall's main patina face. A few short low-to-mid-grade problems with sweet landings provide the entertainment on the Goblin Rock, while downhill from this, the Shock Therapy Boulder has some harder testpieces including the 45-degree overhang of Lounge Lizards (v11). This last has become considerably more sustained than it originally was, after good patina and nice crimps broke off. Also find the excellent and highly popular sit-start, Shock Therapy (v8)—for a long time the ultimate gimme v9, then down-rated by popular demand in the last guide. However another recent break has made it harder again!

GOBLIN ROCK

GOBLIN ROCK

1 Maid of Constant Sorrow v4 ★ ☐
On the west side of the boulder, start standing at a vague "W" feature, traverse right to the smile edge and up the shallow groove.

2 Ainvar v2 ★ ☐
Sit start with the left hand in the hueco and right on a crimp or sidepull, and a low right foothold. Move right and then directly up the wall.

3 The Vibe v0 ★ ☐
Make the same sit start as for the previous line and head right up the dihedral.

4 Baby Wants to Ride v1 ☐
Sit start at the large red block. Pull up to a seam/crack and up left or right. Try not to pull the block off. The stand start is v0.

5 Unnamed v2 ☐
Sit start and pull into the hollow, then up.

6 Able-bodied Goblin v2 ★ ☐
Sit start on a large sloper. Move left to an undercling in the roof and up left to a good hold, and then over.

7 Spoiled Blond v4 ★ ☐
Start as for the previous line, but move straight up using holds out right—squeezing—and grope over the top on slopers to a good hold.

GOBLIN ROCK

see overview map page 383

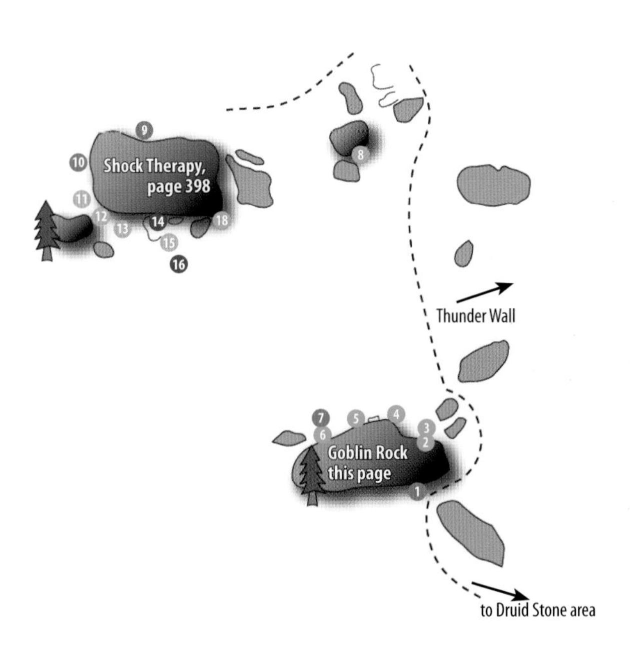

Lisa Rands climbs *Skye Dance* (v5, page 402), on the excellent Skye Stone, which sits on level ground overlooking Bishop and the Owens Valley. Photo: Wills Young.

SHOCK THERAPY BOULDER

Head down the hill from the Goblin Rock to some large boulders forming a line down the slope, the largest of which is the Shock Therapy Boulder.

On the way down, pass a small boulder with:

8 Rainbow Slab v0- ★ ☐
The center of the slab provides a short problem.

On the Shock Therapy Boulder itself, beginning at its west face and rotating rightward, find:

9 The Handcuff Manual v5 ☐
Sit start low and make a butt-dragging short traverse left and then up on good edges.

10 Chaps v4 ☐
The short wall, left of Shock Therapy (below) is climbed on decent edges.

11 Shock Therapy v8 ★★ ☐
Slide into a liedown start using huecos (not the flakes above). Pull up to the flakes, and the distinctive triangular pinch/crimp. Continue up left past tiny edges to a small right-facing flake, and so to the top. Harder since breaks after last guide?

12 Shock Therapy Right v9 ★★ ☐
As for Shock Therapy to the triangular pinch/crimp. From here, move up and right into the scoop by big moves to small vertical crimps avoiding further holds on Shock Therapy. The nice smooth huecos are not really needed on this line, except as footholds.

13 Lizard Therapy v9 ★★ ☐
Begin with the right hand in a good hueco at right, and the left on the sloping hueco at left. Climb straight up via a crimp at the left edge of the upper hueco. Tricky start.

14 Lounge Lizards v11 ★★★ ☐
Begin super-low with both hands in the large hueco. Move out left (knee-scum useful) to a good edge up and left. Grab a smaller crimp and make a big pull back right to a good left-facing sidepull. Match and make another big move up with the right hand. Then persevere with slightly easier moves to the top.

15 Lounge Lizards High Start v9 ★★ ☐
Sit start on the rock base and a thick pad if necessary, with both hands at a good incut above the alcove. Make a big move up left to the sidepull and join Lounge Lizards.

16 Lounge Lizards Direct v11 ★★★ ☐
Sit start very low at left of deep hueco, as for the regular Lounge Lizards. Instead of pulling left out of the large hueco, go direct to a good incut up to the right of the sit-start near the lip of the big hole/hueco. From here make another big pull up left to join the regular line. Could be a lot harder than the original for those coming up short on that first long move.

17 Project ☐
A right exit to Lounge Lizards looks plausible.

18 Turn the Screws v1 ★ ☐
Sit start at a big flake/ledge. Move up to another

Isaac Caldiero crushing the crimps of *Gasperini* (v12) on the back of the Skye Stone (page 402). Photo: Wills Young.

THUNDER WALL AREA

Join Denton Calhoun for a ton of fun at the Thunder Wall. Denton sold his car, but left inside an envelope that had slipped under the seat. It contained a letter from a couple of lady admirers with a pair of photos of them showing, shall we say, a naked display of affection. Denton has been immortalized in the naming of a long, hard traverse across the Thunder Wall, the last section of which, has become more difficult since breaking. But this is not the greatest problem on the wall. Here, find a string of excellent straight-ups on this amazing unforgettable red-brown patina. You may well have come all the way up here on the basis of this piece of rock, and if v3 to v7 is your calling, then you will not be disappointed. Those looking for harder stuff will also enjoy the many hard traverse link-ups and some stimulating sit starts.

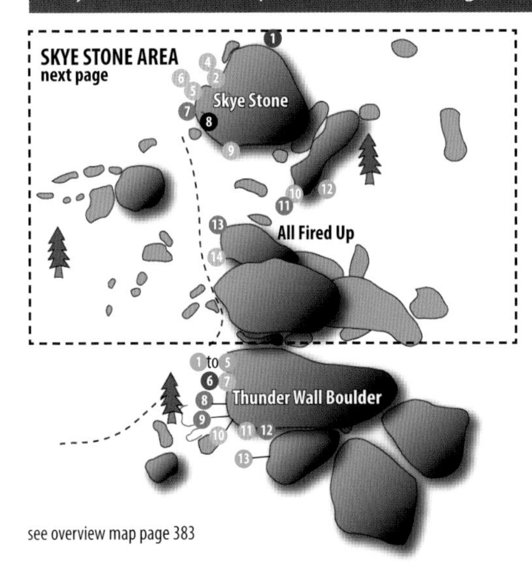

see overview map page 383

THUNDER WALL BOULDER

The problems are listed from the left side of the wall rightward to the east face.

1 Mad Cap Mushrooms ☐
Supposedly start sitting on the left side as for the next line, and climb up (and presumably left) at v5. Perhaps this should start further left(?).

2 Days of Blunder v9 ★ ☐
Sit start with the left hand on a small right-facing crimp-flake, and the right hand on a small crimp. Make a hard move up right to gain two crimps (one above the other). Then climb the wall past a small crimp slot for the right hand. Follow the left edge of the patina as it leads up and right to top out above big jugs in a shallow groove, as for Kredulf (see below).

3 High Start to Blunder v7 ★★ ☐
Basically two-moves in from the previous line: Sit/hang start with hands, one above each other, on crimps about six inches apart. Pull off the ground, set your feet and climb past a small crimp slot for the right hand. Top out up and right on Kredulf (see below).

4 Denton Calhoun v11 ☐
Start as for Days of Blunder, but after the first couple of moves, traverse low across the wall to top out as for Natural Philosophy (see below).

5 Denton's Leftovers? ☐
As for the previous line, but top out on Thunder (see below). Could also start as for the High Start to Blunder for an easier and good traverse.

6 Denton's Remorse v10 ★★ ☐
Sit start with hands low in a large hidden undercling. Move the left hand to a down-pointing pinch/undercling and right to a flat edge out right. Grab the break above and climb up and left to good patina. Move back right and top out as for Kredulf (see below).

7 Denton's Diversion v7 ★★★ ☐
Sit/hang start at the wide horizontal slot. Climb up and diagonally left by hard moves to good patina jugs, and then back up and right to top out on the following line.

8 Kredulf v4 ★★★ ☐
Sit start at the middle of the wall and climb by sustained hard crimp moves to jugs at the lip. Pull over with some difficulty. A straightforward, athletic and excellent climb on great rock. Photo page 394.

9 Thunder v3 ★★★ ☐
The original line on the wall begins toward the right side, just left of the undercut section. Sit start on very low holds and makes a couple of hard pulls to gain jugs leading to a fun finale.

10 Natural Philosophy v7 ☐
Sit start at a high flat edge up and right of the previous line's start. Avoiding hand-holds on that line, make hard moves to grab a flexi flake with the left hand. Make a long move to the lip at right and climb over with relative ease.

11 Old Ei v8 ★★ ☐
The Old Ei (pronounced 'eye') is a German-language influenced term for "Rotten Egg." Sit start at a good hueco and climb the overhang with a hold out left, using long moves and clever technique.

12 Prostrate to the Higher Mind v5 ★ ☐
Sit start at a large flake. Move up and right to a pair of crimps and over on more crimps to good holds. Steep powerful pulling.

Just right of the Thunder Wall Boulder is a slab:

13 Antiquities of Cornwall v0+ ☐
Climb delicately up the lichenous slab.

1
2
4
3
4
6
7
8
9
10
THUNDER WALL BOULDER

11
12
13
THUNDER WALL BOULDER

SKYE STONE

Another outstanding piece of rock, in a glorious situation. Climbing here is like being on stage, with nothing but the wide open valley, the mountains and the sky looking on. The Skye Stone provides a row of great problems over great landings, all with steep starts. The rock is good and the climbing is interesting: a little rough on the skin, a little tricky, a little thuggish, and a little aggro. *All Fired Up* (v7) on the All Fired Up Boulder between the Skye Stone and Thunder Wall is an unusual crimpy and technical climb also listed here.

SKYE STONE

Beginning at the east face and moving right, find:

1 Gasperini v12 ★ ☐
Sit start at edges. Pull up past a shallow hueco and up over on sharp crimps and an undercling. Has broken a few times, but hopefully is settled now.

2 Soul Window v8 ★★ ☐
Sit start at the big flat hueco edge. Pull up and climb the rib above, with shallow huecos on the left and crimps on the right.

3 Through the Window v8 ★★ ☐
Begin on Soul Window and turn the bulge and then make a long move up and left to good edges and move left and up through the large hole.

4 McCallum v6 ★★★ ☐
Sit start at the big flat hueco edge as for the previous line. Traverse low right to join Skye Dance (see below).

5 Guilty Conscience v6 ★★ ☐
Sit start at good huecos. Climb up to underclings at the lip of the roof. Move to the far left undercling and up the vertical headwall beginning with a long move to a good horizontal crimp.

6 Skye Dance v6 ★★★ ☐
Sit start at good huecos. Climb up to underclings at the lip of the roof, pull around and slightly right to good angled crimps. Bust a hard pull up right to a good edge and up the headwall on improving holds.

7 Short Dance v3 ★ ☐
Stand on the low rock. Using a pair of huecos, make a big hard move up left to a good edge and so the top.

8 Project ☐
A low start to the previous line, either from the left or—exceptionally hard—from the right might go.

9 Cayla v7 ★★ ☐
Sit start down and left of a huge hueco. Move up and right to the big hueco, and then over the lip by underclings and small crimps and up the headwall, which stays interesting.

Slightly up and right on a smaller boulder are:

10 That's Embarrassing v6 ☐
Contrived, ridiculous, super grainy and with a boulder under it. Kinda good though. Sit start with the left hand in the hueco. Pull up to good edges and move left using sloping holds just over the lip of the boulder, and a right-hand sidepull in the first hueco

Above: Another pretty line is *All Fired Up* (v7, see below) around to the left of the Thunder Wall. Photo: Wills Young.

to gain a second hueco on the left. Pull around and over the left side.

⓫ **White Man's Overbite** v3 ★ ☐
Sit start with the left hand in the hueco. Pull up to good edges and directly over. You might start even lower to make this harder.

⓬ **Roman Nose** v2 ☐
Sit start on the right side of the low boulder. Move lcft and up.

ALL FIRED UP

Further to the right (toward the Thunder Wall) is a triangular-looking boulder, wider at the top with a beautiful arching arete on its right. Here are:

⓭ **Brother Law** v3 ☐
The left edge of the face is climbed on good rock.

⓮ **All Fired Up** v7 ★★★ ☐
Kinda hard to start if you're short. Kinda hard to finish no matter what. Climb the angled arete, beginning with the right hand on an undercling. Excellent rock and great moves make this one of the area's finest little problems.

THE WAVE AREA

The Wave Boulder is only about 50 yards or so along the ridge from the Skye Stone in a south-easterly direction. It is distinctly recognizable by the 20 feet wide, 15 feet high wave-like overhang facing northwest, which breaks to a vertical, heavily patinaed headwall. Sadly, the overhang itself is virtually devoid of holds. However, around on the east side of the boulder, facing away from the Druid Stone's main area, is a tall gently overhanging wall, with three superb problems representative of the area's best: aggressive moves on positive holds up a tall face with a flat landing. Downslope from the Wave is the Kojak Boulder, also with good landings and relatively easy climbing on a short steep hueco-coed wall. Beyond this again, and easily recognized from a distance is the Wicca Tower.

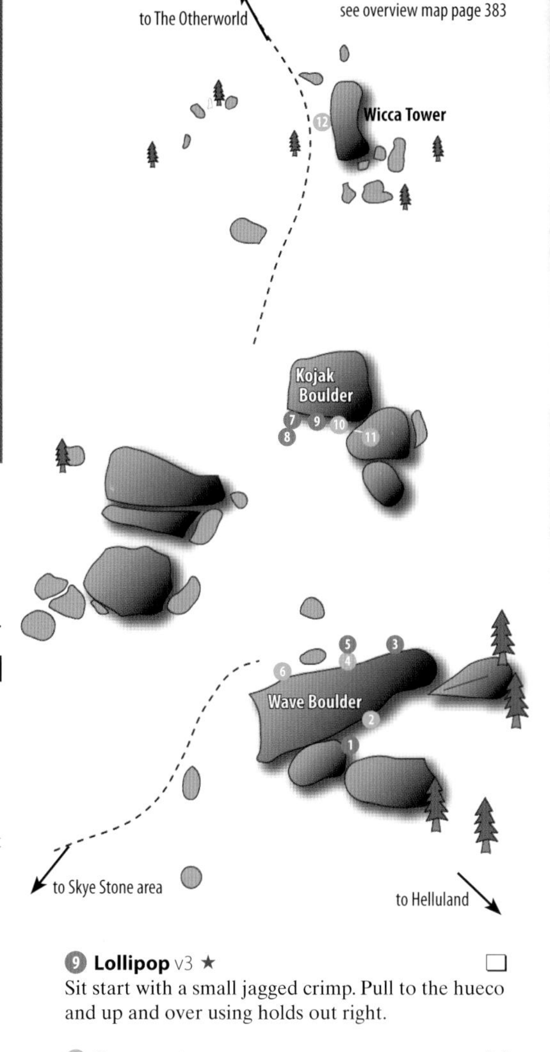

Adjacent to the Wave Boulder itself is a smaller boulder forming a kind of alcove on the Wave Boulder's uphill side. This has:

1 The Hidden Value of a Cheap Thrill v4 ☐
Climb thin patina up a short wall to a sloping topout.

THE WAVE BOULDER

2 Re-write History v2 ☐
Around the back, on the uphill side of the boulder, climb thin patina edges to a positive slab finish.

3 Hook Line and Sinker v5 ★★ ☐
Sit start at a good rail. Move directly up the wall past a right-hand sidepull to good, but sharp edges.

4 Red Light District v8 ★★ ☐
Sit start at a right-facing flake, very low. Make hard moves up and left to a thin, but solid crimp flake. Climb directly up the wall from here through a bulge with difficulty to a good wide edge, and an okay finish. Good, sustained crimping!

5 Suspenders v5 ★★★ ☐
Sit start at a right-facing flake very low, as for the previous line. Move right and up the wall by long moves on good edges. Great climbing on good rock.

6 Cindy Crawford v1 ☐
She's thin and dangerous. Climb onto the ramp and use sketchy patina to gain flakes above. Not the most solid looking line!

KOJAK BOULDER

This is an obvious, small and heavily huecoed boulder down slope from the Wave Boulder.

7 Who Love's Ya Baby? v3 ★★ ☐
Sit start and climb up the left side of the wall.

8 Kojakian Wisdom Reworked v4 ★ ☐
Sit start as for the previous line. Move right across the wall to a big move to a jug in the low scoop.

9 Lollipop v3 ★ ☐
Sit start with a small jagged crimp. Pull to the hueco and up and over using holds out right.

10 Stavros v1 ☐
Sit start on the right of the boulder and climb the wall on good holds.

To the right is a small boulder:

11 Unnamed v2 ☐
Sit start on two low crimps. Climb up and over the small bulge.

WICCA TOWER

The Wicca Tower is a 20-feet high pinnacle located down the ridge from the Kojak and Wave Boulders. It has a golden patina face on its north side that looks more solid than it is, and provides:

12 Wicca Tower v0- ☐
Utterly crusty, but very photogenic climbing up the north face of the tower leads to a treacherous descent off the kitty-litter rock on the back, or a downclimb by the same route.

Perfect stone at the Hall of the Mountain Queens (overleaf). Photo: Wills Young.

THE OTHERWORLD

The Hall of the Mountain Queens slab is an immaculate slab with smooth clean edges offering delightful footwork testpieces over a flat landing. This is surely one of the finest pieces of rock in the entire Bishop area: just high enough to be exciting and just hard enough to be demanding, it really is nearly perfect. What a find! The Otherworld also has, in Morning Glory (v4), one of the best v4s around.

Directions: The Otherworld is the outermost area described here. To get there, head out along the ridge in a north-easterly direction from the Wicca Tower (page 404) staying atop the ridge and aiming for a giant dead tree with wide-spreading branches. See the locator photo opposite. For the Morning Glory Boulder, go around the dead tree to the left and on about 30 yards to a big slab. *Morning Glory* (v4) is on the downhill side of this boulder, facing southeast. For the Hall of the Mountain Queens, go around the dead tree to the *right* and downhill a further 50 yards or so. Note: there are many other boulders in this area that are not covered in this guide.

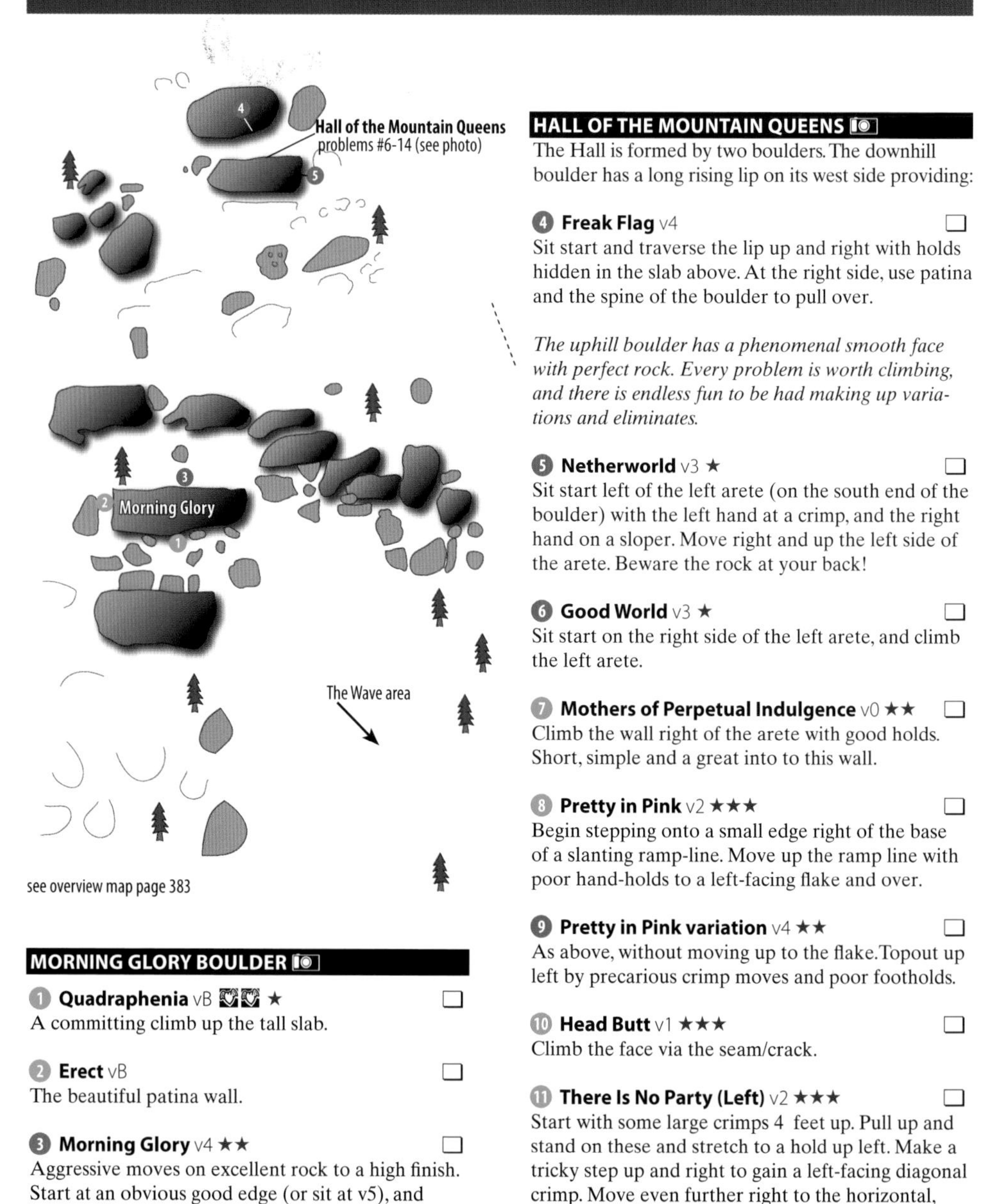

see overview map page 383

MORNING GLORY BOULDER

1 Quadraphenia vB ★ ☐
A committing climb up the tall slab.

2 Erect vB ☐
The beautiful patina wall.

3 Morning Glory v4 ★★ ☐
Aggressive moves on excellent rock to a high finish. Start at an obvious good edge (or sit at v5), and climb directly up by hard moves on small crimps.

HALL OF THE MOUNTAIN QUEENS

The Hall is formed by two boulders. The downhill boulder has a long rising lip on its west side providing:

4 Freak Flag v4 ☐
Sit start and traverse the lip up and right with holds hidden in the slab above. At the right side, use patina and the spine of the boulder to pull over.

The uphill boulder has a phenomenal smooth face with perfect rock. Every problem is worth climbing, and there is endless fun to be had making up variations and eliminates.

5 Netherworld v3 ★ ☐
Sit start left of the left arete (on the south end of the boulder) with the left hand at a crimp, and the right hand on a sloper. Move right and up the left side of the arete. Beware the rock at your back!

6 Good World v3 ★ ☐
Sit start on the right side of the left arete, and climb the left arete.

7 Mothers of Perpetual Indulgence v0 ★★ ☐
Climb the wall right of the arete with good holds. Short, simple and a great into to this wall.

8 Pretty in Pink v2 ★★★ ☐
Begin stepping onto a small edge right of the base of a slanting ramp-line. Move up the ramp line with poor hand-holds to a left-facing flake and over.

9 Pretty in Pink variation v4 ★★ ☐
As above, without moving up to the flake.Topout up left by precarious crimp moves and poor footholds.

10 Head Butt v1 ★★★ ☐
Climb the face via the seam/crack.

11 There Is No Party (Left) v2 ★★★ ☐
Start with some large crimps 4 feet up. Pull up and stand on these and stretch to a hold up left. Make a tricky step up and right to gain a left-facing diagonal crimp. Move even further right to the horizontal, and up.

The approach to the Hall of the Mountain Queens and Morning Glory is described in the intro on the opposite page.

⑫ Variation v3 ★★ ☐
At the top of the previous line, instead of moving right to the horizontal, off-limit the horizontal, and use a right-hand sidepull to make a hard last move with awkward footholds.

⑬ There Is No Party (Right) v1 ★★★ ☐
Begin to the right of the left version with smaller crimps, and climb up and right, and then back left to the horizontal slot to finish.

⑭ You Can Cry If You Want To v1 ★★ ☐
At the far right side of the wall, climb with big moves between good holds up the blunt rib and shallow dihedral.

MORNING GLORY BOULDER

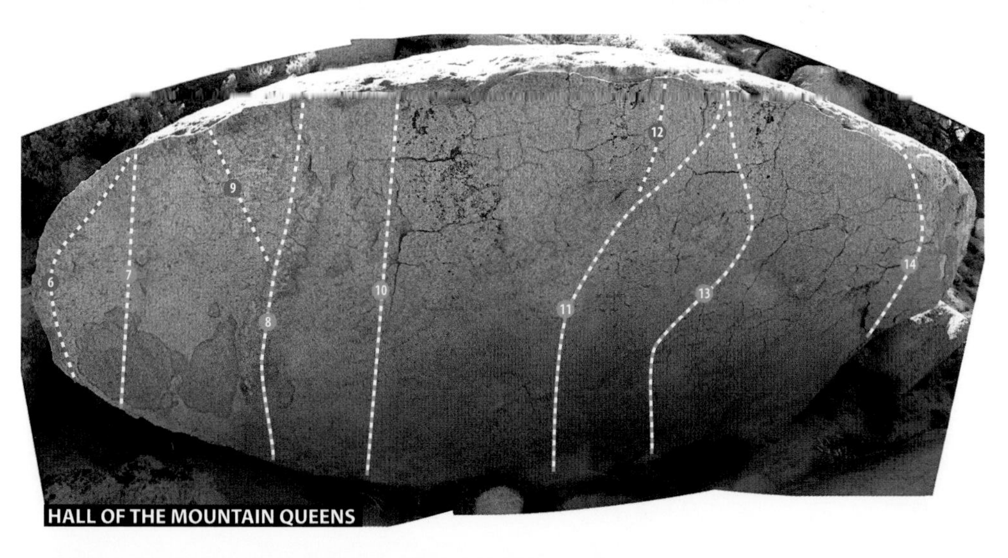

HALL OF THE MOUNTAIN QUEENS

GRADED LIST OF PROBLEMS

v14

Problem	Stars	Page
☐ Mandala Sit Start, The	★★★	292
☐ Goldfish Trombone	★★★	158
☐ Swarm, The	★★★	322
☐ Direct North	★★	277
☐ Mandala Direct Assis, The	★★	293

v13

Problem	Stars	Page
☐ Beautiful and Damned, The	★★★	376
☐ Spectre	★★★	338
☐ Buttermilker, The	★★	259
☐ Direction	★★	276
☐ Oracle, The	★	276
☐ Crankenator, The		286
☐ Realization Traverse		142
☐ True North		276

v12

Problem	Stars	Page
☐ A Maze of Death	★★★	376
☐ Evilution	★★★	270
☐ Mandala, The	★★★	292
☐ Plain High Drifter	★★★	284
☐ Swordfish Trombone	★★★	158
☐ A Scanner Darkly	★★	315
☐ Aquarium, The	★★	205
☐ Babeurre	★★	276
☐ Beautiful Gecko	★★	205
☐ Bubba Lobotomy	★★	114
☐ Butterfinger	★★	292
☐ He Got Game	★★	116
☐ Kill On Sight	★★	128
☐ Mandala Direct, The	★★	293
☐ Michael Caine Sit Start	★★	315
☐ Mystery, The	★★	276
☐ Form Destroyer	★	326
☐ Gasperini	★	402
☐ Plain High Drifter, Right Exit	★	285
☐ Rastaman Vibration	★	270
☐ Sharma's Traverse		142

v11

Problem	Stars	Page
☐ Ambrosia	★★★	272
☐ Bubba Butt Buster, The	★★★	114
☐ Evilution Direct	★★★	270
☐ Fight Club Direct	★★★	296
☐ Haroun and the Sea of Stories	★★★	233
☐ Lounge Lizards	★★★	398
☐ Lounge Lizards Direct	★★★	398
☐ Rorschach Test	★★★	202
☐ Shizaam Sit	★★★	202
☐ Xavier's Roof	★★★	363
☐ Babeurre Short	★★	276
☐ Beefy Gecko	★★	205
☐ Fight Club	★★	296
☐ Les Trois Maunets	★★	282
☐ Mordecai	★★	282
☐ North of Center	★★	277
☐ Slow Dance Right, a.k.a. Mandance	★★	128
☐ Stained Glass Right, Sit	★★	228
☐ Tony's Dyno	★★	66
☐ Already Forgotten	★	260
☐ Blood Sport	★	66
☐ Blue Ribbon	★	63
☐ Bubba: The Legend	★	114
☐ Buttermelter, The	★	260
☐ Dirty Boulevard	★	142
☐ Exit the Dragon	★	180
☐ Scenic Crank Low Start	★	238
☐ Shining Sit, The	★	152
☐ Standing Kill Order	★	128
☐ Thunderbird	★	276
☐ Unnamed	★	316
☐ Wheel of Beef	★	205
☐ Belette, La		270
☐ Dance the Night Away		128
☐ Denton Calhoun		400
☐ Reuniting the Family		142
☐ Sleipnir		392

v10

Problem	Stars	Page
☐ Beefcake	★★★	205
☐ Golden Shower	★★★	342
☐ Luminance	★★★	325
☐ River Face Arete	★★★	58
☐ Saigon Superdirect	★★★	296
☐ Stained Glass	★★★	228
☐ Stained Glass Sit	★★★	228
☐ This Side of Paradise	★★★	376
☐ Zen Flute	★★★	373
☐ Bubba Escapes the Ward	★★	204
☐ Bubba Gump	★★	295
☐ Campground Arete Sit	★★	59
☐ Center Direct	★★	276
☐ Constellation	★★	244
☐ Denton's Remorse	★★	400
☐ Drone Direct	★★	333
☐ Dude Sit Start	★★	66
☐ Hueco Wall Sit	★★	362
☐ Little Forgotten	★★	260
☐ Plain High Dyno	★★	284
☐ Redrum Sit	★★	152
☐ Return Jedi	★★	336
☐ River Face Arete Sit	★★	58
☐ Sharma Traverse, The	★★	299
☐ Sidewinder	★★	254
☐ Slow Dance	★★	128
☐ Water Hazard	★★	204
☐ A Grand Day Out	★	314
☐ Acid Wash	★	128
☐ Aquatic Hitchhiker	★	205
☐ Blood Spud	★	228
☐ Bubba Gets Committed	★	114
☐ Capoeira	★	291
☐ Charlie's New Squeeze	★	288
☐ Iron Slap	★	243
☐ Led Zeppelin, Sit Start	★	368
☐ Osama Sit-Start Eliminate	★	58
☐ Action Jackson		142
☐ Cocktail Sauce		295
☐ Diedrin		316
☐ Fakir School		233
☐ Groovy Sue		66
☐ Human Contra-Ban		142
☐ King Me		306
☐ Low Rider		142
☐ One Mule Wonder		259
☐ Pope's Hat		238
☐ Seriously Twisted		66
☐ Stamen Envy		333
☐ Sue's Groovy Blood		66
☐ Wheel of Cheese		260

v9

Problem	Stars	Page
☐ Campground Arete	★★★	58
☐ Cholos	★★★	142
☐ Dude	★★★	66
☐ Fall Guy, The	★★★	233
☐ Finder's Fee	★★★	335
☐ Hueco Wall	★★★	362
☐ I Am a Beautiful Man, Sit	★★★	92
☐ Iron Fly	★★★	243
☐ Life Ain't Easy	★★★	66
☐ Queen Sweet Nectar Left	★★★	320
☐ Sloth, The	★★★	388
☐ Soul Slinger	★★★	264
☐ Toxic Avenger	★★★	114
☐ Checkerboard Right	★★	306
☐ Chicken Licken	★★	182
☐ Compression Session	★★	62
☐ Flabmaster	★★	118
☐ Footprints	★★	269
☐ Gastonia Sit	★★	362
☐ Golden Child	★★	392
☐ Hit the High Hard One, Sit	★★	114
☐ Lizard Therapy	★★	398
☐ Lounge Lizards High Start	★★	398
☐ Michael Caine	★★	315
☐ Mooned	★★	254
☐ Overzealous	★★	64
☐ Queen Sweet Nectar	★★	320
☐ Saigon Direct	★★	296
☐ Shock Therapy Right	★★	398
☐ Slunk	★★	212
☐ Super-Froz	★★	144
☐ Swanky Sit	★★	335
☐ The Gleaner Sit Start	★★	131
☐ Tim's Fred Traverse	★★	157
☐ Twin Cracks	★★	315
☐ Acid Wash Right	★	128
☐ America's Fit Homeless	★	262
☐ Compression Aversion	★	62
☐ Days of Blunder	★	400
☐ Disco Hulk	★	150
☐ Dove Direct	★	118
☐ Enter the Dragon	★	180
☐ Fast Dance	★	126
☐ Finders Keepers	★	290
☐ Funnel Man	★	92
☐ Grit Dreams	★	250
☐ Harem	★	60
☐ I Was Beautiful Till I Woke Up, Sit	★	92
☐ Jack of Swords	★	106
☐ Large Talons	★	62
☐ Last Dance	★	126
☐ Lean Thinking	★	335
☐ Left Lindner, The	★	305
☐ Matt's Project Sit	★	252
☐ Paralimpet	★	372
☐ Pimp Trick Gangsta Chicks	★	122
☐ Sharma's Flake	★	373
☐ Shining, The	★	152

v4

- [ ] White Man's Overbite ★ 403
- [ ] Agent Orange 367
- [ ] Amazing Cragging Cuisine 94
- [ ] Battleship Earth 371
- [ ] Bob Parrot 196
- [ ] Brother Law 403
- [ ] Church of the Lost and Found Left, The 94
- [ ] Ethan 140
- [ ] Exoframe 360
- [ ] Feral Child 190
- [ ] Fumble in the Dark 176
- [ ] Geriatric Burns Off Young Guns 72
- [ ] Hector 160
- [ ] Hovercraft 190
- [ ] Ice Cream Against Time 182
- [ ] Joseph 131
- [ ] Lay the Candle Lady Later 149
- [ ] Lazy Lion 162
- [ ] More Than Nothing 346
- [ ] Morgan's Traverse 128
- [ ] Nonsuch 124
- [ ] North Face Low Start 373
- [ ] North Face Patina 373
- [ ] Queenie 302
- [ ] Slab 118
- [ ] Slots 267
- [ ] Sorry About That (East Side) 104
- [ ] There Goes a Supernova 84
- [ ] Toothless 196
- [ ] Unnamed 104
- [ ] Unnamed 112
- [ ] Unnamed 116
- [ ] Unnamed 164
- [ ] Unnamed 180
- [ ] Unnamed 184
- [ ] Unnamed 192
- [ ] Unnamed 212
- [ ] Unnamed 233
- [ ] Unnamed 250
- [ ] Unnamed 256
- [ ] Unnamed 262
- [ ] Unnamed 262
- [ ] Unnamed 272
- [ ] Unnamed 272
- [ ] Unnamed 285
- [ ] Unnamed 285
- [ ] Unnamed 296
- [ ] Unnamed 359
- [ ] Unnamed 364
- [ ] Unnamed 352

v2

- [ ] Big Chicken ★★★ 150
- [ ] Bob Parrot (of Maine) ★★★ 196
- [ ] Cover Me With Flowers ★★★ 335
- [ ] Fire Pit ★★★ 208
- [ ] Galerie des Glaces ★★★ 112
- [ ] Green Wall Essential ★★★ 280
- [ ] Hunk, The ★★★ 280
- [ ] Kling and Smirk ★★★ 156
- [ ] Monkey Dihedral ★★★ 296
- [ ] Pig Pen ★★★ 102
- [ ] Pretty in Pink ★★★ 406
- [ ] Secret to Success ★★★ 164
- [ ] Sheepherder ★★★ 226
- [ ] Sixty-Foot Woman Traverse, The ★★★ 155
- [ ] There is No Party (Left) ★★★ 406
- [ ] Three Men and a Crippler ★★★ 74
- [ ] Timothy Leary Presents ... ★★★ 348
- [ ] A Brief Conversation Ending In Divorce ★★ 168
- [ ] Action Potential ★★ 232
- [ ] An Artist of Leisure ★★ 143
- [ ] Bear ★★ 144
- [ ] Beekeeper Standing Start, The ★★ 342
- [ ] Blue ★★ 196
- [ ] Boy ★★ 132
- [ ] Brian's Slab Direct ★★ 364
- [ ] Buzz, The ★★ 320
- [ ] Cheap New Age Fix ★★ 114
- [ ] Cobble, The ★★ 350
- [ ] Coors is Light ★★ 144
- [ ] Dale's Right ★★ 368
- [ ] Diamond ★★ 208
- [ ] Fluke ★★ 140
- [ ] Hobbs' Problem ★★ 250
- [ ] Horseshoe Problem, The ★★ 348
- [ ] It's the Altitude ★★ 124
- [ ] Kevin Cauldron ★★ 80
- [ ] Little Fluffy Clouds ★★ 106
- [ ] Marty Lewis's Ever-Changing Hair ★★ 156
- [ ] Maximum Joy ★★ 80
- [ ] North Face Direct ★★ 276
- [ ] Prozac Nation ★★ 208
- [ ] Psychopath ★★ 72
- [ ] Round Two ★★ 84
- [ ] Run With Me ★★ 126
- [ ] Sleeping Gas ★★ 188
- [ ] Slight Inducement Right ★★ 164
- [ ] Spinal Snap ★★ 154
- [ ] Spinal Snap Right Start ★★ 154
- [ ] Still Life ★★ 194
- [ ] Sunburst Seahorse ★★ 124
- [ ] Thought Seeds ★★ 364
- [ ] Thread the Needle ★★ 211
- [ ] Through the Heart ★★ 388
- [ ] Unnamed ★★ 262
- [ ] Unnamed ★★ 102
- [ ] Unnamed ★★ 241
- [ ] Unnamed ★★ 252
- [ ] Unnamed ★★ 302
- [ ] Up Your Skirt Left ★★ 156
- [ ] Up Your Skirt, Right ★★ 156
- [ ] Valium ★★ 211
- [ ] Wavy Gravy ★★ 136
- [ ] Western Motif ★★ 104
- [ ] Wicca Warrior ★★ 138
- [ ] Winter Sun ★★ 392
- [ ] Xen ★★ 310
- [ ] Able-bodied Goblin ★ 396
- [ ] Ainvar ★ 396
- [ ] Aspen ★ 64
- [ ] Auto-gedden ★ 122
- [ ] Ballorama ★ 141
- [ ] Bear Hug ★ 110
- [ ] Best Bitter ★ 144
- [ ] Cheezy Brit ★ 252
- [ ] Chemical Romance ★ 198
- [ ] Chess ★ 304
- [ ] Comfort of Home ★ 146
- [ ] Dance Mix ★ 122
- [ ] Death Mantel ★ 390
- [ ] Don't Believe the Hype ★ 149
- [ ] Dumb Luck ★ 176
- [ ] Each Day We Get Closer ... ★ 166
- [ ] Emma ★ 200
- [ ] Emotional Rescue ★ 367
- [ ] Extended Mix ★ 122
- [ ] Fargo ★ 138
- [ ] Grandfather Hooler ★ 345
- [ ] Hauck a Loogie ★ 200
- [ ] Hunting Dog ★ 332
- [ ] Ice Shirt, The ★ 392
- [ ] If It's Not Norse It's Scottish ★ 384
- [ ] Jensen Route ★ 340
- [ ] Junk in Your Trunk ★ 385
- [ ] KD Factor Left Start, The ★ 348
- [ ] Knob and Slab ★ 306
- [ ] Kung-Fu Grip Left ★ 178
- [ ] Meth Squealer ★ 126
- [ ] Model Dairy ★ 368
- [ ] Needle Across the Groove ★ 102
- [ ] No Words, No Talk ★ 320
- [ ] Porn Again Christian ★ 208
- [ ] Prow, The ★ 224
- [ ] Scoop ★ 236
- [ ] Separate Grindrite ★ 83
- [ ] Sierra Phantom ★ 311
- [ ] Simpatico ★ 366
- [ ] Sun Spot ★ 194
- [ ] Trollkind ★ 388
- [ ] Unnamed ★ 248
- [ ] Unnamed ★ 156
- [ ] Unnamed ★ 266
- [ ] Unnamed ★ 304
- [ ] Unnamed ★ 368
- [ ] Unnamed ★ 369
- [ ] Unnamed ★ 72
- [ ] Unnamed ★ 90
- [ ] Unnamed ★ 91
- [ ] Unnamed ★ 106
- [ ] Unnamed ★ 232
- [ ] Unnamed ★ 241
- [ ] Unnamed ★ 244
- [ ] Unnamed ★ 266
- [ ] Unnamed ★ 296
- [ ] Unnamed ★ 298
- [ ] Unnamed ★ 304
- [ ] Unnamed ★ 359
- [ ] Unnamed ★ 359
- [ ] Unnamed ★ 360
- [ ] Unnamed ★ 364
- [ ] Visor Left ★ 354
- [ ] Voodoo Doll ★ 78
- [ ] Wanderlust ★ 332
- [ ] Woodman, Woodman... ★ 388
- [ ] Yggdrassil ★ 392
- [ ] Beam Me Up, Scottie 151
- [ ] Buttocks, The 295
- [ ] Charlotte Rampling 335
- [ ] Cry Baby 164
- [ ] Dangerous Brother 334
- [ ] Don't Believe 168
- [ ] E3 5c 386
- [ ] Exit the Rat 126
- [ ] Fish Sticks 178
- [ ] Giggle, Giggle 162
- [ ] Giselle 335
- [ ] Good Day Bruce 372
- [ ] Hawkman 72
- [ ] Home is Where You Hang Yourself 78
- [ ] Inner Sanctum 260

- Unnamed 296
- Unnamed 302
- Unnamed 314
- Unnamed 315
- Unnamed 315
- Unnamed 316
- Unnamed 320
- Unnamed 332
- Unnamed 335
- Unnamed 336
- Unnamed 336
- Unnamed 346
- Unnamed 348
- Unnamed 348
- Unnamed Arete 348
- Unnamed Mantel 359
- Unnamed Slot 359
- Unnamed, Exit Right 364
- Various 370
- Wall 371
- What Mick Missed 371
- Zero 384
- Zero Roof 390
- Zygote 332

v0-

- Arete, The ★★★ 192
- Bourbon IV ★★★ 73
- Groove, The ★★★ 192
- Natural Melody ★★★ 320
- Veruca Salt, I Want You ★★★ 132
- A Flake as Marvellous as You, Veruca ★★ 132
- Celestial Trail ★★ 146
- Frontierland ★★ 104
- Unnamed ★★ 155
- Unnamed ★★ 262
- Unnamed ★★ 262
- Unnamed ★★ 278
- Unnamed ★★ 278
- Aerial Surveillance ★ 160
- Corner, The ★ 149
- Crash Dive ★ 160
- Duck Soup ★ 156
- Erik Bloody Axe ★ 384
- Erik the Bolder ★ 385
- Everlasting Soul ★ 395
- Georgia O'Keefe ★ 308
- Getting Lonely, Getting Old ★ 166
- Latona Basin ★ 112
- Mmm... Nice ★ 156
- My Veruca ★ 132
- Pokeriotous ★ 140
- Rainbow Slab ★ 398
- Unnamed ★ 138
- Unnamed ★ 250
- Unnamed ★ 385
- Unnamed ★ 72
- Unnamed ★ 91
- Unnamed ★ 233
- Unnamed Slab ★ 242
- Wolverine ★ 131
- Wow is Me ★ 124
- Aaarhhhhhh 168
- Bitter Lander Cowboyz 164
- Blameless 164
- Bouldering.com 149
- Brock Bating 168
- Dirty Sound 142
- Double Vegetation 144
- Downclimb 390
- Dumb 156
- Durban Poison 160
- Echo 156
- Elephant Graveyard 160
- Fizzwiggwiggler 133
- F-Squared 82
- Future Planet of Style 164
- Golden 144
- Ha-Ha 131
- If That Augustus Gloop Looks at You ... 132
- I'll Kick the Butt of That Mike Teavee 132
- In Thick of the Woods 94
- Lack Luster 124
- Loop 142
- Marriage-Go-Round 168
- Monkey on My Back 88
- Nagasaki Badger 168
- One Note Sample 142
- Open Sky, The 94
- Painless 164
- Pish 168
- Planet Plush 74
- Plastic-Bandi-Whoopies 149
- Please Please Me 156
- Radio, Radio 164
- Rosalie's Chimney 149
- Scoop 390
- Sentimental African 160
- Shameless 164
- Silence So Red 154
- Split Melon 144
- Strangle Hold 168
- Time to Go 128
- Time to Go 131
- Time to Play 131
- Unnamed 72
- Unnamed 232
- Unnamed 236
- Unnamed 256
- Unnamed 266
- Unnamed 267
- Unnamed 267
- Unnamed 274
- Unnamed 280
- Unnamed 286
- Unnamed 344
- Unnamed Crack 242
- Veruca, I Will Do Anything 132
- Veruca, Veruca 132
- Violet Beauregarde Sucks 132
- Vitamin C 82
- Weak as Piss 144
- What Did the Aliens Say? 154
- Wicca Tower 404
- X-Static 150

vB

- Path ★★ 146
- Which Road ★★ 146
- Brown Slab ★ 176
- Goi ★ 390
- Margo's Arete ★ 156
- Norse Crack ★ 384
- Quadraphenia ★ 406
- Tribal Wisdom ★ 395
- Advanced Rockcraft Arete 272
- All the Way Down 146
- Backside Crack 315
- Biggie Smalls 363
- Blob 350
- Charlatan 364
- Choke the Chicken 366
- Chrysler Crack 122
- Crack and Ramp 305
- Downclimb 384
- Downclimb 352
- Downclimb 395
- East Arete 274
- East Arete 5.10ish 272
- Erect 406
- Fear of a Black Planet 359
- Flake 196
- Flake Crack 320
- Flake Descent 336
- Flush 200
- Frilla 390
- Galar 386
- Hands-On Slab 194
- Holy Slab 315
- Hydra Pilferers 146
- Hysterical Bear Incident, The 208
- Long Ship Crack 384
- Low-Angle Arete 200
- Southwest Arete, The 277
- Toffee Crack 132
- Unnamed 359
- Unnamed 359
- Unnamed 280
- Unnamed 388
- Unnamed 388
- Unnamed 236
- Unnamed 244
- Unnamed 244
- Unnamed 350
- Unnamed 359
- Unnamed 359
- Unnamed 364
- Unnamed 390
- Xav's Problem 146
- Xenolith Slab 367

INDEX

A

B

C

G

H

I

J

K

L

S

T

U

V

W

X

Y

Z

ABOUT THE AUTHORS

WILLS YOUNG has been an avid boulderer for over 30 years. He was born in Los Angeles but raised in England, not far from his beloved gritstone edges of the Peak District where he still feels at home even though he has lived in Bishop for ten years, and spent about half his life in the United States. He graduated with an MA in philosophy from the University of Edinburgh in Scotland, a degree which served him well as he contemplated life from behind a large mug of Nambarrie tea and a plate full of marmalade on toast. Moving to Ventura in Southern California, he became influential in generating the bouldering boom, helping to kick-start development of major bouldering areas around Los Angeles and writing about his exploits and those of his friends. Wills grew up to become a freelance writer and photographer, a frequent voice in the climbing journals. He has traveled extensively, most recently documenting a life of climbing with his wife Lisa Rands, who not only shares his passion for bouldering, but has even surpassed him with her zeal for "the grit." He continues to travel and climb while working with the legendary British climber Ben Moon to import MOON Climbing products to North America.

Born in Blackburn, England, **MICK RYAN** started climbing in 1979 on the gritstone quarries near his home. He soon started climbing new routes and discovering new areas and was active in the sport-climbing revolution in England in the late 1980s.

In 1994 he moved to Boston, Massachusetts, then to Lake Tahoe, California, and eventually to Bishop with his wife Gabriella, son Xavier, and eventually the Bishop-born Felicity. Along the way he published guidebooks to New Hampshire's Cathedral and Whitehorse Ledges, and Rumney; to Rifle, Colorado (*Bite The Bullet*), the limestone of Las Vegas (*Islands In The Sky*), and several editions of the *Bishop Bouldering Survival Kit.* His specialty is digital map and topo drawing, and the design of clear and easily interpreted climbing information.

In Bishop he was instrumental in exploring new areas, he discovered and named the Sad Boulders and the Druid Stones, and made first ascents such as *Morning Dove White, Every Color You Are, Strength In Numbers, Suspended In Silence, The Beekeepers Apprentice, Cover Me In Flowers, Everything and Nothing, The Scent of Magnolia, Maximum Joy, the Church of Lost and Found* and *Arch-Drude.* He was also a driving force behind access and conservation work in Bishop, working closely with the Bureau of Land Management and the US Forest Service, organizing work parties and designing flyers and educational materials for visiting climbers.

Today, Mick lives in England, enjoying the climbing (and the rain). He works as the senior editor and advertising manager for UK Climbing Ltd that runs the websites UKClimbing.com and UKHillwalking.com, and publishes Rockfax guidebooks. He climbs and runs all over Europe, and is still threatening to move back to the USA.

His painting of climbing on Eastern Sierra, part of which illustrates the inside front cover of this guidebook, is available from Wilson's Eastside Sports as a fine-art poster.